The World of the Favourite

The World of the Favourite

edited by

J. H. Elliott and L. W. B. Brockliss

Yale University Press
New Haven and London

Set in Ehrhardt by Best-set Typesetter Ltd, Hong Kong
Printed in Great Britain by St Edmundsbury Press

Library of Congress Cataloging-in-Publication Data
The World of the Favourite/edited by J. H. Elliott and L. W. B. Brockliss.
    Includes bibliographical references and index.
    ISBN 0–300–07644–4 (alk. paper)
    1. Favorites. Royal – Europe – Biography.   2. Statesmen – Europe –Biography.
   I. Elliott, John Huxtable.   II. Brockliss. L.W.B. Brockliss.
  D107.7.W67   1999
  920.04 – dc21   98–49579
                                                        CIP

A catalogue record for this book is available from the British Library.

10 9 8 7 6 5 4 3 2 1

To Sydney L. Mayer
whose generosity made this
volume possible.

Contents

Illustrations

Contributors

Ronald G. Asch is Professor of Early Modern History at the University of Osnabrück. He is the editor of *Politics, Patronage and the Nobility: The Court at the Beginning of the Modern Age* (1991) and the author of *Der Hof Karls I. Politik, Provinz und Patronage 1625–1640* (1993), a study of the English court before the Civil War. His most recent publication is *The Thirty Years War. The Holy Roman Empire and Europe 1618–1648* (1997).

Jean Bérenger is Professor Emeritus at the Sorbonne. His research has concentrated in particular on the development of the Habsburg Empire in the seventeenth century. Publications include *Finances et absolutisme autrichien dans la seconde moitié du XVII siècle* (1975) and *A History of the Habsburg Empire, 1273–1918* (1994–7).

James M. Boyden is Associate Professor of History at Tulane University and the author of *The Courtier and the King: Ruy Gómez de Silva, Philip II and the Court of Spain* (1995). He is currently researching cultural changes in modern Iberia stemming from the experience of overseas empire.

L. W. B. Brockliss is Reader in Modern History at the University of Oxford and a Fellow and Tutor of Magdalen College. His publications include *French Higher Education in the Seventeenth and Eighteenth Centuries: A Cultural History* (1987) and, with Colin Jones, *The Medical World of Early Modern France* (1997). He is currently writing a book on the Enlightenment in Provence and preparing a one-volume history of the University of Oxford.

Jonathan Brown is Carroll and Milton Petrie Professor of Fine Arts at the Institute of Fine Arts, New York University. He has written extensively on Spanish art and on art at the European court of the seventeenth century. His books include *A Palace for a King: The Buen Retiro and the Court of Philip IV*, in collaboration with J. H. Elliott (1980), *Velazquez, Painter and Courtier* (1986) and *Kings and Connoisseurs: Collecting Art in Seventeeth-Century Europe* (1995).

Pauline Croft is senior lecturer in history at Royal Holloway, University of London. She has published extensively on the politics, and parliamentary and commercial history of England in the late sixteenth and early seventeeth centuries. She is currently editing a volume of essays entitled *Patronage, Culture and Power: the Early Cecils.*

J.-F. Dubost is maître de conférence at the University of Caen. He has published *Les étrangers en France, XVIe siècle–1789. Guide des recherches aux archives nationales* (1993), *La France italienne, XVIe–XVIIe siècles* (1997) and, with Peter Sahlins, *Et si on faisait payer les étrangers? Louis XIV, les immigrés et quelques autres* (1999).

J. H. Elliott is Regius Professor Emeritus of Modern History in the University of Oxford, and an Honorary Fellow of Oriel College. His books include *Richelieu and Olivares* (1984), *The Count-Duke of Olivares* (1986), *Spain and its World, 1500–1700* (1989) and, with Jonathan Brown, *A Palace for a King. The Buen Retiro and the Court of Philip IV* (1980).

Antonio Feros is Assistant Professor of History at New York University. He is the author of a forthcoming book on the career of the duke of Lerma and the political history of the reign of Philip III of Spain, and has published articles on royal favourites, power and propaganda, and patronage and clientelism in early modern Spain.

M. Fumaroli has been a member of the Académie Française since 1996 and was made Professor at the Collège de France, Paris in 1986 (Chaire de Rhétorique et Société en Europe XVIe–XVIIe siècles). In 1997 he published *Le Poète et le Roi. Jean de la Fontaine en son siècle.* He is currently working on books on the Count of Caylus and on Chateaubriand's *Mémoires de l'Outre Tombe.*

Paul E. J. Hammer is Senior Lecturer in History at the University of New England, Australia. He has published articles on Elizabethan politics as well as *The polarisation of Elizabethan politics: the political career of Robert Devereux, 2nd earl of Essex, 1585–1597* (1999). He is currently working on a study of the fall of the earl of Essex and the closing years of Elizabeth's reign.

Knud J. V. Jespersen is Professor of Modern European History at Odense University, Denmark and holds the position of Historiographer of the Orders of Chivalry at the Royal Danish Court. His publications include an essay in H. M. Scott (ed.), *The European Nobilities in the Seventeenth and Eighteenth Centuries* (1995), and he is currently working on a *History of Denmark, 1500–2000*, to be published in English.

Antoni Mączak is Professor of Modern History at the University of Warsaw. His most recent publications include *Travel in Early Modern Europe*, translated by Ursula Phillips (1995), *Money, Prices and Power in Poland, 16–17th Centuries. A Comparative Analysis* (1995). He is currently working on a book on patronage, *The Elites of Modern Europe*.

Linda Levy Peck is Professor of History at George Washington University. She is author of *Northampton: Patronage and Policy at the Court of James I* (1982), *Court Patronage and Corruption in Early Stuart England* (1990, 1993) and editor of *The Mental World of the Jacobean Court* (1991). She is currently writing a book entitled *Consuming Splendour: Britain in the Age of the Baroque*.

Orest Ranum is Professor of History at the Johns Hopkins University. His books include *Richelieu and the Councillors of Louis XIII* (1963), and *The Fronde, a French Revolution* (1993). He is currently working on a book on the origins of the modern French state in the 1650s.

I. A. A. Thompson is Honorary Professor in the Department of History of Keele University. He is the author of *War and Government in Habsburg Spain 1560–1620* (1976). A number of his other essays in subjects relating to the government of Spain in the sixteenth and seventeenth centuries have been published as *Crown and Cortes: Government, Institutions and Representation in Early-Modern Castile* (1993).

David Wootton is Professor of Eighteenth-Century History at Queen Mary and Westfield College, University of London. He has published widely on early modern intellectual history, and is currently working on Reginald Scot's *Discoverie of Witchcraft*.

Blair Worden is Professor of Early Modern History at the University of Sussex. He has written widely on the political, intellectual and literary history of early modern England. His most recent book, *The Sound of Virtue. Politics in Philip Sidney's* Arcadia, was published in 1996.

Acknowledgements

The editors' first debt of gratitude is to Mr Sydney L. Mayer for his generosity in supporting the international colloquium which was the starting-point for this book. Along the way they have received much help, in particular from Mrs Felicity Dobbie, whose devoted labours in organizing the colloquium laid the groundwork for this volume, and her successor as secretary to the Regius Professor, Mrs Teena Stabler, who handled the correspondence with the authors and did valuable preliminary work on the preparation of their contributions for press.

They are also grateful to Professor Joseph Bergin, Professor Robert Evans, Dr Robert Frost and other friends and colleagues who took part in the colloquium, and who responded so generously when the editors turned to them for advice.

The authors have shown much forbearance and understanding during the long period of gestation for this volume, and have taken in good part the editors' requests for revisions to their chapter. The staff of Yale University Press have displayed their customary professional skills, and the editors are especially grateful to Sally Nicholls for assembling the illustrations, and to Candida Brazil for the combination of broad vision with meticulous attention to detail which she has brought to the complicated task of transforming the typescripts into a book.

Introduction

J. H. ELLIOTT

Favourites have not enjoyed a good historical press. Writing in 1844 of the Earl of Bute, the young George III's choice for prime minister, Lord Macaulay was characteristically dismissive: 'He was a favourite; and favourites have always been odious in this country. No mere favourite had been at the head of the government since the dagger of Felton had reached the heart of the Duke of Buckingham.'[1]

Macaulay's strictures on Buckingham and Bute place him firmly in a centuries-old tradition of hostility to the overmighty subject who had risen to dazzling and (it was assumed) unjustified pre-eminence through his artful success in winning and retaining the favour of his prince. Piers Gaveston in the England of Edward II; Alvaro de Luna in fifteenth-century Castile; and Olivier Le Daim, the barber of Louis XI of France – all three provoked such fierce contemporary passions as to earn for themselves a lasting place in the national demonologies of their respective countries. The drama that attended their lives was further enhanced by the drama of their deaths. The sword of the executioner became an instrument of divine retribution for cupidity, pride and the tyrannical abuse of power, and provided an appropriate denouement to careers that would serve as exemplary warnings to contemporaries and to future generations.

The appearance of the word *favori* in France at the start of the sixteenth century may reflect something of the impact made on the French collective consciousness by the spectacular rise and fall of Olivier Le Daim.[2] The equivalent word in Spanish was either *privado* or *valido*, used of someone who, like Alvaro de Luna, enjoyed the royal favour, or *privanza*, or was valued and protected by the monarch, whose *valimiento* he enjoyed. By the early seventeenth century the word *privado*, alternating with 'private', had entered the English language, if rather hesitantly. 'The modern languages', wrote Francis Bacon in his essay 'Of Friendship', 'give unto such persons the name of *favourites*, or *privadoes*. . . .'[3] 'A Favourite is call'd a Private', explained the Bolognese historian Virgilio Malvezzi, an apologist for the contemporary

Spanish favourite, the Count-Duke of Olivares, 'because he is to be Private to his will, to all his affections, to all his passions, and transformed only into the service of God and of his Lord.'[4] But in English the word 'favourite' was to win out over 'private' or *privado*, and in 1715 Michael Geddes, in a biography of Alvaro de Luna, described that quintessential Spanish *privado* as 'the top Favorite I have anywhere met with in History'.[5]

The exact word chosen, however, is of less significance than the fact that, during the course of the sixteenth and seventeenth centuries, the phenomenon of the favourite impinged on the consciousness of Europeans forcefully enough to create its own terminology. Yet the phenomenon itself was hardly new. Quite apart from more or less recent historical examples, like Gaveston and Alvaro de Luna, the Bible and the classics both yielded their share of favourites – some good, like Joseph in the service of Pharaoh, others bad, like Haman, the henchman of King Ahasuerus, or Sejanus, who exploited the favour of the Emperor Tiberius to rule imperial Rome.

Indeed, the Renaissance recovery of the works of Tacitus may itself be at least partly responsible for the sixteenth- and seventeenth-century preoccupation with the figure of the favourite. It hardly seems a coincidence that the Spanish royal secretary Antonio Pérez, who carried the secrets of the court of Philip II with him into exile in France and England, was at once a self-appointed authority on favourites and one of the leading Tacitean enthusiasts of the later sixteenth century.[6] Pérez, when in London, moved in the circle of the Earl of Essex, another enthusiast for Tacitus, whom Ben Jonson may well have presented in the guise of Sejanus in his play of 1603.

Tacitus, in his depiction of Sejanus, provided a historical character against whom contemporaries could measure their own overmighty subjects, as Georg Acacius Enenkel von Hoheneck did in his treatise on Sejanus published in Strasburg in 1620.[7] Two years earlier, the French historian and publicist Pierre Matthieu had published two works, one – *La Conjuration de Conchine* – on the recently assassinated favourite of Marie de Médicis, and the other a biography of Sejanus. The clandestine English translation of this biography, under the title of *The Powerful Favorite*, appeared in 1628, two years after Sir John Eliot's famous speech in the House of Commons comparing Buckingham with Sejanus – a speech which elicited Charles I's outraged comment: 'Implicitly, he must intend me for Tiberius.'[8] In some respects, therefore, the seventeenth-century favourite or minister–favourite may be seen as a Tacitean construct.

Yet it is hard to believe that the figure of Sejanus would have loomed so large in the early seventeenth century, or plays like Marlowe's *Edward II* and Mira de Amescua's two *comedias* on the *Prosperous and Adverse Fortune of Don Alvaro de Luna* have had such resonance, if playwrights, spectators and readers had not been convinced that they, too, were living in an age of overmighty favourites. They had, after all, only to look around them to see men who had risen to enormous power and wealth as the result of royal favour – the Duke of Lerma in Spain, Concini and the duc de Luynes in France, Cardinal Klesl at the court of the emperor, George Villiers in England. Naturally they turned to classical history and national memories to set such figures into context.

Later generations were to endorse a perception which, while increasingly prevalent in the later sixteenth century, seems to have acquired a new intensity in the first half of the seventeenth. In 1715 Lesage set his *Histoire de Gil Blas* in the Spain of the earlier seventeenth century, and told the story of a *pícaro* who contrived to become in succession the favourite of each of the two great royal favourites, Lerma and Olivares. The flattery, the court intrigue and the patterns of clientage depicted by Lesage in his life of Gil Blas were as characteristic of the age of Lesage himself as of that of his fictional hero,[9] but he had located his story in a period and a land which had given the word *privado* to Europe, and were to be permanently associated with the figure of the favourite.

The romantic novelists of the nineteenth century followed in the footsteps of Lesage, with Scott, Dumas and Balzac recreating an increasingly remote world in which courtiers jostled for power, and Machiavellian minister–favourites spun their complicated webs of intrigue and made lesser men the agents of their grand designs. But in France at least the age of the minister–favourite was perceived as marking the beginnings of the nation's rise to greatness, and the papers of Richelieu and Mazarin, lovingly edited by Avenel and Chéruel, became monuments to the men who were seen as laying the foundations of the modern French state.[10]

Understandably it was the ministerial aspect of the careers of Richelieu and Mazarin that commanded the attention of historians as they sought to evaluate their contribution to the creation of the modern state. Given the pejorative overtones that the word 'favourite' had acquired, it was not thought applicable to ministers of their calibre, even though contemporaries – usually, but not always, their critics and opponents – had not hesitated to use it of both.[11] Equally, the historical reputation of the Earl of Strafford benefited to some extent from the negative connotations of the word, since neither his character nor the nature of his relationship with the king lent themselves easily to the conventional characterization of a favourite. In the eyes of contemporaries he might be 'libidinous as Tiberius, cruell as Nero, covetous as rich Cressus, as terrible as Phalaris, as mischievous as Sejanus',[12] but for Macaulay he deserved a place alongside Falkland, Clarendon, Shaftesbury, Sunderland and other prominent figures in Stuart England who, 'whatever their faults might be, were all men of acknowledged ability. They did not owe their eminence merely to the favour of the sovereign. On the contrary, they owed the favour of the sovereign to their eminence.'[13]

It was, therefore, as state-builders, or at least as embryonic state-builders, that those minister–favourites of the seventeenth century who were not perceived as incurably frivolous or irredeemably corrupt entered the historiography of the twentieth century. They had played their part in creating

the sovereign and centralized nation-state which was seen as the logical culmination of a thousand years of European history. But historically they tended to
be confined, in the twentieth century as much as in the nineteenth, to their own
national compartments. Although their contemporaries might draw parallels
between them, there was little disposition among historians to consider the
extent to which the circumstances in which they rose to power and their
subsequent manner of exercising it might reflect conditions and assumptions
that transcended national boundaries.

In 1974, however, the French historian Jean Bérenger published an important article in which he suggested that historians of the seventeenth century
were confronted by a 'European phenomenon'. It was not by chance, he argued,
that powerful first ministers – Richelieu, Buckingham and Olivares – emerged
more or less simultaneously in the three principal west European states, thus
initiating a European age of prime-ministerial government. After 1660, however, the figure of the single omnicompetent minister disappeared from the
scene, although he continued to cast a long shadow over the European political
world until the end of the century and beyond.

In seeking possible reasons for this 'European phenomenon', Bérenger
rejected what he called the 'superficial psychological explanations of traditional
political history', with its heavy emphasis on the personal inadequacies of a
Louis XIII, a Charles I and a Philip IV. He pointed, rather, to the growing
complexity of the early modern state, which imposed increasingly heavy
demands on the monarch. Some rulers, like Philip II of Spain, wore themselves
out in the exercise of their governmental duties; others, like the Emperor
Rudolf II, were patently incapable of undertaking them; and all monarchs found
themselves increasingly compelled to delegate their powers to some form of
premier ministre. The result of this delegation of powers was a growing contradiction between the humanist ideal of the prince, the social ideals of nobility
and the practical requirements of kingship. This contradiction was a source of
increasing concern to the European aristocracy, which saw itself as the natural
governing class, and resented the emergence of an all-powerful minister
standing between itself and the monarch. Eventually this concern manifested
itself in the form of a powerful European backlash, which led to the eclipse of
the minister–favourite in the age of Louis XIV. But Bérenger advanced these
explanations only tentatively, and felt that the phenomenon of the emergence of
the *premier ministre* was sufficiently important to justify a systematic enquiry
of international scope into 'its origins, its manifestations, its evolution, and the
violent criticisms that it aroused'.[14]

His appeal elicited no response at the time, and the systematic historical
enquiry which he advocated has yet to be undertaken. But twenty-two years
later the appeal still seemed sufficiently cogent to encourage Laurence Brockliss
and me to organize an international colloquium at Magdalen College,
Oxford, on 'The World of the Favourite, 1550–1700'. The papers presented to
this colloquium form the substance of this book.

In many respects the historical climate is today more propitious for the kind of enquiry for which Bérenger called than it was when he made his appeal in 1974. Both political and institutional history, then out of fashion, have returned to favour, and state-formation in early modern Europe has attracted renewed historical attention at a moment when the sovereignty of the state is being eroded by supra-national organizations.[15] Biography, which for long was under a cloud, has emerged again into the sunlight as historically respectable.[16] Recent years, too, have seen a reassessment of the possibilities inherent in comparative history, a form of history that transcends national boundaries.[17]

These changes in historical fashion have been reflected in, and sometimes encouraged by, a number of works devoted to the study of sixteenth- and seventeenth-century ministers and favourites and the political world in which they operated. Given the importance of the *privado* in the history of Habsburg Spain, it is natural that the theory and practice of the Spanish *privanza* should have been the subject of particular historical attention. Already in 1963 the Spanish legal and institutional historian Francisco Tomás y Valiente, who was assassinated by terrorists in February 1996, had published what proved to be a path-breaking study of the institutionalization of the office of the Spanish *valido*, and of the political theory which grew up around his position and functions.[18] My own researches into the ministerial career of the Count-Duke of Olivares included a political biography and a comparative assessment of him and his arch-rival, Cardinal Richelieu.[19] The count-duke's predecessor, the Duke of Lerma, has been attracting increasing attention,[20] while the career of a sixteenth-century *privado*, the Prince of Eboli, has been surveyed by James M. Boyden, whose essay on the early history of the Spanish *privanza* appears in this volume.[21]

While interest in Cardinal Richelieu has never waned, and biographies continue to appear,[22] Richelieu studies have moved in new directions. Joseph Bergin has thrown new light on his personal finances and his rise to power, and the cardinal's relationship to the king has been reassessed.[23] In the France of the later sixteenth century, the old caricature of the court of Henri III and his *mignons* (pl. 1) is being replaced by a more clear-headed evaluation of political, social and cultural realities.[24] On the English side of the Channel, the Duke of Buckingham has been the subject of a large-scale biography, and recent historical debates about Stuart politics have generated a new interest in the career of the Earl of Strafford.[25] The favourites of Queen Elizabeth, too, are being subjected to fresh scrutiny, partly in response to a rapidly growing interest in the royal court as a sociological and cultural phenomenon.[26]

The relationship of favourites to their princes is a theme that naturally lends itself to psychoanalytical interpretation, but, in general, historians seem to have found the specific context of the court and court culture more illuminating as an explanation of the phenomenon of the favourite than allegedly recurring patterns in interpersonal relationships.[27] The new awareness of the role of the court in the structure of power and social relations in the early modern state has done much to bring the favourite back to centre stage.

The reassessment of the role of the court forms part of a wider reassessment of the character and functioning of the early modern state. The traditional picture of the centralized 'absolutist' state has come to look outmoded as historians have pointed to its essentially 'composite' character, and have devoted their energies to the patient reconstruction of patronage networks and of clientage systems which did much to define the limits within which royal power could operate.[28]

If the sixteenth and seventeenth centuries were notable for the development of new and more sophisticated forms of bureaucratic organization, it has become increasingly apparent that the effective working of governmental institutions, old and new, was heavily dependent on the skill of princes and their ministers in manipulating to the advantage of the crown a system of social relationships tied together by family and personal loyalties, and informed by a strong sense of the hierarchy of authority. Cardinal Richelieu, as Orest Ranum demonstrated in his *Richelieu and the Councillors of Louis XIII*, relied on his *créatures* to get his commands obeyed; Olivares likewise depended on relatives and subordinates who were known as his *hechuras*, or creatures; and in Rome, where the secretary of state headed the papal administration, popes continued to appoint cardinal nephews who could act as their direct agents and were used to advance the interests of their families.[29]

The operation of such family networks and clientage systems, extending from the court into the provinces, is receiving growing attention,[30] as is the court itself as a centre of political patronage.[31] But, as European courts are brought under the microscope, it becomes clear that they cannot be studied simply as self-contained social and political organisms. They were embedded in, and themselves did much to influence, a wider cultural environment which was shaped by values and assumptions that need careful scrutiny. The court, for instance, was at the centre of a gift-giving culture, in which the boundaries between reciprocity and the expected returns for services on the one hand, and 'corruption' on the other, were not easily defined.[32] It spoke a language of loyalty, friendship and dependence which possessed deep classical and Christian roots, and involved subtle shades of meaning.[33] Above all, as the abode of the prince, it spoke a language of power which radiated through the state – a language with sacred and mystical overtones which raised large questions about the nature of 'counsel' and the degree to which a monarch could delegate the authority received in trust from God.

'The wisest princes', wrote Bacon, 'need not think it any diminution to their greatness, or derogation to their sufficiency, to rely upon counsel. God himself is not without, but hath made it one of the great names of his blessed Son; *The Counsellor*.'[34] The question of counsel went to the heart of early modern kingship. What were the qualities of a good counsellor, and what should be his duties? How should the prince's counsellors be chosen? Should he have one or many? Discourses on the favourite inserted themselves into this wider discourse on counsel, which itself was a discourse on the powers and limitations of royal authority and the justification for ministerial (or even prime-ministerial) government.[35]

Discourses on the favourite, attacks on the favourite and apologias for the favourite arose out of a perceived disjunction between the notion of ideal kingship and the troubling realities of a world in which all too often monarchs seemed for one reason or another incapable of exercising to the full their monarchical authority, and devolved substantial parts of it on to a single individual who might or might not be qualified for the task. Either way, as Jean Bérenger pointed out, this meant the interposition of a third party between the sovereign and the subject.[36] This, inevitably, was a situation that gave rise to violent polemic, and generated vigorous attempts both to legitimize and to delegitimize the minister–favourite. The debate was conducted both verbally and visually, and still awaits systematic analysis. But the work done in recent years on the language and the visual imagery of power in early modern Europe leaves us in a better position than in 1974 to respond to Bérenger's appeal that the historical enquiry he advocated should embrace not only the 'origins' and 'evolution' of this 'European phenomenon' but also its 'manifestations' and 'the violent criticisms that it aroused'.[37]

The volume that follows is intended to explore and develop some of the issues raised in Bérenger's article, building on the work that has been done on early modern European politics, culture and society in the years since it was published. It does not pretend to provide a comprehensive coverage of the favourite and his world, and certainly not to examine individually the major favourites or minister–favourites of the sixteenth and seventeenth centuries. While the careers of one or two of the less well-known favourites, like Concini, Enzlin and Griffenfeld, are discussed in some detail, the approach adopted in the volume is essentially thematic. There is little point, for instance, in publishing yet another summary account of the career of a much studied figure like Richelieu, but an analysis of his vocabulary, like that provided here by Orest Ranum, allows us to look at him from an unconventional angle, while exploring the wider theme of the linguistic options available to those who exercised authority in seventeenth-century France.

As will be seen, the book is loosely divided into four parts. The first, 'The Emergence of the Minister–Favourite', is designed to cast light on the origins of Bérenger's 'European phenomenon', by illustrating through individual case-histories and the discussion of institutional, political and social conditions the kind of environment conducive to the rise of favourites, and to their acquisition of ministerial or prime-ministerial functions. The second part, 'Favourites in Office', illustrates some of the challenges facing the favourite or the would-be favourite, and the difficulties inherent in differentiating between 'favourite' and 'minister'. The third part, 'Representations of the Favourite', is devoted to the themes of the creation and projection of the image of the favourite through the visual arts and the written and spoken word, and of his place in the public discourse of political theory and the more personal discourse of friendship. The fourth considers the question of the decline of the favourite as an institutional phenomenon.

Inevitably a book of this nature raises more questions than it answers. Since it ranges over an entire continent and spans a century and a half, it necessarily omits many individual examples that might have been included. It was not possible, for instance, to include the Italian principalities and the papal states, or to examine the favourite in Russia, where his golden age comes in the eighteenth century with the rule of the empresses.[38] While the favourites of female rulers are discussed in the volume, the decision to place the prime emphasis on the ministerial aspects of the royal favourite means that the role of women as favourites has been neglected, although this is obviously a subject deserving of more attention than it has so far been accorded.

The prime purpose of the volume, as of the colloquium that preceded it, is to suggest something of the importance of favour and the favourite in European life of the sixteenth and seventeenth centuries, and to encourage further thinking and research about a phenomenon with European-wide dimensions. It may well be, as some of the chapters in the book would seem to suggest, that national differences are so marked as to make impossible a definition of the minister–favourite and his role in politics and society that transcends national boundaries. On the other hand, a reading of these essays is likely to suggest that, although the careers and images of these favourites may have followed distinctive national patterns, there was also a strong element of international imitation. The spectacular career of the Duke of Lerma, for instance, clearly exercised an influence that extended far beyond his native Spain. Here, as in so much else, the role of mutual influence and of international fashion in a competitive state system would repay further study.

'It is not by chance', observed the Spanish political theorist Diego Saavedra Fajardo in the 1640s, 'that the management of Europe is in the hands of favourites.'[39] It is hoped that readers of this book will come away from it understanding better why it was 'not by chance', although their understanding will be different from that of Saavedra, who saw the hand of Providence at work. For long a supporter of Olivares, whose 'creature' he had been, he was now inclined to attribute the miseries of a war-torn Europe to the alienation of the authority that should be exercised by kings. In this he reflects the change of mood that was coming over the Europe of the mid-seventeenth century, and that foreshadowed the eclipse or semi-eclipse of the minister–favourite in the age of Louis XIV.

As Saavedra was writing, the lights were dimming over a stage on which, for the best part of a century, the rise and fall of favourites had been endlessly re-enacted in a variety of settings. But revivals were always possible, and memories of the drama lingered on. Why that drama should have been presented on a European stage, and what it meant to contemporaries, is the theme of this book.

Notes

1. Essay on 'The Earl of Chatham', *Essays and Biographies*, in *The Complete Works of Lord Macaulay*, Albany edn, 12 vols (London, 1898), x, p. 315.
2. Arlette Jouanana, 'Faveur et favoris: l'exemple des mignons de Henri III', in Robert Sauzet, ed., *Henri III et son temps* (Paris, 1992), pp. 155–65, at p. 155.
3. Francis Bacon, *Essays*, Everyman edn (London, 1946), p. 81.
4. Virgilio Malvezzi, *The Pourtract of the Politicke Christian-Favourite* (London, 1647), p. 59.
5. Cited in Nicholas Round, *The Greatest Man Uncrowned: A Study of the Fall of Don Alvaro de Luna* (London, 1986), p. 218, n. 11.
6. See Gustav Ungerer, *A Spaniard in Elizabethan England: The Correspondence of Antonio Pérez's Exile*, 2 vols (London, 1974–6), esp. ii, p. 339.
7. See below, p. 96.
8. P. M. (Pierre Matthieu), *The Powerful Favorite, or, The Life of Aelius Seianus* (Paris, 1628); and see Kenneth C. Schellhase, *Tacitus in Renaissance Political Thought* (Chicago and London, 1976), pp. 159 and 163. The first Spanish translation of Matthieu's life of Sejanus was published in Barcelona in 1621, and he inspired Juan Pérez de Montalbán's play of 1638, *Amor, privanza y castigo* (see Raymond R. MacCurdy, *Don Alvaro de Luna and Other Favorites in Spanish Golden Age Drama* (Chapel Hill, 1978), p. 78).
9. Charles Dédéyan, *Lesage et Gil Blas*, 2 vols (Paris, 1965), i, p. 143. Unfortunately the author makes little attempt to relate *Gil Blas* to the contemporary French court.
10. *Lettres, instructions diplomatiques et papiers d'état du Cardinal de Richelieu*, ed. D. L. M. Avenel, 8 vols (Paris, 1853–77); *Lettres du cardinal Mazarin pendant son ministère*, ed. P. A. Chéruel, 9 vols (Paris, 1872–1906).
11. See below, pp. 214–15, for the use of the word 'favourite' by Richelieu's apologists.
12. Cited by Terence Kilburn and Anthony Milton, 'The Public Context of the Trial and Execution of Strafford', in J. F. Merritt, ed., *The Political World of Thomas Wentworth, Earl of Strafford, 1621–1641* (Cambridge, 1996), p. 238.
13. Macaulay, 'The Earl of Chatham', *Works*, x, p. 315. For the historical reputation of Strafford see the introduction to Merritt, ed., *Thomas Wentworth*.
14. Jean Bérenger, 'Pour une enquête européenne: le problème du ministériat au XVIIe siècle', *Annales*, 29 (1974), pp. 166–92.
15. See the volumes published or planned by the European Science Foundation on 'The Origins of the Modern State in Europe, 13th–18th Centuries'.
16. See, for example, Derek Beales, 'History and Biography: An Inaugural Lecture', reprinted in T. C. W. Blanning and David Cannadine, eds, *History and Biography: Essays in Honour of Derek Beales* (Cambridge, 1996), pp. 266–83.
17. See my 'Comparative History' and the works there cited, in Carlos Barros, ed., *Historia a Debate*, 3 vols (Santiago de Compostela, 1995), iii, pp. 9–19.
18. *Los validos en la monarquía española del siglo XVII* (Madrid, 1963; revised edn, 1982; 2nd revised edn, 1990).
19. J. H. Elliott, *The Count-Duke of Olivares: The Statesman in an Age of Decline* (New Haven and London, 1986), and *Richelieu and Olivares* (Cambridge, 1984).
20. Articles by Patrick Williams, including 'Lerma, 1618: Dismissal or Retirement?', *European History Quarterly*, 19 (1989), pp. 307–32; Antonio Feros, 'The King's Favorite, the Duke of Lerma: Power, Wealth and Court Culture during the Reign of Philip III of Spain, 1598–1621' (PhD thesis, The Johns Hopkins University, 1994); Bernardo José García García, *La paz hispánica: Política exterior del Duque de Lerma* (Leuven, 1996); Francesco Benigno, *L'Ombra del Rey. Ministri e lotta politica nella Spagna del Seicento* (Venice, 1992).
21. *The Courtier and the King: Ruy Gómez de Silva, Philip II and the Court of Spain* (Berkeley, Los Angeles and London, 1995).

22. Most recently Roland Mousnier, *L'Homme rouge ou la vie du cardinal de Richelieu* (Paris, 1992).
23. Joseph Bergin, *Cardinal Richelieu: Power and the Pursuit of Wealth* (New Haven and London, 1985); *The Rise of Richelieu* (New Haven and London, 1991). For a survey of recent trends in Richelieu scholarship, see Joseph Bergin and Laurence Brockliss, eds, *Richelieu and his Age* (Oxford, 1992).
24. See Robert Sauzet, ed., *Henri III et son temps* (Paris, 1992).
25. Roger Lockyer, *Buckingham: The Life and Political Career of George Villiers, First Duke of Buckingham, 1592–1628* (London and New York, 1981); Merritt, ed., *Thomas Wentworth*.
26. For example, Simon Adams, 'Favourites and Factions at the Elizabethan Court', in R. G. Asch and A. M. Birke, eds, *Princes, Patronage and the Nobility: The Court at the Beginning of the Modern Age, c. 1450–1650* (Oxford, 1991).
27. For a psychoanalytical approach, see in particular Elizabeth Marvick, 'Favorites in Early Modern Europe: A Recurring Psychopolitical Role', *Journal of Psychohistory*, 10 (1983), pp. 463–89, and her monographic studies of Louis XIII and Richelieu.
28. For recent work on the 'absolutist state' see the essays by various hands in John Miller, ed., *Absolutism in Seventeenth-Century Europe* (London, 1990). For the 'composite state', J. H. Elliott, 'A Europe of Composite Monarchies', *Past and Present*, 137 (1992), pp. 48–71, and the works there cited. For the central role of the nobility in the early modern state, H. M. Scott, ed., *The European Nobilities in the Seventeenth and Eighteenth Centuries*, 2 vols (London, 1995).
29. Orest Ranum, *Richelieu and the Councillors of Louis XIII* (Oxford, 1963); J. H. Elliott, *The Count-Duke of Olivares*; Wolfgang Reinhard, *Papstfinanz und Nepotismus unter Paul V, 1605–1621*, 2 vols (Stuttgart, 1974), and *Freunde und Kreaturen. 'Verflechtung' als Konzept zur Erfaschung historischer Führungsgruppen Römische Oligarchie um 1600*, Schriften der Philosophischen Fachbereiche der Universität Augsburg, 14 (Munich, 1979).
30. For example, Sharon Kettering, *Patrons, Brokers and Clients in Seventeenth-Century France* (Oxford, 1986); A. Mączak and E. Müller-Luckner, eds, *Klientelsysteme im Europa der Frühen Neuzeit*, Schriften des Historischen Kollegs, Kolloquien, 9 (Munich, 1988). See also the volume published under the auspices of the European Science Foundation, Wolfgang Reinhard, ed., *Power Elites and State Building* (Oxford, 1996).
31. See Linda Levy Peck, *Court Patronage and Corruption in Early Modern England* (Boston, 1990).
32. *Ibid.*, ch. 8.
33. See, for instance, Sharon Kettering, 'Friendship and Clientage in Early Modern France', *French History*, 6 (1992), pp. 139–58.
34. *Essays* ('Of Counsel'), p. 62.
35. Although there is a large and rapidly growing literature on the theory and practice of early modern kingship, and increasing attention is being paid to the question of counsel in humanist writings, there is as yet no systematic survey of disquisitions on the favourite as a European discourse, or even, outside Spain, as a national discourse. For general guidance see Quentin Skinner, *The Foundations of Modern Political Thought*, 2 vols (Cambridge, 1978), and Richard Tuck, *Philosophy and Government, 1572–1651* (Cambridge, 1993). For Spain see, in addition to Tomás y Valiente, *Los validos*, José-Antonio Maravall, *La Philosophie politique espagnole au XVIIe siècle* (Paris, 1955), esp. ch. 7.
36. Bérenger, 'Pour une enquête européenne', p. 167.
37. For examples of recent work on literature, language and the iconography of power, see Kevin Sharpe, *Criticism and Compliment: The Politics of Literature in the England of Charles I* (Cambridge, 1987); Marc Fumaroli, *L'Âge de l'éloquence* (Geneva, 1980; repr. Paris, 1994); John H. Elliott, *Lengua e imperio en la España de Felipe IV* (Salamanca, 1994); Roy Strong, *Art and Power: Renaissance Festivals, 1450–1650* (London, 1984); Jonathan Brown and J. H. Elliott, *A Palace for a King* (New Haven and London, 1980); R. Mousnier, ed., *Richelieu et la culture* (Paris, 1987).
38. See J. T. Alexander, 'Favourites, Favouritism and Female Rule in Russia, 1725–1796', in Roger Bartlett, ed., *Russia in the Age of the Enlightenment* (London, 1990), ch. 6. I owe this reference to the kindness of Dr Hamish Scott.
39. Diego Saavedra Fajardo, 'Empresa 50', in Quintín Aldea Vaquero, ed., *Empresas políticas*, 2 vols (Madrid, 1976), i, p. 487. The first edition of the *Empresas* dates from 1640. The second, from which the passage on contemporary favourites is drawn, was published in Milan at the end of 1643, the year in which Saavedra's patron, Olivares, fell from power.

Part One
The Emergence of the
Minister–Favourite

I

The Institutional Background to the Rise of the Minister–Favourite

I. A. A. THOMPSON

In January 1647, in a private letter to his confidante, the nun Sor María de Agreda, Philip IV of Spain (pl. 25) sought to justify why, after the fall of Olivares, he had thought it necessary to take another *valido*:

> You will have heard of the prudence and competence with which my grand-father, Philip II, governed this Monarchy, and also that he at all times had servants or ministers in whom he placed his every trust and whom in all his affairs he valued most. Such a form of government has existed in every monarchy at all times, ancient as well as modern, for none has been without a chief minister [*ministro principal*] or trusted servant [*criado confidente*] whom their masters valued above all others, since they could not do all the necessary work by themselves.[1]

Philip was, of course, right. There had been favourites in the past (mistresses of both sexes); there had been ministers in the past; there had been minister–favourites in the past; and there were to be minister–favourites in the future.[2] Can we then talk of *an* age of the minister–favourite at all? If so, when was it? And how is it to be identified? A firm delineation of our target period is obviously crucial to a focused discussion of the institutional or political background against which the phenomenon of the minister–favourite is to be set.

The problem originally raised by Jean Bérenger, in 1974, was centred on 1600–60,[3] and was inspired by what seems to be an exceptional clustering of all-powerful ministers dominating politics for long periods in the great states of western Europe: Lerma, Olivares, Haro in Spain; Sully, Richelieu, Mazarin in France; Oxenstierna in Sweden; Cecil, Buckingham in England. Perhaps no less relevant, there seemed an inability to do without epigoni, secondary favourites to fill the gaps: Uceda between Lerma and Olivares; Nithard and Valenzuela after Haro; Concini, de Luynes, Sillery, La Vieuville between Sully and Richelieu; Carr between Cecil and Buckingham – suggesting that 'favouritism' was not just a superficial question of exceptional individuals, but a deep-seated feature of the age.[4]

It is true that the distinctiveness of the early seventeenth century in this respect is being increasingly questioned. There is much current emphasis on the continuity between the favourites of the early seventeenth century and their sixteenth-century antecedents.[5] Part of the difficulty is definitional. The language of 'favouritism' is both imprecise and protean, covering different relationships and roles – Wolsey, Leicester, Essex, Cecil, Carr; Ruy Gómez, Olivares, Valenzuela; Epernon, Sully, Concini, Richelieu. In a personal monarchy every minister must in some sense have the 'favour' of the ruler, to the extent that his position depended on *beneplacito*, on trust, or acceptance, rather than on his institutional role *per se*. The stress that some historians have placed on the combination of the personal and the ministerial as distinctive of the early-seventeenth-century favourite is not, therefore, entirely helpful. The affective, not to say sexual, connotations of 'favourite' may, indeed, be a distraction. There may have been a strong affective element in the relationship between king and minister (Buckingham), or there may not (Richelieu); close friendship was sometimes the source (Haro), sometimes the consequence (Oxenstierna) of ministerial power. There were favourites and factotums; personal favourites, political favourites, minister–favourites, hegemonical favourites and ministers plenipotentiary, men like Oxenstierna, or Don Juan José de Austria, for example, whose position did not originate in the king's choice at all.[6] For these reasons, it seems to me that the Spanish terms *valido* and *valimiento* are to be preferred to 'minister–favourite', both as being less loaded and as contemporary neologisms which express semantically the sense at the time that the *valido* was in some way different from the *privados* of the past.

The *validos* of the early seventeenth century were clearly not all the same animal; but they did all have similar functions in government, and they were all responses of one kind or other to a common set of problems, political and institutional.

I want to draw attention to four interrelated features which, while perhaps not individually unique, taken together could be said to have been characteristic of the seventeenth-century *valido*, and which defined the range of their political and institutional functions.

First, they were operating in the areas of both power and patronage, *gobierno y gracia*, council and court – and they were predominant, if not monopolists, in both areas. Indeed, the *valido* was commonly denounced at the time for usurping the office of king (or seeming to), and some historians have gone so far as to talk of a complete handover of power.[7] That view is undoubtedly exaggerated. The dominance of the *valido* was neither total nor uninterrupted, and certainly never as total as contemporaries imagined.

That said, and although some sixteenth-century *privados* were also viewed in a somewhat similar way, still it seems to me that overall the determining influence enjoyed (or thought to be enjoyed) by Richelieu, Mazarin, Lerma and Olivares, in both policy and patronage during the fullness of their long ministries, and perhaps by Buckingham for a shorter time, distinguishes them from a Ruy Gómez, a Leicester, a Don Cristóbal de Moura or a Sully, who, however influential, shared or continuously competed for influence with other faction leaders or close advisers (Alba; Burghley; Idiáquez, Chinchón; Villeroy).

Second, they operated outside (or alongside) established institutional channels, and indeed often without any formal ministerial status. The *valido* was different from a private secretary or privy councillor in that he interfered with the normal processes of conciliar business, interrupting, as Alamos de Barrientos put it, the *corriente ordinaria* and diverting through himself the normal flow of access and information to the king.[8]

Third, they stood at the centre of a national network of clientage, a clientage network that was not restricted to the court, nor to a specific local interest, but which was the means of integrating court and country on a broad front.

Fourth, they were 'political' – and that not merely at the basic management level, as a sort of chief whip, to cajole or to put a bit of stick about (Olivares' brutal dressing down of Lisón y Viedma being a classic example); but, more important, they were using influence for a political rather than for just a private purpose, promoting a 'policy', a programme of governmental or constitutional reform, or merely some fiscal arrangement, designed to reinforce the authority and reputation of the state.

Not all *validos* fit all these slots, or they fit into them in different ways. Nonetheless, these are the key features which can be related to a number of broader institutional and political developments which by the end of the sixteenth century were creating the conditions for which the emergence of the *valido* was an intelligible, if not necessarily an inevitable, response.

The Minister–Favourite and Government Growth

If the rise of the minister–favourite is a general phenomenon of the early seventeenth century, undoubtedly some general explanation is needed that goes beyond that old stock-in-trade, a pandemic of idleness and incapacity among the princes of early-seventeenth-century Europe, not least because, the accidents of royal minorities and female regencies apart, the view that related the rise of the *valido* to the accession of a series of *rois fainéants* has become increasingly less tenable. Certainly James I, Louis XIII and Philip IV are no longer being regarded in this way.[9]

A more serious explanation has seen the *valido* as a response to a crisis of government growth. The increasing administrative complexity of the state, which, with the expansion of its spheres of involvement, was outgrowing personal methods of government, had created a burden which had become too great for one man, and especially for a prince educated for the court, not the desk. At the same time, the growing emphasis on the majesty of monarchy made it seem inappropriate for the king to be concerned with the minutiae of administrative detail, with negotiating business and dealing with the *hoi polloi* of place-seekers.[10]

Undoubtedly government was growing, and especially in the last quarter of the sixteenth century, though perhaps not more so than in the 1520s and 1530s. Historically the role of minister commonly took on a greater salience in such periods of administrative reform (Gattinara, Thomas Cromwell, Cobos), and the need for the king to share the burdens of government was the standard contemporary justification for the *valido*. But kings were not incapable of filling a co-ordinating role themselves (Louis XIV), and were not without secretaries and aides to assist them. Nor is it true that kings necessarily thought the essential tasks of government inappropriate for their immediate attention – Louis XIII embarked on an attempt to govern in person in 1622, and Philip IV was clearly not ashamed of his own efforts in that direction.[11]

Something of what it was not thought appropriate for a king to do, Philip IV explained to Sor María de Agreda, in that same letter, quoted above:

> What he [the principal minister] is ordinarily required to do is to hear ministers and petitioners so that he can tell his chief what they want. He is also to follow up the matters of most importance and see that what has been decided is carried out promptly. That is something necessary at any time, but most of all at present when it is so important that decisions are put into effect without delay. This is something that cannot easily be left for the king to do in person, because it would not be compatible with his dignity to go from house to house to see if ministers and secretaries are carrying out promptly what they have been ordered. But with the information passed on to him by his most trusted ministers and servants he can order what needs to be done and know whether it has been done.[12]

These were important functions, and functions with great potential for influence, but they were not functions that any king of the sixteenth century would have carried out in person either, even Philip II, whose problem was not that he had too much to do, but that he did too much that was not necessary for him to do himself.

The heart of the problem was to separate decision-making in routine matters from matters of policy, by allowing routine administrative and governmental matters to be dealt with directly by established institutions. The English Privy Council was perhaps the supreme example, but in Spain as well the councils and the *audiencias* had areas of effective, if much more limited, administrative autonomy. There were, in other words, existing models of solutions to the problems of administrative and government growth that did not involve the concentration of power in one minister, which was, in any case, a solution more to the problem of the royal dignity than to the excessive burden of business. So, even in Spain, where, given the size and the multiple administrative structure of the Monarchy, the expansion of the tasks of government had a much greater impact than in smaller or more uniform states, I am not sure that the growth of government by itself was the main consideration in the emergence of the *valido*.

Rather more pertinent was the nature of the institutional development to which the growth of government gave rise. The institutions of government in Spain were markedly different in character from those in France and England. Partly for jurisdictional reasons, Spain's central institutions were more numerous, more formalized and more differentiated. The presidents and secretaries of the councils were more departmentalized than the ministers and secretaries of state in France, and there was no overarching institution in Spain with the open-ended competence of the English Privy Council. But this high degree of institutionalization and specialization brought with it associated problems of bureaucratic routinization, institutional rivalry and corporatism. Government was obliged by law and due process to work through an administrative and judicial system that had become largely self-regulating and whose component parts were in systemic jurisdictional conflict with each other. Its permanent officers were appointed internally from within a narrow professional coterie, and, protected by law and by their ordinances, pursued an agenda, set by judicialist principles and collegial interests, by no means always coincident with that of the king or his ministers. This was likely to be a particular problem for a new king, encumbered with an administration staffed by the instruments of the previous reign, especially if that reign had been a long one.

The search for an effective mechanism for co-ordinating, controlling and imposing obedience on the central agencies of government in Spain had been a major preoccupation at least from the 1540s, and one made more acute from the early 1580s by the combination of administrative overload and the progressive debility of the king. The *valido* thus emerged in the 1590s as one solution to a long-standing problem of control, one of a line of proposed solutions going back to the great ministerial secretaries in the decades up to the 1560s (Cobos, Vázquez de Molina, Eraso), the ministerial president (Espinosa), the private secretary (Mateo Vázquez), the inner cabinet (*junta de noche*) of Philip II's last years, and the old king's own *valido*, or quasi-*valido*, Don Cristóbal de Moura. Feros is right in this respect, therefore, to point to the elements of continuity between Lerma and the immediate past, a continuity which reinforces the view that the emergence of the full-scale *valimiento* in the seventeenth century was the result not just of the chance of personality and circumstance, but of the broader needs of government.[13]

Where, as in France and England, such a complex and institutionalized administrative development did not occur, or was slower to mature, leaving access to government office more open to political considerations, it was less necessary to impose control on the administration from the outside, from the court. Personal favour and the *ministériat* were, therefore, more likely to remain separate spheres (Essex, Cinq Mars). While in Spain the *valido* came from inside the king's household, in France and England the chief minister was more likely to emerge from within the council or the secretariat (Villeroy, Cecil, Richelieu). Robert Carr's appointment in 1612 as acting secretary of state, slotting the favourite into an already existing government role, is thus interesting as a sort of 'missing link' in the evolution of the *valimiento*.

The rise of the *valido* was visibly the counterpart to the diminution of the secretary, many of whose duties both in the king's private office and as state secretary the *valido* took over.[14] Up to the 1560s the secretaries in Castile had been developing very like the state secretaries in England and France. Men like Francisco de los Cobos, Juan Vázquez de Molina, Francisco de Eraso were departmental pluralists, with supervision over multiple areas of business, and far more important in government than their individual offices. This development was curtailed by the progressive specialization and separation of departments and the multiplication and bureaucratization of the secretariats.[15] Though an undeniable sign of increased business, the effect was to fragment and weaken the authority of the secretaries. The space between the king and the institutions of government left by the downgrading of the secretaries, and those co-ordinating, admonitory and patronage functions, crucial for the political control of the court and the councils, for which a mere secretary was not appropriate, were taken over variously by ministers, cabinet committees or *validos*. Secretary and *valido*, and indeed *valido* and cabinet committee as the repeated alternation between them suggests, were competitive outcomes for particular constituencies. Which solution was to be most appropriate was as much a social and political as a governmental issue.

The *valido* emerged then at a particular moment in the development of the central administration. It was also a moment which presented uniquely favourable opportunities for patronage in the Castilian lay bureaucracy (lay as opposed to the legist bureaucracy of the councils, which was always more institutionally advanced). The period from the 1580s to the reign of Philip IV was precisely the time in the secretarial bureaux when the 'servants' of the secretary were being transformed, first into 'royal officials' and then into 'officials of the secretariats'. For thirty or forty years there was opened a patronage window; by the end of Philip IV's reign, the royal officials, appointed *ad lib*, had become a departmental bureaucracy, with promotion governed by rule and seniority, and that window had again closed.[16]

The *valido* operated not only by inserting clients into key conciliar offices, disrupting the normal paths of bureaucratic advancement – promotion in leaps ('por saltos') not in steps ('por grados'), as Bermúdez de Pedraza complained[17] – but also by diverting essential business from formal, institutionalized channels, the 'via ordinaria', to informal, hand-picked juntas or commissions. He was thus not merely acting as a quasi-secretarial channel between the councils and the king, but also controlling the flow of information and the management of business and resolutions. The *valido* was therefore in a sense taking government back into court. The process is most obvious in Spain, but it does appear to have parallels elsewhere: perhaps in James I's restoration of the bedchamber and privy chamber favourites, which Cuddy suggests was also a way of circumventing administrative sclerosis in the pursuit of new policies.[18]

Viewed, then, as a system of government, the *valimiento* can be seen as a form of de-institutionalization, or politicization; the instrument for the crown to recapture control of government from an administration regarded as ineffective, corrupt, obstructive and irremovable, and to impose on it a policy direction, absent from the normal considerations for appointment and advancement. Indeed, the force (and the weakness) of the *valimiento* lay precisely in the fact that (unlike kingship) it was not an office, and was therefore extra-legal, not regulated by rules and ordinances, but driven by a guiding principle which was not distributive justice, but reason of state.[19] The coincidence of the age of the *valido* with the development of the doctrine of reason of state is not, therefore, accidental. The *valido* was the political persona of the 'Christian Prince', the negative identity of a king who could do no wrong; he was a buffer, a lightning conductor, or at worst a burning-glass interposed between king and people at a time when a moral consensus for government policy could not be relied upon.[20]

The Minister–Favourite and the Court

The *valido* had another constituency – the court, and the court nobility who looked to the new regimes in 1598, 1603 and 1610 to reverse what they saw as their exclusion from government and favour under Philip II, Elizabeth and Henri IV. Closed court rituals, notoriously parsimonious rulers, the narrowing membership of the councils of state, the professionalization of government and, indeed, of war, and the cornering of influence by secret cabinet juntas, ministers and even secretaries were blocking off the channels of magnate patronage upon which the whole nobility depended. And all this at a time when, for economic, demographic, political and cultural reasons, the pressure on the nobility to get its hands, one way or other, on the resources of states, which were absorbing an increasing proportion of the wealth of the community, was irresistible. The shift in the balance of resources between aristocracy and state, with the crisis of noble finances at the end of the long upward swing of the sixteenth century, was dramatic.[21] But no less important was the increasing centralization of honour, and the shift of the basis of clientage from authority in the localities to influence at court that was related to it. Courtiership and court patronage necessarily acquired increasing significance as alternative avenues of social advance and enrichment, not least among them the opportunities offered by war, were narrowing.

The new regimes – seeing enough warning signs of discontent – partly in response to the patronage bottleneck of the late sixteenth century, partly to win the allegiance of the nobility, and partly to create new government clienteles, adopted strategies of accommodation: opening the councils to the great nobility, splashing out on their courts, bestowing honours, freeing access to administrative office. In this process the *valido* had a key role, though by no means everywhere the same role, or even a single role: representative of the aristocratic reaction to the 'government of secretaries' (Oxenstierna, Lerma), or expression of a reaction against the restrengthening of the aristocracy at court (Concini); voice of the lesser nobility against the greater (de Luynes), or promoter of a new nobility against the old (Griffenfeld); front for one aristocratic faction against another (Buckingham), or means of cutting through the factionalism of the re-aristocratized councils (Lerma); linkman between the king and the nobility (Carr), or champion of royal authority over the grandees (Olivares, Richelieu).

Perhaps most important, he was, as Asch has pointed out, the instrument employed by the ruler to control the court, the king's patronage manager.[22] The explosion of patronage needed careful management if it was to serve a political purpose, or even if internal conflict within the court was to be avoided. But the patronage-management role of the *valido* also served a demand from below – the establishment of a single allocation queue, as Peck puts it,[23] was in the interests of both patron and client, which is perhaps why Lerma was once described as 'Protector General and Everyone's Advocate'.[24]

The Minister–Favourite and the Country

The *valimiento* is also to be seen as the expression of a new relationship between crown and country, linked with the two key political developments of the end of the sixteenth century: the increased need for the co-operation of the local elites, and the changing structure of power in the localities.

The strains on government and finance in the 1590s were immense, and, if in places there was some abatement after 1600, they returned with a vengeance in the 1620s. Governments were more and more having to seek parliamentary grants and concessionary revenues. Alongside traditional and novel exactions, the fiscality of the first half of the seventeenth century was characterized by concessionary and voluntary taxation, benevolences, *dons gratuits*, *donativos*, alienations and sales, all of which involved negotiation, persuasion and inducement. In these circumstances the co-operation of the localities with royal policy was more necessary than ever. The need to win compliance was a *continuous* exercise, not least because the political consensus of the late sixteenth century was breaking down and royal policy was getting less wholehearted endorsement.

However, the form of negotiation with the country was determined by the decline of direct aristocratic influence in the localities and by the increasing patrimonialization and venality of office, which increased the autonomy of local political elites, both from the crown and from the local magnate, and resulted in a significant expansion of the *political* nation – as Bacon remarked, 'nowadays . . . there is no vulgar, but all statesmen'.[25]

The standard sixteenth-century means of influencing local outcomes, relying on the good offices of the great local magnate, or sending courtiers and royal officials back to their countries as envoys, seem to be increasingly ineffective or inappropriate. In Castile, certainly, I get the impression not only that the grandees were being used less as local trouble-shooters in the cities, but that their intervention was frequently resented by the city oligarchies, and was often counter-productive. This fragmentation of local influence had the effect of multiplying direct contacts between government and locality and therefore making necessary a much more co-ordinated degree of management within the localities themselves, the lubricant for which was the *valido*'s access to the patronage of the crown.[26]

In Castile this was palpably different from what had been happening in the sixteenth century. That is not to say that in the sixteenth century connections between the country and the court were not important, nor that courtiers did not have local clientage, but they were individual and unsystematic, social not political. Under Philip II there does not seem to have been any coherent policy of extending court influence into the localities; indeed individual attempts to do so might well be blocked by a rival court faction.[27] But in the seventeenth century there was a conscious programme of infiltration into the oligarchies of the cities, which was clearly new and which was directly related to the new political importance of the Cortes of Castile from the 1590s. Lerma's regime sees the first substantial involvement of senior ministers of the crown in the Cortes itself (including Lerma as proctor on two occasions) and the beginnings of a systematic programme of patronage directed at the ruling oligarchies of the cities with a vote in the Cortes. The *valido* was at the centre of a web of patronage and clientage that spread over the entire kingdom of Castile. Lerma himself had offices in eight Cortes cities; Olivares was granted offices in every one of the nineteen cities represented in the Cortes – all served by substitutes of course. I am not aware that there are any parallels to be found among sixteenth-century ministers.[28]

Mutatis mutandis, this sort of intervention in the localities, which was perhaps only possible with, or at the very least facilitated by, the weakening of magnate power, was a common feature of the *valido*'s *modus operandi*. Court patronage and local clientelism were brought within a single system of control. They were also becoming politicized, for ministerial patronage was capable of a prescriptiveness that the king on his own, entrapped in a rhetoric of 'service' too flexible to ensure unquestioning compliance with royal demands, could not legitimately require.

Though kin and dependency ties are important in this, so too is pure patronage. It was patronage more than anything which provided the *valido* with a clientele which generalized his political influence across localities which were previously the separate spheres of influence of individual magnates, a process which, as well as promoting political cohesion, was contributing to the transformation of patronage from a private social relationship to a more prescriptively political one.[29]

Validos were thus part of a process of a social transformation of power in the localities. The building up of local clienteles reduced the local influence of *les grands*. Brokerage moves down the social scale in the seventeenth century.[30] The integration of local elites with the court via the centralized patronage of the *valido* shifted alignments within local society from clan loyalties to associational client relationships, part of a process of centralizing politics, and politicizing them.

The Minister–Favourite and the State

Finally, might it not be possible to see the emergence of the *valido* as a response to what, as a convenient shorthand, we can call 'The Crisis of the 1590s'? I am thinking here of the observations John Elliott made in his concluding contribution to Peter Clark's volume, an essay entitled with a pointed weariness, 'Yet Another Crisis?'.[31] What was different about the principal *validos* of the 1620s was that they were men with a new conviction that something could be done about the ills of government and society, and that they were the men who could do it. The *validos* were reformers, projectors, *arbitristas*. Faced with demands that were stretching the capacities of the state to breaking point, they were to be the means by which the power of the state would be extended. The *valido* was the instrument for the suppression of faction and the unification of the court, for the co-ordination of the machinery of government, the articulation of centre and locality, the mobilization of all the resources of the community for the support of royal policy, the proponent of programmes for the regeneration of the state and the harmonization of kingdoms.[32]

Should we see the *valido*, therefore, like the patronage-broker of which he was, at least in part, a particular kind, as specific to a particular phase in the development of the state?[33] In contrast to a Don Alvaro de Luna in the mid-fifteenth century, who could muster what was virtually a private army, the *valido* exercised a power totally dependent on the favour of the prince and on the resources of the state. His power, and the very transience of that power, was itself an assertion of the pre-eminence of the royal grace and an expression of the shift in the balance of authority as well as of resources within the body politic.[34] Inevitably – although the political cultures of Spain, England and France differed in this respect[35] – the *valimiento* was frequently seen as a subversion of the constitution, an instrument of tyranny, the harbinger of absolutism. But at the same time the state was facing demands at the limit of its capacities which it was not at a stage to meet without the co-operation of increasingly fragmented local and intermediate powers.[36] The *valido* thus had to employ the carrot as much as, and perhaps even more effectively than, the stick. Clientage was compromise; it involved working with existing political structures rather than assaulting their autonomy. Richelieu's handling of the Estates of Brittany is a particularly illuminating illustration of the circumstances in which it was not always advisable to pursue so-called absolutist solutions, and of the mutual benefits, to the crown as well as to the province, to be gained from mutual accommodation.[37] In Brittany, as elsewhere, the *valido* was the interface between loyalty to the local community and loyalty to the interests of the state.

Institutionally, the *valido* emerged in the window of transition between a private and a public bureaucracy, between a judicialist and an instrumentalist conception of government, between the *Rechtsstaat* and the *Verwaltungsstaat*, between the *Respublica Christiana* and *raison d'état*. The question that remains is, to what extent was the *valido* to be instrumental in effectuating that transition?

Notes

1. F. Tomás y Valiente, *Los validos en la monarquía española del siglo XVII* (Madrid, 1963), p. 181.
2. William Doyle, *The Old European Order, 1660–1800* (Oxford, 1978), p. 262: 'The period offers plenty of examples of favourites . . . or adventurers who shook states to their foundations on the strength of personal relationships with rulers' – Law, Alberoni, Squillache, Godoy, Potemkin, Struensee, as well as Tanucci, Pombal and so on; Elizabeth Marvick, 'Favorites in Early Modern Europe: A Recurring Psychopolitical Role', *Journal of Psychohistory*, 10 (1983), pp. 463–89.
3. Jean Bérenger, 'Pour une enquête européenne: ie problème du ministériat au XVIIe siècle', *Annales*, 29 (1974), pp. 166–92.
4. For an exceptional analysis of the phenomenon of the early-seventeenth-century favourite, see Francesco Benigno, *L'Ombra del Re* (Venice, 1992), esp. pp. ix–xxxv.
5. Antonio Feros Carrasco, 'Gobierno de Corte y Patronazgo Real en el reinado de Felipe III' (tesis de licenciatura, Universidad Autónoma de Madrid, 1986), pp. vi, 23; Simon Adams, 'Favourites and Factions at the Elizabethan Court', in R. Asch and A. Birke, eds, *Princes, Patronage and the Nobility: The Court at the Beginning of the Modern Age, c. 1450–1650* (Oxford, 1991), pp. 265–87, at p. 265; Arlette Jouanna, 'Faveur et favoris: l'exemple des mignons de Henri III', in R. Sauzet, ed., *Henri III et son temps* (Paris, 1989), pp. 155–65, as cited by David Potter, 'Kingship in the Wars of Religion: The Reputation of Henri III of France', *European History Quarterly*, 24 (1995), pp. 485–528, at p. 507.
6. For these categorizations, respectively, Marvick, 'Favorites in Early Modern Europe', p. 465; A. Lloyd Moote, 'Richelieu as Chief Minister', in J. Bergin and L. Brockliss, eds, *Richelieu and his Age* (Oxford, 1992), pp. 13–43, at p. 16; Adams, 'Favourites and Factions', p. 272; Antoni Mączak, 'From Aristocratic Household to Princely Court: Restructuring Patronage in the Sixteenth and Seventeenth Centuries', in Asch and Birke, *Princes, Patronage and the Nobility*, pp. 315–27.
7. Tomás y Valiente, *Los validos*, p. 7.
8. Baltasar Alamos y Barrientos, *Discurso político al rey Felipe III al comienzo de su reinado*, ed. Modesto Santos (Barcelona, 1990), p. 92. Antonio Feros, 'Lerma y Olivares: la práctica del valimiento en la primera mitad del seiscientos', in J. H. Elliott and Angel García Sanz, eds, *La España del Conde Duque de Olivares* (Valladolid, 1990), pp. 195–224, at p. 217, and *idem*, 'Gobierno de Corte', pp. 69, 72.

9. Roger Lockyer, *Buckingham: The Life and Political Career of George Villiers, First Duke of Buckingham, 1592–1628* (London, 1981), p. 464; J. Bergin and L. Brockliss, eds, *Richelieu and his Age*, 'Introduction', pp. 1–11, at p. 2; J. H. Elliott, *Richelieu and Olivares* (Cambridge, 1984), p. 47; R. A. Stradling, *Philip IV and the Government of Spain, 1621–1665* (Cambridge, 1988).

10. Geoffrey Parker, *Europe in Crisis, 1598–1648* (London, 1979), p. 56; Bérenger, 'Le Problème du ministériat', p. 166; Richard Bonney, *The European Dynastic States, 1494–1660* (Oxford, 1991), p. 382, and *idem*, 'Louis XIII, Richelieu, and the Royal Finances', in Bergin and Brockliss, eds, *Richelieu and his Age*, pp. 99–133, at p. 122; Elliott, *Richelieu and Olivares*, p. 50.

11. A. Lloyd Moote, *Louis XIII, The Just* (Berkeley, 1989), p. 107; Tomás y Valiente, *Los validos*, p. 181.

12. Tomás y Valiente, *Los validos*, p. 181, letter of 30 January 1647.

13. Feros, 'Gobierno de Corte', pp. 23–4.

14. Francisco Bermúdez de Pedraza, *El Secretario del Rey* (1620), facsimile edn (Madrid, 1973), fol. 12v, 'VM no ha tenido Secretario privado porque los Grandes de España afectos de su servicio toman este cuidado, despachando con su Real persona a boca las consultas y los expedientes del Secretario, con que en la realidad y en la substancia el privado viene a ser el Secretario, pues el exercicio es el que le hace, y no el nombre.' Victor Morgan, 'Some Types of Patronage, Mainly in Sixteenth- and Seventeenth-Century England', in Antoni Mączak, *Klientelsysteme im Europa der Frühen Neuzeit* (Munich, 1988), pp. 91–115, at p. 111.

15. During the last dozen years of Philip II, the previously single secretariats of the Cámara, Finance and Italy were each split into three, and those of War and the Indies into two. The two secretaries of state after 1586 were nonentities. Escudero lists forty-seven secretarial titles issued in 1516–79, sixty-three in 1584–1621, and seventy-six in 1621–30: José Antonio Escudero, *Los Secretarios del Estado y del Despacho (1474–1724)*, 4 vols (Madrid, 1969), iii, pp. 703–13.

16. See my 'War and Institutionalization: The Military–Administrative Bureaucracy of Spain in the Sixteenth and Seventeenth Centuries', in I. A. A. Thompson, *Crown and Cortes: Government, Institutions and Representation in Early-Modern Castile* (Aldershot, 1993), ch. 3.

17. Bermúdez de Pedraza, *El Secretario del Rey*, fol. 20v.

18. Neil Cuddy, 'Anglo-Scottish Union and the Court of James I, 1603–1625', *Transactions of the Royal Historical Society*, 5th series, 39 (1989), pp. 107–24, at p. 122: 'even an established monarch would have found it difficult to purge the bureaucracy, or create new offices in pursuit of policies'. And in a similar vein, Lockyer, *Buckingham*, p. 415.

19. The other side of the coin is that everywhere the institutionalization of counsel and the formal regulation of council membership and procedure were advocated as an essential barrier to the arbitrariness of the *valido* and tyrannical rule.

20. Lockyer, *Buckingham*, pp. 466–7, 473; Feros, 'Gobierno de Corte', p. 93 n. 15.

21. For example, the revenues of the titled nobility in Castile in 1516 were roughly the same as those of the crown; by 1600 they amounted to scarcely more than a third of the king's revenues, and there were twice as many *títulos* to share them.

22. Ronald Asch, 'Introduction: Court and Household from the 15th to the 17th Centuries', in Asch and Birke, eds, *Princes, Patronage and the Nobility*, pp. 1–38, at p. 22.

23. Linda Levy Peck, *Court Patronage and Corruption in Early Stuart England* (London, 1990).

24. Iñigo Ibáñez de Santa Cruz, 'Discurso crítico contra el govierno de Felipe II' (1599), Biblioteca Nacional, Madrid, Ms. 10.635, fols 1–44. Malcolm Smuts, 'Cultural Diversity and Cultural Change at the Court of James I', in Linda Levy Peck, ed., *The Mental World of the Jacobean Court* (Cambridge, 1991), p. 107 and n. 30.

25. Kevin Sharpe, 'Crown, Parliament and Locality: Government in Early Stuart England', *English Historical Review*, 101 (1986), pp. 321–50, at p. 336.

26. John K. Gruenfelder, *Influence in Early Stuart Elections* (Columbus, Ohio, 1981), identifies a new approach to government interference in parliamentary elections after 1614; for similar activity in France at the same time, J. Michael Hayden, *France and the Estates General of* 1614 (Cambridge, 1974), p. 7.

27. Santiago Fernández Conti, 'La Nobleza Cortesana: Don Diego de Cabrera y Bobadilla, Tercer Conde de Chinchón', in José Martínez Millán, ed., *La Corte de Felipe II* (Madrid, 1994), pp. 229–70, at p. 251: Eraso blocks Chinchón's attempt to acquire the office of Alférez Mayor of Segovia, 1566.

28. José Martínez Millán, in the 'Introducción' to his *La Corte de Felipe II*, pp. 13–35, at p. 24, says Cardinal Espinosa also made an intense effort to control the city councils by getting his clients placed in all of them; but the document he cites refers to the appointment of *corregidores* (royal city

governors), not the ruling city oligarchs (*regidores*), and the evidence that I have does not suggest that, if there ever was such a policy, it was persevered with.

29. Lockyer, *Buckingham*, pp. 276, 331; Peck, *Court Patronage*, pp. 52, 91, 214; Sharpe, 'Crown, Parliament and Locality', pp. 329–30. And for an earlier period, Nicholas Round, *The Greatest Man Uncrowned: A Study of the Fall of Don Alvaro de Luna* (London, 1986), p. 19: 'Instead of reflecting a confused balance of the different claims and pressures on the king, with appointees beholden to a dozen secondary patrons, the service of the Crown became . . . a coherent vehicle for a single line of policy.'

30. Arlette Jouanna, *Le Devoir de révolte* (Paris, 1989), pp. 233–4; Sharpe; 'Crown, Parliament and Locality', pp. 330, 343; Peck *Court Patronage*, p. 55. For Castile, I. A. A. Thompson, 'Patronazgo real e integración política en las ciudades castellanas bajo los Austrias', in José Ignacio Fortea Pérez, ed., *Imágenes de la Diversidad: El Mundo Urbano en la Corona de Castilla (S. XVI–XVIII)* (Santander, 1997), pp. 475–96.

31. Peter Clark, ed., *The European Crisis of the 1590s* (London, 1985), pp. 301–12.

32. This is not only the case for Richelieu, Olivares and Oxenstierna; even Buckingham was a champion of financial reform: Lockyer, *Buckingham*, pp. 47–8, 49–50; for Lerma, see Feros, 'Gobierno de Corte', pp. 89–90; for Griffenfeld in Denmark and Enslin in Württemberg see the essays by Jespersen and Asch in the present volume (Chapters 17 and 7).

33. Sharon Kettering, 'The Historical Development of Political Clientelism', *Journal of Interdisciplinary History*, 18 (1988), pp. 419–47, at pp. 432–3; Benigno, *L'Ombra del Re*, p. ix.

34. This is the argument of James M. Boyden, *The Courtier and the King: Ruy Gómez de Silva, Philip II, and the Court of Spain* (Berkeley, 1995).

35. See the essays by Feros, Worden and Dubost in this volume (Chapters 13, 11 and 5).

36. Bergin and Brockliss, eds, *Richelieu and his Age*, p. 3.

37. See K. Dunkley, 'Richelieu's Clients and the Estates of Brittany', *Parliaments, Estates and Representation*, 1 (1981), pp. 1–12.

2

'Fortune Has Stripped You of Your Splendour': Favourites and their Fates in Fifteenth- and Sixteenth-Century Spain

JAMES M. BOYDEN

En route to his retirement at Yuste, the emperor Charles V passed in the autumn of 1556 through the highland village of Pancorbo, north-east of Burgos. The villagers welcomed Charles and his party with joyful pomp, and presented him with a lavish gift. When the welcoming ceremonies drew to a close, the town officials petitioned the emperor to grant them a certain minor jurisdiction. Charles replied by thanking them for their hospitality and gift, but explained that, having renounced his kingdoms, he no longer wielded power or influence over jurisdictional matters. Absorbing this unwelcome news, the town councillors responded that 'if that's so, then we humbly kiss Your Majesty's hands in thanks for your goodwill toward our affairs, and now we'll be taking back our present'.[1]

The attractions of this story are several, and for the most part obvious. Now as – most likely – then, it is funny. It portrays the villagers in the half-flattering, half-mocking manner familiar from some of the *comedias* of the time; simultaneously they are shrewd but clumsily calculating, plainspoken but churlish, unawed yet sycophantic. For the man who preserved the anecdote, however, its significance was more serious. In his *Miscelánea*, compiled towards the end of the sixteenth century, Luis Zapata used this tale to illustrate the themes of 'the World's Nature Revealed', and 'Human Disloyalty'. Perhaps surprisingly, condemnation of the villagers' inconstancy is not the sole or even the principal moral pointed by Zapata; instead the entry ends with a comparison of the emperor to a stream that, at flood, shivers the timbers of the greatest vessels, but that in the subsequent dry season is easily forded by 'little animals'.[2]

This imperial anecdote, then, is presented as a tale of 'how the mighty have fallen'. Everywhere and always, perhaps, there exists a popular appetite for this sort of narrative, although today perhaps the public expects not so much to see the great overturned as to learn that their greatness is a fraud. It has been widely noted, though, that reversals of fortune were favoured topics of early modern literature and philosophy. Writers of the period often seem to utilize biographical narrative merely as a perfunctory set-up for the predictable punchline of the subject's fall from power, prosperity or grace. Juan de Mariana provides an especially bald example of this approach in his *Historia general de España* when he introduces Bartolomé de Carranza at the time of his elevation to the archiepiscopal see of Toledo. Obviously looking forward to Carranza's lengthy ordeal with the Inquisition, Mariana observes that 'it seems that he rose so high [simply] in order that his fall might be the more severe'.[3]

This atmosphere is particularly pervasive in the literature of the period concerning *privados*, the favourites of the Spanish kings. The state of *privanza* is generally depicted as inherently unstable, transitory. Favour consumes those upon whom it is bestowed, or, in the words of one sixteenth-century observer: 'Great confidences [between royal master and favourite] end in precipitous downfalls.'[4] There are a number of reasons for this generalized attitude. One of the most striking will emerge from a brief consideration of the career of Alvaro de Luna, the greatest of Castilian *privados*, at least before the dawn of the seventeenth century (pl. 2). Born in the 1380s, the bastard son of a prominent family and the nephew of the anti-pope Benedict XIII, Alvaro de Luna came to the court of Castile in 1408, and two years later became a page of the child-king Juan II. As so often before and since, special favour – *privanza* – was born in this situation out of the personal service of a young nobleman to a child prince; by 1419, when Juan II came into his majority at age fourteen, Alvaro de Luna was his undisputed favourite.[5]

For the next three decades and more, Don Alvaro remained the king's favourite and was the principal figure in Juan II's government. For his services, he was named Constable of Castile and Master of the Order of Santiago. The king's gifts and his own acquisitiveness made Alvaro de Luna the wealthiest lord in the kingdom, while his political acumen and military skills saved his royal master from domination by the ambitious Infantes of Aragon and the restive nobles of Castile. The wonder of the constable's career was eclipsed only by the stunning horror of its end, for in 1453 Juan II found resolve for one of the few times in his long reign, and ordered the arrest and execution of his long-time favourite. Alvaro de Luna would probably not be particularly consoled by the judgement of modern historians, who praise his efforts on behalf of Juan II for opening the way to royal absolutism in Castile, citing his own arbitrary death sentence as the clinching proof of the newfound powers of the crown.[6]

It is difficult to imagine a more striking illustration of the transitory nature of earthly fortune than the spectacle of the constable's execution in a public square of Valladolid on 2 June 1453. Certainly the event caught the imagination of contemporary poets. 'Look then to that great Constable,' wrote Jorge Manrique, 'the Master whom we knew so deeply favoured by the king / And yet even of him nothing more need be said than that we saw him beheaded. / His limitless treasures, his towns and villages, his power of command / What did they bring him but tears? / What were they to him except sorrows at the leaving?'[7] More famously, Iñigo López de Mendoza, Marquis of Santillana, who hated and resented the constable in life as a lowborn upstart, eulogized him with a sneering pun: 'De tu resplandor io Luna! / te ha privado la fortuna.' Santillana's verses combine taunts and curses, at one point insinuating a parallel between Don Alvaro and Lucifer, who was cast down for excessive pride and for coveting his creator's throne. The poem lingers over images of the inexorable turning of fortune's wheel, disregarded by the constable in his arrogance. 'I'm sure you never thought such a turnabout could take place,' Santillana continues, before tracing a bleak depiction of a lunar eclipse and rendering the cold judgement that 'you get the reward you deserve'.[8] In another poem – the 'Doctrinal de privados', its lessons all derived from the constable's perceived failings – Santillana puts the same admission in Don Alvaro's own mouth. He had enjoyed 'higher station and greater wealth than was ever before seen in Spain / An abundance undreamt of by any other *privado*'. Even these blessings, however, were unable to stay his 'raging appetite for gold'; undone by greed and power-hunger, at the end Don Alvaro found himself 'left with nothing but this scaffold'.[9]

The vivid image of Alvaro de Luna at the execution block dominated literary treatments of *privanza* throughout the early modern period in Spain. According to one scholar, the constable's 'personality and tragic fate . . . were so deeply embedded in the national consciousness that any discussion of favoritism – Spanish or foreign, past or contemporary – inevitably returned to him'.[10] Most obviously, an array of poets and playwrights were inspired by the death sentence and execution of Rodrigo Calderón in 1621 to take up once again the theme of courtly glory curtailed on the gallows; predictably, contemporary concerns were cloaked by resort to historical dramatization.[11] If Don Alvaro's fate comprised tragedy, it is difficult today to avoid regarding Don Rodrigo's as its repetition as farce, since leaving aside their similarly dignified deportment on the scaffold there are few points of similarity between the two figures. But, no matter how criminal Calderón may have been, his end certainly reinforced the contemporary vision of the mutability of a *privado*'s fortune.

For now, though, to return to the constable's case: some further aspects of his story shed light on the lineaments of *privanza* as they were to be perceived at least through the reign of Philip II. First of all, when we look to the reasons why the constable was brought low in 1453, they reduce themselves primarily to a shift in the three-way relationship between Juan II, Alvaro de Luna and the great Castilian lords. Repeatedly during his career, Don Alvaro through his intrigues and campaigns had preserved the king's freedom of action in the face of aristocrats who sought to control him. For this, and for his wealth and arrogance, Alvaro de Luna had been roundly hated by most of the higher nobility; three times, their machinations had led to his banishment, and, as Santillana's verses suggest, many of them celebrated his execution. Juan II, on the other hand, had traditionally shielded his favourite as best he could from the envy and plotting of his high-born enemies. But the constable's arrest in 1453 arose from a reversal of this conjuncture, with the king making common cause with the great families of Estúñiga (Zúñiga) and Mendoza to lay hands on his erstwhile favourite.[12]

The reasons for Juan II's change of heart have been variously assessed. Perhaps the most persuasive interpretation is that the king, knowing that he had only a short time to live, wanted to smooth his son Enrique's succession by removing the overmighty constable from the board. (And in fact Juan II survived Alvaro de Luna by less than fourteen months.)[13] But, while we may never know the king's inner motives or precise calculations, his public explanation was quite explicit. According to Juan II, Don Alvaro's principal crime was that he 'has for a long time held and usurped a chief position near me and in my household and court', and despite having been admonished about his excessive pride and effrontery 'he has persevered in it . . . grasping more power to himself each day, excessively, without temperance or measure, so that there remains to me no room to rule and administer my kingdoms personally, nor to maintain my towns in justice and truth and law . . .'.[14]

Not surprisingly, the constable saw matters in another light. While the king alleged usurpation of his royal authority, Don Alvaro responded with a charge of ingratitude, levelled in a tone meant to convey the sadness and resignation of a loyal servant stripped at last of his illusions. Rather than withdraw into a well-deserved retirement after forty-five years of service, he wrote,

> I chose . . . to serve as I was in duty bound and as I felt the situation demanded; I deceived myself, for this service has been the cause of my misfortune. How bitter that I should find myself deprived of liberty who more than once have risked life and fortune to preserve your highness's freedom! I am well aware that for my great sins I have angered God, and I will consider it a boon if I can placate his rage through these travails.[15]

This appeal to justice was accompanied by an offer of treasure, but neither swayed the king, who was so intent upon Don Alvaro's destruction that he would finally order his execution despite the failure of a hand-picked tribunal to render a clear sentence of death.[16]

At the very end, Alvaro de Luna returned to the theme of royal ingratitude. From the scaffold he is said to have called out to one of the household officers of the crown prince Enrique: 'Go to the prince and tell him for me that when the time comes to reward his own servants he ought not to follow the king's example.'[17] This taunt may have hit home; at least Juan II's apologists took pains to reverse the charges of ingratitude and disloyalty. Thus Santillana's litany: 'On the one hand, the inexhaustible largesse of a magnanimous lord / On the other, the damnable ingratitude of a servile nature / Here, the constancy and virtue of the master / There, the arrogant lackey singing his own praises'.[18]

Here, then, in the sad end of Alvaro de Luna, we find presaged some of the key elements that would condition the relationships of kings and favourites up to the end of the sixteenth century and to some extent beyond. Inevitably the *privado* (and especially a relatively lowborn favourite like Alvaro de Luna) would excite the envy and resentment of the high nobility.[19] This situation could work to the crown's benefit in several ways: first, the *privado*'s political utility might consist in large part in maintaining some distance between these great nobles, their private concerns, and the monarch; secondly, the favourite rather than the monarch would usually attract the bulk of opprobrium for policies antithetical to aristocratic interests (or at least monarchs might hope so);[20] finally, the king by siding with the magnates could at any moment bring the favourite to heel or even to ruin.

Of course, jealous aristocrats were not alone in being capable of resenting the influence and pretensions of *privados*. More dangerously, the king might conclude, as Juan II did or at least claimed to have done, that the favourite had usurped powers that were rightfully the monarch's alone. Here the specific example of Alvaro de Luna undoubtedly exerted a cautionary influence on subsequent *privados* – and may provide a partial explanation of the motivations behind the more explicit and legalistic delegation of royal powers that characterized the seventeenth-century *valimientos* beginning with that of the Duke of Lerma.[21]

Moreover, at least in the sixteenth century, *privados* and to some extent their royal masters as well seem to have operated in the expectation that their relationships would be characterized by ingratitude, inconstancy and fickle reversals of favour and fortune. With the trenchant bitterness that was his literary speciality, Antonio Pérez insisted that 'the favour of Princes is False, Feeble, Deadly, the Shadow of Death: Death itself'.[22] Meanwhile, maritime metaphors, with their ominous suggestion of the constant danger of shipwreck, were quite common: the court, for example, was equated with a dangerous stretch of water, while another writer referred to royal 'favour as treacherous as the sandbanks of Flanders'.[23] Injustice was the rule, according to Antonio de Guevara, who asserted that 'at court . . . the man of great merit is persecuted'.[24] As far as can be judged from the problematic testimony that exists, favourites and courtiers mused openly about the vicissitudes of fortune, casting themselves as long-suffering servants loyally proceeding with their onerous duties despite the inconstancy, envy and perfidy eroding their positions.

As we saw above, Alvaro de Luna was hardly behindhand in striking this attitude. Few of his successors, however, were forced to carry the pose to such lengths – after all, the constable in his final role provided a perfect portrayal of courage, indifference, Christian resignation and ironic bemusement on the scaffold. It is difficult to avoid the suspicion that later *privados* largely feigned stoic acceptance in order to lessen the chances that they would have to act it out on such a grisly stage. As so often, Francis Bacon here provides shrewd guidance about the theatre of the court. '[Y]ou shall observe', he wrote, 'that the more deep and sober sort of politic persons, in their greatness, are ever bemoaning themselves what a life they lead, chanting a *quanta patimur*. Not that they feel it so, but only to abate the edge of envy.'[25] Guevara made a similar point. 'At court,' he remarked, 'everyone curses the court, and then they all follow it.'[26] But, while we may plausibly doubt that Spanish favourites were philosophic men of constant sorrow, the personal and power relationships inherent in *privanza* and the attitudes respecting it that I have begun to sketch were bound to impede the maintenance of the sort of stable, lengthy, trusting relations between monarchs and favourites that could develop into a truly ministerial mode of government.

To elaborate the point that favourites did not easily become ministers, it may be useful to turn now to a consideration of some aspects of *privanza* during the reign of Philip II (pl. 3), and more broadly to the evolving style of rule exercised by the Prudent King. Philip's first and most durable *privado* was Ruy Gómez de Silva (pl. 4), better known to history as the Prince of Eboli. Ruy Gómez was born around 1516, the second son of middling Portuguese nobles, and came to the court of Castile as a young boy in the entourage of Charles V's bride, the empress Isabel of Portugal. He served the prince (born 1527) in his infancy, and was assigned a minor post in Philip's first household in 1535. Over the next decade, the two formed a close bond, cemented with Ruy Gómez's appointment to a privy household post as *sumiller de corps* in 1548.[27] Elsewhere I have studied Ruy Gómez's conquest of political influence, his exercise of a leading role in government in the period of Philip's succession and the opening years of the reign, and his bitter rivalry with the Castilian grandees, captained at court by the Duke of Alba.[28] More to the point here, however, is his fall, which unlike that of Alvaro de Luna was gradual, prolonged and only partial.

In brief, what happened was that over the decade of the 1560s Philip and his favourite drew slowly apart. The king seems to have concluded soon after returning to Spain in 1559 that Ruy Gómez's value as a minister was not sufficient to warrant unlimited defence of the *privado* against the insults and allegations of Alba and other aristocrats. Eboli reacted cautiously, by withdrawing from the public prominence that so incited his rivals. He was further devalued in mid-decade by the prosecution for corruption of his closest ally, the secretary Francisco de Eraso, and by the simultaneous emergence of a more efficient rival in the person of Diego de Espinosa. At the same time, he was saddled with supervising the increasingly erratic heir to the throne, Don Carlos, and doubtless was tainted in the king's perception by association with the prince's sad decline. Finally, Ruy Gómez offered Philip blatantly self-interested counsel of compromise with the Dutch rebels. Rather surprisingly, this string of setbacks did not lead to dismissal from court or worse.[29]

Philip's genuine affection and, more important, Ruy Gómez's extraordinary suavity and uncanny instinct for backing off at the earliest sign of conflict with royal desires combined to preserve Eboli's place near the king if no longer in his intimate confidence. As his governmental power declined, Ruy Gómez devoted his remaining influence at court to acquiring wealth and a landed estate, and eventually a Castilian ducal title.[30]

Recognition of the courtly skill of this feat reportedly led even the *privado*'s bitter rival, the Duke of Alba, to remark that:

> Señor Ruygomez . . . was not one of the greatest Counsellors that there has been, but I acknowledge him . . . as so great a master of that herein [in the king's inner chamber], and of the temper and disposition of Kings, that all the rest of us who pass through here have our heads where we think we are carrying our feet.[31]

Other contemporary appreciations of Eboli's achievements also stress his soft landing. Thus Cabrera de Córdoba, in an elaboration of the maritime metaphor, after characterizing the court as a 'dangerous gulf' eulogized Ruy Gómez as 'the first pilot who, in such huge undertakings, lived and died secure, always choosing the best port'.[32] Eboli's protégé Antonio Pérez was presumably contemplating his mentor's prowess and his own failings when he asserted that 'the Favour of *Privados* is no less treacherous than a light Berber horse, and he must be a fine horseman and have a very good seat who would not be dislodged from the saddle or thrown off altogether'.[33]

Ruy Gómez's accomplishment in the course of his extended *privanza*, as described by contemporaries and narrated here, amounted to self-preservation and the aggrandizement of his lineage. In this, and from a purely personal point of view, he was infinitely more successful than Alvaro de Luna. On the other hand and from the crown's perspective, though, Eboli can scarcely be seen as an advance over the luckless constable in terms of an evolution of *privanza* into a responsible and effective ministry of state. And it does not seem utterly implausible to postulate a connection between recognition of the bitter fate of Don Alvaro and the strategic backing and trimming of Ruy Gómez. Some evidence exists that Eboli was steeped in the sorrowful language of fortune's cruelty to her one-time favourites. Antonio Pérez depicts him as musing often on the fickle winds of favour, and lamenting that his loyalty to the king keeps him at court long after his service has ceased to bring enjoyment or fulfilment.[34] That this ostensible inner pain hardly interfered with his estate-building exertions may lend further credence to the suggestion that the courtly rhetoric of disillusion and stoical resignation was in some cases a stylized form of protective coloration.

But we can hardly be surprised that personal survival and the optimization of fortune's bounty were prime career goals of a royal favourite. Don Alvaro, after all, was in truth the exception, the rare *privado* who, in addition to enriching himself and his friends and family, rendered signal service to the crown's broader interests. His reward emphatically did not encourage emulation, but more importantly the very conditions in which *privanza* typically was born and nurtured were hardly propitious for the production of disinterested statesmen. For, as Antonio Feros has argued, the essence of the relationship between monarch and favourite is friendship, with all its potential vicissitudes.[35]

In most cases it is difficult to envision these particular friendships as other than irregular and innately dysfunctional. Their origins almost invariably lay in the affection of sheltered and lonely child-princes for unctuously solicitous adolescent or young adult males who were their servants and constant companions. With a bit of adjectival alteration here and there, this sentence can stand as a description of the initial relationships of Juan II with Alvaro de Luna, of Enrique IV with Juan Pacheco, of Philip II with Ruy Gómez de Silva, of Philip III with Lerma and of Philip IV with Olivares. Such peculiar friendships would almost inevitably become strained as the friends grew older. Often, the prince's initial attraction must have been akin to hero-worship of an older, more graceful or more worldly male. In adulthood, though, such heroes of childhood often come to appear pathetic, and may be viewed with distaste because of the association with the very weaknesses to which they once appealed. Moreover, the exaggerated attentiveness that originally attracted the prince's attention to the favourite may have had diminished appeal to an adult monarch with broader experience of flattery. Finally, the inherently dramatic inequality between king and even his most favoured subject had to place strains on friendship, which could only grow more severe as the monarch matured into a sense of his power and prerogatives. No matter how ingratiating the *privado*, wrote Antonio Pérez, and 'although he may love the gratification of his inclinations, the Prince will most often turn his face to the honour of the office'. The result is that monarchs 'are habitually abashed with the passage of time, and with the burden of the public's complaints and those of the greatest estates, and adding their own indictment [are wont] to exonerate themselves by means of the punishment and exclusion of the *Privado*'.[36]

Returning, then, to our specific case: in parallel with Ruy Gómez's tactical disengagement from the public aspects of *privanza* and the redirection of his energies into private pursuits we may postulate on Philip II's part a gradual process of disillusionment with his long-time favourite. As Ruy Gómez entered middle age, the athleticism and grace that may initially have commended him to Philip were doubtless waning, and in the very years when the king himself was rather belatedly leaving his awkward youth. The most important aspect, however, of this royal farewell to youth was that in the course of the 1560s Philip seems to have emerged from his father's long and daunting shadow. As he gained faith in his own ability to rule, his estimation of the favourite of his youth waned proportionally, helped along by revelations of Ruy Gómez's failings and character flaws. Twenty years earlier, Philip had clung the more tightly to Ruy Gómez in mildly rebellious response to the emperor's directive that he must leave childhood and lighthearted childish companions behind, as he turned his attention to matters of state under the tutelage of older and wiser men.[37] The suave and youthful courtier Ruy Gómez had been the inexperienced prince-regent's friend and ally in a situation where he was surrounded by the stern old advisers of Charles V. But, as king in his own right in the Spain of the 1560s, Philip II must have begun to see the comforting companion of his youth as an ineffectual and self-serving aide in the business of government.

In 1543, Charles V had warned his son not to delegate too much authority to a single person:

> Not now, not ever, not to [anyone] else, but instead conduct your business with many [advisers] and don't bind or oblige yourself to any single individual; for although this would allow you a more restful existence, it is nonetheless ill-advised . . . because they will then say – quite likely with reason – that you are governed, and moreover any person in whom such confidence was reposed would swell up with pride and become high and mighty . . . in the end everyone else would become aggrieved and querulous.[38]

But, even in his latter-day disillusion with Ruy Gómez, Philip II was not yet ready to accept this paternal advice in its entirety. Instead, he replaced Eboli with the churchman Diego de Espinosa, in a *privanza* that now partook more of business than of affection. The emperor's lesson seems to have taken only with the disgrace and death of Espinosa in 1572. The king regretted having entrusted so many of his affairs to the cardinal. 'Perhaps,' he wrote, 'there were good reasons for it then. But experience has shown that it was not a good thing; and although it meant more leisure and less work for me, I do not think it should be allowed to continue.'[39]

And in fact Philip II never again placed such great political reliance on a *privado*. When he came to pass his accumulated wisdom about ruling to his successor, the king cautioned the future Philip III to 'make use of all, without submitting yourself to anyone . . . but rather hearing out many men and maintaining proper discretion with each'.[40] The echoes of Charles V's advice are unmistakable. Towards the end of his life, the king feared that the close personal relationships of his youth and early manhood had clouded his monarchical judgement. In full maturity he preferred to know his servants and subjects from written reports, and even his lands were more familiar to him from research than from experience: 'He had full reports of all his provinces, cities, towns, sites, wildernesses, rivers, of their advantages civil and military, their finances, manufactures and tributes: and what he neither strode nor saw was represented to him in pictures.'[41] The king's withdrawal from public view (or *retraimiento*) in later life, while obviously a product of personal and psychological predilection, was also then a response to his mounting distrust of *privados* (a distrust soon enough exacerbated by the Antonio Pérez affair). He devoted his life to the state papers rather than confide his affairs – and by extension his trust – in another favourite. And, through the familiar process that converts the whim of a forebear into immemorial family custom, from Philip's *retraimiento* developed the Spanish Habsburg royal style of the 'invisible and inaccessible' king, most recently examined by Antonio Feros, the reclusive and dignified style which would govern courtly arrangements in the subsequent reigns.[42]

Philip's withdrawn style has been subjected to a scathing critique by Fernando Bouza Alvarez.[43] Without fully subscribing to Bouza's condemnation of the so-called Prudent King, one can certainly identify some problematic results of the new sphinx-like style of monarchy. Ironically, one of these may have been to enhance the possibility that the wills of subsequent Habsburg princes would be captivated be scheming favourites. That contemporaries recognized this danger may be inferred from Juan de Mariana's *Historia general de España*, drafted in the last years of Philip II and revised at the outset of the era of Philip III and the Duke of Lerma. Purporting to explain how Juan II had fallen under the influence of Alvaro de Luna, the Jesuit historian – and theorist of monarchy – asserted:

> It is a miserable way to raise a king, leading to the gravest harms, to insist that the lord of all should not move about in public nor be seen by his vassals, to the extent that he does not even recognize the grandees who visit him; it is a shameful thing that they should deprive the Prince of the liberty to speak, to see and to be seen. . . . [Well might he ask] why do you treat me, who was born for toil and exertion, like a capon in the fattening cage?

For Mariana, the inevitable result was that the king would 'forever subordinate himself to the will and command of his courtiers and palace servants'.[44]

Mariana wrote at the dawn of the great age of minister–favourites in the Spanish monarchy, and there is a certain attractiveness to his implication that, rather than biological decline, a cultural legacy bestowed by those whom we once knew as the 'greater' upon the succeeding 'lesser' Habsburgs may account for the pronounced dependence of the latter on favourites. This is not, however, the place for further exploration of the seventeenth-century development of the *valimiento*. Instead I will return in conclusion to my theme of the association of *privanza* with a bleak view of fortune and loyalty, in order to observe that, even in the seventeenth-century golden age of the minister–favourite, the relationships of monarchs and *privados* were no less prone than before to end badly, in regrets, recriminations, expressions of existential gloom, or worse. After all, Lerma, notwithstanding two decades of unparalleled *valimiento*, was exiled from court in 1618, and saw fit to take out the insurance of an ecclesiastical dignity against the eventuality of a more dire fall from favour. Three years later, Rodrigo Calderón re-enacted Alvaro de Luna's appointment with the headsman, reprising the constable's dignity in the face of death even though he had shared few of Don Alvaro's virtues as a *privado*. And even the greatest of the minister–favourites, the Count-Duke of Olivares, had occasion in the disgraced and half-mad exile of his last years to exclaim that the only sure things in life were 'instability and inconstancy and lack of gratitude'.[45] Among the ranks of *privados*, we would, it seems, be hard pressed to find anyone to reject the famous description of attendance upon princes as 'a poor richness; an abundance miserable; a highness that falleth; an estate not stable; a surety trembling; and an evil life'.[46]

Notes

1. Luis Zapata, *Varia historia (Miscelánea)*, i, ed. G. C. Horsman (Amsterdam, 1935), pp. 108–9.
2. *Ibid.*
3. Juan de Mariana, *Historia general de España*, in *Obras*, ii, Biblioteca de Autores Españoles 31 (Madrid, 1909), p. 393.
4. Antonio Pérez, *Aphorismos de las cartas españolas y latinas de Ant. Perez* (Paris, 1598?), fols 14r–15v.
5. See the useful chronology in Raymond R. MacCurdy, *The Tragic Fall: Don Alvaro de Luna and Other Favorites in Spanish Golden Age Drama* (Chapel Hill, NC, 1978), pp. 104ff.
6. See most recently and extensively Nicholas Round, *The Greatest Man Uncrowned: A Study of the Fall of Don Alvaro de Luna* (London, 1986) and Isabel Pastor Bodmer, *Grandeza y tragedia de un valido: La muerte de don Alvaro de Luna*, 2 vols (Madrid, 1992).
7. Jorge Manrique (*c.* 1440–79), 'Coplas por la muerte de su padre', in J. M. Cohen, ed., *The Penguin Book of Spanish Verse* (Harmondsworth, 1988), p. 61. My translation after Cohen.
8. Iñigo López de Mendoza, Marquis of Santillana (1398–1458), 'Otras coplas del dicho señor marqués sobre el mesmo casso', in Manuel Durán, ed., *Poesías completas*, ii (Madrid, 1980), pp. 177, 182–3.
9. Santillana, 'Doctrinal de privados', in *Poesías completas*, ii, pp. 159, 160.
10. MacCurdy, *Tragic Fall*, p. 109. MacCurdy provides an excellent survey of this theme in the plays of the seventeenth century; his coverage may usefully be supplemented by Doris Havener, 'Some Literary Treatments of Don Alvaro de Luna' (MA thesis, Louisiana State University, 1942).
11. MacCurdy, *Tragic Fall*, ch. 2 and *passim*.
12. See Mariana, *Historia general*, pp. 136–7; Round, *Greatest Man Uncrowned*, chs 2–3.
13. See Round, *Greatest Man Uncrowned*, p. 235. The constable's chronicler suggested that, in ordering Don Alvaro's death, the king effectively killed himself through the effects of sadness and remorse. Juan de Mata Carriazo, ed., *Crónica de don Alvaro de Luna, condestable de Castilla, Maestre de Santiago* (Madrid, 1940), p. 434.
14. *Cédula* of Juan II, Burgos, 8 April 1453, in *Memorias de don Enrique IV de Castilla*, ii (Madrid, 1835–1913), p. 43.
15. Mariana, *Historia general*, p. 137.
16. For the key document, see 'Noticias relativas a la condenacion de don Alvaro de Luna', in *Memorias de Enrique IV*, ii, pp. 74–7.
17. Mariana, *Historia general*, p. 138.
18. Santillana, 'Otras coplas', p. 178.
19. For some general remarks on this phenomenon, see Francisco Tomás y Valiente, *Los validos en la monarquía española del siglo XVII*, revised edn (Madrid, 1982), pp. 117ff.
20. But on the 'Achilles' heel' of this lightning-rod theory, see Antonio Feros, 'Twin Souls: Monarchs and Favourites in Early Seventeenth-Century Spain', in Richard Kagan and Geoffrey Parker, eds, *Spain, Europe and the Atlantic World: Essays in Honour of John H. Elliott* (Cambridge, 1995), p. 45.
21. For written delegation, Tomás y Valiente, *Los validos*, pp. 6–7 and apéndice I, p. 157.
22. Pérez, *Aphorismos*, fol. 24v.
23. See Luis Cabrera de Córdoba, *Historia de Felipe II, rey de España* (Madrid, 1876–7), ii, pp. 141–2; and Pérez, *Aphorismos*, fol. 32v.
24. Antonio de Guevara, *Libro primero de las epístolas familiares*, ed. José María de Cossío (Madrid, 1950), i, no. 32 (7 January 1535).
25. Francis Bacon, 'Of Envy', in *The Essays*, ed. John Pitcher (Harmondsworth, 1985), p. 85.
26. Guevara, *Libro primero de las epístolas familiares*, i, no. 32.
27. James Boyden, *The Courtier and the King: Ruy Gómez de Silva, Philip II, and the Court of Spain* (Berkeley and Los Angeles, 1995), pp. 7–16.
28. *Ibid.*, chs 3–5.
29. *Ibid.*, chs 5–6, esp. pp. 128–36.
30. *Ibid.*, pp. 140–50.

31. Antonio Pérez, 'A un gran Privado', *Cartas de Antonio Pérez* (Paris, 1598?), fol. 73v.
32. Cabrera de Córdoba, *Felipe II*, ii, pp. 141–2.
33. Antonio Pérez to Gil de Mesa (*c.* 1594–5), *Cartas*, fol. 76v.
34. Quoted in Boyden, *Courtier and King*, pp. 139–40.
35. Feros, 'Twin Souls'.
36. Antonio Pérez, *Cartas*, fol. 72.
37. See Boyden, *Courtier and King*, pp. 17–18. Charles V's instruction to his son, 4 May 1543, is reproduced in Francisco de Laiglesia y Auset, *Estudios históricos (1515–1555)* (Madrid, 1918), i, p. 75.
38. 'Instrucción secreta de 6 de mayo de 1543', in Laiglesia y Auset, *Estudios históricos*, i, p. 84.
39. Quoted in Geoffrey Parker, *Philip II* (Boston, 1978), p. 30.
40. Quoted by Ciríaco Pérez Bustamente, *Felipe III: Semblanza de un monarca y perfiles de una privanza* (Madrid, 1950), p. 41.
41. Baltasar Porreño, *Dichos y hechos del rey D. Felipe II* (1628), ed. Angel González Palencia (Madrid, 1942), pp. 6–7.
42. See Feros, 'Twin Souls', esp. pp. 33ff. Quoted phrase at p. 35.
43. Fernando Bouza Alvarez, 'La majestad de Felipe II: Construcción del mito real', in José Martínez Millán, ed., *La corte de Felipe II* (Madrid, 1994), pp. 37–72.
44. Mariana, *Historia general*, p. 75.
45. Quoted in J. H. Elliott, *Richelieu and Olivares* (Cambridge, 1984), p. 172.
46. Alain Chartier (*Curial*, early fifteenth century), translated by Caxton, 1484, and quoted in Sydney Anglo, 'The Courtier: The Renaissance and Changing Ideals', in A. G. Dickens, ed., *The Courts of Europe* (London, 1977), p. 35.

3

'Absolute and Sovereign Mistress of her Grace'?
Queen Elizabeth I and her Favourites, 1581–1592

PAUL E. J. HAMMER

At the end of 1581, the collapse of her proposed marriage to the Duke of Anjou finally extinguished any hope that Elizabeth I of England might take a husband, let alone produce an heir.[1] Elizabeth was now forty-eight and all hope of a further generation for the Tudor dynasty was ended. Even before this last desperate attempt at matrimony, the theme of some public entertainments for the queen began to hint at a new attitude towards Elizabeth. Since the start of her reign, these displays had consistently and loudly urged the queen to marry. From about August 1578, however, they instead increasingly sought to idealize her virginity.[2] Advanced at first by opponents of the queen's intended marriage to Anjou, this theme was soon deployed for more positive ends. The result was the growth during the 1580s of a virtual 'cult of Elizabeth', in which the ageing monarch was idealized as the Virgin Queen – a sacred, unmarried female embodiment of England which denied both the passage of time and political reality (pl. 5).[3] Portraits of the queen also took on a curiously timeless quality in these years, as pictures of her became subject to official approval and ceased to be painted from life.[4] With the nation's elite finally defeated in their expectations about a royal husband and child, the queen's image-makers sought to lessen the impact of this blow by denying the reality of their sovereign's ageing through a collective act of artistry and wishful thinking.

If Elizabeth's ageing was effectively overlooked, the same was not true of her leading favourites. In 1581, the queen's oldest and dearest favourite, the Earl of Leicester (pl. 6), was forty-eight or nine, while her other leading favourite, Sir Christopher Hatton (pl. 7), was forty-one. Although both men seemed fit and healthy, Leicester was increasingly anxious about passing his wealth and title to a son. Leicester had once seemed the man most likely to marry the queen – an idea which he may have floated as late as the summer of 1575[5] – but his hopes were always dashed. By 1578, he could wait no longer and in September of that year he secretly married the Dowager Countess of Essex. The public revelation of this marriage a year later caused Leicester intense political embarrassment and for some months seemed likely to wreck his relationship with the queen. Elizabeth never forgave his wife (whom she termed a 'she-wolf') and may have held this marriage against Leicester when she treated him harshly for his opposition to the Anjou match during much of 1580. Even so, Leicester was at least able to console himself with the birth of a legitimate son in June 1581.[6] By contrast, Sir Christopher Hatton remained steadfastly unmarried, placing his immediate political benefit ahead of any dynastic considerations. For him, whether by deliberate choice or otherwise, being a favourite of Elizabeth included avoiding the Virgin Queen's notorious sexual jealousy, even at the expense of his own potential for legitimate procreation.

This essay seeks to explore the issues which confronted Elizabeth, Leicester and Hatton by 1581: notions of ageing, favour and succession. It will examine how Elizabeth interacted with her favourites as she approached and passed her fiftieth year, and how she and her intimates responded to the ambitions of a younger generation of courtiers eager for their own share of royal favour. By the end of the period covered in the essay – the decade following the collapse of the Anjou match – royal favour had been transferred from one generation to another: Elizabeth and her court had moved from the age of Leicester and Hatton to the age of the Earl of Essex. This essay will examine this process, which constitutes both a period of transition in Elizabeth's reliance upon individual favourites and a crucial part of the political history of her reign. In doing so, it will emphasize the theme that, despite the peculiarly personal nature of the queen's relationship with her individual favourites, these bonds must also be seen in the context of her relations with the court as a whole. Obviously enough, most royal favourites were not merely successful individual politicians but men whose presence at court was magnified by family, friends and followers. Such networks are therefore vital to any understanding of the nature of royal favourites. In the case of the Elizabethan court during the 1580s, this point can be made even more strongly. The mixed fortunes of Sir Walter Ralegh suggest that, whereas *choosing* a favourite might be a personal decision by the queen, her ability or willingness to advance her chosen favourite, and the means by which she might do this, could be constrained by the attitudes of her court.

Although the role and significance of female members of the queen's court has begun to attract serious scholarly attention – and rightly so – the focus here will be primarily on the queen's leading male courtiers. This is because only men could play a formal part in the business of government and because I believe that we still do not know enough about leading women at court to make a fully valid assessment of their activities there. Nevertheless, if Dr Charlotte Merton is correct, at least in the courts of Mary and Elizabeth, male favourites always had to reckon with a fair degree of political power among the senior women there.[7] It will be interesting to see how far this claim can be developed, and how far it was also true of other royal courts during the early modern period.

The starting point for any discussion about Elizabeth I must be her sex. Female princes were not altogether uncommon in the sixteenth century but their task was nevertheless a difficult one. The men who advised and staffed early modern governments were decidedly chauvinistic in their attitudes and believed that a woman's true place was under male control. To some degree, female princes were accorded the status of 'honorary men' by virtue of their royal rank but the prevailing attitudes remained entrenched and found common expression behind the queen's back and at a safe distance from her court. Elizabeth suffered from this prejudice throughout her reign, most notably from her generals, who frequently ignored or misinterpreted her orders.[8] However, Elizabeth also played upon such chauvinistic attitudes as a deliberate strategy to control her court. As queen, she used the alleged capriciousness of all women to cover her own uncertainty and changes of decision. She demanded that men seeking her favour cast their actions in the mould of courtly love. Those who were most successful at this game won pet-names which were at once affectionate and demeaning – 'eyes', 'mutton' and even, in the case of the royal Duke of Anjou, her 'frog'.[9] Womanly flirtatiousness also helped to ensure that rewards were distributed among a range of courtiers and that men new to the court might always hope to find royal favour, even if only because the queen sometimes wished to nettle the more established recipients of her largesse.

Although the occasional pricking of great men's pretensions had a personal and often playful element to it, Elizabeth's desire to show favour to a range of men at her court had a clear political rationale. Early in her reign especially, the queen's regime needed to win a broad base of support from within the governing class to rebuild royal influence after the narrowing of power under her predecessors, Edward VI and Mary. Elizabeth also had to reckon with the fact that the man whom she might otherwise have chosen as her sole favourite or even her husband, Sir Robert Dudley (whom she made Earl of Leicester in 1564), was unpalatable to many leading men of her court, as tentative steps in this direction quickly revealed.[10] Above all, Elizabeth's actions were governed by a fear of losing power and personal control. Her nightmare was that her leading male courtiers might form a united front and browbeat this 'mere woman' into accepting their views on such vital issues as her own marriage and the succession. Many female princes of the period succumbed to such pressures but Elizabeth consistently fought against this danger by ensuring plurality, and even occasional friction, among the leading men (and, to some degree, women) of her court.[11] The most famous (and misleading) expression of this policy is the oft-quoted comment of Sir Robert Naunton: 'the principal note of her reign will be that she ruled much by faction and parties, which she herself both made, upheld, and weakened as her own great judgment advised.'[12] This account is particularly misleading because it reads the political practices of the 1620s back into an earlier period, conflating Elizabeth's habit of 'divide and rule' among her courtiers with factionalism. As I have argued elsewhere, following Dr Simon Adams, the appearance of open factions at the Elizabethan court was the product of political crisis and represented a challenge to the queen's control of her court and policy, not a means of securing them.[13]

A more useful characterization of Elizabeth's conduct might be the young Edward Hyde's rephrasing of Naunton's statement: 'that Queen almost her whole reign did with singular and equal demonstrations of grace look upon several *persons* of most distinct wishes one towards another'.[14] In other words, Elizabeth divided her favour among a variety of competitors precisely in order to avoid the kind of reliance upon one man which was embodied in the Castilian practice of acknowledging a *privado* or *valido*. Although a king might delegate power to a single favourite and still retain his authority, this option seemed neither attractive nor safe to Elizabeth. As a result, she sought to ensure that a variety of men sought and gained varying degrees of favour at her court. Many of these men were little more than a nine-days wonder who gave the queen only brief amusement. The most successful and enduring recipients of royal favour, such as Leicester, Sir Christopher Hatton and Sir Thomas Heneage, were true royal favourites in the contemporary sense – men who were recognized by their fellow courtiers as having a special bond with the queen and consequently able to influence her in a variety of patronage and/or policy matters. The wide-ranging and protean influence of such favourites was especially important, for it represented a marked contrast to other officeholders at court whose spheres of competence were delimited by agreed lines of demarcation or the terms of their patents of appointment.

A kind of pattern can be discerned in the careers of Elizabeth's favourites. The first real acknowledgement of their special status came when they gained some office in the royal household, thereby demonstrating that the queen regarded them as permanent fixtures in her court and guaranteeing them access to the inner sanctum of the privy chamber. The most successful and influential of these men ultimately gained a place on the Privy Council. This move formalized their involvement in public affairs and channelled their energies into a body which had strict rules both for the conduct of its business and for precedence among its members. Once they entered the world of policy advice and endless paperwork, these erstwhile rivals tended to develop a sense of corporate responsibility, based upon shared perceptions of the problems and dangers which faced the queen's regime. This experience undoubtedly limited and contained the rivalry among the queen's leading favourites. Ironically, this also gradually made it more difficult for the queen to play these men off against each other. Although she habitually sought consensus among her advisers in matters of policy, Elizabeth also hated losing her freedom to manoeuvre, especially when a consensus began to form around a policy which she did not like.

The work of the council also brought royal favourites into more intimate contact with the queen's leading bureaucrat, Sir William Cecil (pl. 8), who became Baron of Burghley in 1571 and lord treasurer in 1572. Burghley was not a favourite in the sense of being a man of the court: he saw himself as the queen's faithful old servant, whose relationship with her was based upon trustworthiness and length of service rather than the kind of elaborate romantic courtesies practised by Leicester and Hatton. Nevertheless, Burghley undoubtedly had a very strong personal bond with Elizabeth. He was steward of her private lands before her accession to the throne and, as her secretary of state, subsequently exercised an influence on her policies which rivalled both that of more aristocratic members of the council and that of favourites like Leicester. Leicester and Burghley were often viewed as political opponents – rival poles, as it were, in the queen's elaborate balancing act – and historians have tended to emphasize the contrast between the courtly favourite and the master of paperwork. In reality, as Simon Adams has shown, this contrast can be exaggerated. By the 1570s, the relationship between Leicester and Burghley was one of co-operation, broadly common perceptions and only occasional tensions.[15] Moreover, the old emphasis upon the rivalry between these two men ignores other features of this multipolar court, including the influence of aristocrats like the Earl of Sussex and the growing importance of Hatton and of Burghley's successor as secretary of state, Sir Francis Walsingham.

During the early 1580s, the character of Elizabeth's court began to change. Although he remained paramount in the queen's favour, Leicester's rehabilitation after his marriage was perhaps not fully completed until his young son died in July 1584, aged barely three. This tragedy shook Leicester so profoundly that any residue of bitterness harboured by the queen – who received news of the boy's death from Hatton – was converted into sympathy and perhaps also a stronger, if less romantic, affection for him.[16] In terms of ceremony, the court began to witness ever more elaborate celebrations of the 'cult of Elizabeth'. The leading participants in these displays were not men like Leicester and Hatton but aristocrats young enough to have been the sons of Elizabeth. This younger generation of courtiers also sought to win the queen's favour in the now established manner – playing the role of ardent suitors bent upon wooing their courtly mistress. Such behaviour had been understandable in the 1560s and 1570s, but the growing gap in age between the queen and these suitors gave Elizabeth's court an increasingly contrived, even bizarre, quality by the 1580s and 1590s. This sense of incongruity was all the more powerful because of the sexual charge which was inherent in this mode of behaviour. Earlier in the reign, this had encouraged scandalous tales about lascivious conduct between Elizabeth and Leicester or Hatton, but passing time now made this interpretation of the queen's dealings with her mock suitors seem more and more grotesque.[17] Although wooing by young men appealed to her suitably splendid royal ego, Elizabeth increasingly came to seem ridiculous to her younger courtiers, as they complained in private and ventilated in their poetry.[18] Such feelings finally burst into the open in mid-1598, when the Earl of Essex allegedly remonstrated with the queen that 'her conditions were as crooked as her carcase'.[19]

If the style of Elizabeth's court seemed increasingly artificial, even uncomfortable, the striking wealth and influence of Leicester and Hatton, in particular, raised expectations about the special value of royal favour. These expectations were perhaps somewhat inflated because the image of a royal favourite which they presented reflected the culmination of ten or twenty years of intimate service to the queen. Even so, the usual jockeying between ambitious younger courtiers now took place with half an eye to replacing these great favourites whenever they should die or lose the queen's trust. In this quest, two conspicuous failures at court during the early 1580s were Burghley's son-in-law, the Earl of Oxford, and Leicester's eldest nephew, Sir Philip Sidney. Ironically and perhaps significantly, the most successful new suitor for royal favour was a complete outsider, Sir Walter Ralegh (pl. 9).

Although the romantic story of Ralegh laying his cloak in the mud seems to be apocryphal, his rise was hardly less extraordinary. Like Hatton before him, Ralegh lacked influential family or friends to assist his rise to political prominence. In this sense, they shared the distinction of being the only self-made men at Elizabeth's court – or, rather, favourites raised entirely by the queen's own efforts. However, where Hatton's rise during the 1560s and 1570s took more than a decade,[20] Ralegh aspired to the status of a favourite with startling swiftness. While Hatton always sought to seem a bridge-builder at court and the friend of all those with power there, Ralegh often seemed proud and overbearing. Initially a follower of the Earl of Oxford, Ralegh abandoned him for military service in Ireland. From this most unlikely and distant post, he gained royal attention during 1580 and 1581 by carrying back letters from the lord deputy and making oral reports to the queen. Ordinarily, Ireland was the Elizabethan equivalent of Siberia but, at this juncture, the Desmond Rebellion gave news from there a genuine urgency. During his private audiences with Elizabeth, Ralegh ventured to offer his own opinions on Irish affairs, even though they contradicted the written advice given by his superior. Ralegh's views struck a chord with the queen and allowed her to contest the counsel of her alleged experts – a situation which she often seemed to relish because it forced her advisers to argue matters of policy on her terms rather than their own. As contacts between them increased, Ralegh's accomplished behaviour and formidable personality soon attracted broader interest from the queen.[21]

Having caught the royal ear and eye, Ralegh proved remarkably adept at retaining and strengthening his precarious hold on favour. Although at first nominally a client of Leicester (who probably got him his Irish command),[22] he soon parted company with his erstwhile patron. By early 1582, Elizabeth informed the lord deputy that she wished Ralegh to retain his command in Ireland, even though he would remain at court.[23] Beginning in May 1583, she gave Ralegh a succession of lucrative grants, some of them even cutting across other rewards previously given to old hands like Lord Hunsdon, her closest male cousin.[24] This conspicuous demonstration of royal largesse equipped

Ralegh with the financial resources which he needed to sustain himself in suitable splendour as a companion of the queen but also won him growing enmity from others at court. To some degree, this actually aided him because it meant that Elizabeth was loath to lessen her support since this would be seen as bowing to pressure from her own courtiers. Ralegh also played upon his weak political position, sometimes using poetry to express his insecurity, thereby implicitly demanding some concrete sign of reassurance from the queen.[25]

By mid-1585, Ralegh was on bad terms with Leicester, in particular. Around this time, the queen sought to fill several important courtly offices which had been left vacant by deaths among her senior noblemen. According to one report received by the former Spanish ambassador, these promotions were to have included Leicester's appointment as lord steward. However, Leicester refused to surrender his current post as master of the queen's horse, which he had held since the start of the reign, and his promotion was cancelled.[26] Stories passed on to Spanish agents often constitute a very poor source for events at Elizabeth's court, but other information in this report seems to be broadly corroborated elsewhere.[27] If the report about Leicester is accurate, it raises the possibility that he refused to surrender his office at least partly in order to prevent it being given to Ralegh, who lacked a suitable household post. It is also conceivable that Leicester wished to keep the mastership of the horse for his own stepson, the Earl of Essex (pl. 10), who now loomed as Leicester's best hope for a political – if not biological – heir. Certainly, it was at this juncture that Leicester chose to bring Essex to court. After some delays, Essex finally joined Leicester's entourage about the start of September.[28] However, the young earl's arrival at court was barely noticed amid the frantic activity which accompanied Elizabeth's grudging and long-delayed decision to intervene in support of the Dutch rebels against Philip II of Spain. This act not only destroyed the central plank of her foreign policy over the preceding twenty years but initiated the transformation of her government from a peacetime to a wartime regime. This had profound effects upon a country which, for a generation, had enjoyed low taxes and a relatively undemanding central government.

The outbreak of open hostilities made Elizabeth's task of asserting her will upon her regime all the more difficult, for it encouraged dreams of martial glory and exhibitions of machismo among her aristocratic soldiers. Elizabeth's problems were immediately and spectacularly demonstrated by the furious rebukes which she directed at the Earl of Leicester, who went to the Low Countries as commander-in-chief in December 1585. Elizabeth's bitter complaints about Leicester's conduct as a general provided many opportunities for attacks against him (both real and imagined), and the relationship between the queen and her chief favourite briefly oscillated between the extremes of royal wrath and reassurance. Leicester especially blamed Ralegh, who he believed was poisoning the queen against him in his absence. Elizabeth herself, perhaps rather naively, sought to assure Leicester that this was untrue.[29] However, her own outbursts of anger against her absent favourite encouraged other members of the Privy

Council to rally in Leicester's support, out of solidarity with their colleague and, above all, because they saw no political alternative to continuing his command. The war in the Low Countries was a struggle for national and religious survival, and neither Ralegh nor anyone else could afford to be seen to jeopardize its success. As a result, Ralegh's ability to capitalize on Leicester's absence was sharply limited.

Leicester returned to court at the end of 1586, preceded by the freshly knighted Earl of Essex and the body of Sir Philip Sidney, whose death in battle created a bow-wave of sympathy and Protestant solidarity. In Essex, who had spent the last year undergoing an apprenticeship in military command, Leicester now had an eager and well-equipped rival to set up against Ralegh. What followed seems like a concerted campaign to establish Essex in the queen's affections, trading upon his new reputation as a war hero, his personal charm and the youthfulness which he so vigorously displayed in jousting. As with Ralegh before him, Elizabeth seems to have been quickly impressed by this new adornment to her court, opening the way for bitter rivalry between Essex and Ralegh.

Like most princes perhaps, Elizabeth was essentially reactive to the initiatives of others and hence her control of affairs was often erratic. She was also prone to being manipulated by those who knew her well, especially on certain sensitive issues. Perhaps the most dramatic demonstration of these limitations was the execution of Mary Queen of Scots in early 1587. This brought an end to what Professor Collinson has dubbed 'the Elizabethan exclusion crisis',[30] but it also fleetingly turned her nightmare of losing control into a reality: despite her explicit order to the contrary, the Privy Council as a body decided to proceed against Mary before the queen could intervene to stop them. Elizabeth singled out Burghley and Hatton for special blame in this affair, whereas Leicester was able to wring the lord stewardship from the queen and convince her that Essex should take his place as master of the horse.[31] Even before this arrangement was approved, Leicester briefed his stepson on the substantial financial benefits that would accrue to him as master of the horse, which constituted a sweet bonus to the office's politically invaluable requirement of close attendance upon the sovereign.[32]

Despite her fury over the death of Mary Queen of Scots, Elizabeth soon appointed Hatton as lord chancellor. This decision was quite unexpected and dismayed many lawyers. More significantly, it created a unique concentration of political power in a triumvirate of great officers of state, with Hatton, Burghley and Leicester as, respectively, lord chancellor, lord treasurer and lord steward. This also meant that the two senior favourites, Hatton and Leicester, were now increasingly occupied with administrative matters – just like Burghley – and no longer able to spend long hours with the queen. As a result, the rivalry between Ralegh and Essex for royal favour became more direct and obvious, although Leicester's influence served to constrain Ralegh somewhat and to embolden Essex. At one point, in July 1587, Essex even berated the queen for continuing to support Ralegh, questioning whether he could 'give myself over to the service of a mistress that was in awe of such a man'.[33]

It seems quite extraordinary that a young courtier who aspired to royal favour should engage in such a shouting match with his sovereign. It seems even more extraordinary that, despite also storming out of the court in fury, Essex suffered no punishment for his actions. Indeed, he was back in the queen's presence within days. Undoubtedly, the queen's host at the time, the Countess of Warwick, had something to do with this. Yet Essex himself was no ordinary young courtier. Turning twenty-one in November 1586, he was the scion of an old aristocratic family and the son of a man who had won favour at court in the 1560s and early 1570s. Succeeding as a minor, Essex was educated under Lord Burghley and soon also became the stepson of Leicester. Through his mother, he had a number of other influential allies at court. These powerful connections made it very difficult for Elizabeth to punish him, or (perhaps) even to resist his attractions as a frequent companion. For his own part, Essex had very considerable talents and personal charm, as well as a remarkable ability to inspire affection in others – including the queen. 'When she is abroade,' boasted one of his servants in mid-1587, 'noboddy [is] neere her but my lord of Essex. At night my lord is at cardes or one game or another with her that he cometh not to his owne lodginge tyll the birdes singe in the morninge.'[34]

The meteoric rise of Essex into royal favour was powerfully backed and, to some degree, planned by his stepfather. Leicester's sudden death in September 1588 therefore created both a crisis and an opportunity for Essex. With Leicester dead, Essex lost the man who could best advise him on how to shape his actions, but his only serious rivals for royal favour were now Hatton, who was nearly fifty and was friendly towards him, and Ralegh. Absent from court for some months because of Leicester's hostility towards him, Ralegh must have made similar calculations. When he returned to court in late 1588, the rivalry with Essex gained a new level of intensity, even desperation. On one occasion, Elizabeth apparently had to prevent violence between them.[35] Nevertheless, Essex challenged Ralegh to a duel shortly afterwards. The Privy Council hastily intervened to stop it but also sought to conceal the affair from the queen.[36] Duelling had been seen before around the fringes of the court – Ralegh himself had been imprisoned twice within a month for duelling in 1580[37] – but the period of his struggle for supremacy with Essex was perhaps the first time that this behaviour penetrated to the heart of the court. In mid-1587, Ralegh came close to fighting Robert Carey, one of Lord Hunsdon's sons, while Essex actually fought a duel against Sir Charles Blount, perhaps a few months later.[38] Although this violence did not have such fatal effects as when duels tore apart the inner circle of Henri III of France ten years before,[39] the atmosphere at Elizabeth's court was clearly becoming more and more hot-blooded.

Even before Leicester's death, Elizabeth had used 'all . . . ways' to calm her court, and even to try and make Essex and Ralegh become friends.[40] Although she occasionally resorted to furious indignation, her standard tactics revolved around conspicuous displays of royal favour: rewarding Essex when he pleased her, rewarding Ralegh when he pleased her or when Essex had not, and rewarding other men, such as Sir Charles Blount, when both Essex and Ralegh had displeased her. However, by the end of 1588, Elizabeth's methods of control were breaking down. Despite verbal expressions of royal fury, she was unwilling, or unable, to take more serious action. This might be connected to the lingering effects of Leicester's death, which was a shocking reminder of mortality for the queen: to take tough action, such as expulsion from court, would force her to endure losing yet another of her most intimate companions, compounding her sense of loss. Looking at the antics of this younger generation of courtiers, she also seems to have felt unthreatened, and even indulgent towards them, seeing them less as the grown men they were than as adolescents who required guidance.[41] Whatever the reason, Elizabeth had an extraordinary record of forgiveness towards intimates who offended her, despite the explosive anger of her initial reaction to their sins. Perhaps because she lacked children and close family, and because she appreciated the power of forgiveness, Elizabeth always clung desperately to those who were most familiar – in stark contrast to her father, who had readily sacrificed even the oldest of friends.

When Essex ignored her explicit command and joined the naval expedition launched against Spain and Portugal in early 1589, the queen responded with fury against the earl – 'all his hopes of advancement had like to bee strangled almost in the very cradle', as Sir Henry Wotton later put it[42] – and a gold chain for Ralegh. Yet, within six weeks of his return, Essex was able to regain her favour so fully that Ralegh found it advisable to visit his estates in Ireland.[43] Although he now lacked Leicester's powerful advocacy, Essex had established a curiously powerful bond with the queen and was also 'mightelie backt by the greatest in opposition to Sir Walter Ralegh, who had offended manie and was maligned of most'.[44] This weight of support in his favour proved to be a constant force in Essex's rise. When his secret marriage to Sir Philip Sidney's widow was revealed in late 1590 and on several occasions when his conduct as general of the queen's forces in Normandy during the second half of 1591 moved her to threaten him with dire consequences, Elizabeth's royal anger was carefully softened by senior courtiers, before Essex himself completed the process of rehabilitation by speaking to her in person. In late 1591, Elizabeth complained to Sir Robert Cecil that Hatton 'hath ever cockered the earle and would not suffer her to chasten him'.[45] On another occasion, Hatton gave the queen a jewel with the request that she send it to the absent Essex to reassure him of her continuing favour.[46]

Such powerful support – and apparent affection – for his rival made it very difficult for Ralegh to take lasting advantage of Essex's periods of vulnerability. Although Ralegh sought to capitalize on the earl's every slip, Essex had gained a psychological superiority over him by late 1589 which even Elizabeth herself had to recognize. Moreover, each time Essex recovered from a bout of disfavour, his hold upon the queen – and the reputation which he had with other courtiers – seemed to grow stronger. Ralegh also still lacked a household office to buttress his position. Although there had been talk of him becoming captain of the queen's guard when Hatton was appointed lord chancellor,[47] Hatton had declined to surrender the position. It was not until after Hatton's death in November 1591 that Ralegh finally became captain of the guard. Like Leicester before him, Hatton may well have held on to his household post partly to deny it to Ralegh.

By the time Hatton died, the political significance of this breakthrough was greatly diminished, for Essex's ascendancy was already well established. Furthermore, like Leicester and Essex before him (but unlike Hatton), Ralegh now succumbed to a secret marriage in order to fulfil his own dynastic needs.[48] This major new point of vulnerability encouraged him to seek a rapprochement with Essex, presumably on the latter's terms. True to his promise, Essex not only did not expose Ralegh but even stood as godfather to Ralegh's son in April 1592. However, news of the child's birth soon reached Elizabeth and her wrath effectively crippled Ralegh's career. Unlike other royal favourites, not only had Ralegh had the temerity to marry one of the queen's maids of honour but both he and his wife clearly tried to deceive the queen about their relationship even after the birth of their first child. As A. L. Rowse suggests, it was probably this imposture, rather than the marriage itself, which saw Ralegh banned from the court and sequestered from his captaincy of the guard until Essex brokered his return five years later.[49]

With Ralegh's demise, Essex was confirmed as the queen's only real favourite in the 1590s. This is not to say that Elizabeth ceased her policy of also offering royal favour to other men, especially when she wished to remind Essex of her power or to rebuke him for some reason. However, no man dominated the court in the way Essex did and many of his would-be rivals, such as Sir Charles Blount and the Earl of Southampton, soon became his friends and followers. Others, such as Henry Brooke (who succeeded his father as Lord Cobham in 1597), were harried and abused as Ralegh had been. Yet the dominance of Essex was to some extent illusory. Although he won greater grants for himself than any other man in Elizabeth's reign, these were primarily intended as recompense for the vast sums of his own money which he spent on royal service. By contrast, he won little more than minor royal patronage for his followers. Unlike his stepfather, he proved unable to intervene decisively in some key areas of policy, such as the growing official campaign against Protestant nonconformity.

Essex was also unlike Leicester and Elizabeth's other previous favourites in more fundamental ways. Above all, he was an aristocrat, who had been brought up with elevated notions of public service and of his own status. This may have contributed to his support among other courtiers, especially in comparison with an outsider like Ralegh, but it also made him less amenable than other favourites to courtly politics. Essex never received any pet-name from the queen other than Robin (the familiar form of Robert) and most of his surviving poems and letters to the queen complain about the injuries which she has allegedly done to his honour and dignity. He also soon came to dislike life at court and the daily attendance which his post as master of the horse entailed. When the pressures seemed too great to bear any longer, he sometimes secretly departed from the court or hid himself away in 'sudden recesses'.

For Essex, royal favour was not an end in itself but merely a means to the greater goal of securing delegated authority from the queen, especially in matters of war and foreign policy. Ultimately, he believed that he must pursue certain policies for the benefit of the realm, regardless of whether the queen herself was actually prepared to endorse them. His attitude can be gauged from the letter which wrote to Henri IV of France on surrendering his command in Normandy at the start of 1592: 'I am very ashamed that we English have so soon quitted Your Majesty's service. . . . As to myself . . . I hope Your Majesty believes that a nobleman, having given his faith to a prince with so much affection as I have often shown, will not be inconstant in his profession nor fail of his word.'[50] A few years later, Essex expressed his view of Elizabeth's conduct of policy even more bluntly: 'I know I shall never do her service butt against her will.'[51] These are hardly the sentiments of a typical favourite and powerfully demonstrate how far he had outgrown his youthful image as the queen's eager partner at cards.

Essex's ambition to dominate policy inevitably led him to focus on winning a seat on the Privy Council, which was dominated after the deaths of Leicester and Hatton by Lord Burghley. As the earl's former guardian, Burghley had long been a supporter of Essex, whom he saw as a natural ally for his own son, Robert Cecil (pls 18 and 21). However, Essex's political ambitions began to strain this bond because they imperilled Cecil's future. During 1591, these problems were solved by a compromise which Burghley and Hatton seem to have jointly urged upon the queen: Cecil gained a place on the Privy Council and Essex the military command in Normandy. Yet Hatton's death and Essex's newfound ambition 'to intend matters of state' pointed to inevitable conflict in the years to come, especially after the earl gained a seat on the Council in early 1593. The story of this clash and how it poisoned the last decade of Elizabeth's reign has been discussed elsewhere.[52] For the present, however, a few points might be emphasized by way of conclusion.

Perhaps most obviously, the increasing rivalry between Essex and the Cecils helped to destroy the strong base of courtly support which had characterized the earl's rise to power. As the passing years removed key supporters like Walsingham, Hatton, Heneage and Hunsdon, Essex's own aggressiveness alienated men who rose to fill their places, such as Buckhurst, Cobham and Howard of Effingham. Moreover, unlike Leicester and now Robert Cecil, Essex failed to create a network of effective support among the women of the privy chamber.[53] In effect, as the decade progressed, Essex became ever more isolated and dependent upon his favour with the queen. Ironically, this made his position increasingly like Ralegh's in the 1580s.

Secondly, the rivalry between Essex and the Cecils in the 1590s was an indication not only of the earl's drive for political influence but also of how great and pervasive was the power which Lord Burghley had built up during his long years of royal service. As the last of the 1580s triumvirate, Burghley retained a seniority and authority which commanded wide respect, even from Essex, until his death in August 1598. When Burghley pretended to retire from royal service in 1591, Elizabeth simply refused to let her 'Sir Spirit' go.[54] Thirteen years older than the queen, he became almost a kind of surrogate uncle to her – grave, loyal and increasingly curmudgeonly. In some senses, Burghley might almost be called a minister–favourite, for his long and close personal relationship with the queen was combined with an unprecedented collection of offices, including those of lord treasurer, master of the court of wards and (until July 1596) acting secretary of state. However, Burghley himself clearly distinguished his own position from that of a courtly favourite like Essex. The validity of this distinction, which was both deliberately self-effacing and self-serving, would require a lengthy discussion in itself. Nevertheless, even if Burghley was not a minister–favourite, the victory of his son in 1601 (which cost Essex his life) created the conditions for Sir Robert Cecil to become precisely such a figure. After this, Elizabeth had no more courtly favourites in the mould of Leicester, Hatton or Essex. Although Ralegh lived to see his great rival executed, neither he nor anyone else could match Cecil's influence in the last years of Elizabeth's reign.

Finally, what do events in the 1580s suggest about the interrelationship between Elizabeth and her leading male favourites? Sir Robert Naunton, whose writings have been so influential upon subsequent views of Elizabeth and her reign, claimed that 'she was absolute and sovereign mistress of her grace and that those to whom she distributed her favours were never more than tenants at will and stood on no better ground than her princely pleasure and their own good behaviour'.[55] To a degree, this is true. Most royal offices, for example, were bestowed upon their holders only 'during the queen's pleasure' and some key posts were granted without any patent at all. However, events in the 1580s suggest that Naunton's image of an all-powerful Elizabeth in 'absolute and sovereign' control of her court is unrealistic. Since Naunton wrote with more than half an eye to events in the 1620s, this judgement is perhaps not surprising.[56]

The rise of Essex and his struggle with Ralegh demonstrate that the queen was not always fully in control of her royal favour. At the very least, she was sometimes prepared to let others make demands upon it in a remarkably insistent and aggressive manner. Even when her commands were flagrantly ignored, as in the case of Essex's involvement in the Portugal expedition, she also proved unable, or unwilling, to punish the offending party in any serious way. In part, this may be a reflection of Elizabeth's own personality and circumstances. It may also be a demonstration of what it actually meant to be a royal favourite – men who could do things that other subjects could not dare and yet still be forgiven for their actions. However, this essay has shown that Elizabeth's various dealings with her favourites must also be seen in the context of her relationship with that intimate little community which comprised her court, and especially the one or two dozen men and women who comprised its most influential members. It is only in this wider human context that the complexities of Elizabeth's relations with her individual favourites can be fully understood.

Notes

1. S. Doran, *Monarchy and Matrimony: The Courtships of Elizabeth I* (London and New York, 1996), ch. 7; W. T. MacCaffrey, *Queen Elizabeth and the Making of Policy, 1572–1588* (Princeton, 1981), pp. 243–81; *idem, Elizabeth I* (London, 1993), ch. 16; M. Leimon, 'Sir Francis Walsingham and the Anjou Marriage Plan, 1574–1581' (PhD thesis, University of Cambridge, 1989), *passim.*

2. S. Doran, 'Juno versus Diana: The Treatment of Elizabeth I's Marriage in Plays and Entertainments, 1561–1581', *Historical Journal*, 38 (1995), pp. 270–1.

3. See, for example, R. Strong, *The Cult of Elizabeth: Elizabethan Portraiture and Pageantry* (London, 1977); J. Wilson, *Entertainments for Elizabeth: Studies in Elizabethan and Renaissance Culture* (Woodbridge and Totowa, NJ, 1980); P. Berry, *Of Chastity and Power: Elizabethan Literature and the Unmarried Queen* (London and New York, 1989); J. N. King, 'Queen Elizabeth I: Representations of the Virgin Queen', *Renaissance Quarterly*, 43 (1990), pp. 30–74.

4. S. P. Cerasano and M. Wynne-Davies, 'From Myself, My Other Self I Turned', in Cerasano and Wynne-Davies, eds, *Gloriana's Face: Women, Public and Private, in the English Renaissance* (Hemel Hempstead, 1992), p. 12, and the sources cited there.

5. Doran, 'Juno versus Diana', p. 266.

6. S. Adams, 'The Papers of Robert Dudley, Earl of Leicester. III. The Countess of Leicester's Collection', *Archives*, 23 (1996), p. 3.

7. C. Merton, ' "The Forgotten Crowd of Common Beauties": The Women Who Served Queen Mary and Queen Elizabeth, 1553–1603' (PhD thesis, University of Cambridge, 1992), *passim*. A less confident view of the role of women at court is presented by P. Wright, 'A Change in Direction: The Ramifications of a Female Household, 1558–1603', in D. Starkey, ed., *The English Court from the Wars of the Roses to the Civil War* (London, 1987), pp. 147–72.

8. C. Haigh, *Elizabeth I* (Harlow, 1988), pp. 125ff.

9. Leicester was Elizabeth's 'eyes', while Hatton was variously called her 'mutton', 'lids' or 'bellweather'.

10. Doran, *Monarchy and Matrimony*, ch. 3; A. Somerset, *Elizabeth I* (London, 1991), pp. 111ff.; S. Adams, 'Queen Elizabeth's Eyes at Court: The Earl of Leicester', in D. Starkey, ed., *Rivals in Power: Lives and Letters of the Great Tudor Dynasties* (London, 1990), p. 157.

11. See, for example, P. E. J. Hammer, 'Patronage at Court, Faction and the Earl of Essex', in J. Guy, ed., *The Reign of Elizabeth I: Court and Culture in the Last Decade* (Cambridge, 1995), pp. 76–7.

12. Sir Robert Naunton, *Fragmenta regalia or observations on Queen Elizabeth, her times and favourites*, ed. J. S. Cerovski (Washington, London and Toronto, 1985), p. 41.

13. Hammer, 'Patronage at Court, Faction and the Earl of Essex', *passim*. Cf. S. Adams, 'Faction, Clientage and Party: English Politics, 1550–1603', *History Today*, 32 (December 1982), pp. 33–9; *idem*, 'Eliza Enthroned? The Court and its Politics', in C. Haigh, ed., *Reign of Elizabeth I* (Basingstoke, 1984), pp. 55–77.

14. 'The difference and disparity between the estates and conditions of George, duke of Buckingham, and Robert, earl of Essex', printed in *Reliquiae Wottonianae: or a collection of lives, letters [etc.] . . . by . . . Sir Henry Wotton*, 4th edn (London, 1685), p. 188.

15. S. Adams, 'Favourites and Factions at the Elizabethan Court', in R. G. Asch and A. M. Birke, eds,

Princes, Patronage and the Nobility: The Court at the Beginning of the Modern Age, c.1450–1650 (Oxford, 1991), pp. 283–7; *idem*, 'Eliza Enthroned?', p. 63.

16. D. Wilson, *Sweet Robin: A Biography of Robert Dudley, Earl of Leicester, 1533–1588* (London, 1981), p. 244; A. Kendall, *Robert Dudley, Earl of Leicester* (London, 1980), pp. 198–9.
17. For allegations about Elizabeth's sexuality, see C. Levin, *'The Heart and Stomach of a King': Elizabeth I and the Politics of Sex and Power* (Philadelphia, 1994), ch. 4.
18. See, for example, K. Duncan-Jones, *Sir Philip Sidney: Courtier Poet* (London, 1991), pp. 16–18, 146–8.
19. *Dictionary of National Biography*, sub. 'Robert Devereux, 2nd Earl of Essex'.
20. A. G. Vines, *Neither Fire Nor Steel: Sir Christopher Hatton* (Chicago, 1978), pp. xiii–xv and *passim*; MacCaffrey, *Queen Elizabeth and the Making of Policy*, pp. 441, 448–55; W. J. Tighe, 'The Gentlemen Pensioners in Elizabethan Politics and Government' (PhD thesis, University of Cambridge, 1984), p. 389.
21. D. C. Peck, 'Raleigh, Sidney, Oxford and the Catholics, 1579', *Notes and Queries*, 223 (1978), pp. 427–30; E. Edwards, *The Life of Sir Walter Ralegh*, 2 vols (London, 1868), i, pp. 37ff.; P. Lefranc, *Sir Walter Ralegh écrivain* (Paris, 1968), pp. 28–9; S. W. May, *Sir Walter Ralegh* (Boston, 1989), pp. 3–6.
22. Edwards, *Ralegh*, i, p. 43; *ibid.*, ii, pp. 17–18; May, *Ralegh*, p. 4.
23. Edwards, *Ralegh*, i, p. 46.
24. Public Record Office, State Papers (hereafter PRO, SP) 46/20, fol. 229v. For grants to Ralegh, see J. H. Adamson and H. F. Folland, *The Shepherd of the Ocean: An Account of Sir Walter Ralegh and his Times* (Boston, 1969), pp. 100–3.
25. See, for example, S. W. May, *The Elizabethan Courtier Poets: The Poems and their Contexts* (Columbia, Miss., 1991), pp. 119–22, 318–21.
26. *Calendar of Letters and State Papers, Relating to English Affairs, Preserved Principally in the Archives of Simancas*, iii, ed. M. A. S. Hume (London, 1896), pp. 537–8 (hereafter *CSPSpan*).
27. See, for example, R. W. Kenny, *Elizabeth's Admiral: The Political Career of Charles Howard, Earl of Nottingham, 1536–1624* (Baltimore, 1970), pp. 25ff.; PRO, SP 12/178, fol. 24r.
28. Longleat, Devereux Ms. 5, fol. 69r; Christ Church, Oxford, Evelyn Ms. 285b, unfol., entry for 7, 8 and 20 September 1585. I am grateful to the Marquess of Bath for permission to cite from the papers at Longleat. The date of Essex's arrival at court is conventionally, but wrongly, placed almost a year earlier.
29. Edwards, *Ralegh*, ii, pp. 33–4.
30. P. Collinson, 'The Elizabethan Exclusion Crisis and the Elizabethan Polity', *Proceedings of the British Academy*, 84 (1994), pp. 51–92.
31. John Stow, *The annales of England . . . untill this present yeere 1601* (London, 1601), p. 1243. Modern commentators erroneously date Leicester's promotion to 1584 or 1585.
32. Folger Shakespeare Library, Washington, DC (hereafter FSL), Ms. L.a.39. This is printed in W. B. Devereux, *Lives and Letters of the Devereux, Earls of Essex, in the Reigns of Elizabeth, James I and Charles I, 1540–1646*, 2 vols (London, 1853), i, p. 185.
33. Bodleian Library, Oxford (hereafter BLO), Tanner Ms. 76, fol. 29v (printed in Devereux, i, p. 188).
34. FSL, L.a.39 (printed in Devereux, i, pp. 185–6).
35. *CSPSpan*, iv, p. 504.
36. PRO, SP 12/219, fol. 115r.
37. Edwards, *Ralegh*, i, p. 50; Adamson and Folland, *Shepherd of the Ocean*, p. 46.
38. British Library (hereafter BL), Lansdowne Ms. 96, fol. 69r; F. M. Jones, *Mountjoy, 1563–1606: The Last Elizabethan Deputy* (Dublin and London, 1958), pp. 23, 187–8.
39. F. J. Baumgartner, *France in the Sixteenth Century* (Basingstoke, 1995), pp. 260–1.
40. BLO, Tanner Ms. 76, fol. 29v (printed in Devereux, i, p. 188).
41. For example, she rebuked Essex as a 'rasshe & temerarious youthe' even as late as January 1594 (Lambeth Palace Library, Ms. 650, fol. 26r). See also her riposte to Sir Robert Cecil in February 1603: E. Jenkins, *Elizabeth the Great* (London, 1958), p. 323.
42. Sir Henry Wotton, *A parallel betweene Robert late earle of Essex and George late duke of Buckingham* (London, 1641), p. 3.
43. Edwards, *Ralegh*, ii, p. 41.
44. BL, Egerton Ms. 2026, fol. 32r.
45. University College London, Ogden Ms. 7/41, fol. 19r. 'To cocker' means to pamper or coddle.
46. *Ibid.*, fol. 34v.

47. BL, Lansdowne Ms. 96, fol. 69r. Modern commentators have universally (but erroneously) assumed that Ralegh did replace Hatton in 1587.
48. Arthur Throckmorton's diary entry suggests Ralegh married in early or mid-November 1591: A. L. Rowse, *Ralegh and the Throckmortons* (London, 1962), p. 160. Cf. P. Lefranc, 'La Date du Mariage de Sir Walter Ralegh: un document inédit', *Etudes anglaises*, 9 (1956), pp. 193–211.
49. Rowse, *Ralegh and the Throckmortons*, p. 161.
50. E. M. Tenison, *Elizabethan England*, 12 vols in 13 (Leamington Spa, 1933–61), viii, pp. 573–4.
51. Hammer, 'Patronage at Court, Faction and the Earl of Essex', pp. 79–80.
52. See, for example, *ibid.*, pp. 72ff; W. T. MacCaffrey, *Elizabeth I: War and Politics, 1588–1603* (Princeton, 1992), pp. 472ff.
53. Merton, 'The Forgotten Crowd of Common Beauties', ch. 6.
54. BL, Reserved Photocopy 2895.
55. *Fragmenta regalia*, p. 42.
56. Adams, 'Favourites and Factions', pp. 281–3.

4
Monopolizing Favour: Structures of Power in the Early Seventeenth-Century English Court

LINDA LEVY PECK

In 1636 a Dutch broadside used the powerful image of the sleeping prince and his corrupt favourite to rouse the English to war against Spain. While the English fleet lies at anchor at Dover, Charles I dozes in the chair of state. Louis XIII tries to wake Charles to defend the Palatinate but 'De Engelsche gespaniolezeerede Favorit' fends him off, supported by the Spanish ambassador offering a trunk filled with gold plate (pl. 11).[1] The print situates the royal favourite both in the structure of the early modern court and in the politics of the Thirty Years War.

The dominance of Cardinal Richelieu, the Count-Duke of Olivares and the Duke of Buckingham (pls 34–40) in seventeenth-century European court politics forced many contemporaries and later historians to analyse the reasons for their hold on power. In his seminal article on the minister–favourite in the seventeenth century, Jean Bérenger emphasized structural changes in the seventeenth-century European state to explain the political control wielded by Richelieu.[2] Most recently, A. Lloyd Moote has argued that the conjuncture of a weak king, state-building and warfare provides the context for the minister–favourite across early modern Europe.

Yet James VI and I (1603–25) (pl. 19) was *not* a weak king and Britain was at peace from 1604 to 1618. Therefore, in this essay I wish to complicate Bérenger's and Moote's model. Several areas of structural change in the early seventeenth-century English court affected the power of the favourite beyond the conjuncture of a weak king and warfare. The centralization and diversification of royal bounty, in particular the increase in monopolies, manufacturing and licensing, extended court favour into everyday life. In addition, the creation of multiple kingdoms and colonies abroad widened the stage for the favourite. Furthermore, the favourite's control and marketing of royal favour generated a language of complaint that went beyond the traditional terms of abuse. In part this was due to the issues of intimacy and display that Bérenger and Moote omit from their analysis of the role of the favourite in the early modern state.[3]

We also need to enquire whether the French model proposed by Bérenger and Moote should be applied to Britain in the first half of the seventeenth century. For the historiographical use of the term 'minister–favourite' to distinguish those who exercised important control over policy from the personal favourites of the monarch needs to be interrogated.[4] How favourites are named – *mignons*, *privados*, *validos*, minister–favourites – is not only an analytical tool but also an ideological construction, one that indicates the cluster of positive and negative attributes ascribed to them by contemporaries and later historians. Indeed, somewhat different historiographies of the favourite have emerged from the differing structures of the medieval and early modern British, French and Spanish states.[5] Perhaps because of Spain's more elaborate conciliar structure and secretariat[6] Philip III ordered in 1612 that the will of the Duke of Lerma should be obeyed as if it were his own, power never enjoyed by Richelieu or Buckingham.

Characteristic of the favourite is the monopoly of royal favour, real or imagined, based on the personal relationship between the king and the favourite.[7] Favourites were, of course, well-known components of court societies, acknowledged in the contemporary advice literature of kings such as Charles V, Philip II and James VI and I, their trajectory dutifully documented in the correspondence of foreign ambassadors and writers of domestic newsletters.[8]

Piers Gaveston, favourite to Edward II in the 1320s, lived on well into the seventeenth century, galvanized by the new print culture, in a literature of complaint. Plays and tracts about Gaveston were reprinted at moments of political tension in both England and France.[9] Sir Robert Naunton, looking back to the Elizabethan court in the 1630s, wrote:

> Her ministers and instruments of state . . . were favourites and not minions, such as acted more by her own princely rules and judgement than by their own will and appetites . . . for we find no Gaveston, Vere or Spencer to have swayed alone during forty-four years.[10]

'The Kingly Cocke' (see pl. 11), the broadside with which this essay began, illustrates the role of the Duke of Buckingham, the Stuarts' greatest favourite. There are, however, significant differences between the Dutch and English versions of the print. Dorothy George argues that the Dutch print alludes to Sir Francis Cottington, formerly English ambassador to Spain, but the English version labels the favourite as the Duke of Buckingham. Moreover, George notes that the English version of the Spanish ambassador's speech refers, mistakenly, not to Charles but to James. This confusion of identity of both king and favourite demonstrates, I would argue, that James and Buckingham, the king devoted to peace and the favourite devoted to entertainment and display, were appropriated as emotive icons into the 1630s. Thus 'the English Favorit' gives a more elaborate speech in the English than in the Dutch version, stressing his concentration on consumption and display, corruption by Spanish gold and disdain for war, saying to Louis XIII:

> Holla, French King, who taught you to be so rude,
> So near our King who sleepes thus to intrude?
> . . .
> Tis better dance, be merrie, jovial still,
> With Spanish pistollets our purses fill,
> Better with pictures gaie to feed our sight
> Than naked corpses gor'd with blood in fight
> In hunting spend our time than all in vaine
> With losse of men and monie warre with Spaine.[11]

Buckingham had been assassinated eight years before, but the cluster of attributes ascribed to him by the broadside (and by other contemporary literature), his intimacy with the king, consumption, display, corruption and leanings towards Spain continued to resonate in contemporary propaganda.

'Our Purses Fill': The Expansion of Royal Bounty

What was new in the narrative of the rise and fall of the favourite in the seventeenth century? Structurally, the minister–favourite who oversaw the dispensation of crown patronage emerged in England out of the centralization of the state and the secularization of church property in the sixteenth century that allowed successive Tudor monarchs to re-endow the crown itself and create the court as the centre for favour. From the reign of Henry VIII, the crown used statute and proclamation to regulate the use of land, capital and labour, and to control the prices and terms of trade, of both imports and exports.

At the same time, Renaissance prescriptive literature increasingly stressed the importance of liberality as a central attribute of monarchy.[12] When James VI of Scotland became King of England in 1603 he found himself monarch of a multiple kingdom of England, Scotland and Ireland with a much larger clientele clamouring for patronage and the imperative to increase his bounty. Patronage relationships, which permeated the society, were the means by which the crown rewarded local elites in whose hands local government rested.

I have argued elsewhere that the early seventeenth century saw an expansion in royal bounty in response to the pressure of demand from the increasing numbers of those who thought themselves entitled to royal favour. Lloyd Moote notes a similar phenomenon in France, suggesting that 'Richelieu's generation of fortune-seeking nobles of sword and *robe* extraction . . . were more frantic in their quest for favour than the tamed nobility of Louis XIV's Versailles.'[13] If the English population doubled between 1541 and 1641, the numbers of those who could consider themselves 'gentle' grew even more dramatically. And they owned an increasing share of landed wealth due to the dissolution of the monasteries and chantries as well as royal land sales to finance war.[14] The expanding number of justices of the peace in the late sixteenth and seventeenth centuries suggests the growing numbers of gentry whose support the crown needed as local governors and who, in turn, brought pressure on court patronage relationships to gain access to land and economic privileges, such as licences and customs farms. In particular the demand for offices, regarded by judicial decision as private property, expanded in response not only to the state's need but to the demands of growing numbers of the political elite.[15]

Why did James deliberately create a monopoly of favour? In *Basilikon Doron* James VI and I had warned his son Prince Henry not to:

> use one in all things, lest he waxe proude, and be envied by his fellowes. . . . Acquaint your selfe so with all the honest men of your Barrons and Gentlemen, and be in your giving accesse so open and affable to every ranke of honest persons . . . to make their owne suites to you themselves, and not to employ the great Lordes their intercessors; for intercession to Saints is Papistrie.[16]

In the 1590s when he wrote *Basilikon Doron* James was concerned with the overweening power of the Scottish nobility that he had recently tamed. Nevertheless, in the 1620s the strength of Buckingham's control over the king was such that contemporaries described Buckingham as a good angel, and even a saint, as he served as a broker between the petitioner and the king.[17]

King James deliberately chose to place the monopoly of favour in the hands of a single favourite between 1612 and 1628 because of the increase in royal bounty. James' own personal inclination, experience and even perhaps emulation of foreign practice, I would argue, led him to place the distribution of his bounty in the hands first of Robert Carr, Earl of Somerset (pl. 12), and then of George Villiers, Duke of Buckingham, each of whom he created so as to be dependent only on himself. Somerset and Buckingham played different roles from that of Esme Stuart, James' French cousin, in Scotland because the economy and political structures over which they exercised control were strikingly different. In Scotland Esme Stuart's role as personal favourite countered the influence of the nobility and the kirk.[18] In the new British imperium Somerset and Buckingham oversaw the dispensation of royal bounty on a much larger scale and a much larger canvas. While favourites continued to receive pensions and lands from the crown they now were also rewarded with monopolies and the brokerage of the sale of titles and offices.[19]

James I first met the young Scot Robert Carr after he was injured at a royal tournament. By 1610 Carr's importance was noted by other courtiers, who emphasized the personal intimacy between him and the prince.

Robert Carr is now most likely to win the Prince's affection. . . . The Prince leaneth on his arm, pinches his cheek, smoothes his ruffled garment. . . . We are almost worn out in our endeavors to keep pace with this fellow in his duty and labour to gain favour, but all in vain; where it endeth I cannot guess, but honours are talked of speedily for him.[20]

By 1613 the Scottish knight had become Viscount Rochester and by 1614 the Earl of Somerset.

After the death of Salisbury in 1612 King James chose to do without a principal secretary of state, reasserting his own power by relying on the favourite, Carr, as his secretary. James recalled that he placed the monopoly of patronage in Carr's hands deliberately: 'ye have deserved more trust and confidence of me than ever man did: in secrecy above all flesh, in feeling and unpartial respect, as well to my honour in every degree as to my profit'.[21]

Carr attended the king and conveyed his instructions to the lord privy seal, Henry Howard, Earl of Northampton. Indeed, between 1611 and 1613 the Howards, led by Northampton and Thomas Howard, Earl of Suffolk, the lord treasurer, worked consistently to attach the favourite firmly to themselves. Northampton described Carr as the 'primum mobile of our court, by whose motion all the other spheres must move, or else stand still; the bright sun of our firmament, at whose splendour . . . all our marigolds of the court open or shut'. Seekers of office were told to contact Carr and Northampton; and Northampton wrote to one candidate for the secretary of state: 'I am very glad to hear of the good correspondence between you and noble Rochester and make no doubt but it will be fortunate to you in the end of the banquet.'

Carr controlled royal patronage in conjunction with his allies the Howards. For example in 1611 when the title of baronet was created for sale, Cecil, Northampton, Carr and others helped to select the grantees. The power the king entrusted to Carr extended beyond the bedchamber and Carr played a role in the parliamentary sessions of 1610–11 and 1614. King James himself acknowledged the political reach of Carr and the Howards. 'Do not all court graces and place come through your office as Chamberlain, and rewards through your father-in-law's that is Treasurer? Do not ye two, as it were, hedge in all the Court with a manner of necessity to depend upon you?'[22]

After his fall, Carr recalled his power. At the death of John Holles, Earl of Clare, Somerset told Gervase Holles:

I was once upon the top, when I was able to confer favours, and I did so to some (though I must say to my Lord of Clare I never did one considerable courtesy; yet I must tell you had I stood he had risen) but in my calamity and when I was underfoot (whether I looke upon your nation or my owne country-men that I had deserved well of) I found not one faithfull freind but my Lord of Clare.[23]

Nevertheless Carr never enjoyed the extensive control of patronage and policy enjoyed by the Duke of Buckingham, who succeeded him in the king's favour in 1615.[24]

While King James used Buckingham, as he did Carr, to filter petitions, Roger Lockyer notes the intensity of the king's dependence on the new favourite. Thus James recognized Buckingham's 'continued attendance upon my service, your daily employments in the same, and the incessant swarm of suitors importunately hanging upon you without discretion or distinction of times'.[25] Buckingham was the only English or Scottish favourite to achieve the power of the great continental minister–favourites, Cardinal Richelieu and the Count-Duke of Olivares.

The issue of the favourite was much on the minds of their contemporaries when Sir Francis Bacon (pl. 31), then attorney general, wrote to Buckingham in 1616 that 'it is no new thing for Kings and Princes to have their *privadoes*, their favourites, their friends'.[26] But Bacon was writing to Buckingham before the age of Richelieu and Olivares. His use of the term *privado* suggests that he had in mind Francisco de Sandoval y Rojas, Duke of Lerma, who in 1616 was still favourite, even if in decline, to Philip III. Gondomar, the Spanish ambassador to England, claimed that James I had said of Lerma that no king in the world ever had such a minister (pl. 33).[27] The Howards and their clients were Spanish pensioners. Northampton sent Lerma a jewel via Gondomar. Indeed it is possible that James patterned the favourite's monopoly on the model offered by Lerma as the king centralized bounty in the hands of Somerset in the household, and his allies the Howards on the Privy Council; and later refused to name a secretary of state after the death of Salisbury.[28]

Lerma may also have served as the model for both Carr and Buckingham. Display was an essential feature of the performance of almost every favourite. But why did Somerset and Buckingham collect Italian Renaissance, Mannerist and Baroque painting? It was not unusual for earlier ministers to have important collections made up of tapestries, jewels and portraits of the great. Wolsey and Leicester come immediately to mind.[29] But the consummate collector of the period was the Duke of Lerma, whom Sarah Schroth calls 'the first large-scale aristocratic collector in Spain'.[30]

The inventory taken at Somerset's arrest in 1615 documents not only his gilded wardrobe but also his important art collection (pl. 13). Daniel Nys and Sir Dudley Carleton began to put together collections for Somerset the same year.[31] Who was the model? Surely the Duke of Lerma. Schroth points out that Buckingham visited Lerma's collection in 1623 and suggests that later royal favourites, in particular the Duke of Buckingham and Cardinal Richelieu, followed the pattern established by Lerma.[32]

Bacon's advice to Buckingham also offers important comment on what was new about the emergence of the minister–favourite in the seventeenth century; why the position appeared; how power was grasped, sustained and lost. Bacon described the increased span of the seventeenth-century favourite's control, ranging from law, matters of state, diplomacy and war to foreign plantations, colonies and trade.

Bacon's very practical counsel to Buckingham focused on how to give favour on the king's behalf and thereby control the essential flow of patronage that linked the crown and its elites and the centre and localities.[33] It also reflects Sir Henry Wotton's statement that Buckingham was 'illiterate'.[34] Reflecting practice under the Cecilian regime (and specifically that of the Earl of Dorset), Bacon told Buckingham to insist that important petitions be put in writing and to have his secretary appoint a day for their answer. Secondly, he advised Buckingham to spend an hour or two a day sorting the petitions (Bacon noted that this would not be too hard to do because Buckingham's secretary could 'draw lines under the matter'). Buckingham should then refer these to specialists, not just his private friends. By spending another hour or two a week perusing the petitions and opinions of the referees, 'within a short time you shall be able to judge of the fidelities of those you trust and return answers to petitions of all natures as an oracle'.

Like Lerma, Somerset and later Richelieu, Buckingham did not attend the Privy Council often. As Somerset was advised 'to set such a sharp edge upon your Lordship's favour as may cut off impediments',[35] so Buckingham demanded fidelity from his clients and, like Richelieu, singular fidelity at that. At the beginning of the new reign in 1625 Buckingham's personal ascendancy was transferred from James VI and I to Charles I, and one courtier wrote to another that 'if you saw the fashion of his treating of suitors (whereof he is as full as ever), and with what elevation he comports himself with the greatest . . . you would say he hath gained le hault bout and that he knows himself fixed past jeopardy of relapsing'.[36] Again like Richelieu and Olivares, Buckingham and his allies fashioned plans to reform royal administration, specifically the household, the navy and the Treasury.[37] In the 1620s, Buckingham controlled an administration that tried to restructure the finances and military strength of the early modern British state.

Although James began to create new peers from the beginning of the reign, further expansion coincided with Buckingham's rise in 1615. In Britain the sale of titles was a means to raise money in the absence of parliamentary support or of a *paulette*, the French tax on offices. Between 1615 and 1628 the king created forty-five more peers and the peerage came to total 126, more than double the size of Elizabeth's peerage. The size of the Irish and Scottish nobility increased too. The sale of titles was handled by Buckingham and his agents. Sir John Holles, a disappointed client of Somerset's, bought first a barony and then an earldom. His kinsman Gervase Holles described why:

For this dignity he payd the then favourite (the Duke of Buckingham) ten thousand poundes sterling. For after the entrance of King James the sale of honours was become a trade at Court; and whilst that Duke lived scarse any man acquired any honour but such as were either his kindred or had the fortune (or misfortune) to marry with his kindred or mistresses, or paid a round summe of mony for it. . . . I have heard the Earle of Clare . . . often inveigh bitterly against it, and he would usually call it temporall simony. I remember I once tooke the liberty (hearing him so earnest upon that subject) to aske him why he would purchase himselfe seeing he condemned the King for selling. He answered 'that he observed merit to be no medium to an honorary reward, that he saw divers persons who he thought deserved it as little as he (either in their persons or estates) by that meanes leap over his head, and therefore seeing the market open and finding his purse not unfurnished for it he was perswaded to ware his mony as other men had done'.[38]

The favourite was situated in a culture of exchange that permeated early modern society in which gift-giving sat uneasily beside the market. Creating a market for titles and offices was an allocative device that addressed the frenetic clamour for favour. Nevertheless, the sale of titles was one of the charges brought against Buckingham in the parliament of 1626 where one of his chief accusers was the ungrateful Earl of Clare.

Most importantly, the sixteenth and seventeenth centuries saw a changed framework for the scope of the favourite because of the state's increasing regulation of the economy, the development of projects designed to diversify the economy, and the privatization of power in the hands of informal agents of the state. The crown, concerned to promote employment and economic growth in order to prevent disorder, established policies both to discourage imports and to encourage home industries, a policy known today as import substitution. The term 'monopoly' denoted a variety of activities, including privileges granted by the sovereign for new inventions and exclusive trade in some commodity.

This expansion of government regulations and monopolies shaped a pattern of behaviour known as rent-seeking that exploited government regulation 'as if it were part of the market sphere'.[39] Rent-seeking was a policy encouraged in sixteenth-century European prescriptive literature in order to avoid taxing the commons. In the suppositious *Advice of Charles V to Philip II* which circulated in late sixteenth-century Europe, Charles V advised: 'When occasion is offered rather to sett hand to the sale of offices, and rents, then to beate your heade about any newe kinds of aggrievance to the people.'[40]

In the early seventeenth century, monopolies were increasingly organized by the favourite – first by Carr and then by Buckingham. Beginning in the 1580s, patents had been granted not only to establish new industries but also to raise moneys for the crown and to reward courtiers. An especially large number of patents were granted in the period between 1610 and 1620, between the failure of the Great Contract and the meeting of the parliament of 1621 which strongly attacked monopolies. By 1621 the distribution of monopolies as bounty had become as crucial to the crown as the encouragement of home industry. Yet the favourites merely implemented royal policy.[41] Rent-seeking behaviour continued to characterize both petitioners and the crown even in the absence of the minister–favourite so long as mercantilist policies persisted.

Along with monopolies emerged the privatization of law and order. The judges reluctantly agreed that the crown could reward private individuals for the prosecution of penal statutes after the king had received forfeiture under the law. Despite promises to the contrary in *The Book of Bounty*, the king's proclamation in 1610 that he would limit the distribution of favour, the crown began to farm its own judicial functions on a larger scale. Whether with monopolies or with the farming of the enforcement of penal statutes, such grants under Queen Elizabeth and James were increasingly accorded to the political elite. In Britain colonial ventures of the late sixteenth and seventeenth centuries expanded the reach of the favourite. Thus Leicester insisted that his battery works included the patent for Ireland; Essex made knights on the battlefield in Ireland; Somerset and his allies helped to shape the planters for Ulster; and Buckingham's clients such as Francis Blundell organized the sale of the Irish baronetcy for the duke.

Patronage networks spanned the multiple kingdoms of early modern states. Sharon Kettering argues that Cardinal Richelieu crafted networks that integrated the metropolis and the provinces, allying provincial leaders by making them his clients, creating clienteles dependent on himself, taking away clients from great nobles.[42] John Elliott describes how Olivares used his patronage in the multiple monarchy of the Spanish Habsburgs. Though Buckingham certainly tried to assert his power over provincial governors he was less successful, as the failure of the Forced Loan demonstrated. Patronage worked as a means of integration when other issues were less important than the benefits bestowed. But the complaint of corruption that emanated from the venal practices of the early modern monarchy was destabilizing politically. In 1626 the House of Commons tried to impeach Buckingham. Charles I dissolved parliament rather than allow the removal of the favourite. For the king the administrative role of the seventeenth-century favourite was only part of the story.

Gender and the Court: Family, Sex and Marriage

Bacon underlined the familial and personal aspect of the minister–favourite long before the House of Commons tried to impeach Buckingham for, among other things, promoting his relatives, a charge also levelled against Richelieu and Olivares.[43] Bacon wrote, 'For the affairs of Court, you are much better able to instruct yours than any man else can. . . . In the disposing of the offices and affairs of Court, the King hath a latitude for his affection, which in matters touching the public, he must deny to himself where he is more properly *Paterfamilias*; in the other *Pater Patriae*.'[44] That powerful combination of court, family and state was the domain of the seventeenth-century minister–favourite.

Early modern favourites differed in their age, function, previous connections at court, social origin and control over royal bounty. Thus the Duke of Lerma was a father figure to Philip III; the youthful Earl of Essex was presented to Elizabeth by his uncle the Earl of Leicester, her contemporary and greatest favourite. In a psychological study of the favourite, Elizabeth Marvick drew attention to the paternal and sibling models of the relationship of favourite to monarch.[45] Both Leicester and Essex had military pretensions. Henry Howard, an Essex adherent, wrote, 'the time serveth now most fitly for expeditions of war which no man understands amounge the councell in respect of the . . . sloth and rest of peace or if any did in former times, discontinuance and ease have cancelled it'.[46] Richelieu and Olivares oversaw the Thirty Years War. In contrast, Buckingham, fashioned in the form of a king who favoured peace, only saw service under Charles I at the Isle of Ré.[47] Buckingham effectively controlled patronage in the second half of James' reign while Essex, who jeopardized his position at court by going off on expeditions, was able to garner few favours for his followers.[48]

Where favourites resembled one another was on the matter of intimacy.[49] Indeed, intimacy was the key to the power of the favourite, whether the poetic 'lovers' of Queen Elizabeth, the physical lovers of James I or the friends of Charles I. Thus the power of the favourite was situated in the king's privy chamber or, in the case of a queen regnant, in the household.[50] Often the favourite's power was signalled by the possession of an important household office. If Richelieu was controller of the household of Marie de Médicis and Olivares was groom of the stole, in England the Earl of Essex and the Duke of Buckingham were masters of the horse and Robert Carr was gentleman of the bedchamber. Whether drawn from the nobility, like the Earl of Leicester, the Earl of Essex, Cardinal Richelieu and the Count-Duke of Olivares, or younger sons of gentry like George Villiers, Duke of Buckingham, or 'foreigners' like Concini and Robert Carr, Earl of Somerset, the key to the power of the royal favourite was the perception that he had unique access to the monarch and to the allocation of royal bounty.

Buckingham was seen by contemporaries as the creation of James I. As Sir Henry Wotton, a client to both Essex and Buckingham, wrote:

> the Duke of Buckingham had another kind of Germination; and surely had he been a Plant, he would have been reckoned the *Spontes Nascentes*, for he sprang without any help, by a kind of congenial composure (as we may term it) to the likeness of our late Sovereign and Master of ever blessed memory who taking him into his regard, taught him more and more to please himself, and moulded him (as it were) Platonically to his own *Idea*; delighting first in the choice of materials, because he found him susceptible of good form, and afterwards by degrees, as great Architects use to do, in the workmanship of his Regal hand. . . . After he had hardened and polished him about ten years in the School of Observance (for so a Court is) and in the furnace of trial about himself (for he

was a King could peruse men as well as books) he made him the Associate of the heir apparent.[51]

The erotic aspect of Jacobean life has received less notice than it should from historians. The power of the favourite was inscribed on the king's two bodies: on the monarch himself and on the body politic. Simon Adams points out that *Leicester's Commonwealth* attacked not only his 'absolute reign' in court but also 'his spectacular sexual appetites'.[52] Having prevented the French match,

> this tyrant for his own private lucre (fearing lest hereby his ambition might be restrained and his treachery revealed) . . . gave out . . . that he was assured to her Majesty and consequently that all other princes must give over their suits for him. . . . Neither holdeth he any rule in his lust besides only the motion and suggestion of his own sensuality. Kindred, affinity, or any other band of consanguinity, religion, nor honesty taketh no place in his outrageous appetite. . . . given to procure love in others by conjuring, sorcery, and other such means . . . by the Italian ointment procured not many years past by his surgeon . . . whereby . . . he is able to move his flesh at all times, for keeping of his credit, howsoever his inability be otherwise for performance. . . . I am ashamed to have made mention of so base filthiness.[53]

Such language was found not only in contemporary propaganda against Leicester. The erotic aspect of kings' relationships with their favourites is shown most strikingly in the Leaguer complaint literature about Henri III's *mignons* which used vivid accusations of sodomy to delegitimize the ruler.[54] Courtiers too were explicit. Northampton, who cemented the alliance between Carr and Frances Howard, wrote to the favourite: 'think not that I can find pain in that which gives me greatest pleasure which proceeds out of your pen and flows from your mind . . . though it were but what which a man takes in cracking a sweet nut to taste the kernel or but like the pain my Lady Frances shall feel when the sweet stream follows'.[55]

At the same time the court of James I was perhaps the most uxorious court in England until that of Queen Victoria. Unlike Queen Elizabeth, King James encouraged the marriage of his courtiers, notably the Essex and Cecil groups, and, later, the marriage of both his and the queen's favourites, going so far as to force his bishops to declare the married Frances Howard a virgin, so that she could marry Somerset. Queen Anne sought a major role in the making and breaking of her husband's favourites. She pleaded with James to send Somerset away, a contemporary wrote, going so far as to threaten to return to Denmark. Of Buckingham she wrote, 'the king will teach him to despise and hardly entreat us all, that he may seem to be beholden to none but himself'. When the Howards attempted to replace the disgraced Somerset with another, the queen blocked him and favoured the rise of Buckingham.[56]

James' letters to Buckingham demonstrate the overlapping of family, sex and marriage in the seventeenth-century court. He wrote to Buckingham in the hope that:

> we may make at this Christmas a new marriage ever to be kept hereafter . . . as I desire only to live in this world for your sake, and that I had rather live banished in any part of the earth with you than live a sorrowful widow's life without you. And so God bless you, my sweet child and wife, and grant that ye may ever be a comfort to your dear dad and husband.[57]

Reconsidering the Paradigm

How useful is the French paradigm? In order to support the French model of minister–favourite, Bérenger and Moote both suggest that Archbishop Laud (pl. 69) and Thomas Wentworth, Earl of Strafford (pl. 70), became minister–favourites after the death of Buckingham. In fact, neither Laud nor Wentworth can be considered minister–favourites since neither controlled 'the court'. As lord deputy of Ireland from 1632 to 1640, Wentworth spent most of his time after 1633 in the environs of Dublin. He did however insist on controlling Irish patronage and profiting from Irish monopolies.[58] He persuaded Charles I to agree 'that the places in the Deputy's gift, as well of the civil as the martial list, be left freely to his dispose; and that his Majesty will be graciously pleased not to pass to any upon suit made unto him here [in England]'.[59] Despite Laud's hold on the king's conscience he does not appear to have tried to control Charles' court patronage. Instead, after the death of Buckingham, whose influence spanned both court and state, the scope of the favourites retreated to the royal households of King Charles and Henrietta Maria, with power diffused among courtiers such as Hamilton and Holland who held positions in the household, in combination with leading officials such as Laud, Wentworth and Weston in church and state.[60]

Further, even great favourites were not hegemonic. The power of Richelieu and Olivares was initially rooted in the queen and king's households.[61] So too other great Tudor ministers had clients in the household even as they sought to control the Privy Council.[62] The need to control both was understood by seventeenth-century monarchs, even those with great favourites. Thus Philip III, who had made Lerma his *valido*, insisted that Gondomar have confidants in the English Privy Council as well as the household. Contemporaries understood the importance of both foci of power. No one was able to span both after the death of Buckingham.

In conclusion, what was the significance of the emergence of the minister–favourite? Situated in the structure of the early modern state, the minister–favourite dealt with increasing pressure from clients on the patronage system. In addition, the favourite as collector and impresario of courtly entertainments celebrated the power of the king. Finally, the seventeenth-century favourite was the focus of a literature of complaint, the English equivalent of the *Mazarinades*, pamphlets attacking Cardinal Mazarin, or, closer in time, those attacking Cardinal Richelieu.

In England, the language of the favourite that emerged in the fourteenth century was applied to the minister–favourites in the seventeenth century.[63] Many contemporaries understood the monarch's needs for friends he could trust to act as a buffer between the crown and the great nobility and as filters for petitions. At the same time the traditional attack on the rise of baseborn upstarts who gave the monarch evil counsel had a long shelf-life. It extended even to such unlikely characters as Judge Jeffreys, James II's hanging judge, called 'the unfortunate favourite' in a tract of 1690, and to colonial governors at the time of Bacon's rebellion in 1674 who were accused of having low-born favourites.[64]

In particular, the reaction against the favourite was repeatedly demonstrated in the attack on monopolies in 1601, 1621 and 1624 and the unsuccessful attempt to impeach Buckingham in 1626. Elizabeth had said during the famous debate on monopolies in 1601:

> yet did I never put my pen to any grant but upon pretext and semblance made me, that was for the good and avail of my subjects generally, though a private profit to some of my ancient servants, who have deserved well; but that my grants shall be made grievances to my people, and oppressions, to be privileged under color of our patents, our princely dignity shall not suffer it.[65]

During the impeachment proceedings, Buckingham echoed her. In his reply we hear the voice of the seventeenth-century favourite. Buckingham responded:

> He may without blame, receive and retain that which the liberal and bountiful hand of his master has freely conferred on him; and it is not without precedents both in ancient and modern times that one man, eminent in the esteem of his sovereign, has at one time held as great and as many offices. But when it shall be discerned that he shall falsify or corruptly use those places . . . or that the public shall suffer thereby . . . he will readily lay down at his royal feet not only his place and offices but his whole fortunes and his life to do him service.

Although Bacon had advised in 1616 that one aspect of the role of favourite was to fall from power to prevent political damage to the king, this counsel was ignored by both Buckingham and Charles.[66] In 1642, however, Charles I had to promise an outraged assembly to give up his favourites: 'the Prince may not make use of this high and perpetual power to the hurt of those for whose good he hath it, and make use of the name of public necessity for the gain of his private favourites'.[67]

By 1659 a paradigmatic shift had taken place in both the position and analysis of minister–favourites, one that focused less on the court and more on the state, and explicitly linked the position of minister–favourite to the state's control of money, arms and thereby loyalty. Thus William Cavendish, Earl of Newcastle, urged his pupil Charles II on the eve of his restoration to the English throne to emulate Cardinal Richelieu:

> The Cardinal De Richelieu was the wisest and greatest statesman. . . . hee had butt two thinges, which hee did all, with all, which was money and Armes, saying if the money would not doe, the Armes would, and if the Armes fayled, the money would, and if They were singly to weake, Being Joyned they would Effecte moste thinges in this world for they are very few above the price of money.[68]

It is significant that Newcastle advised Charles II not to *have* a Richelieu but to *be* a Richelieu. Buckingham was no Richelieu. But, if not Buckingham, then who? The Civil War and Protectorate devastated the court system. But there was a contemporary British statesman who was singularly successful with arms and money. We might speculate whether Oliver Cromwell, in fact, was not a Richelieu, a minister who most successfully put together arms and money and whose name for obvious reasons Newcastle does not mention. But then we are left with the question of whether it is possible to have a minister–favourite in the absence of a king. To pose the question helps to make the point that, while favourites played important roles in court society, they were possibly no more than epiphenomena in state formation.

Notes

1. British Museum, *Catalogue of Political and Personal Satires* i (London, 1978), #133.
2. Jean Bérenger, 'Pour une enquête européenne: le problème du ministériat au XVIIe siècle', *Annales*, 29 (1974), pp. 166–92. See also A. Lloyd Moote, 'Richelieu as Chief Minister: A Comparative Study of the Favourite in Early Seventeenth-Century Politics', in Joseph Bergin and Laurence Brockliss, eds, *Richelieu and his Age* (Oxford, 1992), pp. 23–5.
3. See Louis Montrose, 'The Work of Gender in the Discourse of Discovery', *Representations*, 33 (1991), pp. 1–2.
4. Moote categorizes favourites as personal, political and minister–favourites: 'Richelieu as Chief Minister', p. 16. See also Roger Lockyer, 'An English Valido? Buckingham and James I', in Richard Ollard and Pamela Tudor-Craig, eds, *For Veronica Wedgwood These* (London, 1986), pp. 45–58, and Antonio Feros, 'Twin Souls: Monarchs and Favourites in Early Seventeenth-Century Spain', in Richard L. Kagan and G. Parker, eds, *Spain, Europe and the Atlantic World: Essays in Honour of John H. Elliott* (Cambridge, 1995), pp. 27–47.
5. See for instance Francisco Tomás y Valiente, *Los validos en la monarquía española del siglo XVII* (Madrid, 1963); J. H. Elliott, *Richelieu and Olivares* (Cambridge, 1984); Bergin and Brockliss, eds, *Richelieu and his Age*; Lockyer, 'An English Valido? Buckingham and James I', pp. 45–58.
6. On Spanish governmental structures see J. H. Elliott, *Imperial Spain, 1469–1716* (London, 1963).
7. See Bérenger, 'Pour une enquête européenne', and Moote, 'Richelieu as Chief Minister'. For a discussion of patronage see L. L. Peck, *Court Patronage and Corruption in Early Stuart England* (London, 1990).
8. Karl Brandi, *The Emperor Charles V*, trans. C. V. Wedgwood (London, 1949), pp. 488, 490. Yale University, Beinecke Library, Osborne b 31: Karl V, 'The summe of diverse directions of

68 The Emergence of the Minister–Favourite

Government which Charles 5th lefte unto his sonne Philip the II K of Spaine' (see also British Library (hereafter BL), King's Ms. 166): 'Every man needs advice, and so I ask you to make Don Juan de Zuniga your watch and your alarm in all things. . . . Sleep is often sweet and an alarum is commonly a nuisance; therefore remember that he acts only out of devotion and duty to me, and be grateful to him' (p. 488).

9. Michael Drayton, *Piers Gaveston Earle of Cornwall, His Life, Death and Fortune* (London, 1594?); E.F., *The History of the Life, Reign, and Death of Edward II, King of England, and Lord of Ireland with the Rise and Fall of his Great Favorites Gaveston and the Spencers Written by E.F. in the year of 1627* (London, 1680), Henry Viscount Falkland, *The History of the Most Unfortunate Prince King Edward II with Choice Political Observations On Him and His Unhappy Favorites, Gaveston & Spencer* (London, 1680), reprinted as *The Parallel or the History of . . . Edward the Second* (London, 1689). *L'histoire ou Fable de Pierre de Gaveston* (Paris, 1588), cited in Joseph Cady, 'The "Masculine Love" of the "Princes of Sodom", Practicing the Art of Ganymede at Henri III's Court: The Homosexuality of Henri III and his Mignons in Pierre de L'Estoile's *Mémoires-Journaux*', in Konrad Eisenbichler and Jacqueline Murray, eds, *Desire and Discipline: Sex and Sexuality in the Premodern West* (Toronto, 1996), p. 140. For the translation of French complaint literature into English see for instance *The Character of an Ill-Court Favorite: Representing the Mischiefs that flow from Ministers of State when they are more great than good, the arts they use to seduce their masters, and the unhappiness of Princes, that are curs'd with such destructive servants* (London, 1601).

10. Quoted in Simon Adams, 'Favourites and Factions at the Elizabethan Court', in Ronald G. Asch and Adolf M. Birke, eds, *Princes, Patronage and the Nobility: The Court at the Beginning of the Modern Age, c. 1450–1650* (Oxford, 1991), p. 281.

11. British Museum, Prints and Drawings: 'The Kingly Cocke', 1636 (Dorothy George #133).

12. See L. L. Peck, 'For a King not to be Bountiful Were a Fault', *Journal of British Studies*, 25 (1986), pp. 31–61.

13. See Peck, *Court Patronage and Corruption*. Moote, 'Richelieu as Chief Minister', p. 26.

14. Christopher Clay, *Economic Expansion and Social Change: England, 1500–1700*, 2 vols (Cambridge, 1984), i, pp. 2, 142–58.

15. James had the Scottish parliament pass a statute establishing procedures to insulate him from clients. The *Book of Bounty* (1610) excluded grants that were illegal or 'are fitt to be wholly to our owne use until our estate be repaired', including the benefits of penal law, royal land, leases and rents, leases in reversion, pensions and freedom from customs duties. Royal officials also considered 'a French ordinance concerning certain petitions and suits'. Were the king to make such grants, the secretary of state was not to expedite and the chancellor and keeper of the seals not to grant them. See Peck, *Court Patronage and Corruption*, pp. 36–8.

16. *The Political Works of James I*, ed. C. H. McIlwain (Cambridge, 1918), pp. 25, 33, 50.

17. See L. L. Peck, 'Benefits, Brokers and Beneficiaries: The Culture of Exchange in Seventeenth-Century England', in Bonnelyn Young Kunze and Dwight D. Brautigam, eds, *Court, Country and Culture* (Rochester, 1992), pp. 109–28. In retrospect, such language was also applied to Somerset by Anthony Weldon: 'Lord, how the great men flocked then to see him, and to offer to his shrine in such abundance.' Robert Ashton, ed., *James I by his Contemporaries* (London, 1969), p. 118.

18. James Melville wrote in his diary: 'That year arrived Monsieur d'Obignie from France, with instructions and devices from the House of Guise, and with many French fashions and toys; and in effect, with a plain course of Papistry, to subvert the estate of the Kirk new planted both with true doctrine and discipline.' Quoted in Ashton, ed., *James I by his Contemporaries*, pp. 115–17. 'Put never a forrainer, in any principall office of estate: for that will never faile to stir up sedition and envie in the countrymen's hearts, both against you and him: But (as I said before) if God provide you with more countries then this; choose the borne-men of every countrey, to bee your cheif counsellors therein.' *Political Works of James I*, ed. McIlwain, p. 32.

19. Similarly, Richelieu enjoyed not only the liberality of Marie de Médicis and Louis XIII but also the benefits of state regulation, specifically provincial governorships, participation in the tax farms and rentes of a variety of types. See Joseph Bergin, *Cardinal Richelieu: Power and the Pursuit of Wealth* (New Haven, 1985), *passim*.

20. Thomas Birch, *The Court and Times of James I*, 2 vols (London, 1849), i, pp. 390–7, Lord Thomas Howard to Sir John Harrington, *Nugae Antiquae*, 2 vols (London, 1804), i, pp. 390–7.

21. G. P. V. Akrigg, ed., *Letters of James I* (Berkeley, 1984), pp. 339–40.

22. *Ibid.*, pp. 339–40.

23. Gervase Holles, *Memorials of the Holles Family, 1493–1656*, Camden Society, 3rd series, 55 (1937), p. 113.

24. See Maurice Lee, *Great Britain's Solomon* (Champaign–Urbana, 1990), pp. 233–60; Peter Seddon, 'Robert Carr, Earl of Somerset', *Renaissance and Modern Studies*, 4 (1970), pp. 46–68.
25. Roger Lockyer, *Buckingham: The Life and Political Career of George Villiers, First Duke of Buckingham, 1592–1628* (London and New York, 1981), pp. 55, 28.
26. James Spedding, ed., *The Letters and the Life of Francis Bacon*, 7 vols (London, 1861–74), vi, p. 14. Bacon discusses favourites in his *Essays* on 'Ambition', 'Fame', 'Friendship' and 'Envy'. 'Filthy privado' is also used in *Leicester's Commonwealth* to describe Leicester's servant who helped convince Eric of Denmark that the queen was assured to Leicester. *Leicester's Commonwealth*, ed. D. C. Peck (Athens, Ohio, 1985), p. 80.
27. Public Record Office, State Papers 31/12/34, fol. 114, 5 October 1613. Gondomar's correspondence with Philip III and the Duke of Lerma underscores the power of the Howards and of Somerset, who were Spanish pensioners, and later notes the moment of Somerset's fall and Buckingham's rise.
28. On Lerma see Patrick Williams, 'Lerma, Old Castile and the Travels of Philip III of Spain', *History*, 73 (1988), pp. 379–97; 'Lerma, 1618: Dismissal or Retirement', *European History Quarterly*, 15 (1989), pp. 307–32; Antonio Feros, 'The King's Favorite, the Duke of Lerma: Power, Wealth and Court Culture during the Reign of Philip III of Spain, 1598–1621' (PhD thesis, The Johns Hopkins University, 1994).
29. See, for example, Tom Campbell, 'Cardinal Wolsey's Tapestry Collection', *Antiquaries Journal*, 76 (1996), pp. 73–137.
30. Sarah Schroth, 'The Private Picture Collection of the Duke of Lerma' (PhD thesis, New York University, 1990), pp. 4, 99–100.
31. On Carr see Peter Seddon, 'Robert Carr, Earl of Somerset', *Renaissance and Modern Studies*, 14 (1970), pp. 46–68; A. R. Braunmuller, 'Robert Carr, Earl of Somerset as Collector and Patron', in L. L. Peck, ed., *The Mental World of the Jacobean Court* (Cambridge, 1991), pp. 230–50. Timothy Wilks, 'The Picture Collection of Robert Carr, Earl of Somerset (*c.* 1587–1645), Reconsidered', *Journal of the History of Collections*, 1 (1989), pp. 167–77.
32. Sarah Schroth, 'Private Picture Collection of the Duke of Lerma', pp. 4, 99–100.
33. For recent work on patronage see Peck, *Court Patronage and Corruption*; Sharon Kettering, *Patrons, Brokers and Clients in Seventeenth-Century France* (New York and Oxford, 1986); A. Mączak, ed., *Klientelsysteme im Europea der frühen Neuzeit* (Munich, 1988).
34. Sir Henry Wotton, *Reliquiae Wottonianae*, 3rd edn (London, 1672), p. 173.
35. BL, Cotton Ms. Titus CVI, fol. 110, Northampton to Carr, before November 1613.
36. Quoted in Lockyer, *Buckingham*, p. 169.
37. See Peck, *Court Patronage and Corruption*, pp. 106–33.
38. Holles, *Memorials of the Holles Family, 1493–1656*, p. 99. Seven years later he paid another £5,000 to become an earl. Later he was a leader in the effort to impeach Buckingham in the House of Lords. See Peck, *Court Patronage and Corruption*, pp. 190–6.
39. Rents provide profits above costs because of property rights. See Robert Ekelund and Robert Tollison, *Mercantilism as a Rent-Seeking Society: Economic Regulation in its Historical Perspective* (College Station, 1981).
40. Yale University, Beinecke Library, Osborne b 31: Karl V, 'The summe of diverse directions of Government which Charles 5th lefte unto his sonne Philip the II K of Spaine'.
41. Ronald G. Asch, 'The Revival of Monopolies: Court and Patronage during the Personal Rule of Charles I, 1629–1640', in Asch and Birke, eds, *Princes, Patronage and the Nobility*, pp. 357–92.
42. Kettering, *Patrons, Brokers and Clients*, p. 209. In analysing the clientelism of Cardinal Richelieu, Sharon Kettering writes that 'The politicization of great noble clienteles accelerated in response to the state building efforts of Richelieu, Mazarin, Colbert, and other royal ministers, who created and used extensive ministerial clienteles to help govern distant provinces' (p. 159).
43. On the promotion of relations by French favourites see Moote, 'Richelieu as Chief Minister', p. 28.
44. Spedding, ed., *Letters and the Life of Francis Bacon*, vi, p. 24.
45. Elizabeth Marvick, 'Favorites in Early Modern Europe: A Recurring Psychopolitical Role', *Journal of Psychohistory*, 10 (1983), pp. 463–89.
46. Durham University Library, Howard Ms. 2, fol. 119. 'The necessarie use of such a person in this time. . . . The Councell of the state waxinge olde . . . which dulleth and abateth oftentimes the edge of the most pregnant witts.'
47. See Wotton, 'Of Sir Robert Devereux, Earle of Essex and George Villiers, Duke of Buckingham. Some Observations by Way of Parallel in the Time of Their Estates of Favour', *Reliquiae*

Wottonianae; BL, Egerton Ms. 2026, fol. 32: 'that it is exceeding dangerous to a favourite to be long absent from his Prince'.

48. See *Reliquiae Wottonianae*, pp. 161–83, and L. L. Peck, 'Peers, Patronage and the Politics of History', in John Guy, ed., *The Reign of Elizabeth* (Cambridge, 1995), pp. 87–108.

49. See David Starkey, 'Representation through Intimacy', in I. Lewis, ed., *Symbols and Sentiments* (London, 1977), pp. 187–224.

50. See Moote, 'Richelieu as Chief Minister,' p. 23.

51. *Reliquiae Wottonianae*, p. 164.

52. Adams, 'Favourites at the Elizabethan Court', in *Princes, Patronage and the Nobility*, p. 271.

53. Peck, ed., *Leicester's Commonwealth*, pp. 78–89: 'there are not . . . two noblewomen about her Majesty . . . whom he hath not solicited by potent ways; neither contented with this place of honor, he hath descended to seek pasture among the waiting gentlewomen of her Majesty's great Chamber whereof my Lord is nothing squeamish for satisfying of his lust but can be content . . . to gather up crumbs when he is hungry, even in the very laundry itself or other place of baser quality' (pp. 88–9).

54. Joseph Cady argues, *pace* Foucault, that homosexuality was defined clearly if critically in those pamphlets and was not a later historical invention. See Cady, 'The "Masculine Love" of the "Princes of Sodom"'. It might also be suggested that such complaint literature also secularized criticism of the church in the works, for instance, of John Ponet and John Bale attacking the 'buggery' of monasticism. See Donald R. Kelley, 'Elizabethan Political Thought', in J. G. A. Pocock, ed., *The Varieties of British Political Thought* (Cambridge, 1993), p. 58. See also Alan Bray, *Homosexuality in Renaissance England* (London, 1982).

55. Cambridge University Library, Mss DD 3, 63, fols 54, 35, 36v–37v. Referring to her first husband as 'my Lord the gelding' he wrote to the favourite: 'If my Lord would draw his sword in defence of a good prick it were worth his pains but never make such a poor pudding's apology.'

56. See Leeds Barroll, 'The Court of the First Stuart Queen', in Peck, ed., *Mental World of the Jacobean Court*, pp. 191–208; quoted in Ashton, ed., *James I by his Contemporaries*, pp. 119–20, 127.

57. Quoted in Alvin Kernan, *Shakespeare, the King's Playwright* (New Haven, 1995), pp. 9, 118, December 1623. Glyn Redworth notes that at much the same time Charles I wrote to Gondomar as his 'pimp' during the Spanish marriage negotiations but whether such usage was due to his poor Spanish he delicately refuses to decide: Glyn Redworth, 'Of Pimps and Princes: Three Unpublished Letters from James I and the Prince of Wales Relating to the Spanish Match', *Historical Journal*, 37 (1994), pp. 401–9.

58. Hugh Kearney, *Strafford in Ireland, 1633–1641* (Manchester, 1959); J. F. Merritt, ed., *The Political World of Thomas Wentworth, Earl of Strafford, 1621–1641* (Cambridge, 1996).

59. Quoted in Paul Hardacre, 'Patronage and Purchase in the Irish Standing Army Under Thomas Wentworth, Earl of Strafford, 1632–1640', *Journal of the Society for Army Historical Research*, 67 (1989), p. 42.

60. See for instance Kevin Sharpe, 'The Image of Virtue: The Court and Household of Charles I, 1625–1642', in David Starkey, ed., *The English Court from the Wars of the Roses to the Civil War* (London, 1987), pp. 226–60.

61. See Elliott, *Richelieu and Olivares*.

62. See Starkey, ed., *English Court*.

63. Peck, *Court Patronage and Corruption*, pp. 173–81.

64. The tract applies all the usual language about ambition, rising above one's birth and flattery to Judge Jeffreys, a leading judge in the reign of James II who had no personal relationship with the king. Bacon's 'Declaration of the People' in 1674 attacked the imposing of taxes 'upon specious pretences of Publick works for the advancement of private Favourites and other sinister ends'. Such favourites had experienced 'the sudden Rise of their Estates compared with the Quality in which they first entered this Country'. Quoted in Edmund Morgan, *American Slavery–American Freedom* (New York, 1975). I am grateful to Terry Schneider and Richard Bushman for these citations.

65. Quoted in Harold G. Fox, *Monopolies and Patents* (Toronto, 1946), p. 92n.

66. House of Lords Record Office Manuscript Journal of the House of Lords, p. 657, 8 June 1626, Yale Center for Parliamentary History transcript, pp. 930–1.

67. See Richard L. Bushman, *The King and the People* (Williamsburg, 1985), p. 99n.

68. Thomas Slaughter, ed., *Ideology and Politics on the Eve of the Restoration: Newcastle's Advice to Charles II* (Philadelphia, 1984), p. 57.

5

Between Mignons *and Principal Ministers: Concini, 1610–1617*

J.-F. DUBOST

Concino Concini (pl. 14) is a most peculiar and original example of a court favourite. Though it is not easy to define the sixteenth- and seventeenth-century understanding of the term favourite succinctly, we can use words written at the end of the 1610s – exactly the era when Concini was a favourite – depicting Albert de Gondi, the duc de Retz, and the favourite of Charles IX:

> The aforementioned Albert . . . formerly master of the royal wardrobe . . . has, with his keen understanding and his wise conduct, ingratiated himself with the king. Consequently he has reached the kingdom's most honourable offices and set up an illustrious House, possessed of considerable means and well connected. . . . His unfailingly wise and agreeable conduct, avoiding ceremony and ostentation, yet remaining virtuous and courageous, has enabled him, through valour and patience, to overcome all opposition and setbacks.[1]

Friendship with the prince, closeness to his person, courtesy and delicacy in social relations – following Castiglione's precepts – provided the basis for Albert's fortune and the founding of his dynasty. Concini's career scarcely fits such a pattern. His assassination on 24 April 1617 ruled out the founding of an aristocratic dynasty; the patronage he enjoyed was not that of the king, who neither liked nor valued him, but only that of the queen mother; and if Concini's lifestyle was that of a free-spending cavalier, he remained a poor courtier, unable to avoid the pitfall of 'ostentation'. Yet for all this Concini managed to make his mark in the political life of the 1610s, to the extent that contemporaries are unanimous in their recognition that he came to exercise considerable – even inordinate – power.

But it is difficult to define the realms of Concini's power. Indeed, two diverging interpretations are to be found among historians. The first, based largely on Sully's memoirs, and recently restated by Hélène Duccini's biography, contends that Concini wielded considerable political power from as early as 1610.[2] The second, to be found in the late nineteenth- and early twentieth-century works of J. Nouillac, Berthold Zeller and F. Hayem, acknowledges the Florentine's influence at court and among Marie de Médicis' entourage, but stresses that this served his own personal advancement before evolving, belatedly, into real political influence.[3] These differing readings prompt a reconsideration of Concini's career.

Maintaining that Concini had political power as early as 1610 is excessive. Rather, it is clear that his power, not fully established at the start of the regency in 1610, developed in three major stages. Between 1610 and 1614, Concini and his wife Leonora concentrated on amassing their fortune, and on acquiring land and office through Leonora's close relationship with the queen: as one of Leonora's entourage stated, 'the queen mother never bestowed any gifts or favours without first seeking the counsel of the marshal's wife' (pl. 15).[4] Leonora's influence over the queen meant financial reward for the Concinis. Above all, control over the assignment of office in the royal households and in the *parlements*, and over the appointment of bishops, was a means of financial gain. Wealth in turn helped to consolidate social status, in Concini's case, epitomized by the acquisition of the marquisate of Ancre in 1610 and of a marshal's baton in 1613. But throughout this phase power remained in the hands of the minister Villeroy.

The second phase was one of broadening influence for Concini. From 1614 to 1616, he made his first interventions in politics, supporting the Spanish marriages and then the rebel princes to restore or maintain civil order. The turning point is 1615, a change reflected in the increase in criticism of Concini in contemporary pamphlets.[5] This change is linked to the proclamation of the king's majority in 1614: once Marie de Médicis was confirmed as head of the government (pl. 16), the Concinis were in a position to intervene in the political sphere.

Dating from the Peace of Loudun in 1616, the third phase saw Concini play a full part in the political direction of the kingdom. Here, Leonora and her husband inspired a radical change in general policy. Initially favourable to concessions to the princes (the Loudun settlement had cost the state the equivalent of a year's budget in various bequests and gifts), they subsequently promoted a diametrically opposed policy that sought to reinforce royal authority. As a consequence the Prince de Condé was imprisoned on 1 September 1616, and, after the dismissal of Henri IV's old ministers, a young and 'strong' ministry was constituted with Barbin as finance minister, Mangot as keeper of the seals and Richelieu (pls 26 and 47–57) as foreign minister. These changes reflect Concini's political leanings and convictions. As the son and nephew of the absolutist ministers of the Grand Dukes of Tuscany, he readily adopted an authoritarian attitude. Did his conduct in 1616 reveal a Machiavellian cunning? Did he first press for peace the better to impose his own authoritarian approach afterwards? It seems more probable that he simply let himself be swept along by the course of events. But to his contemporaries and to the princes, his sudden change appeared as a failure to keep his word.

The means Concini used to secure his influence and facilitate his access to power, expanded in similar fashion. Proximity to the royal person was essential here and was made possible by the possession of court offices. Initially, the favourite was Leonora Galigaï. As the queen's lady-in-waiting since 1601, she held a position which brought her into direct daily contact with her mistress. Concini himself only became the queen's first *maître d'hôtel* in 1605. He then became her first equerry in 1608 and was finally the king's first chamberlain from 1610 to 1617. Despite its importance, this last office failed to bring Concini open access to the favour of the king, a very different situation from that of Olivares in Spain, where the latter's role as *sumiller de corps* certainly brought royal favour. Meanwhile, proximity was also secured through accommodation at the Louvre: first a chamber adjoining the queen's for Leonora, then in 1612 a house directly adjacent to the Louvre beside the Seine. From 1615, the Concinis lived exclusively in this new house, abandoning their sumptuous residence on the rue de Tournon. This relocation to the Louvre coincided exactly with the extension of Concini's political power.

Keeping close to the royal person enabled Concini to influence government appointments. In the early stages of the regency, the Concinis gave special attention to the posts of *intendants* of finance, and managed to secure the appointments of two of their most loyal clients, the physician Noël Duret in 1610 and the lawyer Louis Dollé in 1612. All the evidence indicates that in the first years of the regency the Concinis were far keener to further their personal fortune than to deal in high politics: appointed counsellor of state with a seat on the Council of finances late in 1610, and with his own placemen in the central administration of finances, Concini was now well positioned to protect his own financial interests.

With the formation of a new ministry in November 1616 Concini's standing changed radically. No one doubted that Barbin, Mangot and Richelieu were Concini's creatures. As the nuncio Bentivoglio wrote: 'The marshal also spoke to me of these three new ministers as his own men, and showed great pleasure at my praise of Mangot and Luçon, whom I had already visited, and told me that I was to esteem Barbin still more, since he could be the master of the other two in important matters.'[6] They were Concini's creatures since they owed him their rise, and their relatively modest social status meant that they were nothing without him. Here a striking parallel may be observed between Concini's choices and those made by Richelieu when he became principal minister and ruled with the help of his own creatures. Concini directed the affairs of the realm through the intermediary of these ministers, situating himself outside the institutional framework the better to control the wheels of state.[7]

Ministers received their instructions by letter, or through visits to and from the marshal. To take a specific example, after several weeks of fruitless negotiations over the Grisons the Venetian ambassadors made a direct approach to the maréchal d'Ancre. The very next day, they met with an answer from the secretary of state, Richelieu, confirming that he had ironed out all the difficulties, as he told them: 'yesterday the maréchal d'Ancre came to see me, spoke warmly of your mission and instructed me to do everything possible to help you'.[8] As for Mangot, the keeper of the seals, he simply asked Concini to provide ready-made copies of the documents he was due to send out, a practice his colleagues came to imitate.[9] Unquestionably, Concini's power had evolved considerably since the start of the regency.

However this power did not develop consistently. There were phases of semi-disgrace because of Concini's involvement in court intrigues and because of his tactical alliances with various princes and factions.[10] This shows that, for several years, he was just one among many on the political scene. Unlike his successor de Luynes (pl. 17), he was far from having a clear ascendency over the other *grands* from an early stage. This ambiguous, fragile position corresponded to a well-established pattern where the favourite had to take account of princes, other favourites and the members of the incumbent government. This situation, seen under Charles IX and Henri III, was still applicable to Concini's position at court where, until November 1616, he sometimes had to rely on the princes of the blood and sometimes on the Guises. Thus in Concini's time rival aristocratic clans continued to use the favourite in their political games, whereas later the favourite's political pre-eminence would be more clearly established, placing him above such issues.

A further archaic feature of Concini's power is the importance given to non-governmental responsibilities. He was involved in provincial administration, in Picardy in 1611 and Normandy in 1616, and in the army as a marshal (from 1613), although fondly cherishing the hope of rising to the rank of constable, a promotion which de Luynes was to secure after him.

But Concini's power also featured new aspects that had a promising future ahead of them. First, the favourite became a standard conduit for the distribution of royal graces and favours. Provided the princes remained included in these decisions, and were able to combine their influence with Concini's, they tolerated the favourite's role. Guise was well-disposed towards the Florentine because he himself was also favoured by the queen regent as one of her main advisers and supporters. Ultimately, the relationship between the two men became embittered, once Concini's position became too strong and threatened to end Guise's effective participation in government affairs, undermining his network of patronage. What the other grandees found intolerable was the position of an unavoidable intermediary which Concini had attained by the start of 1617. This was not the first time that a monopoly of royal favour was held to be intolerable. In 1588, for example, – under pressure from public opinion and from the nobility – Henri III was forced to get rid of d'Epernon, who had become the king's chief *mignon* after the death of the duc de Joyeuse in 1587.

Furthermore, Concini's persistent attachment to the discourse of authority did nothing to improve his relations with the other grandees. His aim in political affairs was for 'power and authority always to rest with the king'.[11] He was at one with his ministers, Mangot and particularly Richelieu, who was already intimating that some heads should roll like that of Lesdiguières in Dauphiné, who took his instructions from the Council too lightly.[12] The authoritarianism with which government was carried out aroused shock and condemnation, sentiments which found an echo in the despatches of the Venetian and Florentine diplomats. Such a style of government was said to be inconsistent with the French tradition, a pertinent criticism, and, in fact, a thinly disguised accusation of failure to respect the unwritten constitution of the realm. As the secretary of the Tuscan ambassador wrote, 'The French have come to believe that the queen mother will gradually adopt the Spanish style of government in this kingdom.'[13]

This attack was founded on the regular presence of the Spanish ambassador, the Duke of Monteleón, in the meetings of the Council. Spain had become France's main foreign support since traditional allies (England, the Protestant princes) had shied away, threatening to support the princes. But this attack also showed that Castile and its bureaucratic government were held to represent the antithesis of the limited form of monarchy considered appropriate for France. The issue at stake now appears clearly. Concini stood accused of encouraging the forging of a modern state in the 'Spanish style', sacrificing in the process 'the ancient customs of the kingdom' which catered for the claims of the princes and tolerated their displays of independence. As an authoritarian favourite, Concini was determined to impose this new style, by force if necessary.

To illustrate these views we must retrace our steps for a moment. From the moment he became lieutenant general in Picardy (1611), Concini embarked upon a strategy of fortifying the areas assigned to him: in Amiens the fortress posed a direct threat to the town and its inhabitants. This method of imposing royal authority influenced other initiatives after Concini's death – in Montpellier (1622), Marseille (the fortress of Saint-Nicolas in 1660) and in Bordeaux (the castle of Trompette in 1675). In the building of these fortresses, Concini called upon the finest specialists of his time, the Italian engineers who had served the Spaniards in Flanders. Pompeo Frangipani, Apollon Dougnano and Giuseppe Gamurrini soon made their appearance at court, all being employed by the marshal between 1615 and 1617. Furthermore, as a marshal of France, Concini owned his own regiment. After Condé's arrest, he strengthened his forces by recruiting both from abroad (from Liège) and from within France, which led to the creation of the Normandy regiment. His aim was to establish a permanent royal army worthy of the name, constantly at arms and ready to operate at the first sign of trouble.[14] Diplomats were much impressed by this new method and disturbed by its effectiveness. As one Tuscan diplomat noted, troubles used to persist because the king's troops were never ready in time, but now all that had changed.[15] Again, the lesson did not go unheeded, as Richelieu's reminder to Louis XIII in 1624 demonstrated:

> to control the *grands* under that royal authority which is the mainstay of the State, it is necessary . . . to increase the fund for the upkeep of the militia in order to keep the kingdom armed with adequate forces . . . it being impossible that his

Majesty . . . be obeyed . . . without maintaining a powerful force which will hold everyone to his duty out of fear of swift punishment.[16]

Whether in 1617 or in 1624, the discourse is identical: force is fundamental to the triumph of the absolutist state.[17]

Should we be surprised by Concini's final downfall? The major weakness of his power was that he was the favourite of the queen mother rather than the king – obviously an essential point, though not, in itself, enough to account for his fall. Since contemporaries kept comparing the situation with Spain, we shall do the same. Olivares' accession to power in 1622 was justified by the defence of a cause (the reform of the state and *limpieza de manos*) and it relied on the support of an aristocratic clan.[18] Concini's position lacked both these dimensions. In 1617, the intent of the Concini ministry was to implement the triumph of royal authority, but public opinion only saw self-interest in the marshal's actions. As for reform of the state, there was no reference to this, an omission which allowed de Luynes and his team to exploit this theme the better to distinguish themselves from the previous government.

As a foreigner newly arrived in the kingdom, did Concini succeed in establishing a solid network of aristocratic patronage around which to base his power? Contrary to the evidence found in pamphlets written largely after his death, Concini was far from being an isolated, universally hated figure among the nobility. In Picardy, for instance, seat of the marquisate of Ancre, he headed a prosperous clientele, hence his determination to retain his post as lieutenant general of the province.[19] Nor was he isolated in Normandy, thanks to his relationship with the uncle of the duc de Montmorency, the marquis de Portes, whose sister, the abbesse de Caen, used her influence in the province to Concini's advantage.[20]

Yet, though Concini was far from lacking aristocratic support, it was still quite restricted. There are several reasons for this. First, because of his use of bribes. There was nothing unusual in this practice and some of the greatest fortunes of the *ancien régime* were built on bribes. But in Concini's case it was seen to be scandalous in that it benefited foreigners. Strong xenophobia marked the early seventeenth century, and the elite, still far from possessing a cosmopolitan outlook, was no exception. Furthermore, it was unclear what special services could justify such enrichment by royal favour. Most of all, while the Concinis elevated bribery to an art form, they practised it so widely that they ended up alienating a great many of their victims, whether courtiers, members of sovereign courts, bishops or even close friends such as Barbin. Because the patronage of the Concinis came only at an extortionate price, the relations they developed among the nobility and other leading groups lacked that vital emotional dimension which converts a dependent relationship into genuine patronage. On top of this, some of those who chose to assist the Florentine favourites spent years waiting in vain for their reward.[21] Thus we find Concini surrounded by all too many ill-rewarded servants, too many embittered financiers and too many nobles alarmed at the venality of a system of protection carried on at their expense. All these factors ruled out genuine loyalty in the service of the Florentine and stood in the way of the formation of a powerful network. The only remedy to the situation was for the Concinis to weld themselves to an existing aristocratic clan by marrying Marie Concini into a great family of the realm. Her death in January 1617 had dramatic consequences for the favourite.

Finally, the decision to remove Concini must be placed in the context of the crisis ignited in January 1617 by the start of a fresh civil war. As secretary of state Richelieu explained, in two pamphlets, that what was at stake was the triumph or defeat of royal authority.[22]

Concini's unpopularity was general. All witnesses agree. This began to rebound on Marie de Médicis and threatened ultimately to affect the monarchy. The danger was such that, in February 1617, Louis XIII himself did not dare to leave the Louvre to visit the Saint-Germain fair.[23] The rebellious princes resorted to the old ploy of keeping their options open, claiming that the king was ill-advised whilst thinking otherwise. At this point the royal government found itself in the exceptional position of being unanimously opposed. As the nuncio said of the ministers, 'these few men form a party opposed by another party, the whole kingdom'.[24]

The great weight of opinion and the king's well-known antipathy towards the marshal reassured the princes that their actions were legitimate, even if Concini's ministers were acting in the name of the king. Thanks to the military preparations to which we have referred, the princes' revolt had all but been put down by April. But this must not lead us to neglect its importance. In February 1617 France was on the point of lurching into rebellion, as the majority of governors and lieutenant generals declared themselves hostile to the ministers. In the spring of 1617, even if victory was a few rounds of cannon fire away, the major risk was that there would be a deep, lasting breach between the monarchy and the *grands*, and thus between the monarchy and the nobility. All things considered, Louis XIII did not want such a triumph for royal authority.

Initially concerned to exploit his wife's special relationship with the queen, Concini came to exercise a genuine monopoly of royal favour. Politically, the brief experience of the Concini ministry was characterized by the primacy given to force as a means to secure the triumph of royal authority, a policy defended by ministers devoted to their patron, whose creatures they remained. Concentrated into a few months, this constituted the essence of Concini's programme and of the measures developed over the course of the seventeenth century to consolidate the absolute authority of the sovereign power. But in 1617 this was to ask for too much too soon, as the early seventeenth century was still imbued with the ideal of limited monarchy.

Concini's failure as a favourite was palpable: his patronage of the nobility remained incomplete and ultimately ineffective; and, driven by an aristocratic ethos of consumption and ostentation, he inspired almost unanimous disapproval on four counts. First, he disobeyed the recommendation of Justus Lipsius – recalled by Antonio Feros (Chapter 13 below) – to avoid the display of riches gained from the king or by his consent. Second, his expenditure did not seem appropriate – to take up one of the key terms of the seventeenth century stressed by Orest Ranum (Chapter 9 below) – to his social stature or his origins. And third, the wealth which underpinned this expenditure had been built up in a manner that was, if not immoral, at least dubious. Finally, in his addresses to the king, Concini was unable to find the right words or the right tone, and, as Sir John Elliott has pointed out (Chapter 8 below) such things were vital. Quite the reverse, his arrogant and authoritarian behaviour seemed to debase the royal majesty. In short, Concini came to epitomize what a favourite should not be.

Notes

1. J. Gassot, *Sommaire mémorial*, ed. P. Champion (Paris, 1934), pp. 65–7.
2. H. Duccini, *Concini: grandeur et misère du favori de Marie de Médicis* (Paris, 1991).
3. J. Nouaillac, *Villeroy, secrétaire d'Etat et ministre de Charles IX, Henri III et Henri IV, 1543–1610* (Paris, 1908); F. Hayem, *Le Maréchal d'Ancre et Léonora Galigaï* (Paris, 1910); B. Zeller, *La Minorité de Louis XIII: Marie de Médicis et Villeroy* (Paris, 1897); W. Monter's appraisal of Concini in the *Dizionario biografico degli Italiani* (Rome, 1960), xxvii, pp. 725–30, takes the same stance.
4. Deposition of Lizza in Hayem, *Le Maréchal d'Ancre*, p. 310.
5. H. Duccini, *Une 'campagne de presse' sous Louis XIII: l'affaire Concini (1614–1617)*, *Histoire sociale, sensibilités collectives et mentalités*, *Mélanges offerts à Robert Mandrou* (Paris, 1985), pp. 292–301.
6. G. Bentivoglio, *Lettere*, ed. Stefani, 4 vols (Florence, 1863–7), i, p. 32, letter of 17 January 1617.
7. 'He manipulates his ministers as he pleases. Since he appointed them they are entirely under his control': Paris, Bibliothèque Nationale (hereafter BN), Ms. ital. 1770, fol. 237, 13 January 1617.
8. BN Ms. ital. 1770, fol. 240, 13 January 1617.
9. Florence, Archivio di Stato (hereafter ASF), Carte strozziane I 55, fol. 512.
10. Good examples of the changing nature of favour can be found in the works already cited by Hayem and Nouaillac, and in P. Chevallier's *Louis XIII* (Paris, 1979).
11. Quoted by F. Pouy, *Concini, maréchal d'Ancre, son gouvernement en Picardie, 1611–1617* (Amiens, 1885), p. 136.
12. BN Ms. ital. 1770, fol. 196, 20 December 1616.
13. ASF, Carte strozziane I 55, fol. 522.
14. BN Ms. ital. 1770, fol. 39.
15. ASF, Mediceo 6008, fols 22–3.
16. Memoir of 1624, 'A remedy to the most pressing disorders', in *Les Papiers de Richelieu*, ed. P. Grillon, 6 vols to date (Paris, 1975–), i, p. 141.
17. Initiatives such as the creation of a council of war and the proliferation of police measures in Paris had the same purpose.
18. J. H. Elliott, *The Count-Duke of Olivares: The Statesman in an Age of Decline* (New Haven and London, 1986).
19. Deposition of Montaubert in Hayem, *Le Maréchal d'Ancre*, p. 264.
20. In 1616, Portes was able to raise 'twelve companies of over twelve hundred men . . . through his sister the abbess of Caen, who employed several wealthy and eminent persons to take charge of the companies': Fontenay-Mareuil, *Mémoires*, ed. Michaud and Poujoulat, *Nouvelle Collection de mémoires pour servir à l'histoire de France*, 2nd series (Paris, 1837), v, p. 90.
21. In addition Concini's reluctance to support the Italians in France (such as the financier Philippe Gondi), alienated the strong Italian networks in the kingdom.
22. *Réponse au manifeste publié par les perturbateurs de l'État* (Paris, 1617), and *Déclaration du roi sur le nouveau sujet des nouveaux remuements de son royaume* (Paris, 1617).
23. ASF, Carte strozziane I 55, fols 571^{v}.
24. Bentivoglio, *Lettere*, i, p. 44, 27 January 1617.

Part Two
Favourites in Office

6

Can a Bureaucrat Be a Favourite?
Robert Cecil and the Strategies of Power

PAULINE CROFT

The English language creates the problem, for it would be absurd to argue that Robert Cecil (pl. 18) was a favourite in the same sense as Piers Gaveston or Robert Dudley or George Villiers. Yet he might more persuasively be regarded during the years of his pre-eminence as a *valido*, the English equivalent of Eboli or Lerma or Olivares in Spain, or a minister–favourite like Richelieu in France. Favour in such cases could be defined first by the holding of great power, more power (though not necessarily supreme power) than that of any other minister serving the monarch. Secondly, favour demanded a bond of friendship, with easy access and a degree of personal familiarity, between king and minister. Both these criteria also imply a position of considerable trust, in which the sustained support of the monarch could be relied on by the minister. How does Robert Cecil fit this formula?

There can be no doubt that Cecil enjoyed great favour, since he had an extraordinarily successful career, at the highest level of power politics, under two very different monarchs, Elizabeth I (pl. 5) and James VI and I (pl. 19). However, he rose from the top, for his early success was built on the achievements of his father Lord Burghley (pls 8 and 21), who trained the boy up with relentless determination and pushed him forward in his own declining years. The correspondence between father and son shows just how intensive and relentless that bureaucratic upbringing was; 'son Robert' was subjected to endless pressurizing and hectoring, with orders for the prompt execution of secretarial business and an insistence on immediate replies that would keep his absent father in touch with every development at court. 'I looke before I slepe to heare from you, how far her Majesty do allow of my simple opinion for the Irland causes,' wrote Burghley from his great house at Theobalds in December 1593.[1] However, Burghley's efforts at promotion would have been to no avail if Cecil had not possessed the ability to benefit from them. The decision to mould his younger son for a brilliant career rather than his elder son Thomas was based on a shrewd assessment of their relative capabilities. Thomas was to become an outspoken member of the Elizabethan House of Commons and subsequently a competent lord president of the Council of the North, but no amount of paternal effort would have got him much further.[2]

Robert Cecil was only twenty-eight, remarkably young, when he joined the Privy Council in August 1591. During Burghley's increasingly frequent periods of weariness and ill-health, Cecil handled the innumerable letters and suits connected with foreign policy. After much manoeuvring, in 1596 he obtained the principal secretaryship of state for which he had already served an arduous apprenticeship.[3] Burghley's strategy was vindicated. The father had created the opportunity but the son had demonstrated his capacity and his value to the queen by his willingness to undertake a heavy workload. In 1597 Cecil consolidated his position by obtaining the prestigious and lucrative chancellorship of the Duchy of Lancaster. Then came Burghley's death in August 1598. His enemies hoped that, without paternal support, Cecil's career would fade, but in May 1599 he was sworn master of the Court of Wards. The court controlled a vast range of patronage both in London and in the counties, as well as considerable potential power over the major landed families of England. By appointing Cecil, Elizabeth decisively signalled that she was convinced of his worth and ability. However, the Wards was not a sinecure but an onerous task adding to the endless paperwork he already undertook. Three months later, in August 1599, Cecil could not even be spared for a few summer days away.[4]

By the age of thirty-six Cecil had achieved a major career under one sovereign, although the queen's extreme parsimony in her later years limited the financial rewards that might have been expected from his position. He also enjoyed great royal favour, and Elizabeth's public praise of him, in jesting and affectionate terms, made it clear that there was a personal relationship, not least because she had been genuinely devoted for forty years to his father. Elizabeth called Cecil her elf and her sprite, but more cruelly from his earliest days in her service she also used what Cecil described as 'her sporting name of pygmy'. He found her allusion to his deformity distressing and made a discreet protest, although similar sneers were to pursue him throughout his life and beyond the grave.[5]

Whatever Elizabeth called him, Cecil was perfectly willing to deploy courtly skills, not merely bureaucratic grind, in the pursuit of advancement. Unlike Burghley, he entered into the lover-like style that the ageing queen required. Describing Elizabeth as God's 'celestiall Creature, who pleasethe out of Angellyke grace, to pardone and allowe my carefull and zealous desires', he told her in 1592, 'I can please none because I thirst only to please one.'[6] In the summer of 1602 Elizabeth skittishly seized from the young Lady Derby, Cecil's niece, a jewelled miniature probably by Hilliard. Finding it to be of her principal secretary, she pinned it at first to her shoe and later to her elbow-sleeve. Commemorating the incident, Cecil wrote a poem to Elizabeth, which he also had set to music. Describing himself as 'a servant of Diana', 'that Angelicke Queen', he declared he was resolved to die at her feet where she had placed the jewel. Perhaps more revealingly, the poem adds, 'She at her elbow wore it, to signify that hee / To serve her at her elbowe, doth ever love to bee.' Even in poetry, the emphasis was on assiduous service as well as courtierly attendance.[7]

However willingly Cecil played this game, he could not win it. The great favourite had been the Earl of Essex, and one observer contrasted the two of them as 'the pygmy' and 'Hercules'.[8] Cecil's short stature and curved spine must have seemed all the more unimpressive when contrasted with the physical glamour of the tall and martial Essex (pl. 10).[9] Lacking the appearance of a court favourite, he had to compensate in other ways, and he chose to continue as the workaholic that Burghley had created. Well aware that Elizabeth was using him as a counterbalance to ensure that Essex did not dominate her court or council, Cecil attempted to avoid conflict wherever possible. It was only after the first trial of Essex in June 1600 that he moved into open opposition. The final drama, Essex's rising in London in February 1601 and his execution two weeks later after a second trial, demonstrated the vulnerability and precariousness of a favourite's position once royal affection had cooled. In both his flamboyance and his desperation, Essex was a world away from Robert Cecil. The trauma of these events must have reinforced the latter's conviction that his safest place was in the grey world of administration. In his capacity to handle immense amounts of paperwork lay his best hope of indispensability. 'God knoweth I labour like a Pack horse, and know that if success be nought it wilbe scorn to me,' he wrote to his friend Sir George Carew in Ireland, seven months after Essex's execution.[10] Similarly Sir Henry Wotton, reflecting years later on court favourites, concluded that Cecil had 'no other advantage as the earl of Essex and others had in person, to justify him in an ordinary estimation, but by eminent services'.[11]

In May 1601 Cecil joined the inner circle of those corresponding secretly with James VI of Scotland. After the death of Essex, his former confidant, the king needed to reconcile himself to Cecil, who was already worrying over the problems created by the queen's obduracy in not naming an heir. Yet, even if a smooth succession were accomplished, there was no security of position into the next reign. Cecil enjoyed power and favour largely by virtue of the principal secretaryship. In the order established by the Act of Precedence of 1539, the principal secretaryship had been one of the great offices of state, but it was demoted after Thomas Cromwell's fall in 1540. Nevertheless, under Elizabeth it revived to become one of the three or four most powerful positions in the Privy Council.[12] A good secretary required the combined skills of a minister, a senior civil servant and a courtier; he was probably the privy councillor who saw the queen most regularly and success depended on the personal rapport between sovereign and servant.

Cecil's own treatise on the secretaryship strikingly compares the secret counsels between the prince and the secretary to 'the mutual affections of two lovers, undiscovered to their friends'. When those matters are subsequently revealed in council discussion, 'it is like the conference of parents, and solemnisation of marriage'. If this close relationship soured, the position would become untenable, or as Cecil put it, 'A suspicion of a Secretary is both a trial and condemnation, and a judgment.' Even more sombre is his comment, 'the state of a secretary is dreadful if he serve not a constant prince'. Although the tract was probably composed for the incoming King James, it did not exaggerate the power and precariousness of the position, but rather reflected an Elizabethan consensus. Nicholas Faunt, writing in 1592, also emphasized the secretary's 'special loue and affeccion hee beareth towards his Master' and 'his masters reciprocall loue borne vnto him'. Such intimacy, as established with Elizabeth in so idiosyncratic an office, might not transfer to the new regime. As the intelligencer Thomas Phelippes shrewdly commented as early as August 1591, 'the Secretary's place . . . is dangerous in the declination of a reign and in a doubtful succession'. James was not accustomed to anything similar in Scotland.[13]

Nor could Cecil rely on any general support. There are plenty of hints in the secret correspondence that those most deeply involved in it, although committed to a Stuart succession, did not trust one another. Cecil knew perfectly well what poisonous rumours circulated about him – that he plotted to become king by marrying Arbella Stuart, or that he favoured the Infanta-Archduchess Isabella, as Essex had alleged – and he must have feared that James' trust was already being corroded, despite the numerous compliments in the king's letters from Scotland. Rumours that he had made earlier attempts to thwart James' accession by arranging a marriage between Arabella and the son of the Prince of Parma were still circulating in May 1603, and there was a widespread expectation that James would take his revenge for the execution of his mother, Mary Queen of Scots, by demoting Burghley's son.[14]

On a personal as well as a political level, Cecil needed to look to his future. Although Burghley had made substantial provision for him, in 1598 the bulk of the family lands and the title inevitably went to Thomas. After 1601, as the succession pressed ever more on his mind, Cecil threw himself into a fury of land speculation, becoming one of the half-dozen largest purchasers of crown estates then flooding on to the market to fund the escalating costs of the Irish campaign. Besides spending around £30,000 in 1601–2, Cecil borrowed heavily from London aldermen at 10 per cent to snap up prime crown properties. In addition, by October 1602 he was writing to Sir George Carew to invite him to visit the room especially arranged for him in what he proudly described as 'my new house (called Cecil House)', next to the Savoy on the Thames river-front.[15] This central position give him a high political profile in the capital and asserted his place and status among the aristocratic owners of great town houses.[16] If all went well under James, that place and status would continue, and the London house would be his main residence.

But if it did not go well? Cecil's other aim seems to have been to build up a great country estate to which he could retire if his political career ended. If he should fall from favour after the queen's death, he could live a secluded life as a very substantial landowner, enjoying the country activities of hawking and gardening which he loved but could rarely pursue. Even worse, if there should be some political disaster, if he were imprisoned or even perhaps executed as the crown passed to another claimant, then his gains from office, embodied in a landed estate, stood a much better chance of passing to his two children than would a hoard of cash or jewels. All the landed acquisitions were normally held by agents and servants on Cecil's behalf. This was a common legal stratagem, but, as Lawrence Stone points out, land conveyed to trustees for uses was fairly immune from confiscation and would offer a degree of protection for his family. On the proclamation of Queen Jane Grey in 1553, William Cecil had at once made conveyance away of his lands, part of his goods, his leases and even his raiment. Cecil must often have heard his father speak of that earlier succession crisis.[17] Awareness of the malleability of fortune at the end of an era is very clear in this orgy of land accumulation.

Despite these fears, in March 1603 the succession went with amazing smoothness, largely thanks to the enormous amount of work and planning that Cecil had devoted to it. Writing in April to Sir Thomas Parry, the ambassador in Paris, he still could scarcely believe it. 'We are now so strangely and unexpectedly made the spectacle of happiness and felicity, in enjoying so quietly and peaceably of such a prince,' he exclaimed, well aware that Parry would spread the word about England's domestic stability. Others felt the same way; Lord Kinloss thought it had been a divine miracle.[18] James' debt of gratitude was great, and on his journey south from Edinburgh he made it known that he intended to keep Cecil on as principal secretary. 'He said', reported Cecil's brother from York, 'he heard you were but a little man, but he would shortly load your shoulders with business.'[19]

Yet James also made it clear that it was to a group of English councillors, not to Cecil alone, that he felt a deep obligation, praising 'the wisdom, providence and policy of our dearest friends' and promising 'condign renumeration'.[20] The king was intent on widening the circle of Englishmen with access to power. Lord Henry Howard was promoted to the Privy Council and the earldom of Northampton, while Lord Thomas Howard became a privy councillor, lord chamberlain and Earl of Suffolk. Lord Mountjoy, conquerer of Tyrone in Ireland, became Earl of Devonshire. Southampton was immediately released from the Tower, where he had been imprisoned since Essex's revolt; his earldom was restored in July 1603, when he also received the Garter. The Earl of Northumberland, usually regarded as the spokesman for loyal crypto-papists and out of favour with Elizabeth, also became a privy councillor.

In May 1603, Cecil received his reward. He was created Baron Cecil of Essendon, and he also kept the mastership of the Wards, although only after a period of indecision in which the king apparently considered granting it elsewhere.[21] The promotions showered on others, however, indicated that James valued ancient nobility rather more than 'mere penclerks', as the Cecils' enemies had long since called them. Cecil had to wait until 1605 for the earldom of Salisbury, and a further year for the Garter. Although he could reflect that his father had never achieved an earldom and had waited fourteen years for Elizabeth to make him a Knight of St George, the rewards bestowed on him in the first year of James' reign were not outstandingly generous.

From 1603 onward, Cecil had to learn a new routine if he was to maintain his grip on power. There was a real possibility that James might quickly tire of him, especially as he had brought his own Scottish advisers with him.[22] He must accommodate to a monarch with a very different style, and the flexibility with which he accomplished this change of routine demonstrated an aspect of his talents which helps explain his success in steadily increasing his control over Jacobean political business. Already, before the accession, James' praise of Cecil had been couched in terms of his efforts, 'those daily so honorable, judicious and painful labours for the furtherance of my greatest hopes'. Once again the way ahead was clear; as the king had jested at York, Cecil's shoulders would have to prove worthy of a weight of business.[23]

English historians no longer despise James I. As early as 1584, foreign observers had condemned him for laziness and for too much time spent hunting; but the king was also prepared to commit considerable effort, particularly to diplomacy and religious policy.[24] Cecil's diplomatic labours, especially the extensive negotiations surrounding the peace with Spain in 1604, brought him into close contact with James and they forged a strong and enduring working relationship. The king showed his appreciation of his principal secretary's efforts. In August 1606, when Cecil kept to his town house for a day in a 'distemper' after a bitter dispute with the Spanish ambassador over the suspects in the Gunpowder Plot, James paid him a personal visit. He told Cecil to take better care of his well-being, 'for if he should once fail there were no more safe hunting for the King of England'. This signal mark of favour embittered Northampton, who had been near death's door for a week without any royal visitors.[25] The alliance continued, for it was the consensus of ambassadorial opinion right through to Cecil's death in 1612 that the duo of the king and the principal secretary shaped foreign policy between them, with little input from other councillors. As late as November 1611, with Cecil already seriously ill, when the ambassador of Savoy arrived to discuss the possibility of a match for Prince Henry, he immediately had an hour's private conference with the king, and another hour with Cecil.[26]

Another factor which accentuated Cecil's position was James' rapidly increasing distaste for London. He was often absent, on his endless sorties to Theobalds, to Farnham, to Bagshot, and above all to his beloved Royston. When the Privy Council assembled at Whitehall the void was very apparent, since the council chamber faced the king's bedchamber. As those who themselves had lodgings at court were expected to be regular attenders at the Privy Council, the message was reinforced; they were there but the king was not.[27]

The situation emerges with particular clarity in the correspondence of the Venetian ambassador. In October 1607, just back from a lengthy summer progress, James stayed only a few hours in London before heading for Royston.

He came to London again on 15 November, intending to leave the next day, but was detained by an attack of colic; he was at once surrounded by the whole diplomatic corps all insisting on audience. The king returned to Royston to write his book on the oath of allegiance, attacking Father Persons; although expected back in London he spent most of Christmas at Theobalds. On 30 December he came to the city for a day, then rode off to Hampton Court. On one occasion the desperate ambassador tried to talk to him while the royal foot was already in the stirrup. James himself compared his visits to London to a flash of lightning.[28] Envoys of all states frequently had great difficulty in speaking to the king, and his absences caused widespread annoyance. Cecil protested about these peripatetic habits and deplored the inconvenience that they caused for himself and others.[29]

Despite these appearances, James kept a firm control on the general direction of foreign policy; but ambassadors trying to deal with specific items of business struggled vainly to attract the royal attention. Not surprisingly they turned with relief to a highly regarded, apparently omnicompetent secretary of state. The king's chosen style of life thus served to enhance Cecil's importance. Ambassadors came to rely on him, not only as their go-between with the distant king, but often also as the source of decisions. James did nothing to counteract this impression, going so far as to say to the Venetian ambassador in 1605, 'Speak to my secretary; he is better informed than I am, for I only know what is told me.'[30] His comment reveals the degree of delegation of conspicuous control over a central area of royal decision-making, and goes a long way to supporting the contention that Cecil enjoyed a uniquely favoured position. The same Venetian ambassador, commenting on Cecil's elevation to the Order of the Garter in May 1606, provided a carefully nuanced assessment. 'No-one seeks but to win his favour. It is thought that his power will last, for it is based not so much on the grace of His Majesty, as on an excellent prudence and ability which secures for him the universal opinion that he is worthy of his great authority and good fortune.'[31] The uncertainties over Cecil's position that had been apparent in 1603 had vanished by 1606.

The most striking proof of Cecil's success under James was to come in 1608. After the death of Lord Treasurer Dorset, Cecil took over the urgent task of attempting to reform the royal finances, while retaining the principal secretaryship and the Wards. Far from dwindling into a subordinate role after James' accession, Cecil had seen off the challenge from the Scots and other English competitors to emerge with an unprecedented trio of great offices. The new appointment occasioned some comment, since the secretaryship and the treasurership were each regarded as labours demanding a man's whole attention. James let it be known that he held Cecil's abilities sufficient to enable him to fill both posts.[32] Arguably after 1606, certainly after 1608, Cecil might be regarded as the equivalent of Lerma or Richelieu, a great minister who by virtue of enjoying his sovereign's confidence had acquired control over the central bureaucracy of the state.

Although James' inability to live within his means could not be remedied, as lord treasurer Cecil proved far more effective than his predecessor in controlling disbursements. The 'Book of Bounty' which Cecil and Sir Julius Caesar drafted in 1608 established a weekly hearing for suitors, and in 1610 Cecil made further proposals for tightening up procedure. On occasion, pensions granted directly by the king were stayed by Cecil at the receipt. Most importantly, he established a system of prioritizing payments, and the letters which flooded in from merchants and contractors seeking long-delayed settlements of royal bills acknowledged his powers. As late as summer 1611, when he was already seriously ill, he continued his detailed supervision of the regular expenditures. Faced with an account of monthly court expenses, he appended a trenchant memo, 'Pay ye navy £500.' Caesar, writing in August with a lengthy list of matters for Cecil's attention, sent him 'a note of those payments now most pressing (of which it may please your lordship to express which shalbe first paid, of the next moneys which we shall receive)'. Cecil also retained firm control over the Court of Wards. In spring 1612 he journeyed to Bath in a last unavailing effort to regain his health, but left very precise instructions regarding the business which the court might conduct in his absence.[33]

The immense administrative and financial power wielded by Cecil unequivocally demonstrated James' exceptional trust in him. The deployment of a distinctive style of language, from monarch to minister and vice versa, was a more unusual manifestation of favour. Where the courtship style had been required by Elizabeth, a new mode was essential in addressing a male monarch. Under James the vocabulary changed but the note of intimacy continued. The pre-eminent example is the appellation 'little beagle', sometimes 'my little cankered beagle', applied to Cecil by a hunting-crazy king. It was not the only label; James loved extravagant language and also called Cecil 'my little fool' as well as 'Tom Derry' (the dwarf), 'parrotmonger' and 'monkeymonger'. As with Elizabeth's 'pygmy', these epithets privately enraged Cecil. It cannot be denied that they embody a degree of both cruelty and condescension, as well as intimacy.[34] However, they were not inaccurate, since Cecil avidly collected animal rarities, sending a servant to the East Indies for them, and also frequently gave them to the royal family as presents.[35] James employed similarly jocular language to the three or four members of the inner circle of the Privy Council. He wrote to Cecil, Northampton and Suffolk as 'a trinity of knaves'; he twitted Suffolk about his overweight and Northampton, 'your fellow hound', about his 'black' countenance. The language indicates a personal relationship, embodied in rough humour, between the king and a handful of senior councillors who were seen as predominantly in his favour. Others just as senior, such as Ellesmere and Dorset, were addressed with formality by James. Cecil felt bound to respond. His early letters to the king attempt a bucolic style very different from the businesslike, cool tone of his other correspondence. In March 1604, he wrote 'from Theobalds this fryday where a pack of Brettons have presumed to drink a helth to ye king of Brittany'.[36] Cecil was willing to use language with chameleon-like adaptability as a means of ensuring not merely continued administrative power but a place in the royal inner circle.

Another aspect of adaptation can be seen in Cecil's conspicuous consumption, in sharp contrast with the threadbare later years of Elizabeth. King James and Queen Anne were almost obsessive purchasers of jewels, and Cecil in 1603 bought himself an enormous diamond ring weighing 53 carats, to keep up appearances at court. He bought more diamonds and a gold chain to the value of £1,257 from the royal jeweller Sir John Spilman. Similarly the procession he arranged for himself when he was given the Garter in 1606 was outstandingly elaborate.[37] Most noteworthy was the bountiful hospitality he lavished on the royal family. Burghley had left Robert Cecil his great house at Theobalds, where he had staged immensely costly entertainments for Elizabeth. Theobalds was regarded by contemporaries such as the poet Sir John Harington, who was moved to quote Ariosto after a visit, as 'paradise'. James paid his first visit in May 1603, staying for four nights on his long progress down to London from Edinburgh.[38] It was not long before the locals were prohibited from passing through the park, where they disturbed the game and hindered the king's sport. At Theobalds in June 1606 Cecil received James and Anne for four days, along with Anne's brother the King of Denmark. He was 'overwhelmed in preparations', but despite his efforts the elegant entertainment in English and Latin devised by Ben Jonson and Inigo Jones degenerated into a Bacchic rout.[39] This social disaster did not stop the flood of Cecilian hospitality. When James insisted on exchanging the semi-derelict royal manor of Hatfield for Theobalds, Cecil responded by mounting a grand entertainment. The king, the queen, the Prince of Wales and the visiting Duke of Lorraine were given dinner in the gallery before a masque by Ben Jonson. Banquets, jousts and hunting parties followed, to celebrate the exchange and demonstrate that Cecil held no animosity at losing the family home that Burghley had left him.[40]

Until the completion of Hatfield House (pl. 20) in 1611, Cecil had no grand country estate where he could entertain the royal family. To compensate for what might have been a major disadvantage, he devised receptions for them in London. On assuming the lord treasurership, he invited the royal family and the court to a sumptuous banquet. Shortly afterwards he again entertained the king, who viewed the Garter processions of the earls of Dunbar and Montgomery from the vantage point of Salisbury House.[41] Then, in April 1609, the king, the queen, Prince Henry, Princess Elizabeth and Prince Charles all came to the extravagant and fantastical opening of the new exchange that Cecil had built in the Strand. He had chivvied his servants and the tenants of the shops so that it would be ready in time. In a display of ceremonial giving, suitably appropriate and lavish presents were handed to the royal family as Cecil showed them around. The king himself named the exchange 'Britain's Burse'.[42]

Meanwhile, at Hatfield House separate sets of apartments were constructed to enable both the king and the queen to visit at the same time, an expensive architectural statement of confidence in future royal favour. In the summer of

1611, as soon as the house was ready, James viewed Hatfield and, while on progress from Salisbury, visited Cecil's much smaller house, Cranborne Manor in Dorset, which was well placed for hunting on Cranborne Chase. These two visits were an important sign of continued royal support in the difficult year after the failure of Cecil's Great Contract in parliament. Considerable efforts were made to prepare the ornamental east garden at Hatfield, with its centre-piece of a great cistern with artificial rocks and a painted statue of Neptune. The elaborate water display was intended as a highlight of the king's visit.[43] Once again the combination of personal attendance and generous hospitality marked out Cecil's efforts to remain in the innermost circle of power. Attention was also devoted to Prince Henry, notably in the magnificent ceremony devised by Cecil to mark his parliamentary installation in 1610 as Prince of Wales. Cecil signalled that he was a supporter of the Stuart dynasty, not simply of the king. Investing time and effort that might assure the favour of the next monarch reflected his hard-won experience of making the successful but nerve-wracking earlier transition from Elizabeth to James.[44]

There is no difficulty in demonstrating that Cecil was a great minister. His determined efforts to remain within royal favour are also evident. Does all this entitle him to be regarded as a minister–favourite in the French or Spanish mould? In many ways the similarities are striking. Cecil profited from favour on a grand scale. In his last two years, 1610 to 1612, he was receiving at least £25,000 per year, when the greatest landed income in the country was more of the order of £8,000 per year.[45] Like Richelieu, he placed his family in the highest ranks of the aristocracy. Like Lerma or Olivares, after 1608 there could be no doubt of his pre-eminence in the king's councils. Yet reservations remain.

First, although Cecil held great power, it is clear that the Privy Council continued as an active and functioning body in the early years of James' reign. There was an inner circle of five or six men, including Cecil, and he adapted not only to working with the king himself, but also to working with them. Above all he managed an effective relationship with Northampton, whom he had little cause to trust and who revealed after Cecil's death how much he had hated him.[46] Cecil also had to adapt to the Scottish bedchambermen, who remained the king's companions of choice, and to the Earl of Dunbar, to whom James delegated powers in Scotland that were effectively vice-regal. Dunbar and Cecil warily recognized each other as great potentates in their different political spheres and extended elaborate courtesies to one another in their careful management of the king. Dunbar was thought of as a 'Favourite' and shrewd observers perceived his support as one of the central pillars of Cecil's impor-tance.[47] So, although Cecil was the most powerful of James' English council-lors, particularly after 1608, he still found it necessary to negotiate and manoeuvre for the support of others. It may well be that this suited him. By training under Burghley and by his own observation of the meteor-rise and fall of Essex, he tended to distrust solitary eminence. Already in 1603 he reproved

Sir Thomas Parry, ambassador to France, for the assumption that he alone could communicate with the king. 'You abridg both your owne liberty and cast an envy upon me of sole dealing in such things which I am very loath to beare,' he wrote back. In particular, he told Parry not to try to prevent Scotsmen writing direct to James, and made great efforts to reconcile Englishmen and Scots at James' court. These techniques, along with his studied courtesy to members of the older aristocratic families and his refusal to pursue those who defamed him on stage or in libels, were part of a strategy which Bacon called 'abating the edge of envy'.[48]

Secondly, English usage obstinately continued to deploy the word 'favourite' for a different style of relationship. Neither the word nor the concept of the *valido* ever took hold. 'Grandee' appears to have come into English in 1589, while Lord Chancellor Dunfermline wrote to Cecil with pleasure in 1605 on the rebuff of the Earl of Huntly, remarking that it would be a lesson to the great Scots 'ydalgos'. Buckingham, himself labelled a grandee, had his own 'privadoes'. By contrast, the language of *valimiento* never Anglicized itself.[49] Nevertheless, during his ascendancy Cecil proved adept in ensuring that those who were 'favourites' in the English sense did not achieve political influence. Elizabeth's personal favourites had also been men of political substance – Leicester, Hatton, even Essex.[50] Until 1612, James' were not. Contemporaries regarded the twenty-year-old Sir Philip Herbert, later Earl of Montgomery, as 'prime favourite of his majesty'. In Cecil's lifetime, Montgomery (who was married to Cecil's niece, Susan de Vere) did not achieve major office, and there is no evidence that he craved it. As Clarendon remarked, he claimed only to understand dogs and horses very well. Among the Scots, the light-weight Lord Hay was regarded as a particular favourite of James.

The transition began with Sir Robert Carr (pl. 12), who replaced Montgomery; in February 1609 he was described as 'now the specially graced man'. Undoubtedly a sexual favourite, he was elevated by James to the peerage in 1611, and took his seat on the Privy Council in April 1612. Cecil clearly feared the political ambitions of Carr, who was himself under the influence of the duplicitous and cunning Sir Thomas Overbury. Cecil tried both to ingratiate himself with the rising favourite and to summon the support of Prince Henry against him. It seems noteworthy, however, that it was only as Cecil himself fell victim to increasingly severe illness that James moved to promote Carr to political power. In his perceptive discussion of James' favourites in both Scotland and England, Maurice Lee Jr points out that, from the disgrace of the Master of Gray in 1587 to Cecil's death in 1612, 'none of the handsome young men of whom the king was fond – and they were plentiful – had any political influence'. Carr was the precursor of Buckingham and of an entirely different style of governance by James. Sir Roger Wilbraham, writing in 1615 just as Carr's career was beginning to unravel, described him as 'the most potent favourite in my tyme'.[51] Herbert and Hay, Carr and Buckingham were favourites in a sense that Englishmen knew Cecil was not. It was only foreign observers such as the Venetian ambassador, familiar with a different and arguably more subtle concept of royal favour, who applied the term to him.

Thirdly, even if in several respects Cecil can be seen as the equivalent of a *valido*, his time was too short for him to compare with Lerma or Olivares. After 1603 he successfully rebuilt, to even greater heights, a career that might have been under threat; but it was only after 1608, with the lord treasurership, that his position became truly exceptional. Although the old assumption that he fell from favour after 1610 is exaggerated, there can be no doubt that the collapse of the Great Contract was a serious blow to his position. He might well have recovered, if fatal illness had not overtaken him by 1612, but his period of unique pre-eminence lasted only two or at most three years.[52] Cecil's career was a series of struggles to overcome the hurdles placed in his way; he was a very successful swimmer in rough seas rather than a powerful favourite above challenge.

Lastly, despite all his deployment of the skills of the courtier, Cecil's power rested predominantly as it had always done on his bureaucratic abilities, his willingness to be a packhorse. His rewards were immense but so was the effort he devoted to the service of the crown.[53] Significantly, the portraits of him follow the dour and restrained style set by Burghley, and the fictional portrait of father and son together holding the same insignia of office makes the deliberate continuity explicit (pl. 21).[54] Like Burghley, Cecil dressed in rich fabrics, but sombrely. Only the Garter portraits of father and son break out into vivid colour. Clad in black, holding the white staff of office, standing by a table with papers and the secretary's seal, sometimes with a small bell to summon a messenger to take the urgently penned missive, Cecil in his portraits projected an image of arduous bureaucratic labour that was worlds apart from the lavishly costumed display of Essex or Carr or Buckingham, those peacocks of sartorial brilliance. Even in the great Somerset House portrait his position as 'gran secretario del rey' is emphasized by the pewter inkpot, quill and paper in front of him, although in reality he was by far the most frequent speaker in the 1604 negotiations, not merely their recorder.[55]

The unprecedented combination of great positions after 1608 forms the strongest argument for seeing Cecil as a minister–favourite, but it created a crushing workload. In 1612 after Cecil's death his closest associate Sir Walter Cope wrote a defence of his late master, wrestling with the most common criticism of him. 'But what are the greatest imputations that this unthankful time doth lay upon this noble lord? First, that he undertook three great offices, and in a general distraction left them all ill executed.'[56] Cope rebutted the allegation, and the vast archive that Robert Cecil left behind is testimony to the enormous effort that he put into the tasks that faced him. But the charge carries weight. Faced with James' blithe confidence in his omnicompetent abilities, Cecil had little choice but to soldier on. Lacking the effortless charm and glamour of Essex or Carr, or the ancient nobility of the Howards, his bid for favour depended as always on those 'eminent services' that contemporaries like Sir Henry Wotton admired but did not warm to.

For all the bonhomie of the royal letters, Cecil's relationship with James was never entirely easy; it seems to have been at its best in their joint supervision of foreign policy. Both were grown men, highly experienced in the handling of power when they first met at York in April 1603. Cecil was a mere three years older than the king. There could not be that avuncular relationship of guidance and tutelage that Lerma and Olivares, or Richelieu and Mazarin, brought to the young monarchs in their charge. Cecil could never presume on favour and was always ultra-sensitive to any hint of coldness on the king's part, often to James' amusement.[57] So Cecil was a great minister certainly, a minister who enjoyed remarkable royal favour and an astonishing harvest of the fruits of office. But a minister–favourite? To English ears at least, the term will not really fit, although the comparison with the great Spanish *validos* has some merit.

Ironically, however, there was one brief moment when Cecil apparently played the role. In 1628, Wentworth remarked of Buckingham after his assassination that 'it is said at Court there is none now to impute our faults unto'. Faults were certainly imputed to Cecil, as the outpouring of venomous libels in the summer of 1612 testifies. It was also noted that, despite the pleas of the Cecil family and retainers, the king did nothing to defend his late minister and rebuke the libellers. The hatred of Cecil that was apparent immediately after his death echoes the hatred aroused by Leicester and prefigures that which poured out in 1628. If one aspect of the traditional function of the favourite was to serve as political whipping-boy, then for the three months after his death, Cecil came closer than he had done in life to serving James I as a favourite.[58]

Notes

1. Thomas Wright, *Queen Elizabeth and her Times*, 2 vols (London, 1838), i, p. 428. Wright printed only a selection of these letters, of which over a hundred survive, mostly in holograph, in Cambridge University Library, Mss Ee. 3–56, in the State Papers Domestic at the Public Record Office (hereafter PRO) and in the Cecil Mss at Hatfield House.
2. P. W. Hasler, ed., *The History of Parliament: The House of Commons, 1558–1603*, 3 vols (London, 1981). He was relieved of his presidency in obscure circumstances probably related to the accession of James in 1603. Cecil Mss, Hatfield House, 100/49. I am grateful to the Marquess of Salisbury for permission to cite this and other Cecil manuscripts.
3. *Historical Manuscripts Commission: Calendar of the MSS of . . . the Marquis of Salisbury . . . at Hatfield House* (hereafter *HMC Salisbury*), iv, p. 623.
4. *The Sidney Papers: letters and memorials of state . . . collected by Arthur Collins*, 2 vols (London, 1746), ii, pp. 117–19.
5. PRO, State Papers (hereafter SP) 15/30/80. There were worse epithets from his enemies. Antonio Perez referred to Cecil as 'microgibbus' when writing to Essex: Gustav Ungerer, *A Spaniard in Elizabethan England: The Correspondence of Antonio Perez's Exile*, 2 vols (London, 1974), i, p. 336. See also Pauline Croft, 'The Reputation of Robert Cecil', *Transactions of the Royal Historical Society*, 5th series, 1 (1991), pp. 43–69.
6. *HMC Salisbury*, iv, p. 632.
7. Katherine Duncan-Jones, '"Preserved Dainties": Late Elizabethan Poems by Sir Robert Cecil and the Earl of Clanricarde', *Bodleian Library Record*, 14 (1992), pp. 136–44.
8. E. M. Tenison, *Elizabethan England, Being the History of This Country in Relation to All Foreign Princes, from Original MSS.*, 12 vols (Leamington Spa, 1958), xi, p. 392.

9. Cecil's curved spine, although often attributed to an accident in babyhood, was almost certainly hereditary scoliosis. Both his mother Lady Burghley and his daughter Frances (the future Lady Clifford) suffered from it. In his formal portraits it is barely evident, but this was probably painterly tact, since even contemporary admirers such as Sir Robert Naunton described him as a little, crooked person. *Fragmenta Regalia: or, observations on the late queen Elizabeth, her times and favourites* (London, 1824), p. 137. The hump is clearly visible in the sketch of him walking in Elizabeth's funeral procession, British Library (hereafter BL), Additional Ms. 35, 324.

10. *Letters from Sir Robert Cecil to Sir George Carew*, ed. John Maclean (Camden Society, 1884), p. 26.

11. Sir Henry Wotton, *Reliquiae Wottonianae* (London, 1651), p. 7.

12. David Kynaston, *The Secretary of State* (Lavenham, 1978), pp. 30–69; David Starkey, ed., *Rivals in Power: Lives and Letters of the Great Tudor Dynasties* (London, 1990), p. 70. Mindful of the formal ranking, in Elizabeth's funeral procession, Cecil walked between Sir John Fortescue, chancellor of the Exchequer, and Sir Edward Wootton, controller of the household. John Nichols, *The Progresses and Public Processions of Queen Elizabeth*, 3 vols (London, 1823), iii, pp. 620–6.

13. Cecil's treatise, entitled 'On the state and dignity of a secretary's place with the care and perill thereof' (printed in *Somers Tracts*, 2nd edn, 13 vols (London, 1748–52), v, pp. 552–54, from PRO, SP 14/69/62, and BL, Harley 805 and 354). There are no surviving drafts among Cecil's papers which would allow the treatise to be dated, though it may relate to James' reorganization of the Privy Council in May 1603. Charles Hughes, 'Nicholas Faunt's Discourse Touching the Office of Principal Secretary of Estate and etc., 1592', *English Historical Review*, 20 (1905), pp. 499–508; PRO, SP 14/239/159.

14. PRO, SP 14/279/72. For Lord Henry Howard's duplicities, and the treachery of Lady Kildare against Cecil (though married to his brother-in-law Lord Cobham), D. D. Hailes, *The Secret Correspondence of Sir Robert Cecil with James VI King of Scotland* (Edinburgh, 1766), esp. pp. 19–22. *Calendar of State Papers Venetian* (hereafter *Cal. SP Ven.*), *1603–1607*, pp. 41, 515.

15. *Letters from Sir Robert Cecil to Sir George Carew*, p. 144.

16. The renamed Salisbury House was large enough for Cecil in 1610 to invite the House of Lords to adjourn with him to it. Elizabeth Read Foster, *Proceedings in Parliament 1610*, 2 vols (New Haven and London, 1966), i, p. 19.

17. Lawrence Stone, *Family and Fortune: Studies in Aristocratic Finance in the Sixteenth and Seventeenth Centuries* (Oxford, 1973), pp. 36–7; Starkey, ed., *Rivals in Power*, p. 252.

18. BL, Cotton Caligula E.x.fol. 217; *Cal. SP Ven.*, *1603–1607*, p. 47.

19. Cecil MSS 99/88, 4 April 1603, Lord Burghley to Cecil.

20. *Letters of King James VI and I*, ed. G. P. V. Ackrigg (London, 1984), p. 208.

21. *Calendar of State Papers Domestic* (hereafter *Cal. SP Dom.*), *1603–1610*, p. 8; *Cal. SP Ven.*, *1603–1607*, p. 41.

22. The case made by Neil Cuddy, although overstated, is broadly convincing: 'The Revival of the Entourage: The Bedchamber of James I, 1603–1625', in David Starkey, ed., *The English Court from the Wars of the Roses to the Civil War* (London, 1987), pp. 173–225.

23. *Letters of King James VI and I*, ed. Ackrigg, p. 184.

24. *Calendar of Papers State Scotland*, vii, p. 274.

25. PRO, SP 14/23/10.

26. *The Letters of John Chamberlain*, ed. N. E. McClure, 2 vols (Philadelphia, 1939), i, p. 313.

27. BL, Add. Mss 34324 fol. 238; Pauline Croft, 'Robert Cecil and the Early Jacobean Court', in Linda Levy Peck, ed., *The Mental World of the Jacobean Court* (Cambridge, 1991), pp. 136–9. For the rapid rise in expenditure on the royal hunting lodges after 1603, Howard Colvin, *The History of the King's Works, 1485–1660* (London, 1983), iv, pt 2, esp. under Royston, Thetford, Ampthill, Bagshot, Newmarket and Eltham.

28. *Cal. SP Ven.*, *1607–1610*, pp. 46, 59–60, 67, 71, 73–4, 82, 87, 92, 95–6, 106, 115–16; *Letters of King James VI and I*, ed. Ackrigg, p. 242.

29. *Letters of King James VI and I*, ed. Ackrigg, pp. 220–1. *Cal. SP Ven.*, *1603–1607*, p. 353.

30. This was on a technical question of cargo restitution, but similar commercial matters were central concerns of both Anglo-Spanish and Anglo-Venetian diplomacy in the first decade of the reign: *Cal. SP Ven.*, *1603–1607*, p. 297.

31. *Ibid.*, pp. 353–4.

32. *Cal. SP Ven.*, *1607–1610*, p. 131.

33. Pauline Croft, 'A Collection of Several Speeches and Treatises of the Late Lord Treasurer Cecil', *Camden Miscellany*, 29 (1987), pp. 249, 254–9; PRO, SP 14/65/41, 60, 65; SP 14/66/43; H. A. Bell,

An Introduction to the History and Records of the Court of Wards and Liveries (Cambridge, 1953), pp. 18–19.
34. PRO, SP 14/15/105. *Illustrations of British History . . . selected from the mss. of the noble families of Howard, Talbot and Cecil*, ed. Edmund Lodge, 3 vols (London, 1838), iii, p. 262; Cecil Mss 228/30a; Lois Potter, 'The Politics of Language in Early Modern England', *Journal of British Studies*, 34 (1995), pp. 536–42.
35. *Calendar of State Papers Colonial East Indies, 1513–1616*, p. 146.
36. *Letters of King James VI and I*, ed. Ackrigg, pp. 221, 257, 300; PRO, SP 14/13/16.
37. *Cal. SP Dom., 1603–1610*, p. 60; Cecil Mss 140/200; Croft, 'Robert Cecil and the Early Jacobean Court', p. 140.
38. Cecil Mss 93/117; John Nicholls, *The Progresses . . . of King James I*, 4 vols (London, 1828), i, pp. 135–40.
39. *Cal. SP Dom., 1603–1610*, p. 138; Nicholls, *Progresses . . . of King James*, ii, pp. 70–4.
40. Nicholls, *Progresses . . . of King James*, ii, pp. 128–31. By contrast Bacon lost the favour of Buckingham when he protested, at the latter's attempt to take York Place, that he would not yield the house where his father had died: David Wootton, 'Francis Bacon: Your Flexible Friend' (p. 198, below).
41. 'Their majesties put off their departure for Greenwich to attend it': *Cal. SP Ven., 1607–1610*, pp. 133, 137.
42. Cecil Mss P. 2233. *Cal. SP Ven., 1607–1610*, p. 269.
43. Stone, *Family and Fortune*, p. 89.
44. Pauline Croft, 'The Parliamentary Installation of Henry Prince of Wales', *Historical Research*, 65 (1992), pp. 179–93.
45. Stone, *Family and Fortune*, p. 27.
46. Linda Levy Peck, *Northampton* (London, 1982), esp. pp. 78–87; PRO, SP 14/71/3 and 16.
47. Cecil Mss 125/47, 128/168; *Letters of King James VI and I*, ed. Ackrigg, p. 262; *Cal. SP Ven., 1607–1610*, p. 131.
48. PRO, SP 78/50 fol. 83r; Thomas Heywood, *An apology for Actors* (1612), discussed in B. N. de Luna, *Jonson's Romish Plot: A Study of 'Catiline' and its Historical Context* (Oxford, 1967), p. 25; *Francis Bacon: The Essays*, ed. John Pitcher (Harmondsworth, 1985), p. 85.
49. Linda Levy Peck, 'The Mentality of a Jacobean Grandee', in Peck, ed., *Mental World of the Jacobean Court*, p. 148; Cecil Mss 190/66.
50. For the range of Elizabethan usage, Evelyn Plummer Read and Conyers Read, eds, *Elizabeth of England: Certain Observations . . . by John Clapham* (Philadelphia, London and Oxford, 1951). Clapham was a long-standing Cecil servant.
51. *Letters of King James VI and I*, ed. Ackrigg, pp. 311–12. Maurice Lee Jr, *Great Britain's Solomon: James VI and I in his Three Kingdoms* (Urbana and Chicago, 1991), pp. 240–1; *The Diary of Sir Roger Wilbraham*, Camden Miscellany, 10 (1902), p. 115.
52. On 7 December 1611, Sir Julius Caesar assumed the central duty of the lord treasurer, receiving the weekly certificates from the officers of the Receipt: L. M. Hill, *Bench and Bureaucracy: The Public Career of Sir Julius Caesar* (Cambridge, 1988), p. 184.
53. As pointed out by Joel Hurstfield, *Freedom, Corruption and Government in Elizabethan England* (London, 1973), pp. 187–92.
54. Erna Auerbach and C. Kingsley Adams, *Paintings and Sculpture at Hatfield House* (London, 1971), p. 127. I am grateful to Lady Cranborne for showing me this painting at Cranborne Manor.
55. Roy Strong, *Tudor and Jacobean Portraits*, 2 vols (London, 1969), i, p. 351; ii, plates 50–61, 536–41.
56. Sir Walter Cope, *An Apology for the Late Lord Treasurer Sir Robert Cecil*, originally circulated in ms. and printed in *Collectanea Curiosa*, ed. J. Gutch, 2 vols (Oxford, 1781), i, p. 122.
57. *Letters of James VI and I*, ed. Ackrigg, pp. 311–12.
58. Roger Lockyer, *Buckingham: The Life and Political Career of George Villiers, First Duke of Buckingham, 1592–1628* (London, 1981), p. 473; Croft, 'The Reputation of Robert Cecil', pp. 63–6.

7

Corruption and Punishment?
The Rise and Fall of Matthäus Enzlin
(1556–1613), Lawyer and Favourite

RONALD G. ASCH

Bureaucracy or Personal Rule: Württemberg in the 1590s

In 1620 a treatise entitled *Sejanus seu de praepotentibus regum ac principum ministris commonefactio* was published in Strasburg. It dealt with the rise and fall of favourites and with remedies against both. The author of this little book was an Austrian nobleman, Georg Acacius Enenkel von Hoheneck, and his reflections were clearly inspired by the fall of one of the best-known favourites of the period, Cardinal Klesl in 1618.[1] For Enenkel, Klesl's fate was just one example of the fate of many favourites since the days of imperial Rome. In Enenkel's tract, however, the reader found not just the names of favourites who had lived in ages past but also examples of royal or princely servants who had risen to prominence in more recent times. In this context Enenkel mentioned the Elizabethan Earl of Essex, the French maréchal d'Ancre, and Emperor Rudolf II's favourite Wolfgang Rumpf. But he also mentioned the name of Matthäus Enzlin (pl. 22).[2]

Enzlin had been the most important counsellor of Duke Friedrich of Württemberg (pl. 23), who governed the duchy between 1593 and 1608. A few months after the duke's death his successor had Enzlin arrested on a charge of corruption and embezzlement. Never tried by a proper court of law, Enzlin signed a confession in 1609. He swore to accept imprisonment for an indefinite period and to forgo his right of appeal. Nevertheless Enzlin's family appealed to the Chamber Court of the empire in Speyer. When they tried to orchestrate a public outcry outside Württemberg against the alleged miscarriage of justice in Enzlin's case, the fallen favourite was tried and sentenced by a special ducal commission on a charge of perjury, high treason and *crimen laesae majestatis*. He was executed in November 1613 in the market square of Urach.

Enzlin's career and the reasons for his rise but also for the fate he suffered after 1608 can be understood only in the context of the constitutional and administrative structures of the German territorial state of the later sixteenth century in general, and of Württemberg in particular. In Germany, as in other parts of Europe, the first half of the sixteenth century had seen a move towards more bureaucratic forms of administration. In the later Middle Ages, counsellors and officeholders had been entrusted with various tasks on an *ad hoc* basis and had given advice either as individuals or as members of committees which lacked a clear corporate identity. But now conciliar bodies with clear responsibilities and a fixed membership were formed. At the same time the princely household largely lost its role as a centre of administration.

All this is familiar enough, but it was not the end of the story. Most princes were not prepared to leave politics and administration entirely to the newly constituted councils, or even to decide controversial matters during the sessions of the relevant conciliar body held in their presence. Rather they reserved a number of important matters, such as dynastic policy, for example, or secret financial transactions, for their own decision. Papers relating to these *Reservatsachen*, reserved matters, were processed not by the normal councils nor by the central chancellery, but by a personal secretary who worked either in the prince's privy chamber or in a room in its immediate vicinity. This secretary was therefore often called *Kammersekretär*, chamber secretary. During the later sixteenth and early seventeenth centuries the office of the personal secretary often became the nucleus of a separate chancellery, the court chancellery. If the prince required any advice on 'reserved matters' he asked some of his more important officeholders for their opinion on an *ad hoc* basis. These officeholders often received the official title of privy or secret councillor but they did not yet constitute a separate conciliar body with a permanent administrative identity. In most territories such bodies were not created until the end of the sixteenth or the beginning of the seventeenth century.[3]

This general model of administrative development, which was outlined many decades ago by Gerhard Oestreich, also applies to Württemberg. Here we find three central administrative bodies in the later sixteenth century. First, the *Oberrat*, the so-called Upper Council (the name was derived from the fact that the council held its sessions on the first floor of the Stuttgart Castle); secondly, the Treasury or *Rentkammer*, which again was organized as a conciliar body; and, thirdly, the Church Council (*Kirchenrat*) which not only dealt with theological matters but also supervised the administration of the ecclesiastical property which had been secularized during the Reformation.[4] The *Oberrat* was undoubtedly the most important institution but its influence on political decisions was limited. Rather it concentrated on legal matters and was in fact at least as much a court of law as an administrative body. Politically sensitive issues, as well as questions of patronage, were dealt with by the duke himself.

However, under Duke Friedrich's predecessor, Ludwig, who governed from 1568 to 1593, this often meant in practice that they were decided by Ludwig's personal secretary, Melchior Jäger von Gärtringen. Duke Ludwig was not too keen on reading official papers and even less on getting involved in the intricacies of the financial administration of his duchy, so more often than not he left these matters to Jäger. In fact Jäger's career shows that in the administrative system which obtained in Württemberg in the later sixteenth century the position of personal secretary to the duke was the natural stepping stone for a potential favourite. Jäger, whose influence was so pervasive that he was sometimes referred to as 'Duke Melchior', ceased to perform the task of personal secretary himself in later years and was content to preside over the court chancellery as aulic and privy councillor. Nevertheless he had started his career as a humble clerk and had achieved his influence only because he handled the duke's personal papers and correspondence.[5]

The tensions between a bureaucratic central administration dealing with routine matters and the far less bureaucratic personal rule of the prince, and even the rise of a personal secretary to the position of favourite which we find in Württemberg in the later sixteenth century, were quite common in the German principalities of this period. However, what distinguished Württemberg from other territories was the absence of an estate of noblemen in the duchy and the strong position of the Diet, the *Landtag*. There were, of course, a number of noblemen holding fiefs from the duke in Swabia but they had managed to retain their independence and recognized only the emperor as their lord, that is they were *Reichsritter*, imperial knights. Some of these imperial knights did enter the service of the duke, served in his household or supervised the local administration as *Obervögte*, head bailiffs, but they were not represented in the assembly of Estates.[6] Rather this assembly was dominated by the mayors and aldermen of the mostly quite small towns of the duchy. What is more, most of the ducal officeholders were recruited from this urban elite, a sort of patriciate, known as the *Ehrbarkeit*, and the same was true for the clergy. In fact, some senior Protestant theologians, the titular abbots of fourteen former monasteries, were also *ex officio* members of the territorial Diet and exerted a considerable influence on its discussions. The leading officeholders of the duchy were often related to the leaders of the Estates and senior clergymen, and one might in fact say that in Württemberg everybody who was anybody was related to everybody else.[7]

A closely knit elite dominated state, church and Diet. The Diet itself held an exceptionally strong position. In 1514 Duke Ulrich of Württemberg was forced by a popular rebellion to sign a treaty with his Estates, the famous Treaty of Tübingen (*Tübinger Vertrag*). The treaty established or confirmed a number of important privileges and liberties. Later political developments, in particular Duke Ulrich's exile between 1519 and 1534, had further reinforced the position of the Estates.[8] Nevertheless after the death of Duke Ulrich in 1550 relations between his two immediate successors and the Estates had largely been quite harmonious. The dukes, their officeholders and the representatives of the Estates were all united in the effort to defend the Reformation settlement, which came under severe pressure in the later 1540s and early 1550s, and their political attitudes were largely inspired by the same set of confessional values.[9]

Duke Friedrich, however, who succeeded Ludwig in 1593, resented the power of this traditional network of families which dominated state and church alike.[10] He was himself largely a stranger to the duchy. Although he had been educated in Stuttgart and Tübingen he was a member of a cadet branch of the ducal dynasty and had governed the small county of Montbeliard or Mömpelgard before 1593. As Count of Mömpelgard he got involved for a time in the French wars of religion and his political and intellectual horizons were certainly much wider than those of Duke Ludwig, not to mention those of the average Württemberg officeholder. In fact he not only knew France quite well, but he also visited other European countries, for example England. Friedrich was proud to be created a Knight of the Garter in 1603 and had received the French Order of Saint-Michel even earlier.[11]

When he succeeded as duke, Friedrich was determined not to have his freedom of action restricted by the network of officeholders, theologians and aldermen who traditionally dominated the duchy. It was therefore not surprising that his predecessor's more intimate advisers lost their influence under the new ruler. This applied in particular to Melchior Jäger, the once all-powerful *Kammersekretär* and privy councillor, who was almost totally excluded from important decisions once Friedrich had become familiar with his new principality.[12] On the other hand, Friedrich could hardly remove all members of the Upper Council, the Treasury and the Church Council from their positions. He therefore had to be content with recruiting a limited number of new men whom he employed to supervise the administration in general, to enforce his will against the old network of officeholders, and to deal with the great political projects he wanted to realize.

One of these new men was a nobleman and courtier, Christoph von Degenfeld, who seems to have concentrated on handling patronage matters. Another was Georg Eßlinger, who was appointed to the new office of *Landprokurator* in 1597.[13] The *Landprokurator*, a sort of fiscal general, had the task of improving the duchy's financial administration and was expected to put an end to the widespread corruption among officeholders. The most important of the new men, however, was undoubtedly Matthäus Enzlin.[14] Enzlin had acted as Friedrich's counsellor when the latter was still Count of Mömpelgard.[15] When Duke Ludwig's last will was officially read in Stuttgart in August 1593, Enzlin was already present as Duke Friedrich's personal adviser. Similarly he stood beside the new duke when the latter received the representatives of the Estates in audience in November 1593.[16]

Enzlin's influence was quite clearly based on his expertise and knowledge as a lawyer. Although Friedrich apparently was not overly concerned about legal niceties and did not have much respect for lawyers in general, he needed their advice to realize his ambitious projects in domestic affairs as much as in his relations with the emperor and other princes. In 1598 his privy councillors, including Enzlin, advised him not to show his disrespect for the traditional privileges of the Estates too openly. He replied that the doctors 'might well cook their own pudding' but he was determined to govern free of any traditional restraints, otherwise he would prefer not to remain duke at all.[17] Friedrich was by inclination an autocratic ruler. He was a short-tempered man who did not suffer fools gladly, and in his opinion most people who contradicted him were fools. When, for example, the Estates protested against the new academy for noblemen which the duke had founded in Tübingen, one of the first of its kind in Germany,[18] Friedrich's laconic comment was 'treschen ufs mhull', in other words that the representatives of the Estates deserved a thorough beating.[19] And when his councillors, again including Enzlin, advised him that not only the Treaty of Tübingen but also the statutes enacted by the Diet of the Holy Roman Empire entitled his subjects to a proper trial in a regular court of law, the duke wrote that his councillors should not 'waffle' so much. If anybody acted against him, he would simply punish him, no matter what his status was.[20]

However, in practice matters were not quite so straightforward and the duke needed somebody who was able to transform his quest for power into legal arguments. In late-sixteenth-century Germany, the dominant language of politics was the language of law. This was true for relations between the various princes of the empire but also for domestic politics in the various principalities of the empire, and if Enzlin's services were indispensable for the duke this was because he spoke this language so well. Moreover, by origin Enzlin belonged himself to the old-established governing elite of the duchy, and was therefore familiar with the principality's most important administrative and political problems, and, of course, with the prevailing patronage relations. He had studied in Tübingen, where he was made a doctor of law in 1576, had subsequently worked in Speyer at the Imperial Chamber Court and had later held a chair in the faculty of law in Heidelberg. In 1583 he returned to Tübingen as a professor and acted twice as *Rektor* of the university. He was employed as counsellor not only by Duke Ludwig, Friedrich's predecessor, but by quite a number of princes in southern Germany, whom he provided with legal advice. Enzlin's father had been director of the Church Council under Duke Ludwig and Enzlin was related to many important Württemberg families.[21]

One of the first great memoranda which Enzlin wrote for Duke Friedrich after 1593 was on Württemberg's relations with the Habsburgs. Ever since 1534 the duchy had been a fief of the House of Habsburg. This meant that although the dukes retained their seat in the imperial Diet and their status as princes of the empire, their immediate liege lord was the most senior Habsburg archduke, not the emperor in his capacity as feudal overlord over all German princes. In his memorandum of March 1594 on the problem of Württemberg's subinfeudation to Austria, Enzlin assessed the legal merits of the case at great length.[22] He became the driving force, after the duke himself, behind the negotiations with Innsbruck and the imperial court in Prague which were undertaken to restore Württemberg's status as a direct imperial fief.[23] At the same time he was in charge of the complicated discussions with the Estates, the Diet and its committees, for it was the Estates which were to provide the emperor and the imperial dynasty with the costly compensation in cash which they demanded for the repeal of the subinfeudation. After five years of protracted diplomatic and domestic bargaining the subinfeudation was finally repealed and the Württemberg Estates agreed to pay a huge sum of money to the House of Habsburg as compensation.[24] In return the Diet had insisted that Duke Friedrich should confirm the cherished Treaty of Tübingen and their traditional liberties once more. The duke was, however, extremely reluctant to do so. The very name of the treaty had, as he wrote, become odious to him by now and he wished that the devil should take those who had persuaded him in 1593 to confirm it in the first place – the duke was probably thinking of Jäger, his father's favourite. Finally, however, Enzlin and the members of the duke's entourage persuaded him to make some concessions to the Estates and a compromise could thus be reached.[25]

The end of the subinfeudation was a personal triumph for Enzlin. In April 1594 he had been appointed the duke's councillor and in October 1596 his secret or privy councillor.[26] From the latter date onwards he seems to have taught less and less at his old university in Tübingen, and in 1602 he finally resigned his professorship, concentrating all his energy on his work as the duke's legal adviser. However, his title of councillor did not imply permanent membership of any corporate body.[27] He was *Rat von Haus aus*, that is he was allowed to submit his advice in writing from his lodgings in Tübingen. And in fact he continued to live mainly in Tübingen, although he also acquired a house in Stuttgart.[28] Because Enzlin was often absent from court he did not control access to the duke. Nor was he able to filter the petitions submitted to him, as Secretary Jäger had clearly done. In fact, the duke insisted on reading all petitions himself.[29]

A Mere Locator Operarum

Nevertheless Enzlin's influence was considerable. Around 1600 he was already called 'cor et os principis', that is the heart and mouth of the prince. In a poem publicly recited at his brother-in-law's wedding he was addressed thus and apparently did not object.[30] Official correspondence relating to secret matters, in particular diplomatic negotiations, was often sent directly to Tübingen to be dealt with by Enzlin.[31] But his influence was not limited to diplomatic affairs or negotiations with the Estates. Apparently Duke Friedrich had begun to channel an increasingly large share of his revenues not through the Treasury but through his privy purse. Large sums of money from this source were devoted to the purchase of manors, villages and whole lordships from the impoverished nobility living beyond the borders of the duchy or were used to provide these noblemen with loans and mortgages in the hope that they would have to cede their property to the duke, should they fail to repay the money.[32] Enzlin was apparently the duke's principal agent in these rather complicated and somewhat shady financial transactions, in which Jewish moneylenders and merchants were frequently employed as brokers.[33] Thus large sums of money went through

Enzlin's hands. Unlike the officials of the duchy's Treasury Enzlin had never sworn a special oath binding him to act faithfully in financial matters. He had sworn only a normal councillor's oath which did not mention financial affairs at all. Later, when Enzlin was accused of corruption, of having embezzled some of the money the duke had given him, his opponents argued that the lack of a proper patent of office and the fact that the favourite had not been sworn in as the duke's treasurer or financial agent proved that Enzlin had interfered in matters which were beyond his responsibilities.[34]

Enzlin, not surprisingly, saw matters differently. He agreed that he had been only *locator operarum* for the duke, as he put it, that is a sort of private contractor who had performed certain tasks, but by no means an officeholder. However, in his opinion this implied that he could not be judged as an officeholder, in particular not for perjury as he had never sworn an oath of office, at least as far as these financial transactions were concerned. Enzlin went even further and said that the letters patent appointing him a councillor did not make him an officeholder in any sense at all. After all, he had in earlier years also acted as counsellor for foreign princes and thus his relationship with the duke was not much closer than if he had been the King of Poland's adviser, giving his advice from his house in Tübingen.[35] This may have been somewhat disingenuous, but it was nevertheless true that Enzlin's position was extremely ill defined and never rested on any clear commission or patent. This did not prevent him, however, from procuring the dismissal of other councillors – on charges of corruption for example. Some of them were even imprisoned.[36]

By 1600 Enzlin had certainly already made a lot of enemies. For example, in 1602 the former vicar of Untertürckheim, a small town near Stuttgart, who had left the duchy some time before, published a sermon. The vicar, a certain Thomas Birck, seems to have been a quarrelsome man, but it is nevertheless remarkable that he compared his opponents, and Enzlin was clearly one of them or perhaps rather their supreme patron, to the Saxon chancellor Krell. Birck gave his readers to understand that those who acted like Krell would suffer his fate too. Krell had been a sort of crypto-Calvinist who had made life uncomfortable for the Lutheran clergy of Saxony in the late 1580s. In 1591, after the death of his electoral patron, however, he had been arrested. Ten years later he was executed, after an impeachment by the Estates of Saxony.[37] Ironically enough Enzlin had been among the lawyers and legal experts who had provided the prosecution with legal advice.[38]

Clearly by 1602 Duke Friedrich and his most influential adviser – although neither had any recognizable sympathies for Calvinism – had already fallen foul of the leaders of the Württemberg clergy. This was partly because they were pursuing a more liberal policy with regard to Jewish merchants, and partly also because they were trying to reduce the influence of the prelates in the Diet. In fact after 1599 relations between the duke and the Diet deteriorated rapidly. The duke was now determined to free himself of the constraints of the Treaty of Tübingen. Again it was Enzlin who provided him with the decisive legal arguments. Enzlin did not advise Friedrich to revoke entirely the privileges which the Estates enjoyed, and it his doubtful whether he can be described as an advocate of 'absolutism', but he argued that the treaty needed to be modified in a special declaration to which the Diet was to give its assent. The duke was not only to be allowed to raise new customs duties and indirect taxes without the consent of the Estates, but Enzlin considered it even more crucial that the Diet should recognize its responsibility to provide the funds needed to pay for mercenaries should Württemberg be involved in a major war.[39] In 1607, when the tensions which were to lead to the outbreak of war in the empire in 1618 were already very much in evidence, this was certainly not an entirely implausible argument.

The Estates put up considerable resistance against the intended changes. Early in 1607 the Diet was dissolved by the duke because the delegates had proved too stubborn. The next Diet, after carefully manipulated elections, proved more amenable. In 1607, the Treaty of Tübingen was amended according to the duke's wishes.[40] This was another triumph for Enzlin, who had been responsible for the negotiations with the Estates. However, in January 1608 Duke Friedrich died. Relations between the duke and his eldest son Johann Friedrich had been fraught with tension in the years before 1608. Not only had the father kept about a dozen mistresses, something his son clearly resented,[41] but he had also refused to finance the prince's luxurious lifestyle.[42] As Enzlin had advised the duke on the education of his son, as on many other matters,[43] it was not surprising that Johann Friedrich now dismissed him. Melchior Jäger and a number of other councillors who had either been deprived of their offices during the preceding years or lost their influence now returned to favour.

Jäger was apparently the driving force behind the imprisonment and indictment of Enzlin in summer 1608, but other councillors agreed that Enzlin knew so much that he could not be allowed to go free.[44] The indictment against him raised no strictly political charges. Rather the fact that he had spent money from the duke's privy purse without keeping proper records and accounts provided his opponents with most of the material against him. After signing a confession under the threat of torture and a death sentence which the town court of Stuttgart was only too likely to pronounce, Enzlin was imprisoned in the fortress of Urach.[45] During his imprisonment he tried to mobilize support for his release outside Württemberg and instructed his wife and children to appeal to the *Kammergericht* in Speyer.[46] As a result new charges were brought against him in 1612. Again, however, none of these charges was directly related to the part he had taken in the late duke's attempts to subdue the Diet before 1608.[47]

Some councillors were indeed of the opinion that such charges would have made the trial a much more straightforward affair, as Enzlin now claimed for himself the legal privileges of the Treaty of Tübingen, which stipulated that nobody was to be convicted without a proper trial. These councillors thought that Enzlin should be charged with having persuaded the late duke to pursue a policy which aimed 'ad eversionem totius status, oblitteranda omnium subditorum privilegia et mores patrios inducendumque extremum seditionis periculum', but clearly Johann Friedrich, who had since 1608 had a number of rather unpleasant encounters with the Estates himself, objected to such a political charge.[48]

Thus Enzlin was convicted because he had broken his promise, given under oath, not to appeal to a court outside Württemberg, because he had besmirched the reputation of the duke and his officeholders, and finally because he had allegedly tried to provide Württemberg's enemies with material and papers which would have allowed them to claim a large part of the duchy as their own property.[49] In any case now more than ever Enzlin's release was seen as too dangerous. He had to die, for as it was argued twenty-eight years later during the impeachment of another powerful and unpopular early-seventeenth-century minister, the Earl of Strafford, 'stone dead hath no fellow'. And thus Enzlin was duly executed in Urach on 22 November 1613.[50]

The Structure of a Career

At first glance Enzlin was a very unlikely figure as a favourite. He never really controlled access to the duke, neither in the physical sense nor in the sense that all or most petitions to the duke went through his hands. In fact, for weeks or perhaps even months on end he was not even present at court, dealing with business from his home in Tübingen.[51] Nevertheless his contemporaries clearly saw him as a favourite, and given that Enzlin was so powerful but that this power was based not on any office with clear responsibilities but on the duke's personal favour, it would in fact be difficult to describe Enzlin as anything but a favourite. Indeed, in late-sixteenth- and early-seventeenth-century Germany the rise of lawyers to the position of favourite was not exceptional. In the 1620s there was the case of the *Generalaudienzier*, provost martial general, Günther in Hesse-Kassel. Günther presided over the military jurisdiction of the principality and also held the position of *director causarum criminalium* and fiscal general. In 1628 he, like Enzlin, was tried and executed on the initiative of the Estates.[52] Earlier there had been Chancellor Nikolaus Krell in electoral Saxony, mentioned above, who had dominated politics in the prince electorate between 1585 and 1591. Krell was also executed, though not until 1601.[53]

What, however, are we to make of the charges of corruption raised against Enzlin after his fall? Were they just a cynical move in a political game or are they to be taken seriously? Does Enzlin's career and that of other favourites in Germany as well as in other European countries demonstrate that administrative practices had indeed become more corrupt during the course of the later sixteenth century? Linda Levy Peck has stated in her study *Court Patronage and Corruption* that in England the taking of bribes and official venality had indeed acquired a new dimension around 1600 and that in response to this development 'the types of practices labelled corrupt were extended . . . and bribery was defined more narrowly'. Furthermore she has argued that charges of corruption constituted a political discourse which was employed to give voice to political opposition which would otherwise have been difficult to articulate.[54]

However, it should not be forgotten that parliaments and estates were not alone in accusing officeholders of corruption. Rulers could speak the same language if they felt like it. Indeed men like Enzlin and his companion the *Landprokurator*, the fiscal general, Eßlinger, owed their career to the fact that Duke Friedrich considered most of his servants to be corrupt and that a large part of his revenues disappeared into their pockets.[55] And his son, Johann Friedrich, came to share this view once his honeymoon with the old-established elite, the *Ehrbarkeit*, was over.[56] Thus the discourse of corruption could, at least in Germany, be employed by the prince as much as by his officeholders and the Estates. In fact, in Enzlin's case it is plausible to call the discourse of corruption a language of consensus and not of opposition. For limiting the charges against Enzlin to embezzlement and corruption clearly allowed the real political issues to be avoided.

Legal proceedings against favourites, even when their original princely patrons were no longer alive as in Enzlin's case, were always politically explosive. Enzlin was not the only favourite to be brought to trial in the late sixteenth and early seventeenth centuries in Germany on the initiative of the Estates or members of the ruling elite of officeholders and clergymen closely connected with the Estates. There were the cases – already mentioned – of Chancellor Krell in Saxony and of Fiscal General Günther in Hesse.[57] These examples show that impeachment was a procedure by no means limited to England, where the charges brought against Buckingham in 1626 are perhaps the most prominent example; if the Earl of Strafford were to be considered a favourite for the last stage of his career immediately before the meeting of the Long Parliament, his trial would offer another important example.[58]

The problem with such judicial proceedings in England as well as in Germany was always that the defendant was likely to argue that he had only obeyed orders. It could seem preposterous to accuse of treason princely servants who had only tried to strengthen the authority of their master. There were essentially two answers to this defence. It was possible to concentrate on misdemeanours which were politically less explosive, such as the favourite's 'avarice' and the allegedly corrupt exploitation of his influence over the ruler. Thus the charge of corruption could be used to downplay the real issues and to maintain consensus between the prince and the Estates. If this most obvious line of attack failed, however, treason had to be redefined as a crime against a God-given objective order, not just against the personal will and the personal interests of the prince. Such a charge was much more explosive. To bring a favourite down in this way the entire position of the ruler within the legal system had to be redefined. The natural person of the ruler had to be distinguished from his 'body politic', which could be identified with the legal order. This could easily lead to a major political crisis, as events showed in England in 1626–7 during and after the Duke of Buckingham's impeachment and even more so in 1641 when the Earl of Strafford was impeached and finally condemned by bill of attainder.

In Germany matters were different, as the trial against Krell in Saxony, which took place about ten years before Enzlin's execution, demonstrates. Of course the fact that Krell's former patron and master, Prince Elector Christian, had died when the chancellor was imprisoned made matters much easier. But this was not the whole story. Krell was accused of having acted against the Peace of Augsburg, one of the fundamental constitutions of the empire, and against the *Landfrieden*, the Perpetual Peace, of 1495.[59] Thus the objective legal order embodied in the imperial constitutions could provide a standard for defining treason in such a way that it was possible to charge favourites with having given counsel against the principles of this order. It was not necessary to redefine the position of the ruler, which was essentially limited in Germany by the constitution of the empire, thereby avoiding the risks of a major political crisis. However, there were clear limits to attempts to invoke the laws of the empire against 'evil counsellors' and in the Estates' favour. After all, at the end of the day the empire was constituted by its princes and high nobility, under the supervision and rule of the emperor, and the solidarity of the princes was unlikely to favour the territorial Estates. In Enzlin's case the chance was too great that other German princes, allies and friends of the late duke in particular and the law courts of the empire, especially the Chamber Court in Speyer, would intervene in his favour, as they in fact did.[60] Here the normal legal procedures as applied by the highest law courts of the empire were likely to work in Enzlin's favour. This was why all politically explosive issues were avoided in his trial and the prosecution essentially limited to charges of corruption. When the Imperial Chamber Court nevertheless ordered Enzlin's release from prison he was sentenced and condemned without further ado.[61]

The young duke, the officeholders and the Estates all welcomed charges of corruption against Enzlin because they allowed them to avoid the really sensitive issues. Although Enzlin's personal enemies, often men who had accepted gifts just as willingly as Enzlin in their time,[62] clearly exploited the widespread criticism of corrupt practices to further their own ends and to undo their rival, there is no doubt that there was a widespread feeling that counsellors should not really behave in the way Enzlin had. Nor was this merely a question of private morals, of personal greed and avarice. Ultimately what was at stake here was the tension between the private and the public sphere.[63] This can be illustrated by looking at the tract written by Enenkel mentioned at the beginning of this essay. In his treatise Enenkel stressed that one of the favourite's defining features was that he did not respect the God-given order of society. He did not just have ideas above his station, he also acted above his station by interfering in business and in conflicts which did not really concern him, or should not have concerned him. Moreover, and this is an important point, the favourite used his influence to work against the common good and the public interest of the commonwealth, not just by pursuing his own interests in a reckless way but also by keeping others, who otherwise might have given the prince better advice, busy by nourishing their private feuds and enmities. What was more, favourites tried to render suspect to the prince the 'conventus subditorum in quibus de bono publico et utilitate universorum consulatur', that is the Estates and their assemblies, which promoted the common interests of everybody. In the last resort they tried to prevent the meeting of the Diets altogether.[64]

Enenkel's definition of the favourite – commonplace enough in the early seventeenth century – quite clearly hinged on the distinction between the private and the public sphere, a distinction which Enenkel saw as necessary but which favourites did not respect. On matters of political significance princes in Enenkel's opinion should consult properly constituted officeholders and the Estates of their dominions, not their personal friends or private counsellors without a proper office or commission. In practice, of course, the distinction between the private and the public on which Enenkel and other authors insisted[65] was highly problematic in a political system in which the court and the personal entourage of the ruler were often the real centre of government and in which patronage networks were all-pervasive. However, one might say that the special position of the favourite in the period under discussion here was defined by this very tension between two equally valid but conflicting moral codes: on the one hand an ideal of public consultation and of the common good, and on the other an ideal of friendship, of mutual loyalty between patron and client, and of course of personal devotion to the prince.[66] Men like Enzlin exploited this tension. They demonstrated that personal loyalty to the ruler, which a prince such as Duke Friedrich expected, and, what is more, their administrative skills provided the prince with a counterweight against a bureaucracy which he controlled only very incompletely because offices had become the virtual freehold of those who held them or because officeholders were too closely connected to the Estates and local interests. But at the same time favourites were liable to become the victims of the tension they exploited. It was not just their wealth acquired in questionable ways which provoked resentment, but the very fact that they moved outside the normal system of administration and consultation, that they were, like Enzlin, only *locatores operarum*,[67] men of business, counsellors and attorneys serving the ruler in a private, not an official capacity. In a manner of speaking favourites had to be corrupt, regardless of their personal vices or virtues, because they stood outside the normal hierarchy of offices and because only patronage and the accepting and giving of gifts allowed them to acquire the power they strove for. For other officeholders such practices were the foundation perhaps for their private wealth and social advancement. For the favourite they were the very foundation of his political power.

In Württemberg, however, the entrenched caste of officeholders and the Estates were to triumph over the favourite in the seventeenth century. Not only was Enzlin executed, but fifteen years after his death a special Secret or Privy Council was created on the initiative, at least to some extent, of the Estates. The new council was to deal with the *Reservatsachen*, the secret business, which in the past had been the responsibility of the duke's personal secretaries and those counsellors who happened to enjoy his special trust. One might say the position of favourite was transformed into or rather replaced by a bureaucratic institution with a corporate identity.[68] The Estates now faced an administrative body with a clearly defined membership which allowed them to hold the privy councillors to account for any violations of their privileges. Private secretaries and favourites like Enzlin had been able to plead that all controversial decisions had been taken by the duke himself or under the influence of other councillors. In the end, however, this was not much help to Enzlin, who became the victim of the social group to which he belonged and against which he revolted, the all-powerful *Ehrbarkeit*.

Notes

1. Georg Acacius Enenkel, Liber Baro Hoheneccius, *Sejanus seu de praepotentibus regum ac principum ministris commonefactio* (Argentorati, 1620).
2. *Ibid.*, p. 39.
3. G. Oestreich, 'Das Persönliche Regiment der deutschen Fürsten am Beginn der Neuzeit', in *idem, Geist und Gestalt des frühmodernen Staates* (Berlin, 1969), pp. 201–34.
4. J. A. Vann, *The Making of a State: Württemberg, 1593–1793* (Ithaca, NY, 1984), pp. 53–88; W. Bernhardt, *Die Zentralbehörden des Herzogtums Württemberg und ihre Beamten, 1520–1629*, 2 vols (Stuttgart, 1972), i, pp. 15–64.
5. For the reign of Duke Ludwig and Jäger's influence see M. Rudersdorf, 'Herzog Ludwig, 1568–1593', in R. Uhland, ed., *900 Jahre Haus Württemberg* (Stuttgart, 1984), pp. 163–73; Bernhardt, *Zentralbehörden*, i, pp. 402–6; K. Pfaff, *Wirtenbergischer Plutarch* (Esslingen, 1830), pp. 1–9; Vann, *Making*, p. 62.
6. D. Mertens, 'Württemberg', in M. Schaab and H. Schwarzmaier, eds, *Handbuch der Baden-Württembergischen Geschichte*, ii: *Die Territorien im Alten Reich* (Stuttgart, 1995), pp. 1–163, at pp. 89–90, 94. For the development of the Landtag see W. Grube, *Der Stuttgarter Landtag* (Stuttgart, 1957) and F. L. Carsten, *Princes and Parliament in Germany: From the Fifteenth to the Eighteenth Century* (Oxford, 1959), ch. 1.
7. For the *Ehrbarkeit* see H. Decker-Hauff, 'Die geistige Führungsschicht Württembergs', in G. Franz, ed., *Beamtentum und Pfarrerstand, 1400–1800* (Limburg, 1972), pp. 51–80; cf. Grube, *Landtag*, pp. 226–7, for the status of the prelates in the Diet.
8. Mertens, 'Württemberg', pp. 74–82.
9. H. Maurer, 'Herzog Christoph als Landesherr', *Blätter für württembergische Kirchengeschichte*, 68/69 (1968–9), pp. 112–38; Grube, *Landtag*, pp. 224–36.
10. There is no adequate modern biography, but cf. E. Schneider, *Württembergische Geschichte* (Stuttgart, 1896), pp. 200–13; H. Gmelin, *Über Herzog Friedrich I. von Württemberg und seine Stände* (PhD thesis, Tübingen/Stuttgart, 1885); A. E. Adam, 'Herzog Friedrich I von Württemberg und die Landschaft', *Württembergische Vierteljahreshefte*, new series 25 (1916), pp. 210–29; O. Borst, *Württemberg und seine Herren* (Esslingen, 1987), pp. 101–9; G. Raff, *Hier gut Wirtemberg allewege*, ii (Stuttgart, 1993), pp. 4–55.
11. R. Uhland, 'Herzog Friedrich I (1593–1608)', in Uhland, *900 Jahre*, pp. 174–82, at pp. 177–8.
12. Bernhardt, *Zentralbehörden*, i, p. 33; Landesbibliothek Stuttgart, Cod. hist. fol. 320, 'Georg Hengher, Württembergische Chronik', p. 264.
13. Bernhardt, *Zentralbehörden*, i, pp. 34, 226–7, 275–6, and G. Lang, 'Landprokurator Georg Eßlinger', *Zeitschrift für Württembergische Landesgechichte*, 5 (1941), pp. 34–87.
14. For Enzlin's biography see Bernhardt, *Zentralbehörden*, i, pp. 263–70; Pfaff, *Plutarch*, 11–35; [Anonymous], 'Der Prozeß des Kanzlers Dr. Matthäus Enzlin', *Württembergische Jahrbücher* (1827), pp. 271–326; and (1828), pp. 171–200. See further the entries in the *Allgemeine Deutsche Biographie* and the *Neue Deutsche Biographie*.

15. A. E. Adam, ed., *Württembergische Landtagsakten*, 2nd series, *1592–1620*, 3 vols (Stuttgart, 1910–19), i, p. 76, n. 4.

16. *Ibid.*, pp. 79–81, 86.

17. *Ibid.*, pp. 557–9: Degenfeld, chancellor and Enzlin to duke about negotiations with the Estates, 11 December 1598, and Duke Friedrich's answer.

18. On the *collegium illustre* in Tübingen see N. Conrad, *Ritterakademien der Frühen Neuzeit* (Göttingen, 1982), pp. 154–200.

19. Friedrich's comment on the grievances raised by the Diet against the *collegium*, 14 February 1599, relating in particular to the fact that most grants would go to foreign students: *Landtagsakten*, ii, pp. 47–8.

20. *Landtagsakten*, ii, p. 41, 13 February 1599, cf. pp. 39–41 for the much more moderate advice of the ducal commissioners.

21. See above, note 14, for biographical information on Enzlin.

22. Hauptstaatsarchiv Stuttgart (hereafter HStA), A 107, Fasc. 13 a, no. 8a, 23 March 1594.

23. For Enzlin's activities see in particular HStA Stuttgart, A 107, Fasc. 14 a, nos 22–5 and 32 b.

24. Grube, *Landtag*, pp. 251–63; *Landtagsakten*, i, pp. 456–83; ii, pp. 1–30, 88–176.

25. The duke initially refused to have the Treaty of Tübingen even mentioned in the final resolution of the Diet: *Landtagsakten*, ii, p. 136, 10 March 1599; cf. *ibid.*, pp. 137–48, and see further i, p. 559 (quoted above, note 17); also Grube, *Landtag*, pp. 262–3.

26. Bernhardt, *Zentralbehörden*, i, pp. 263–4; cf. HStA Stuttgart, A 48 A, Fasc. 13, no. 83, letters patent appointing Enzlin as councillor, 23 April 1594, and no. 85, appointment as privy councillor (with lodgings in Tübingen!), 30 October 1596.

27. As James Allen Vann has put it, the *Geheime Räte* (privy councillors) were 'a pool of advisors rather than a functioning agency, though records survive of sporadic committee meetings in the first three years of the seventeenth century' (Vann, *Making*, p. 68). The Privy Council as a separate institution was not founded until 1628.

28. See above, note 26, with reference to Enzlin's appointment as privy councillor in 1596 and the correspondence between Duke Friedrich and Enzlin, HStA Stuttgart, G 59, Fasc. 11. See also Bernhardt, *Zentralbehörden*, i, p. 264, on Enzlin's travels.

29. See 'Hengher, Chronik', p. 264, and Enzlin's own testimony in his justification, HStA Stuttgart, A 48 A, Fasc. 17, fol. 54r.

30. Thus Thomas Birck, *Letze Predig Thomae Birckii* (Speyer, 1602), preface, pp. 72–4; cf. R. Stahlecker and E. Staiger, eds, *Diarium Martini Crusii*, iii: *1600–1605* (Tübingen, 1958), p. 434, 18 May 1602. For Birck see also below, note 37.

31. Duke Friedrich to his *Kammersekretär* Sattler from Urach, 14 November 1599, HStA Stuttgart, G 59, Fasc. 11, instructing him to send all important correspondence to Enzlin in Tübingen; only the routine business ('gemeine sachen') was to be dealt with by the chancellery in Stuttgart.

32. See the records of Enzlin's trial, in particular HStA Stuttgart A 48 A, Fasc. 2, no. 98, 'Protocoll', 19 November 1608, esp. fols 3v–5v, and Fasc. 3, no. 109, 'Hauptbedenckhen', fols 30r–33r. Cf. Fasc. 3, no. 117, Enzlin's 'Deprecationsschrift', October 1608. See also Pfaff, *Plutarch*, pp. 20–3, and for the duke's attempt to extend his territory Schneider, *Geschichte*, pp. 208–9.

33. This was one of the charges raised against Enzlin ('Protocoll', fols 2r–3v); see also HStA Stuttgart, A 48 A, Fasc. 1, *passim*.

34. HStA Stuttgart, A 48 A, Fasc. 2, no. 98, 'Protocoll', fols 3r–5v: charge relating to interference in 'alienum negotium'. It would have been the *Rentmeister*'s (treasurer) responsibility to deal with these matters.

35. HStA Stuttgart, A 48 A, Fasc. 12, no. 77, Enzlin's interrogation by the ducal commissioners, 3 February 1613: 'bey Herzog Friedrich sey er nur locator operarum gewesen ohne beaidigung und derselben anderst nit verbunden gewesen als wann einer bestallung vom König von Polen habe' (no pagination). Cf. 'Hauptbedenckhen', fol. 66v.

36. Bernhardt, *Zentralbehörden*, i, pp. 242–3 and 195–6. For the part the dismissed councillors took in the proceedings against Enzlin see HStA Stuttgart A 48 A, Fasc. 17, Enzlin's justification, fols 13r–18r, 36r–38r and 40v, 56r.

37. Birck, *Predig*, pp. 82ff., refers to Krell's trial and quotes a funeral sermon on Krell (Nicolaus Blumius, *Leichpredigt über den custodierten D. Nicolaum Krell* (Magdeburg, 1601)) which gave an extremely hostile account of Krell and his trial. For Krell and his fate cf. T. Klein, *Der Kampf um die zweite Reformation in Kursachsen, 1586–1591* (Cologne, 1962), in particular pp. 20–35; B. Bohnenstädt, *Das Processverfahren gegen den kursächsischen Kanzler Dr. Nicolaus Krell, 1591–1601*,

pt i (Halle a. d. S., 1901), and A. V. Richard, *Der Kurfürstlich sächsische Kanzler Dr. Nicolaus Krell*, 2 vols (Dresden, 1859).

38. Richard, *Krell*, ii, pp. 258–66, prints the 'Bedenken' by Dr Varnbüler and Enzlin, both professors of law in Tübingen, dated 2 July 1594.

39. See Enzlin's memorial, HStA Stuttgart, A 34, Fasc. 28 b, no. 1, 25 January 1607, and an earlier version of the same memorial, *Landtagsakten*, ii, pp. 511–30, 27 November 1606.

40. Grube, *Landtag*, pp. 265–73; *Landtagsakten*, ii, pp. 542–764.

41. Raff, *Wirtemberg*, ii, p. 39.

42. See for example HStA Stuttgart, G 66, Fasc. 2, Duke Friedrich to Prince Johann Friedrich, 3 May 1607.

43. See HStA Stuttgart, A 274, Fasc. 72.

44. HStA Stuttgart, A 48 A, Fasc. 2, no. 98, 'Protocoll', November/December 1608, fols 9r–v, in particular Dr Bozer's *votum*.

45. See HStA Stuttgart, A 48 A, Fasc. 3, no. 109, 'Hauptbedenckhen'; Fasc. 5, no. 127 b, Enzlin's submission, 13 March 1609 (Enzlin had to accept life imprisonment and had to pay compensation of 119,496 fl. for the money which he had allegedly embezzled).

46. See e.g. HStA Stuttgart, A 48 A, Fasc. 6, no. 4, Enzlin's wife and sons to Duke Johann Friedrich, 22 August 1612; Fasc. 11, no. 6, Enzlin's sons to the brother of the reigning duke, Ludwig Friedrich, 22 August 1612; Fasc. 11, no. 11, mandate of the Imperial Chamber Court, presented 10 December 1612, asking the duke to justify his procedure against Enzlin or to release him. See further HStA Stuttgart, C 3, Fasc. 926, in particular the memorial by Enzlin's attorney (undated), in which he castigated the original proceedings against his client who had been blackmailed into signing his own confession.

47. See HStA Stuttgart, A 48 A, Fasc. 13, no. 98, report by ducal councillors, 29 July 1613, and Fasc. 11, 'Iudicialprotocoll' 1613. See also Fasc. 8, no. 92, report by councillors 20 February 1613.

48. HStA Stuttgart, A 48 A, Fasc. 13, no. 98, report 29 July 1613, art. viii. For Enzlin's attempt to invoke the privileges of the Treaty of Tübingen: Fasc. 11, 'Iudicialprotocoll' 1613, p. 26.

49. See above, note 47, and Grube, *Landtag*, p. 277.

50. C. V. Wedgwood, *Thomas Wentworth, First Earl of Strafford, 1593–1641: A Revaluation* (London, 1961), p. 369, quoting Clarendon's *History of the Great Rebellion*.

51. See above, notes 26 and 28.

52. L. W. Grotefend, 'Der Prozeß des landgräflichen Raths Dr. Wolfgang Günther (1627–28)', *Hessenland*, 12 (1898), pp. 226–38, 270–2, 298–301; W. Keim, 'Landgraf Wilhelm V. von Hessen-Kassel vom Regierungsantritt 1627 bis zum Abschluß des Bündnisses mit Gustav Adolf 1631', pt 1, *Hessisches Jahrbuch für Landesgeschichte*, 12 (1962), pp. 130–210, esp. pp. 164–9.

53. For Krell, see above, note 37. For his position as first minister in the central administration, cf. W. Ohnsorge, 'Die Verwaltungsreform unter Christian I. Ein Beitrag zur Geschichte der zentralen Behördenbildung Kursachsens im 16. Jahrhundert', *Neues Archiv für Sächsische Geschichte*, 63 (1943), pp. 26–80, at pp. 57–80.

54. L. L. Peck, *Court Patronage and Corruption in Early Stuart England* (Boston, 1990), pp. 163 and 185–207.

55. See for example Enzlin's memorial of 25 January 1607, HStA Stuttgart A 34, Fasc. 28 b, fol. 45r; Bernhardt, *Zentralbehörden*, i, p. 34, and Lang, 'Eßlinger', pp. 41–4.

56. In December 1610 Johann Friedrich referred to the 'devilish corruptions' ('teuffelische corruptiones') among his officeholders: *Landagsakten*, iii, pp. 279 and 281; see also the duke's justification for employing noblemen as officeholders and *Obervögte*, *ibid.*, p. 274 (9 December).

57. See above, notes 37 and 52.

58. For the impeachment in England see C. G. C. Tite, *Impeachment and Parliamentary Judicature in Early Stuart England* (London, 1974); cf. C. Russell, 'The Theory of Treason in the Trial of Strafford', *English Historical Review*, 80 (1965), pp. 30–50.

59. Richard, *Krell*, ii, pp. 179–81, articles 42–5 of Krell's interrogation relating to ecclesiastical matters, with reference to the Peace of Augsburg (the Peace had, according to the strict Lutheran and Catholic interpretation, declared Calvinism illegal, a religious denomination which Krell was supposed to have supported) and p. 187, articles 7 and 8, interrogation in political matters referring to the empire's 'constitutions' which Krell was accused of having undermined by pursuing a warlike policy and having granted support to the French Huguenots.

60. Enzlin's wife and sons did argue in 1612 that his imprisonment was an insult to the entire estate of princes in the empire ('Reichsfürstenstand') as he had served one of them, the late duke, so faithfully. See HStA Stuttgart, A 48 A, Fasc. 6, no. 4, and Fasc. 11, no. 6 (as above, note 46).
61. As above, note 46 (mandate by Chamber Court). Enzlin's companion Eßlinger was tried by the town court of Stuttgart, but in December 1613 the Imperial Chamber Court peremptorily ordered his release from prison, an order which the Württemberg authorities reluctantly obeyed just over a year later; see Lang, 'Eßlinger', pp. 63–4 and 73–83.
62. The tension between conflicting moral codes is illustrated by the criticism which Enzlin faced by other councillors. Dr Eisengrein argued that Enzlin, as opposed to other officeholders, had accepted gifts as a reward not only for work which he had really done himself – this was clearly seen as acceptable – but also for the efforts of others which he later claimed as his own (HStA Stuttgart, A 42, Fasc. 25, no. 190, 28 March 1608). Cf. A 48 A, Fasc. 17, Enzlin's justification, fol. 54v, stressing that it was quite normal to receive gifts ('Verehrungen') in his position.
63. For contemporary opinions on the separation between private and public and between the prince's private friends and public councillors see Christoph Besold, *De Consilio politico axiomata* (Tübingen, 1615), § 134, p. 88; cf. the general invective against favourites, §§ 79–99 and 129, as well as § 135, pp. 88–9; cf. § 140, p. 91 against the 'secretarii intimi'. For the notion of the private and public see further [Bartholomeus Keckermann], *Cursus Philosophici disputatio xxxiv . . . de aula principis . . . praeside Bartholomeo Keckermanno, respondente Simone Clugio Dantiscano* (Danzig, 1608), in particular part II, problema vii; and Bartholomäus Keckermann, *Systema disciplinae politicae* (Hanoviae, 1608), liber I, cap. XXIII, pp. 367ff.; cf. W. Weber, *Prudentia Gubernatoria: Studien zur Herrschaftslehre in der deutschen politischen Wissenschaft des 17. Jahrhundert* (Tübingen, 1992), p. 213, with reference to Lipsius, and p. 255, n. 53. See also most recently G. Chittolini, 'The "Private", the "Public", the State', *Journal of Modern History*, 67, supplement (1995), pp. S34–S61.
64. Enenkel, *Sejanus*, pp. 43, 57–8.
65. Cf. Besold, *Axiomata*.
66. Cf. Peck, *Court Patronage and Corruption*, p. 173: 'If the language of law and religion enphasised responsibility to the public commonwealth, writings on the courtier stressed his or her private relationship to the king.'
67. See above, note 35.
68. See Vann, *Making*, pp. 85–6. Still useful is L. T. Spittler, 'Geschichte des wirtembergischen Geheimen Ratscollegiums', in *idem, Sämmtliche Werke*, ed. K. Wächter, xiii (Stuttgart and Tübingen, 1837), pp. 279–452, at pp. 331–9. The new Privy Council was expressly created to prevent favourites and chamber secretaries or mere courtiers from exercising political influence and its members had to swear an oath to act not just in the prince's but also in the country's and the Estates' interest.

8

Staying in Power: The Count-Duke of Olivares

J. H. ELLIOTT

One day in September 1625, some four years after the accession of Philip IV as King of Spain, a Madrid scrivener interrupted the lunch of a royal official responsible for public order in the capital, saying that he had urgent news for his ears alone. A neighbour of his, a maker of leather jerkins called Antonio Díaz, had discovered that his wife had been administering him certain potions to make him 'love her well'. These potions had been provided by another neighbour, a woman called Leonor. When he taxed Leonor with attempting to cast a spell over him, she told him what she had already told his wife – that the potions would do him no harm, and that no less a person than the king was living proof of this. For the very same potions had been administered to his Majesty on the orders of the Count of Olivares (pls 24 and 41–6), to ensure that he would retain his hold over the king's affections. Later investigations indicated that, in addition to the administration of potions, Leonor's magical arts had included casting spells over the king's handkerchief and strips of the royal shoe-leather.[1]

Allegations of sorcery and enchantment were common currency among those who aspired to bring about the overthrow of favourites. In Madrid, where they provided a continuous accompaniment to the twenty-two years of Olivares' rule, they surfaced in an unusually sophisticated form in 1635 when Calderón presented his court spectacle, *El mayor encanto, amor*, on the island that had been built in the lake of the gardens of the new palace of the Buen Retiro. This was transformed for the occasion into Circe's island. It was widely alleged at the time that the king was being prevented by Olivares from leading his armies on campaign against the French, and the audience, beginning with Philip himself, would have had no difficulty in equating Circe with Olivares and Ulysses with the king held in thrall by his favourite.[2] This was a text that needed little decoding. Philip, like Ulysses, must open his eyes to the truth, turn his back on the seductive delights of the pleasure palace built for him by his favourite, and rise to the responsibilities of his royal office.

The allegation that a monarch had fallen victim to the exercise of magical arts was a convenient device for criticizing his rule without subverting the majesty of his kingship. But it may also have responded to a psychological need in the political culture of early modern European societies, susceptible as they were at every level to allegations of the role of malign influences in human affairs. It was not easy for nobles and grandees who saw themselves collectively as the king's natural counsellors to accept the fact that, of his own free will, he had placed all his trust in a single individual, an omnicompetent minister. If, as happened in the Spain of Olivares, that minister remained dominant for year after year, in spite of glaring mistakes and failures of policy, it was natural to assume that he had acquired some special and improper influence over the monarch. At the very least, such an assumption made it easier for the opposition to explain, not least to itself, what otherwise seemed inexplicable – its continuing failure to dislodge an unpopular minister from the royal favour.

Although explanations of allegedly irrational royal behaviour in terms of bewitchment contained a large element of self-deception, they also hinted at an underlying truth. The magic might not be so crudely administered as it was by Leonor with her magic potions, but in a system of government in which the personal and the institutional coexisted in uneasy combination the minister–favourite needed gifts and skills beyond the ordinary, first to win, and then to retain, the confidence of his king. In particular, he needed, if not the arts of the magician, at least a high degree of psychological insight – an ability to see into the darker recesses of the monarch's personality – in order to respond to every changing royal mood and avoid some fatal step which would lose him his master's trust. Both Olivares and Richelieu possessed this insight to an almost uncanny extent, and it played a vital part in their retention of power for twenty years or more.[3]

In making the most of this insight, Richelieu possessed one important advantage that Olivares lacked – the influence and prestige conferred by clerical status. Richelieu played with great skill the role of the stern but forgiving father-confesssor to a monarch racked by a morbid fear of the devil and damnation. Given the complexities of Louis XIII's tortured personality, the cardinal no doubt needed this additional advantage in his dealings with his royal master. But even Philip, with his more docile temperament, required careful handling. The obsequious self-abasement that Olivares imposed upon himself in order to win the initial favour of a prince to whom at the beginning he was personally antipathetic included the famous episode of his kissing the prince's chamber-pot;[4] and, even when Philip's confidence was gained, the count could never take it for granted. Philip was malleable but he also possessed a streak of obstinacy, and Olivares' enemies were ready to pounce at any hint of a false move.

Retaining Philip's favour therefore required as much thought and energy as the initial winning of it – something that does not seem to have been true of the relationship between Philip's father and *his* favourite, the Duke of Lerma (pl. 33). All we know about Philip III suggests that his sense of personal inadequacy when confronted by the awesome burdens of his royal office made him turn with a profound sense of relief to Lerma as his *alter ego*. Philip IV, too, suffered from feelings of personal inadequacy, but he was more conscious than his father of the need to rise to the occasion and perform his royal duties. He also had more spirit, and a livelier intelligence. This demanded of Olivares constant circumspection in his dealings with his royal master.

The circumspection, however, was accompanied by a high-risk strategy. Olivares' own sense of the high importance of Spanish kingship, and of the political necessity of deploying the full panoply of royal power in order to promote his programme of reforms, forced him to write a script for Philip IV which, if carried to its logical conclusion, would eventually involve his own exclusion from it. Olivares' programme demanded a *Felipe el Grande* – Philip the Great – a king of Spain as politically astute as Ferdinand the Catholic, as heroic in war as Charles V, and as just and conscientious as Philip II. But, by definition, such a paragon would have no need of a favourite. If Philip could indeed be transformed into this paragon, what place remained for Olivares in the order of things?

The grooming of the king for greatness would, of course, take time. Philip was sixteen when he came to the throne in 1621, and for much of the decade Olivares could successfully present himself to the young monarch as the man best equipped to educate him in the varied arts of kingship. This gave him the opportunity to rebuke Philip when he strayed from the path of duty, and in so doing to increase the dependence upon him of a monarch whose aspirations to glory were accompanied by a dispiriting awareness of his own need to be kept up to the mark if they were ever to be realized. In a famous exchange in 1626, when Olivares, not for the first nor for the last time, requested permission to retire from the royal service because the king was failing to apply himself to his duties, Philip replied in words which speak volumes about Olivares' success in establishing himself in the role of guardian of the king's better self. 'Count,' the royal reply began, 'I am determined to do as you ask of me both for my own sake and yours, and your request can in no way be looked upon as excessive temerity by someone as conscious as I am of your zeal and your love. I will do what you ask, Count, and I return your paper with my reply so that you can include it in your entailed estate, to show your descendants how they should speak to their kings. ... '[5]

Those words, 'how they should speak to their kings', emphasize the supreme importance to the favourite of finding the right language in which to address his royal master. This language, as Philip makes clear at the end of his reply, must not be self-serving – it must, he writes, be 'free of human consideration and interest'. Olivares succeeded in forging such a language for himself in his dealings with Philip, although it had to be adapted to new circumstances as the king matured and the relationship changed. It was a language at once deferential and frank, and its persistent theme was that of disinterestedness – a theme depicted on the title-page of *El Fernando*, a heroic poem by Olivares' friend the Count of La Roca, where the Atlas figure of the count-duke is portrayed on the left as naked of interest and, on the right, as clothed with valour (pl. 24).

In choosing to emphasize this theme above all others, Olivares was consciously pitting himself against the traditional image of the self-serving favourite. He refused to use the word *valido* or *privado* of himself, preferring always to be known as a 'minister', or as 'the king's faithful minister'.[6] This same theme of disinterested minister was echoed by his admirers and publicists – by the Count of La Roca in his *Fragmentos históricos de la vida de Don Gaspar de Guzmán*, completed at the end of 1628, and by Francisco de Quevedo in his sycophantic play of 1629, *Cómo ha de ser el privado*, even if Quevedo himself continues to use the offending word *privado*, albeit with a clear intention of sanitizing it.[7] The play's hero, the Marquis of Valisero (a transparent anagram of Olivares), adopts exactly the same stance and the same kind of language as those adopted by Olivares when he sought to guide and control the policies of his royal master.

The stance was that of the minister who tells the truth, however unwelcome, while insisting that it was for the king himself to make the final decision. It was precisely in 1629, the year of Quevedo's play, that the relationship between Olivares and the king went through an unusually rough passage, which for many at court seemed to presage the count-duke's imminent downfall. The two men came into conflict over Philip's expressed determination to leave Spain to assume personal command of his armies in Italy, at a time of acute crisis for the Monarchy both in Flanders and in the Mantuan War. Philip was being openly urged by the count-duke's enemies to assert his independence, and their carefully orchestrated campaign was well designed to play on the young king's well-known cravings for glory on the battlefield.

In the flurry of papers exchanged between king and favourite over this contentious issue, Olivares assumes the role of the cautious counsellor who insists on pointing out the practical difficulties that a headstrong monarch seemed determined to ignore.[8] 'This', he writes at the end of one of his memoranda, 'is the overall plan for this great movement of arms, drawn up by someone who is totally opposed to it. . . . '[9] In producing the plan, however reluctantly, the count-duke was simply performing his ministerial duty as he conceived it. That duty, as he explained in another of his papers, was the logical outcome of historical developments. Ever since affairs of state in Europe had been conducted, as he put it, with 'policy and method', no prince had been able to attend to them full-time. It was therefore the duty of the minister to prepare carefully digested statements of the pros and cons of a particular line of action, so that the prince could make as informed a choice as possible.[10]

This, as Olivares saw it, was the fundamental argument for the existence of a single, omnicompetent minister, a figure far removed from the old-style favourite. Possessed at once of a mastery over the mass of business generated by the new bureaucratic state, and of a rectitude which sprang from absolute dedication to the royal service, such a minister was ideally placed to provide the wise and disinterested counsel that would enable a hard-pressed monarch to reach his solitary decisions. The idealized image of the minister–favourite's role was to provide the foundations for the working relationship established between Olivares and the king once the storms of 1629 were past. The days of Philip's tutelage were now over. In August 1629 the king produced a state document of a kind which – in the admiring words of Olivares to his colleagues – no other ruler of Spain since Ferdinand the Catholic would have been capable of producing by his own unaided effort.[11] The working minister had now created what he had always claimed it had been his intention to create – the effective counterpart to a working minister in a working monarch.

The new relationship held, in spite of periodic difficulties, like those of 1635 when Philip's aspirations to become a warrior–king reasserted themselves. It was a relationship cemented by a shared servitude to the overwhelming necessities of the state. During the 1630s Philip was putting in long hours at his desk. Olivares, for his part, worked without respite, and let everyone know it. The parade of unremitting labour was itself a useful weapon in his armoury, since it helped to foster the impression of his indispensability in the eyes of the king. Careful, as always, to leave the decisions to the monarch, his language remained a language of deference, laced at moments of crisis with expressions of self-abasement. Periodically he would ask for permission to leave office, as in a letter of 1642 in which, after prostrating himself yet again at the king's feet, he observed that the most miserable university professor is allowed to retire after twenty years of service, and he had already served twenty-one.[12] But these offers, however genuine they may have been at the time, were nonetheless made in the knowledge that the king's need of him was, if anything, even greater than his own need of the king. Philip had become dependent on the untiring efforts of a sleepless minister who gave him unstinting devotion and addressed him with a reverence that bordered on adulation.

The king later admitted this condition of dependency, at least implicitly. When he finally gave Olivares leave to retire in January 1643, he announced his intention of ruling on his own, explaining in a letter to the count-duke's son-in-law that 'the burden of government and the management of affairs will now depend directly on my person, for with the Count gone I dare not entrust to anybody what I entrusted to him'.[13] Some months later he wrote to his confidante, Sor María de Agreda, assuring her that he was resolute in his determination to turn away from his former style of government. Although, he wrote, 'there are some who aspire to *valimiento* (for this is a very natural human condition), they are deceived. I will try to *valerme* [make use of] all of them, each and every one where most appropriate. ...'[14] For the second half of his reign he struggled hard to keep his word, although in practice Don Luis de Haro discreetly carried out many of the duties formerly exercised by his uncle the count-duke. Always in the background there must have loomed over Philip the shade of Olivares, summoning him to greatness (pl. 25).

The count-duke's skill in moulding a monarch who would continue to see the world through his eyes, and who would still struggle to play the part written for him after the man who combined the roles of playwright and stage-manager had left the scene for good, suggests the strength of the hold that he gained over the king. It was a hold which understandably drove his enemies, during those twenty-two long years, to frustration and despair. But is that hold – achieved, as here suggested, by a shrewd insight into the personality of his royal master, and by a capacity to involve him in a shared world of service to the ideal of the greatness and *reputación* of a king of Spain – sufficient of itself to explain his survival in power for so long?

In Spain, as in the other monarchies of early-seventeenth-century Europe, no constitutional mechanism existed for removing an unpopular minister or favourite from power, although the English were at this moment struggling to achieve this through the parliamentary device of impeachment. Short of armed revolt or assassination, therefore, favourites were irremovable without the consent of the monarch. In France, the enemies of Concini removed him by assassination, while those of Richelieu tried, and failed, to remove him by revolt. They ordered such matters differently in Spain. A relatively domesticated nobility might mutter and cabal, as it seems to have done in the Duke of Medinaceli's house in the 1630s,[15] but this was a nobility that had lost the habit of revolt. With no upper chamber in the Cortes of Castile to provide a constitutional forum for opposition, all the grandees could manage by way of concerted action was collective withdrawal from court, as happened in 1634 and again in 1642 during the count-duke's final months of power.[16] While such mass abstentions presumably sent a strong message to the king, they still left the initiative in his hands.

The joint action of the grandees, in any event, came very late in the day, and looks like a manifestation more of collective weakness than of collective strength. This weakness is all the more striking when their loathing of the count-duke is taken into account. The Duke of Lerma had remained in power for twenty years, but he had used his massive influence and powers of patronage to bind the great aristocratic houses to his own, constructing in the process a vast network of kinship and clientage which aimed to leave nobody out in the cold.[17] Olivares, by contrast, almost seems to have gone out of his way to slight and humiliate the grandees, eschewing the favours and the *douceurs* which, as they receded into the past, made the years of Lerma's ascendancy look increasingly like a golden age for the great houses of Castile.

Yet, in spite of refusing to play by the rules, Olivares held on to power for even longer than Lerma. If his skill in shaping the king to his own designs was the key to his success, other important elements too must surely have come into play, for (as the career of Alvaro de Luna had shown) not even the most favoured of royal favourites can hold on to power indefinitely when the political establishment is ranged solidly against him. Olivares clearly benefited from the unwillingness of the aristocracy to challenge openly the king's choice of minister–favourite in a society in which loyalty to the monarch had been inculcated by countless theoretical arguments reinforced by at least a century of effective political practice. But no favourite operates in a political and social vacuum, and the count-duke naturally made use of a whole range of devices to buttress his hold on power.

In some ways the devices he did not use, or used to only a limited degree, are almost as revealing of his approach and style as those to which he did in fact resort. Fear undoubtedly played a part in his retention of power, but the apparatus of repression deployed by Olivares looks unimpressive in comparison with that deployed by Richelieu. The censorship laws were tightened in 1627, but even in their revised form they do not seem to have been very effective in preventing the circulation of pasquins and anti-Olivares tracts.[18] A special junta for the enforcement of obedience was set up in 1634,[19] and there were one or two spectacular cases of persecution of individuals who had fallen foul of the regime, like Don Fadrique de Toledo, or Francisco de Quevedo, arrested under cover of darkness in December 1639 and summarily incarcerated in the convent of San Marcos in León, where he remained in miserable captivity until after the count-duke's fall from power.[20] But these seem to have been relatively isolated episodes, and there is little indication of the ruthless repressiveness with which Richelieu treated dissidents and rivals.

Nor did pomp and circumstance represent essential concomitants to the power of Olivares, as they did to that of Richelieu. There could hardly have been a more striking contrast than that between the cardinal, looking every inch a prince of the church as he swept into a room with his impressive entourage, and the count-duke bustling around the palace with state papers stuck into his hatband and dangling from his waist, reminding those who saw him of nothing so much as a scarecrow.[21] At least from the mid-1620s his table was austere, his personal expenditure moderate for someone of his status and position,[22] and neither his apartments in the palace nor his country retreat at Loeches boasted the splendours that surrounded Richelieu in the Palais Cardinal.

If neither the apparatus of terror nor the apparatus of pomp played a significant part in Olivares' retention of power, we must turn elsewhere for explanations of his political longevity. Patronage, inevitably, was a potent weapon in his hands, but it was a patronage used far more sparingly and selectively than it had been used by Lerma. Given the programme with which he identified himself as he staked out his claims to power and favour, this relative parsimony in the dispensing of patronage was inevitable. He had set out to represent himself as the antithesis of the Duke of Lerma, whose profligacy had reduced the royal finances to their current straits, and it is not therefore surprising that his first known memorandum for the king should have been a manifesto against the indiscriminate distribution of *mercedes*.[23] Once he had taken his stand on this issue, it became impossible for him, even if he had so wished, to imitate the profligacy of his predecessor.

But, like all seventeenth-century favourites, he used his command of the resources of the crown to surround himself with his own 'creatures' (*hechuras*), and to build up a following of loyal supporters. In common with his contemporaries elsewhere in Europe, he turned in the first instance to his own extended kinship group, the Guzmáns, the Haros and the Zúñigas, rewarding them with palace appointments, viceroyalties and seats at the council table. By seventeenth-century standards his own hands were relatively clean, but some of his relatives, like his brother-in-law the Count of Monterrey, who was appointed to the lucrative viceroyalty of Naples, made fortunes from their offices.

The building up of his family clan – the *parentela*, as it was called – created a power-group at court and around the person of the king which effectively held rival family groupings at arm's length, and to some extent kept the monarch isolated from criticisms of the favourite which could have endangered his hold on power. At the same time Olivares cast the mantle of his favour and protection over selected members of the royal administration, who in turn would dedicate themselves as unremittingly as himself to the royal service, and support him loyally when the going became rough. In this way he created over the years, from among the ranks of the aristocracy and the bureaucracy alike, a group of *olivaristas*, all of them, as the count-duke once observed, 'embarked on our ship'.[24] It was only when some of the *olivaristas*, and especially a handful of his most influential relatives, turned against him towards the end, in a bid to save themselves from the shipwreck which they saw was coming, that the count-duke became vulnerable to a concerted assault from his enemies.

Control of the king and control of the court and administration were both essential to the survival of a seventeenth-century minister–favourite. But increasingly there was a third desideratum – the control of public opinion. 'It is always important', wrote Olivares in his famous secret memorandum of 1624 for the king, 'to pay attention to the voice of the people.'[25] Diego Saavedra Fajardo, whose political philosophy was shaped by his experience of the Olivares years, echoed this observation in his *Idea of a Christian Prince*: 'The *valimiento* is very subject to the people, because if the people abhor the favourite, the prince cannot sustain him against the *voz común*.'[26]

For much of his period of office Olivares was in fact a walking refutation of this axiom. Although almost universally detested from the later 1620s onwards, he was effectively sustained by his prince year after year against the *voz común*. But he was and remained very conscious of the need to present his case as effectively as possible before the court of public opinion, or at least of that section of public opinion represented by the elite in Madrid and the provinces. He and his friends had swept to power in 1621 on a wave of reformist sentiment. In the Cortes of Castile, in sections of the royal administration and in the municipal oligarchies, the tide of opinion had moved strongly against a dying regime which was identified with corruption and gross mismanagement at home and humiliation abroad. Making the most of the groundswell of sentiment in favour of change, Olivares effectively shaped a language of power which would play as well before the public as before the king.

With its heavy reliance on such words as *reformación* and *reputación* it was a language well attuned to the harsher and more austere age that was dawning in the 1620s as Europe returned to war after two spendthrift decades of at least relative peace.[27] It was also a language indebted to the fashionable writings of Justus Lipsius, whose insistence on such concepts as 'obedience', 'discipline' and 'authority' held a natural appeal for ministers desperately seeking to tighten their grip on societies in which corporate privilege and archaic custom impeded effective mobilization for war.

This Lipsian language of duty, service and obedience became pervasive in the Spain of Olivares as the struggle to sustain its enormous military commitments became increasingly intense. 'We Spaniards', wrote the count-duke in 1632, 'are very good when subject to rigorous obedience, but if we are left to our own devices we are the worst of the lot.'[28] This was the message purveyed by the publicists and spin-doctors of the Olivares regime, the jurists who insisted on the overriding importance of 'necessity', and the playwrights who exalted the absolute authority of the king.

But it remains uncertain how far this authoritarian language, or the accompanying glorification of the king and the regime in the theatre and in the visual imagery of the Hall of Realms, the great hall in the palace of the Buen Retiro,[29] effectively contributed to the count-duke's continuing hold on power. The identification of the authority of the king with the wishes of the minister undoubtedly made opposition more difficult, since resistance to the minister looked like treason to the king. On the other hand, by the later 1630s the image that the regime had sought to fashion for itself was raising grave problems of credibility. It spoke of the need for sacrifice, and yet spent millions on indulging the king in his pleasure-palace of the Retiro. It trumpeted its victories, but failed to win its wars. It rode roughshod over privilege in the name of 'necessity', and yet claimed that its actions enjoyed the sanction of law. When another of the count-duke's spin-doctors, the regime's official historiographer Virgilio Malvezzi, wrote in 1639 that 'this monarchy is a government of the king and of law, or rather of law alone, not because the king cannot do what he wishes, but because he does not wish for more than what he should',[30] his remark could only provoke incredulity. This was not how the king's government was perceived in the country at large.

Control of the king, control of the court, control of public opinion – it was the last of these that was the first to go. The tide of opinion seems to have turned against the count-duke as early as 1627, when the king's nearly fatal illness laid bare the full extent of his government's unpopularity.[31] The outbreak of war with France in 1635 may have brought a momentary respite, but any solidarity provoked by an upsurge of patriotism in Castile was rapidly dissipated by the king's failure to abandon his pleasure-palace and lead his armies into battle.

Thereafter, the hatred of the regime, inside as well as outside Castile, was almost palpable.

And yet it survived for another seven years. Given the chasm that had now opened between the language of the regime and the language of the country, its manipulation of the language of power would hardly seem to have been integral to its capacity for survival. This was a regime which, like that of Charles I in England, was talking during the 1630s largely to itself.

Clearly we must look beyond the language to the substance – to the massively imposing figure of a hyperactive, astute and immensely dedicated minister, whose fertile mind ranged creatively across the European military and diplomatic chessboard as he prepared for each new move, and who possessed the energy, the stamina and the sheer force of personality to browbeat into compliance the generals, the ministers and the bankers on whom he depended to sustain the vast effort required for the prosecution of the war. In many ways, at least until his world began to collapse around him in 1640 with the rebellions of Catalonia and Portugal, it was a virtuoso performance, which itself seemed to offer the best of arguments for his retention of power.

But it was a performance that was called forth, and made possible, by the demands of international diplomacy and war, as the two titans, France and Spain, strove for hegemony in Europe; and it is even possible that in part at least Olivares survived because Richelieu survived, with the converse no less valid. If either minister had fallen during the course of the 1630s, the other's hold on power might well have been weakened by the disappearance of the enemy; and it would hardly seem a coincidence that the death of Richelieu was followed within a matter of weeks by the overthrow of Olivares. With the cardinal gone, the count-duke hardly seemed as indispensable as he had seemed while he lived.

Yet indispensability is itself a relative concept, and one heavily dependent on the terms in which it is defined. The man who did most to define it in the Spain of Olivares was Olivares himself. By insisting first that only his programme of reforms could save Castile from disaster, and then that war was the only way to peace, he effectively created an environment in which he could hold himself out as uniquely qualified to serve as the king's right-hand man. As he presented it, there was no alternative either to the policies or to the man. Within his own terms of reference he may indeed have been right. The king, at least, believed him. Contemporaries preferred to put it differently: Circe had worked her magic arts and held Ulysses in thrall.

Notes

1. Gregorio Marañón, *El Conde-Duque de Olivares*, 3rd edn (Madrid, 1952), pp. 195–8; Adolfo de Castro, *El Conde-Duque de Olivares y el Rey Felipe IV* (Cadiz, 1846), libro VII ('Ilustraciones') for the *Informe* of Miguel de Cárdenas; Archivo Histórico Nacional (Madrid), Inquisición, legajo 494, no. 38, fols 70–3, 'Nacimiento, vida y costumbres de Don Gaspar de Guzmán, Conde Duque de Olivares'.

2. See Margaret Rich Greer, *The Play of Power* (Princeton, 1991), pp. 87–94.
3. See J. H. Elliott, *Richelieu and Olivares* (Cambridge, 1984), ch. 2 ('Masters and Servants'), for an examination of the relationship of the two ministers to their monarchs.
4. J. H. Elliott, *The Count-Duke of Olivares: The Statesman in an Age of Decline* (New Haven and London, 1986), p. 30.
5. John H. Elliott and José F. de la Peña, *Memoriales y cartas del Conde Duque de Olivares*, 2 vols (Madrid, 1978–80), i, doc. xi.
6. Francisco Tomás y Valiente, *Los validos en la monarquía española del siglo XVII*, 2nd revised edn (Madrid, 1990), p. 106.
7. See 'Quevedo and the Count-Duke of Olivares', in J. H. Elliott, *Spain and its World, 1500–1700* (New Haven and London, 1989), ch. 9, esp. pp. 196–201.
8. Elliott and la Peña, *Memoriales y cartas*, ii, docs i–x.
9. *Ibid.*, p. 31.
10. *Ibid.*, p. 57.
11. Elliott, *Count-Duke*, pp. 385–6.
12. Elliott and la Peña, *Memoriales y cartas*, ii, doc. xviii, p. 219.
13. Elliott, *Count-Duke*, pp. 648–9.
14. *Cartas de Sor María de Jesús de Agreda y de Felipe IV*, ed. Carlos Seco Serrano, Biblioteca de Autores Españoles, 108 (Madrid, 1958), p. 7, letter of 16 October 1643.
15. Elliott, *Count-Duke*, p. 557.
16. *Ibid.*, pp. 479 and 646.
17. The ramifications of Lerma's patronage network are explored by Antonio Feros in his doctoral dissertation, 'The King's Favorite, the Duke of Lerma: Power, Wealth and Court Culture during the Reign of Philip III of Spain, 1598–1621' (The Johns Hopkins University, 1994).
18. Elliott, *Count-Duke*, pp. 307 and 364.
19. *Ibid.*, pp. 478–9.
20. See 'Quevedo and the Count-Duke of Olivares', in Elliott, *Spain and its World*, ch. 9.
21. Elliott, *Count-Duke*, p. 283.
22. See Antonio Herrera García, *El estado de Olivares* (Seville, 1990), esp. pp. 223–4.
23. Elliott and la Peña, *Memoriales y cartas*, i, doc. i.
24. Archivo General de Simancas, Estado, legajo 2713, Olivares to Monterrey, 30 October 1629.
25. Elliott and la Peña, *Memoriales y cartas*, i, doc. iv, p. 62.
26. Diego Saavedra Fajardo, *Empresas políticas: Idea de un príncipe político-cristiano*, ed. Quintín Aldea Vaquero, 2 vols (Madrid, 1976), i, p. 483 (*empresa* 50).
27. For further discussion of the language of the Olivares regime, see J. H. Elliott, *Lengua e imperio en la España de Felipe IV* (Salamanca, 1994).
28. Elliott and la Peña, *Memoriales y cartas*, ii, doc. xi, p. 76.
29. See Jonathan Brown and J. H. Elliott, *A Palace for a King: The Buen Retiro and the Court of Philip IV* (New Haven and London, 1980), ch. 6.
30. Virgilio Malvezzi, *La libra de Grivilio Vezzalmi* (Pamplona, 1639), p. 113.
31. Elliott, *Count-Duke*, p. 314.

9
Words and Wealth in the France of Richelieu and Mazarin

OREST RANUM

In recent years Richard Bonney and Joseph Bergin have not only helped to establish the public and private fiscal and financial history of France under Richelieu (pls 26 and 47–57) and Mazarin (pl. 27), they have brought to light some particularly revealing phrases and words about money which they discovered in the mass of archival material that has yielded more secrets than anyone thought possible.[1] What perhaps remains to be done is to sharpen the analysis of phrases and thoughts that were typically used by the governing elites at the time. The meaning that specific words about wealth held for various groups and professions is at present unclear. Scrutinizing words and phrases about wealth may help to clarify attitudes not only about rank and wealth, but about the state, commerce, consumables and religious beliefs. In this essay I explore what the two cardinals say about money, the state and their personal fortunes.

Would it be historically sound to suggest that the words, the metaphors and the innuendo that prompted thought about money changed little or not at all in the decades that separate 1624 and 1661? If the semantic fields of the words about wealth changed little in this period, it would be particularly significant given that this was a time when French as a language was being reformed. The movement generally known as classicization obliged not only the literary but the political and the religious elites to choose their words in conformity with cultural principles of *bienséance*, or risk being characterized as vulgar or out of date. Prompted by a more general courtly social and cultural movement, this effort to rid French of off-colour and popular words resulted in an increased reluctance to speak specifically about money in polite conversation.[2] And never, perhaps, before the 1630s had there been so much borrowing, lending, office purchasing and luxury spending; yet it became increasingly less *bienséant* to talk about money. These were also decades of unprecedented increases in the fiscal power of the state. Never before had so much revenue been raised with consequent political and social protest, yet the increased power of the state seems not to have resulted from new words about wealth or from new meanings given to existing words.

There were three quite distinct sets of words about wealth that the two cardinals and the governing elites could use during this period. Not a language, not a discourse, not quite a historical tradition, each of these sets of words had historical and cultural links to distinct professional groups.[3] Hearing one or more of these words from a prelate, a man of the law or a projecting banker–merchant would prompt distinct mental associations with other words. The professional and cultural characteristics of these groups gave specific meanings to words that were part of the general French vocabulary. *Bienfaits, crédit, grâces* and *corruption*, along with *argent* and *accroissement*, had quite distinct meanings for each of these groups. Indeed, the distinctiveness of each set of words was so great that it permitted Richelieu to live as he did without feeling culpable when the reforming Catholic clergy spoke to him about ecclesiastical poverty. This same distinctiveness permitted him to ignore, for example, *parlementaire* charges that he was financially corrupt, because he believed it was in the nature of kingship to reward subjects liberally for their services. As both a statesman and a thinker, Richelieu never found it necessary to refute arguments about ecclesiastical vows of poverty, or about corruption as violation of public trust for private gain. His stance derived from the distinctiveness of each of the sets of words.

The first set of words about wealth had early Christian origins, but it had recently been restated and given exemplary force at the highest level of the governing elites by such prelates as Bérulle.[4] The insistence on poverty for consistency with the life of Christ, and on charity as an active life principle, constituted a logically coherent ensemble of words that could be used to stimulate reform or launch attacks against the clergy for living in luxury. Every prelate in the period 1624–61 heard these words forcefully articulated in sermons by preachers, notably those belonging to the reforming religious orders.

The second set of words had neo-Stoic origins; and among the nobility, and more particularly the robe, it was solidly articulated both in public legislation about recusation in cases involving kin to the sixth degree and in philosophies of life expressed by Montaigne, Charron, du Vair and others.[5] The words 'service' or 'duty', 'office', 'reward', 'benefit' and *grâces* constituted a veritable civic and individual code of conduct that carefully prescribed attitudes towards wealth. The controversy over the *paulette*, as summarized in the differences of opinion between Bellièvre and Sully, is indicative of the richness and complexity of this set of words – which Sully in the end rejected, pressing Henri IV for the edict that made office heritable according to specific terms that, for Bellièvre, violated principles of probity in rendering justice.[6]

Richelieu's political thought rests on an emphatic notion of service to an abstract principle, that is, the state, and of reward for this service.[7] Mazarin also used the word 'service' when writing about the state, but his usage carries older, sixteenth-century meanings.[8] For Mazarin, service also often meant something more personal – that is, service for the king or the regent, and not for the state.

His sense of state service has resonances not unlike what John Guy has found in the feudal, rather than the neo-classical, meaning of counselling.[9]

If 'poverty' was the most operative word in the first set of words, the word 'appropriate' (decorum, *bienséance*) played this role in neo-Stoic thought about wealth and rank. It is almost impossible to overemphasize the all-pervasiveness and force of the Ciceronian notion of appropriateness for seventeenth-century governing elites. J.-P. Labatut's findings about the correlation between rank and fortune among the dukes and peers confirm the hypothesis that there was a relationship between the meaning of words, the force and the conviction with which they were used, and statistically verifiable correlations between wealth and rank.[10] Clearly the notion of appropriateness extended far beyond the confines of robe corporations and culture. And when Louis XIII created a new duchy, an appropriate amount of land that would produce an appropriate income to sustain the lifestyle appropriate for a duke was either in hand or was provided as a gift from the crown to a favourite.[11] Indeed, these gifts may often be interpreted as the result of the notion of appropriateness at work. When the *frondeur* Councillor Broussel, with his reputation for probity, continued his attacks on Mazarin's ministry, *frondeurs* spoke of raising funds to provide dowries for the old man's daughters, so that they might make appropriate marriages.[12] And in the thirteen house designs published in the first French treatise on general domestic architecture, which Le Muet intended 'for all sorts of persons', the allocation of spaces, the decoration and the other marks of prestige considered appropriate for a given rank are worked out.[13]

To be sure, the conspicuous consumption by tax farmers and fiscal families that judges attacked so passionately with their neo-Stoic words 'peculation' and 'corruption' for inappropriateness, or *malséance*, was, in fact, expenditure necessary for the *financiers'* credibility among their own social and financial groups.[14] Borrowing huge sums, or ensuring that the advances involved in bidding for tax contracts would be repaid, required visible signs of wealth. High consumption among fiscal officials dates at least from the days of Jacques Coeur. Deemed a 'mal nécessaire' by Richelieu, who probably did not consciously understand the need for the *financiers* to keep up an opulent front before their colleagues, it is evident that the word *corruption* in the neo-Stoic sense is rarely found in the correspondence of the *financiers* or in the cardinal's prose.[15] Building country houses, collecting art and coins and accumulating capital surpassed what was appropriate for their social rank. We shall see how Richelieu's understanding of and use of Laffemas' words about *argent* and growth impeded him from moralizing about financiers' behaviour. Strange as it may seem it was possible for Richelieu to use all the neo-Stoic words about state service, and yet avoid alluding to appropriate wealth and the dangers of avarice and display.

The third set of words about money had more recent origin: the thought of sixteenth-century Spanish casuists, of jurists such as Bodin and of non-university-trained projectors such as Henri IV's personal accountant, Barthélemy de Laffemas.[16] Through the latter's writings and his years of experience with merchants and virtually everyone at court, Laffemas launched a set of words about gold, silver and the state, and about growth understood as increased wealth and power. For the projectors, the words 'exchange', 'value' and *biens* did not merely connote things and actions, they had conceptual powers as words, and they almost equate the increased wealth of France with the growth of the state. The increased wealth of France, and of the French, at the expense of foreigners, is deemed not only a necessary but an ethically upright activity. In this set of words, the accumulation of wealth is described as a moral good. The projectors' set of words about wealth almost directly contradicted the neo-Stoic notion about appropriateness according to rank.

Not all words about money were part of these three groups of words, but together these groups, their distinctiveness and their corporate foundations, made up what the governing elites could say and think about money. To be sure, there were also rhetorical techniques, and rabble-rousing cries such as *maltôtier*, but these were rarely used by the elites except, in that world that was upside-down, by the writers of *Mazarinades*. A rhetoric about numbers on fiscal statements is also apparent in Richelieu's or Mazarin's desire for an activist foreign policy that might well include a costly war. Letters to Louis XIII are filled with assurances about the availability of funds.[17] When the rebellious judges of the Parlement wanted to raise troops in 1649, the figures they cited about costs and revenue sources were largely pulled out of the air.[18] Though these estimates were quite fanciful, they carried the day. Usually it was impossible to verify the figures bandied about in council, so a decision would be made to raise troops with no very precise idea of their cost.

With these sets of words in mind, it is possible to ask why the monarchy as a whole seems to have used no one distinct set. The question at first seems *mal posée*. Clerics, lawyers and projectors could not have been expected to talk about the monarchy in the same way, except to express their love for it; yet they might all have thought the crown's rights and estates immense, despite the loss of revenue from their alienation. However, Louis XIII's subjects did not describe him as wealthy, nor was the king known to be magnanimous. Devout, neither a builder nor a collector, he did indeed live in a manner that seemed barely appropriate to his rank among other European monarchs.[19] Reformist circles urged funding the repurchase of the royal domain; but of course, like the repurchase of all venal offices, the proposal was never seriously acted upon.[20] When Richelieu accepted the royal anchorage rights on all foreign shipping into all ports as a reward (not a gift!) for his services at the siege of La Rochelle, he said not a word about the need to repurchase royal rights in order for the king to increase his own wealth.[21]

By its own set of words, the church was understood to be immensely wealthy. Large donations to the crown were therefore deemed not only appropriate, but necessary. Here is Louis XIII speaking to representatives of the clergy assembly of 1628:

Messieurs, I sent for you in order to tell you that I desire that you finish your assembly as promptly as you are able. As for the sum you offer me, 2,000,000 livres, I want much more, or nothing at all. It is a great shame for the welfare of the church and for all the realm ... that you do not wish to contribute a third of your wealth [*biens*]. It would be better used in this way than in the feasts you give every day. You show me necessity but are you not so many prelates and ecclesiastics who have a 100, 25, or 30 thousand livres of income? It is on these that the tithes and new levies should be raised, and not on the poor *curés.* ...[22]

The shift in thought from the whole church to the incomes of individual clergymen is significant, for the set of words about ecclesiastical wealth centred on the reform of the clergy as individuals, and not on the wealth of the church. However, when the king reported to Richelieu what he had said, it is doubtful that he was upbraiding him for being a rich prelate. The sense of household, of protection for his ministers and domestics, was very strong in Louis XIII, in a way that suspended typical or general criticism of their conduct to outside the council or household.

As a reforming and activist prelate–minister, Cardinal Bérulle was well known for his vow not to take church benefices. Writing to Richelieu, Bérulle said: 'It has pleased the king to give me the abbey of La Reaulle, and I have thanked him for it, but I must go to the source of this benefaction, and many others that I must cover over in silence because I do not know how to speak of them worthily enough.'[23] After suggesting that Richelieu was leading him to break his resolution to decline benefices, Bérulle continued: 'You wish me to take the liberty of informing you of my feelings and thoughts. I complain therefore, and grow sad ... and I say to Jesus Christ our Lord that I do not want any benefices at all that serve in the place of a recompense which on earth diminishes what I most desire, a portion of his holy *grâces*.'[24] In the following year, 1629, and while Father Joseph was close to the king, Louis informed Richelieu that he would be receiving the two 'best' abbeys of the recently deceased Grand Prieur Vendôme.

Richelieu humbly and immediately thanked the king but declined to accept them. After noting that it is possible to make inopportune requests of great kings, but that one ought not refuse their liberality, he humbly asked Louis to accept his refusal, saying:

I admit that my reluctance would be a crime, were it not founded on reason; His Majesty will approve since it comes, Sire ... from being in your council when the interests of your state obliged you to arrest this person [the Grand Prieur]; and thus it seems to me that I would go against the heart that it pleased God to give me if I were to profit from his misfortune and take a part of his remains [*dépouille*].[25]

Schoolboy casuistry? This was only the beginning of the story about the fate of the Grand Prieur's two best abbeys.

Louis then decided that Bérulle would have the abbeys.[26] The political atmosphere in early 1629 was already divisive in the council, as the devout party began firmly to express their doubts about the Italian campaign that was about to begin. Bérulle reports to Richelieu what he describes as the thoughts that are expressed here and there, all of which cast doubt on the current policy that would deepen the collision with Spain.[27] Having learnt of Richelieu's refusal of the two abbeys, Marillac wrote to him:

> The action you took regarding the benefices has two fine qualities: one involves a singular generosity, the other, a great and upright charity shorn of personal interest; it is greatly praised, and has upon the mind several very advantageous effects to show the affection that you bear for M. the Cardinal de Bérulle, and the esteem in which you hold him.[28]

Bérulle's subsequent thank-you letters to Richelieu suggest a less generous interpretation. First, Richelieu had informed him that he must take the revenues from these abbeys personally, and not turn them over to his new order, the Oratory. Bérulle writes:

> You continue to oblige me with so much excess that I receive more confusion than contentment from it, but you continue your projects and perfect your work. You have placed me in this condition, and you want to maintain it, owing you what I owe you, and which cannot be sufficiently expressed. . . . It is true that in honouring me, raising me up and obliging me according to the world, I remain weighed down before God with such a heavy weight that I must fear that it crushes me and causes me eternal confusion.[29]

The question of whether it was possible, under certain circumstances, to decline a royal reward merits much more scrutiny than can be given here. It is evident that Richelieu not only took personal satisfaction in creating an impression of disinterestedness and generosity towards another one of Marie de Médicis' collaborators, he personally engineered a rationalist undermining of the principle of (limited) ecclesiastical poverty as practised by one of France's most high-ranking and reforming prelates. Would the jeopardy to his soul not have given Bérulle a justification for declining the abbeys? Would accepting the abbeys involve more than spending a longer time in Purgatory? It is also possible that Richelieu knew Bérulle's character and could gamble that he would accept client dependency. The stakes were high. Bérulle's powers of persuasion were considerable. Had he lived until the Day of the Dupes, would he have rejected the obligation to Richelieu that was implicit in accepting these abbeys? Bérulle had the opportunity to settle accounts with the Master Accountant in Heaven, rather than face the choice between Richelieu's and Marie's foreign policies.

A last example of the use of the ecclesiastical set of words about poverty for the clergy concerns Richelieu's brother Alphonse, Cardinal Archbishop of Lyon and Primate of the Gauls, who complained to his brother that the superintendent of finance, Claude de Bullion, would not give him a special fund with which to pay domestics to spy on prelates who were attending an assembly of the clergy. It was customary to distribute *grâces* to facilitate voting large sums to the crown; but Alphonse wanted something more, and Bullion had refused him the special account for spies. The amounts were small, but it is evident that Alphonse did not want to use his own revenues for such a purpose. In reply Richelieu wrote: 'It is difficult and impossible to dispose M. de Bullion about what is necessary in such matters; but, if you please, inform me in cipher if you have some important occasion to use such funds; I shall do the impossible to provide them promptly.'[30] Richelieu does not specify the account from which he would draw the funds for spying, or whether they were ecclesiastical in origin.

Turning to the neo-Stoic set of words – that is, 'service', 'duty', 'benefit', 'gratitude', 'office' and *grâces* as well as 'peculation' and 'corruption' – their usage is so pervasive that it is possible to speculate that these words no longer had specific historical-ethical resonances. This was certainly not the case for Richelieu, for although not himself one of the philosophers who impressed the age with the originality of their thought, the cardinal nonetheless commented continually and philosophically on the ethical debates of his day, and these were largely between neo-Stoics and Catholic Reformation anti-Stoic reformers. For example, he warns against excessive royal liberality, arguing instead that recompensing service was more capable of establishing order in the realm.[31] He thus implicitly rejects the Senecan notion that giving an unsolicited gift, or favour, best assures the bonds of friendship between the prince and his councillor friends. Criticism of Louis XIII's liberality towards Cinq Mars remains oblique in the letters around the trial of the conspirators, but it was there for the king to read after the cardinal's death. The fruits of favour are rebellion. It is therefore not surprising that, in his thank-you letters to Marie and Louis, Richelieu always insists that the *grâces* he accepts are rewards for his service. These *grâces* may be more than he merits, or at least he claims they are, but they are rewards or recompenses, not gifts or favours. Before glancing at those letters, it is interesting to note that the cardinal alluded almost off-handedly to Louis and to 'the king's humour, which brings him to like to do things for persons who are almost unknown, more than he likes to do things for his intimates, allies or the friends of those who have the honour of serving him near his person'.[32] This bears testimony to the dilemmas and frustrations resulting from the expectations and competitiveness that characterized relations among sovereigns, ministers and householders in a court culture.[33]

In a reflective mood, Richelieu said: 'It is proper to kings to be *libéral*, and it is in imitation of God that they do good to their creatures, and those who are often considered the greatest kings did this the most. . . .'[34] This was written in reply to the thank-you letter from young Saint-Simon, who was rising rapidly in the king's household. Saint-Simon answered: 'I shall not attempt to pay with words for the honours that I receive from you . . . and the joy that is greater than my pen can convey.'[35] The metaphors about meanings beyond words were carefully honed in thank-you notes. The emphatic distinction between reward and gift (*récompense* and *grâces* or *faveur*) so important to Richelieu does not derive easily from Cicero's or Seneca's thought.[36]

In the *Testament politique* the cardinal takes up the subject of whether punishment or reward is the more fundamental instrument for wielding power, and he casuistically concludes that, if one had to get along without one of them, it would be better to dispense with punishment than with reward. While Machiavellian inspiration is evident, there are also indications that he was familiar with the general sixteenth-century debates over the question, notably those of Spanish moralists whose works were well represented in his library.[37]

In his own letters of thanks to sovereigns, Richelieu usually mentions the state, in effect depersonalizing the person who has rewarded him.[38] He seems to do everything the neo-Stoic set of words permits, to describe what he receives as rewards rather than gifts. There were, of course, gifts, not usually money, but objects such as the rosary he gave Marie de Médicis, and the crucifixes she gave him with the usual order to wear them 'pour l'amour de moy'.[39] To reward him for his services at La Rochelle, as Joseph Bergin has already noted, Marie gave Richelieu money to buy a château.[40] She specifically states that this is a reward for his services, and adds: 'You will have a better place to take relaxation and serve the king better. . . . If I could better express how much I esteem your services, it would also be with a good heart . . .'[41] When Marie de Médicis gave Richelieu money as a reward for his services, she specified what it was to be used for, almost as if she wanted the object purchased, and not the money itself, to be the reward.

Louis XIII did not usually write about rewards or gifts in his privy seal correspondence with the cardinal, or perhaps with anyone else. The letters patent granting Richelieu anchorage rights on all foreign vessels stopping in French ports were, their timing suggests, also a recompense for his service at La Rochelle.[42] Only prayers for their mutual health and categorical assurances of his support and affection were expressed in the privy seal letters to Richelieu. It seems likely that the alienation of royal domain such as customs rights had, by law, to proceed through a royal council, the chancery and a number of sovereign courts. Louis probably had a fairly good idea of the enormous recompense he was giving the cardinal, and was willing to quash protests from *grands* such as Guise in the inevitable litigation over these rights.

Louis' largesse with favourites such as Saint-Simon and Cinq Mars, like his mother's with Concini, suggests that they occasionally practised the Senecan gesture of free liberality as a technique of binding these persons to them. For Seneca the gesture of giving, not the gift, is the ultimate friendly act.[43] Only further research will clarify whether Louis had a philosophy about gift-giving and rewards that was consistently followed. His first minister, by contrast, attempted to act according to principles cast in neo-Stoic terms and to win others over to his views. Richelieu's rejection of Seneca's specific views on both clemency and benefits did not, however, remove him from the Stoic school of thought, or inhibit his ability to act forcefully with those who followed Seneca's views. Quite the contrary.

Stating that a recompense exceeds one's merit or asserting that 'words cannot express my gratitude' were conventional replies that linked service, reward and merit; but, while the first statement was continually used by Richelieu, the second was not. His views are consistent with his theology about grace, and the symmetry of these views is evident. While God's grace alone assured man's salvation, a sinner's ability to contribute to his personal salvation by good works remained an article in his faith. For him, service to the state was therefore a divinely required duty, and it was this conviction about working for the 'reign of God' that gave him the courage to pursue his policies, despite the sense of isolation, opposition and foreboding that inevitably followed. The congruence of divine and royal power would lead him to reject, in certain critical instances, the neo-Stoic principle of appropriateness, and put above all other principles the belief in an ethically grounded, limitless, divine power in the state.

There is no doubt that Richelieu was entirely familiar with neo-Stoic, largely robe, thought about corruption, which it defined as private gain from public trust. Though he did not totally engineer La Vieuville's disgrace, the cardinal undertook the quite difficult task of clearing the disgraced minister's clients from fiscal offices and tax farms. He wanted to know how the *chambre de justice* in the reign of Henry III had proceeded against tax farmers,[44] and he quickly developed a policy of systematic threat and terror to force disgraced *financiers* to pay heavy fines. As was always the case with the cardinal, his words about justice reflect the Greek concept of more-or-less-guilty, rather than the Roman guilty-or-not-guilty. And, for him, all this belonged to the sphere of expedients, that is, aspects of government that were ethically doubtful or wrong, but a *mal nécessaire*. Fines, he believed, would lead these officials to mend their ways. Information about the fines should be announced in churches, which suggests that he was trying to shame these officials and tax farmers into greater conformity to the neo-Stoic ideal of disinterestedness in fiscal matters. And he was enhancing his public image as a reformer. Marigny, he noted, had been sentenced to death for the immensity of his fortune, and there was no doubt about the origin of his wealth.[45] Referring in general terms to the *financiers'* activities, he said: 'The laws that do not wish anyone to be obliged to explain where the property one possesses comes from, apply only to those who have not dealt with public funds.'[46]

Even so, the projector word *accroissement*, or 'growth', when used about commerce, manufacturing and the state, would enable Richelieu to apply selectively, in good conscience, neo-Stoic thought about corruption and the appropriateness of wealth according to rank. This is not to suggest, however, that the principle of appropriateness was entirely rejected. The cardinal's attempts to curtail *Surintendant* Bullion's rapacity may be interpreted in this light.

Permitting Bullion to enrich himself was not the issue; allowing him to become as wealthy as some of the most powerful great nobles – and as the cardinal himself – was out of the question.[47]

Partly from lack of time, and also, certainly, to protect himself, the cardinal called in bankers and estate managers to pull the maximum income from his rapidly growing estate; but Joseph Bergin is right to stress that Richelieu's grip never really lessened over the bigger issues, such as land acquisition, exchange of royal rights for other royal rights, and revenues that the cardinal collected from abbeys that were part of a political and geographic strategy for increasing power and wealth (pl. 28).[48] Throughout his writings runs the refrain that persons without wealth receive no *considération*, even if they are kings.[49] The cardinal did his utmost to ensure that he would never be in this pitiful condition. There is no indication that he felt guilty about having amassed too much wealth as he lay near death in Narbonne, dictating his will.

Thus the third set of words, that is the words *crédit*, *argent*, *or*, *commerce*, *Etat*, *biens* and *accroissement*, was of the utmost importance. An activist in a hurry by comparision with Louis' other ministers, Richelieu adopted projector ideas about global commerce, empire, fleets, in order to define the state spatially and commercially as something that required great power if it was to enforce royal rights and customs.[50]

The ideas of the projectors received considerable attention from historians before the Second World War, yet their thought remains obscure. Debates over monetary policy, royally sponsored manufacturing, colonization, urban planning and transport networks were enthusiastically proposed by one or another of the projectors. Laffemas, and still more François du Noyer de Saint-Martin, believed firmly in the need for a royal council to shape royal commercial and imperial policies. Men with commercial experience, a knowledge of accounting and skill at smelting metal worked in Sully's shadow to shape a utopian vision of a wealthy France that was powerful on the high seas and able to sell more luxury goods than it imported.

Richelieu was too young to belong to this group. It is not certain that he read the pamphlets published by Laffemas and du Noyer, but in the reformist years that saw the Assembly of Notables and other initiatives Richelieu applied his theologian's logic to the perennial problem of the monarchy's inadequate financial resources, and he concluded that the Parlement would block efforts to increase taxation. Turning to colonization, to the gabelle and to monetary juggling in order to raise funds for the campaigns against the Huguenots and the Spanish in the late 1620s, frantic borrowing and office-selling laid the groundwork for what can scarcely be described as a policy after 1635: namely, do whatever was necessary to find the money to defeat Spain.

What, for Laffemas and his circle, had been public projecting as formulated by a royal council now became, however, secret management, almost arcana for assuring the state's fortune – and his own. The cardinal's specific role in determining monetary policy remains obscure; he seems to have let his trusted supporters, among them Laffemas' son Isaac, carry out minting and alloy experiments. If there is a magical and alchemical dimension (recall Dubois' fate!) to the cardinal's thought about gold and wealth, it was grounded firmly on the thinking of the projectors rather than on Aristotelian notions of gold and wealth, as expressed, for example, by Montchrétien.

Richelieu could be passionately patriotic about the practices of Dutch and Spanish shippers.[51] All this is well known, but a brief review of the cardinal's thought about letters of exchange clarifies his position on the ethical questions regarding *crédit*, a word that Sharon Kettering has shown to be at the semantic crossroad between money and political power.[52] The word means belief, confidence and trust, that necessary feature of both private and public action that ensured the ability to borrow and to influence one person to do another's bidding.

Richelieu inveighs against merchants who draw up letters of exchange simply as instruments for borrowing and lending, the so-called dry letter of exchange,[53] that is, a letter of exchange that was used not to pay for goods purchased in another location, but merely to borrow and lend at interest. The cardinal wanted legislation to stop this practice, but he realized how difficult it would be to draft it, and then enforce it. His reasons reveal his thought about commerce. Contrary to what one might expect from a seventeenth-century moralizing prelate, he is not troubled by profit from interest on loans. Instead, it is the *traffic* in money that he opposes. If a merchant can make a living merely by taking interest on bills of exchange, he will not risk buying and selling in the market. The implication is that France needed more risk-taking merchants than it had. Obviously finding it difficult to understand money as just another commodity, the cardinal nonetheless shared Laffemas' views on competition as a means of acquiring more and more precious metals through commerce – and at foreigners' expense.

Although Richelieu's last bold plan for reforming the fiscal administration has not been overlooked, historians have not given it the attention it deserves.[54] His fundamentally economic understanding about the relations between prices, taxes and increasing wealth is of particular importance. To be sure, the *peuple* would not be dutiful unless taxed, but the cardinal argues in favour of minimizing the fiscal weight once government expenses have been drastically reduced. The implication is that wealth, even opulence, creates more wealth, and that higher taxes and duties raise prices, thereby reducing consumption.[55] Richelieu's critiques of the fiscal system and of the venality of office were not cast in the neo-Stoic group of words, but were more commercial and projecting – these ever necessary financial expedients rather than the 'corruption' of the neo-Stoics being the real source of future weakness and impoverishment. Rendering the *peuple à son aise* while paring down the state was not contradictory. He concludes:

> I well know that it will be said that it is easy to draw up such plans, similar to those in Plato's *Republic* which, while beautiful as ideas, are chimerical in effect.

But I dare say that this plan is not only so reasonable, but so easy to carry out that if God gives the king the gift of having peace soon, and preserving it for this realm, along with his servants, of whom I consider myself one of the least, instead of leaving this advice by testament, I hope to be able to accomplish it.[56]

Omissions are also a sign of the projector's influence. There are no attacks on luxury, and no recommendations for amassing a royal war chest.

When the cardinal wrote about the *relation* between the condition of the *peuple* and the need for revenues so that the state can sustain itself in grandeur and glory, was he not drawing on the neo-Stoic principle of 'appropriateness' and propriety? Not necessarily. His understanding of the relations between tax rates and economic and social conditions is just that – a *relation* or dynamic grounded on the principle that certain conditions increase wealth, and others do not. The two chapters in the *Testament politique* that immediately precede the chapter on fiscal reform deal with sea power and commerce, the success of the latter being dependent on the former.

This same set of projectors' words about commerce, utility, colonies, fleets and growth also served the cardinal to justify his amassing a personal furtune. He could easily have reached back into French history to find models of noble but impoverished prelates who grew wealthy from state service, but his turn of mind was more philosophical. Fond of maxims, and tending to take pride in coining them himself, Richelieu wrote: 'At court, the minister must not think of increasing his fortune, except through the good and growth of the state.'[57] Here again is a *relation* in axiomatic terms, and quantitatively unlimited because of the limitless power of the state. There is no allusion to appropriateness regarding the fortunes of dukes and peers, or of politically engaged prelates. The order of the words is very significant: first the good, and then the growth, of the state. But Richelieu – the minister who had excluded the Huguenots from state power, obliged the *grands* to conduct themselves like subjects, returned the powers of governors to just limits, built a fleet, founded commercial companies, redressed French prestige in Italy and in the Low Countries – had little doubt that he had been responsible for the growth of the state. Put succinctly, Richelieu died believing that he had increased the state in such a way that it justified his massive increase in fortune. There are no traces of either ecclesiastical or neo-Stoic sets of words about godliness and poverty, nor is there talk of 'appropriateness' in his last will and testament.

Almost the same may be said of James Howell's attempt to sum up the matter in 1646, as he lay writing and rotting in the Tower of London. After the inevitable comparison with Wolsey – who, he says, surpassed Richelieu in train and in building – Howell narrates what a gentleman of quality told him:

> a marchant of Paris brought him [Richelieu] a jewel of high price to shew and sell, he was so taken with it, that he offered 50,000 crowns for it, the marchant demanded 15,000 more and would not go a penny less: a few days after the marchant carrying the jewell to a great lady to see, was suddenly in some place of

advantage surprised, muffled, and so unjewelled: a little after the marchant going to the cardinal's secretary upon some other business, the cardinal hearing of his being their, sent for him, and making grievous mone of his jewell, the cardinal fetched out of his cabinet a box, and drew thence a jewell, and asked whether that was his; the marchant in a kind of amazement answered, I dare not say 'tis mine because 'tis in your Eminence's hand, but were it in any other hand I would swear it were mine. Go, saith he, and keep a better conscience in your dealing hereafter, for I know what this jewell is worth as well as you, and out of that I offered you already, you may draw very fair gaines; so he gave order his 50,000 crowns should be pay'd him, and the business was hushed up.[58]

The notion of 'faire gaine' in this story is revealing of the ethical and rhetorical understandings about exchange in the seventeenth century. The principle of 'appropriateness' would again seem to underlie the words, but it is not certain that someone who uttered those words in an exchange believed them as a neo-Stoic might. If the story is true, and I believe it is, Richelieu used his rank and power as a ducal prelate to frame an exchange the merchant could not refuse. And his weakness for books, paintings, jewels, duchies, sculptures and a gold vermeil altar service was just that: a weakness, not a sin, a stimulant to French opulence, not impoverishment.

While Chéruel's edition of Mazarin's letters is only partial, it is doubtful that sets of words about ecclesiastical poverty and state growth through commerce have been edited out of thousands of letters. If these sets of words are missing, it is because neither is present in the thought of the Roman diplomat.

The neo-Stoic ensemble of words was, however, at the heart of Mazarin's understanding of social relations, and of wielding power. Along with *grâces* and *gratitude*, the words *intérêts* and *gagner* are found much more frequently in Mazarin's prose than in that of his predecessor. Indeed, the ontological aspect so important to Seneca, namely that the gift is in the thought and the gesture, rather than in the material object given, is more frequently sensed (though rejected) in Richelieu than in Mazarin. The word *grâces*, when coupled with *intérêts* and *gagner*, that is, to win over someone with a gift, is particularly frequent in his letters written during the Fronde. At one point Mazarin wrote to Abbé Fouquet, an intimate, that Turenne had to be 'bought' (*acheter*), suggesting that he really understood clientage in monetary terms.[59] Still, both cardinals repeated the lament about how the French had short memories and became ungrateful too quickly, a commonplace in the neo-Stoic group of words that dates at least from Machiavelli.

When someone continued to *fronder*, or in some way upset Mazarin after receiving a *grâce*, he would be disconcerted. It is not always true, the cardinal commented, that 'les honneurs changent les moeurs'. And when some benefit failed to inspire the recipient to change his politics, he would simply remark, 'C'est étrange.'

Fidelity to the king and service to the state were principles that Mazarin clearly noticed in such loyal officials as Le Tellier, but he seems to have been less willing than Richelieu to coerce, or attempt to coerce, obedience away from rebellion by appealing to these principles. Seeking to *gagner frondeurs*, perhaps a bit too quickly, by appealing to their *intérêts*, on many occasions Mazarin lost the initiative when he found the appeals to loyalty and service to be either ineffective or particularly difficult to make for someone who was only a natural-ized Frenchman. Though it may be an exaggeration to suggest that appearances and gestures counted even more for Mazarin than they did for Richelieu, it is clear that when his contemporaries alluded to the Roman diplomat's reputation for 'belles paroles', it was a harsh criticism. The Fronde was in no small way a matter of who could keep his word; and on this point Mazarin simply had a different personality and attitude from those of his predecessor – and of some *frondeurs*.

In his long letter to Abel Servien of 14 August 1648, just as the latter was receiving final instructions for the negotiations at Münster, Mazarin described in detail his own financial status. It certainly would be a factor in the peace-making, he thought; and so he chose to stress his poverty. The *relation* between appearances and his financial status was, according to him, almost an inverse correlation: 'It is superfluous to take the precaution to tell you that in appear-ances I bear things with more pride than ever'[60] – after which he describes how he must borrow daily in order to be able to live and keep his household going.

Mazarin had already pointed out to Servien that he had no forts, offices, governments, duchies or establishments, nor did he have a relative who had become rich during the eighteen years he had served France, or the six he had been first minister. This portrait of the totally disinterested, untarnished royal servant in 1648 was more than rhetorical (and it certainly was that). He seemed to recognize that, in diplomatic negotiations, this image would improve Servien's chances for a settlement.

In the same letter the experienced diplomat becomes more evident still, when he assures Servien that the 100,000 livres in presents – gold chains, flatware, tapestries, diamonds and money – will be shipped to him in a week, to distribute among the foreign diplomats as he sees fit. Though insignificant by comparison with the enormous fortune in money, fine fabrics, paintings, sculptures and jewels that the cardinal possessed at the time of his death, it is nonetheless a clue to how important appearances were to European diplomacy. Nor is it clear that the 100,000 livres in presents came from the royal treasury, which was virtually bankrupt at the time, or from Mazarin's own purse.

In conclusion, if there were no new words about money or wealth, there was in fact one quite recently formulated projector set of words, the key word being *accroissement*. Cardinal Richelieu used this particular set of words to speak of the state, and of his own estate, to make them both more economic in meaning, thereby fusing increased wealth, heightened dignity and power. By contrast, Mazarin's thought about the state was grounded in the hierarchy of international dignities and the appearances that sustained it. He did not think of the growth of the state in economic terms.

For Richelieu, the statesman and private person, casuistic argumentation grounded on the distinctiveness of three sets of words not only helped him overcome moral doubt about his policies, but strengthened the single-mindedness with which he pursued the execution of those policies. The cardinal–theologian differed very much from his fellow state servants, whose education and experience scarcely extended beyond a vague neo-Stoic notion of state and personal service. Mazarin, the consummate courtier, suffered *ad hominem* attacks not only because his *belles paroles* were vapid, but because he followed on the heels of a minister for whom words were things, like swords, guns and the eucharist.

Like the high-level consumerism of the tax farmers and royal-debt financiers, the appearances of international diplomacy may have made Richelieu's neo-Stoic understanding of gift-giving-as-intention quite parochial. Mazarin's understanding of *grâces* was perhaps more cosmopolitan, more materialistic and more in accord with the gift-giving that was part of diplomacy. What Richelieu admired most in the young Roman diplomat was his faultless self-control, and perhaps his willingness to trust fortune and to let time bring what it might – two things the poor Poitevin theologian could not do. Their words about wealth and power differed considerably, and the French of their generation contested the policies grounded on these words; but their love for things beautiful and prestigious – the appearances of power – was enthusiastically shared not only by them but by the new classes of moneyed royal officials for whom *éclat* rather than appropriateness would express their thought regarding culture and power.

Notes

1. R. J. Bonney, *The King's Debts: Finance and Politics in France, 1589–1661* (Oxford, 1981); and J. Bergin, *Cardinal Richelieu: Power and the Pursuit of Wealth* (New Haven, 1985), and articles too numerous to be cited here. See also J. Dent, *Crisis in Finance: Crown, Financiers and Society in Seventeenth-Century France* (Newton Abbot, 1973).
2. The first round of this movement primarily concerned 'grossièreté et indécence'; the second, epitomized in Molière's social mirror of French society, very probably has neo-Stoic origins. See the old but still useful M. Magendie, *La Politesse mondaine* (Geneva, 1970, reprint of the 1925 edn), and M. Fumaroli, 'Le Génie de la langue française', in P. Nora, ed., *Lieux de mémoire* (Paris, 1993), iii, pt 2, pp. 911–73.
3. The literature on language theory and social history is vast. See Arthur L. Herman Jr, 'The Language of Fidelity in Early Modern France', *Journal of Modern History*, 67 (1995), pp. 1–24, for a critical bibliography, and a study of a word and social–political *relation* that complements this paper. A more personal confirmation of how I think as I read sources can be found in J. H. M. Salmon's *Renaissance and Revolt: Essays in the Intellectual and Social History of Early Modern France* (Cambridge, 1987), pp. 1–24. On Richelieu's mode of thinking see Françoise Hildesheimer, 'Le Testament politique de Richelieu, ou le règne terrestre de la raison', *Annuaire Bulletin de la Société de l'Histoire de France* (1994), pp. 17–34.

4. The immense literature on reform of the church has short summaries and occasional sentences regarding ideas about ecclesiastical poverty in the early seventeenth century. For Bérulle in particular, Henri Bremond, *Histoire littéraire du sentiment religieux en France* (Paris, 1935), iii, *passim*. J. Bergin elucidates the effects of La Rochefoucauld's lack of fortune in his *Cardinal de la Rochefoucauld* . . . (New Haven, 1987), p. 45, but does not sum up his financial situation at his death or specific views on ecclesiastical poverty. Jacques Depauw, 'De la pauvreté: à propos de *De la Sagesse* de Pierre Charron, questions de définition', *XVIIe Siècle*, 171 (1991), pp. 107–18, sums up Bodin's and Charron's attitudes towards the wealth of the church. Regarding regulars with vows of poverty, the ensemble of words was clearly articulated, but according to L. J. Lekai: 'Was the fiscal administration of the college suited to the observance of the vow of poverty? Or, was the college a den of thieves, as the reformers charged? To be sure, no monk, with the exception of the procurator, was supposed to hold and spend money. Those who did possess money, must have been fully aware of their wrongdoing. That they [sic] were some abuses, seems to be undeniable. The question how widespread was the independent handling of money among the members of the College, cannot be determined with any degree of certainty.' 'The Parisian College of Saint Bernard in 1634–35', *Analecta Cisterciensa* (1969), pp. 180–208, which includes the report of La Rochefoucauld's visitation.

5. Since this chapter attempts to discern these sets of words about wealth at the most personal rather than institutional level, I shall privilege such sources, beginning with Montaigne, the *Essays*, iii, p. 9, where it would seem that his thought must be taken literally and directly. See President Henri II de Mesmes' speeches in Bibliothèque Nationale (hereafter BN), Mss fr. 523–4, and Omer Talon's *testament* in H. Mailfait, *Omer Talon* (Paris, 1902). On the importance of Lipsius as editor and translator of neo-Stoic ideas on wealth see Mark Morford, *Stoics and Neostoics* (Princeton, 1991), pp. 177ff.; and G. Oestreich, *Neostoicism and the Early Modern State*, trans. D. McClintock (Cambridge, 1982). Georges Matoré found no need to include either *accroissement* or *bienséance* in his *Vocabulaire et la société du XVIe siècle* (Paris, 1988), which suggests that these words were gaining in conceptual strength in the early seventeenth century.

6. Roland Mousnier, 'Sully et le Conseil d'Etat et des finances . . .', *Revue Historique*, 192 (1941), pp. 68–86; and J. Russell Major, *Bellièvre, Sully, and the Assembly of Notables of 1596*, Transactions of the American Philosophical Society, new series, 64 (Philadelphia, 1974).

7. William F. Church, *Richelieu and Reason of State* (Princeton, 1972). See also the numerous works on the *Etat d'offices*, the service state, that centre on interpreting Loyseau, notably Roland Mousnier's early work, *La Vénalité des offices sous Henri IV et Louis XII* (Paris, 2nd edn, 1971).

8. Despite all the research and writing about Mazarin, his writings have not been studied as political thought in his age.

9. 'The Rhetoric of Counsell in Early Modern England', in Dale Hoak, ed., *Tudor Political Culture* (Cambridge, 1995), pp. 292–310.

10. *Les Ducs et pairs en France au XVIIe siècle* (Paris, 1972), p. 326. The value of their movables was on the average, however, about the same: p. 300.

11. *Ibid.*, p. 148.

12. 'Relation de ce qui s'est passé . . . à Paris le 26 août 1648', BN, ms. fr. 5218, fol. 346. It was also noted that Broussel lacked a country house: BN, ms. fr. 25026, fol. 168v.

13. The first edition appeared in 1623, the second in 1648.

14. F. Bayard, *Le Monde des financiers* (Paris, 1988); D. Dessert, *Argent, pouvoir et société au Grand Siècle* (Paris, 1984).

15. Bayard, *Le Monde des financiers*, found some evidence of sincere attachment to the *Etat* by some of the financiers: pp. 303ff.

16. Such old works as Paul Harsin, *Les Doctrines monétaires et financières en France du XVIe et XVIIe siècle* (Paris, 1928), and C. W. Cole, *French Mercantilist Doctrines before Colbert* (New York, 1931), have only partially been superseded by the works of Bernard Barbiche and David Buisseret in and around their edition of Sully's *Œconomies royales*, of which Barbiche's 'Une Tentative de réforme monétaire à la fin du règne de Henri IV: l'édit d'août 1609', *XVIIe Siècle*, 61 (1963), pp. 3–17, is a cogent early example. Norman Doiron's 'Neostoicisme et nouveaux mondes: le voyageur et l'archer dans le *De Ratione cum Fructu Peregrinandi* de Juste Lipse', in *La Découverte de nouveaux mondes* . . . , ed. Cecilia Rizza (Fasano, 1993), pp. 181–90, is exemplary of the type of close reading that must be done in order to discern the projector's sense of space, power and wealth. Despite the attractiveness of the title, Pierre Dockès' *L'Espace dans la pensée économique du XVIe au XVIIIe siècle* (Paris, 1969) is much too general to shed light on du Noyer's and Richelieu's ideas about commercial and statist space.

17. As an example see the 'Mémoire pour le Roi' of May 1626, where Richelieu writes that things seem to 'conspire now to beat down Spanish pride' while assuring the king that there is money for war, but there could also be a rebellion if funds ran out. P. Grillon, ed., *Les Papiers de Richelieu* (Paris, 1975), i (1625), 41. (Citations show first the volume, then the year in parentheses, and finally the numeral of the document – plus the page when the document is long.)

18. See Jean Le Boindre's *Journal des Débats du Parlement de Paris*, AN, U 336, ed. R. Descimon and O. Ranum (Paris, 1997).

19. A. Lloyd Moote, *Louis XIII, the Just* (Berkeley, 1989), ch. 13.

20. J. Petit, *L'Assemblée des Notables de 1626–1627* (Paris, 1936), pp. 95–104.

21. Grillon, ed., *Papiers*, iii (28 December 1628), 655. As a reader of casuistic treatises, did Richelieu believe that he had literally increased the power of the state in order to increase these port duties, and that as a result he had a special title to these duties? As a casuistic thinker, did he think that these moneys were not French but foreign, and that therefore he had some greater moral right to them? The duties would simply have been passed on to French consumers, but it is possible that the cardinal did not see these funds in this way.

22. Grillon, ed., *Papiers*, iii (1628), 264.

23. *Ibid.*, 171.

24. *Ibid.*

25. *Ibid.*, iv (1629), 65. In the *Advis au Roy* of a month earlier he wrote: 'Que j'ay refusé vingt mil escus de pension extraordinaire, qu'il pleust au Roy m'offrir, quoyque je despense grandement. ...' Grillon, ed., *Papiers*, iv (1629), 11 (p. 41). There are many other revealing details about his personal finances in this passage.

26. Richelieu wrote to Rancé that Marie de Médicis was to inform Bérulle of the decision, which obviously left Bérulle beholden not only to the king and Richelieu, but to Marie, and it made it virtually impossible for Bérulle to decline them.

27. Grillon, ed., *Papiers*, iv (1629), 77.

28. *Ibid.*, 86.

29. *Ibid.*, 76.

30. *Lettres, instructions diplomatiques et papiers d'état du Cardinal de Richelieu*, ed. D. L. M. Avenel, 8 vols (Paris, 1853–77), v, CLXXXV (January 1636).

31. *Testament Politique*, ed. Françoise Hildesheimer (Paris, 1995), p. 258. *Bienfaits* are quickly forgotten. See my 'Richelieu and Corneille on Clemency', *Cahiers d'Histoire*, 16 (1996), pp. 80–100, and Sharon Kettering, 'Gift-Giving and Patronage in Early Modern France', *French History*, 2 (1988), pp. 131–51.

32. Grillon, ed., *Papiers*, iv (1629), 11 (p. 41).

33. Richelieu remarks that the office of king keeps Louis from touching money, an intriguing remark given that the French sovereign's sacred character enabled him to touch and heal. Or was it a constitutional matter? *Ibid.*, i (1626), 68: 'et les formes de l'Etat ne permettant point que le Roy touche ses deniers par luy-mesme, estant nécessité que ce soit par les officiers qui en donnent leurs quittances ...'. *Citrons* is used as a metaphor for money.

34. *Ibid.*, iii (1628), 115.

35. *Ibid.*, 124.

36. See the comparison between Corneille's and Richelieu's thought about clemency in the play *Cinna* and the Cinq Mars Affair, where Corneille seems to follow Seneca quite specifically; and, while rejecting Seneca's views, the cardinal does not seem to do so with Seneca specifically in mind. This would suggest the influence on his thought of other still to be determined and presumably modern writers.

37. Jorg Wollenberg, *Les Trois Richelieu*, trans. Edouard Husson (Paris, 1995), pp. 287, 293.

38. This is a general practice, but there are exceptions. See his letter of thanks when he suggests that his brother might serve well as archbishop of Lyon. Grillon, ed., *Papiers*, iii (1628), 451. The king expressed his desire to give Lyon to his brother in a letter dated the same day.

39. *Ibid.*, 101.

40. *Richelieu, Power and the Pursuit of Wealth*, ch. 3, which offers a precise overview of all that Richelieu received from the crown, as a royal official.

41. Grillon, ed., *Papiers*, iii (1628), 630.

42. *Ibid.*, 655.

43. *Les Oeuvres*, trans. F. de Malherbe (Paris, 1659), Des Bienfaits, 'le vray bienfait est la volonté seule de celuy qui donne' (p. 10). On the Baradat Affair of 1626, Richelieu wrote: 'Le remède de ce mal consiste ou à faire de grands biens non seulement à sa personne, mais encore à celle de ses parens.'

Je dis: grand biens, parce qu'il tesmoigne clairement que leur donner des charges mediocres, c'est plustost l'iriter que le contenter.' Grillon, ed., *Papiers*, i (1626), 317.

44. Grillon, ed., *Papiers*, i (1624), 62.
45. *Ibid.*, 63.
46. *Ibid.*, 62 (p. 121).
47. Bonney, *King's Debts*, pp. 181–4.
48. Bergin, *Richelieu: Power and the Pursuit of Wealth*, p. 68.
49. *Testament politique*, p. 343.
50. The standard work is by H. Hauser, *La Pensée et l'action économiques du cardinal de Richelieu* (Paris, 1944).
51. Grillon, ed., *Papiers*, i (1626), 333.
52. 'Brokerage at the Court of Louis XIV', *Historical Journal*, 36 (1993), pp. 76–7.
53. Grillon, ed., *Papiers*, i (1626), 333.
54. *Testament politique*, pp. 343–68.
55. 'Le vray moyen d'enrichir l'Estat est de soulager le peuple et décharger de l'une et l'autre de ses charges en diminuant celles de l'Estat': *ibid.*, p. 358.
56. *Ibid.*, p. 368.
57. Grillon, ed., *Papiers*, iv (1629), 66.
58. *Lustra Ludovic, or the Life of the Late Victorious King of France, Lewis the XIII* (London, 1646), p. 184.
59. *Lettres du cardinal Mazarin pendant son ministère*, ed. P. A. Chéruel, 9 vols (Paris, 1872–1906), v, 16 January 1652, IV.
60. *Ibid.*, iii, LXXXVI.

10

Favourite, Minister, Magnate: Power Strategies in the Polish–Lithuanian Commonwealth

ANTONI MĄCZAK

The Structure of Power

The power structure of the Polish–Lithuanian state[1] was peculiar. From the Union of Lublin in 1569, it was a close federation of the Kingdom of Poland and the Grand Duchy of Lithuania, with an elective king-and-grand-duke as its cornerstone. From 1385 to 1569 the kings of Poland were elected by the Sejm (the Diet) from among members of the Jagiellon dynasty, which claimed undisputed hereditary rights to the grand duchy. In the mid-fifteenth century this had led to short-lived conflicts. For a brief period – 1444–7 – both countries, in personal union since 1385, had two brothers as separate rulers. In the next century there was no serious danger of such a split, but the different interests of the two states (*avant la lettre*) and the particularist interests of provincial elites often led to open conflicts. It is of importance that in Lithuania the assemblies of the nobility emerged only in the sixteenth century and the ruling elite consisted of princes and boyars. This changed when, after 1569, the grand duchy adopted the Polish system of *sejmiki* (county assemblies, or dietines, of the nobles, which included even the poor nobility).[2] The position of the great lords changed too. The problem is: how did the new power structure of the Commonwealth influence individual careers; what strategies were effective; and what room was left to royal favourites?

From 1569, the Senate of the Commonwealth was composed of ecclesiastical lords (archbishops and bishops), palatines and castellans.[3] The crown (that is, Poland) and the grand duchy had their separate structures of offices and *cursus honorum*. The Act of Union secured for the Lithuanian lords seats in the Senate according to their respective dignities, equally with the Poles. It was of crucial importance that all offices were held for life, and not at the king's pleasure; for all practical purposes, officeholders retained their position until promotion to a higher or more profitable post. The ministries were separate for the kingdom and the grand duchy, and ministers had their places in the Senate as well.[4] No *Herrenstand* existed in Poland, but Dr Henryk Litwin has proved statistically that between the mid-fifteenth and the mid-seventeenth century the upper stratum of the nobility established a new identity based on informal *connubium*. A national elite replaced the former provincial elites, and with growing intensity the magnates intermarried beyond the borders of their native counties and provinces.[5] Members of prominent families acquired offices in distant parts where they were not residents. At this high level the *ius indigenatus* could be fairly easily bypassed.[6] The Senate was their forum, but networks of relationships were multiple and dense. The magnates maintained sumptuous households at the heart of their estates. Although they built palaces in and around Warsaw, their points of contact with the other notables, with their 'friends' (that is, real and potential clients) and finally with the independent nobility were their own households.[7] The role of the magnates' residences was growing from the sixteenth to the eighteenth century but in the north-west (Great Poland) it never became so marked as in Lithuania and in the Ruthenian south-east, the Ukraine of today.

What may be called the spatial structure of power, which was so peculiar in the Commonwealth of Poland–Lithuania, was caused by a complex of legal, social and economic factors. The fifteenth-century statutes, and particularly those of 1454, gave to the Noble Estates freedoms similar to those acquired by the Estates in Hungary, in the Czech lands and in most countries of the West. However, the freedoms of the nobility (in the broad, continental sense of the term) found no counterweight in the wealth and strength of the Commonalty (the Third Estate). Secondly, the nobility succeeded in hampering the build-up of a royal administration; from the mid-fifteenth to the mid-sixteenth century the state gradually became something of a federation of counties run by their respective assemblies of the nobility. To a great extent, the situation (in terms of power and politics) within a county depended on the relationships between individuals and/or various strata of the nobility. It is important to add that, whereas the influence from the centre on the localities was minimal, the dietines expressed their opinions on general state issues, internal and foreign, and obliged their deputies to follow their instructions closely. Neither the landed gentry nor their mighty neighbours and patrons, the magnates, were interested in making the royal administration and juridical power strong; local self-government seemed preferable.

Thirdly, the country was very large – around 1632 it was up to one million square kilometres and in the border lands the king was very distant and could hardly be approached except with the friendly help of a magnate–patron. The modern notion of 'citizen', as opposed to 'subject', was current in early modern Poland. Yet this modern trait was hardly compatible with the social and economic structures. The lesser nobility entrenched in the Chamber of Deputies, where all the dietines were represented, achieved in the mid-sixteenth century a great degree of real political freedom from the magnates but were losing their wealth and economic independence. On top of all this, the authority of the 'freely elected' king was declining. He was regarded as 'the true husband of this

Commonwealth'.[8] His person as a sovereign was rarely mentioned separately: the term often used was 'his Majesty the king *and the Commonwealth*'. And yet the Diet was regarded as an important forum. The king-in-parliament was able to display his favour and disfavour, chiefly by grants of offices and leaseholds of the royal domain. He could also play the factions against one another. In the seventeenth century, the Vasas[9] more and more ruled through royalist factions. This created special rules of the game for prospective royal favourites. But in such a decentralized system who was a favourite and who was a minister? What was the relationship of the term 'magnate' to the terms 'minister' and 'favourite'?

Favourites–Ministers–Magnates: A Report from the British Isles[10]

Let me begin with the testimony of an anonymous alien who had spent a long time in Poland and compiled a 'Relation of . . . Polonia . . . Anno 1598'.[11] It was the fruit of a profound knowledge of the Polish polity: both the constitution and the structure of politics. The author must have been connected with Chancellor Jan Zamoyski (1542–1605), whose viewpoint he was presenting. Whoever he was, the author – who came from the British Isles – was critical of the Polish polity, and explained it in terms borrowed from Tacitus' *Germania*.[12] The concepts we are interested in – if not all the terms – can be found there. 'Favourite' we encounter in a marginal note summarizing a paragraph: 'Stephan assured of the State by making his favourites greate.'[13] The former note ran as follows: 'The Kinge may make himselfe stronge.' Both notes accompanied a paragraph on King Stephan's (ruled 1576–86) wise choice of Zamoyski and on the latter's wisdom. The original term 'favour' was in use, as in the following sentence:

> So that bothe spirituall and secular prefermentes allmost onely serve for the mainteyning of greate howses in theire greatnes, they having the hability of following the course of ambition, and the advauntage of favoure with the Prince, whoe bestoweth all charges uppon those which can best pleasure hym, by suche meanes obliging to hymselfe the mightie famelies.[14]

This described not the rise of the royal favourites but rather the method of obliging the great houses: the way of 'maintain[ing] the great houses in their greatness'. The author focused on them. He did not use the term 'minister'. Instead he wrote of 'Officers that are Dignitaries', or 'the greate officers admitted into the Senate . . . the Marshalls, Chauncellors, and Treasurers'.[15] Elsewhere he called them simply 'officers', and contrasted them with 'Terrestres Officiarii'.[16] These dignitaries were however ministers, if this term was not regarded as *singularis tantum*.

Our author related quite accurately the positions and functions of diverse principal officers, but the most valuable parts of his report are the paragraphs devoted to the magnates. The term itself did not appear in his text. This corresponded with Polish usage. The observations touching 'the greate Lordes' belong to the most interesting sections of the 'Relation, 1598'.[17]

> Bothe the greate Lordes, and private riche gentlemen keepe greate traynes, commonly in the uttermost of theire hability, and somme farre beyonde. . . . the Radzivils, Ostrog, Zbaras . . . or other Dukes of Lithuania, and Russia . . . have no other place, then is afforded them by suche office as they gett, howbeit that they are mighty in theire owne terretories, especially Ostrog, whoe hath 4000 feudataries besydes Bawres, Townesmen etc. But theire mighte is not feared because they neyther have pretension nor absolute commaunde other then other of the Nobility.

The author, who did not disguise his criticism of Polish political customs and the Polish constitution (including elective monarchy), saw a political rationale in the 'correspondency of patrone, and Cliente' in Poland, and particularly in Lithuania and Ruthenia: a relationship which he regarded as strange, and described quoting long paragraphs from *Germania*.[18]

> So that whether the Polish Noblemen keepe suche great and ryotuous traynes in that reason of State, or uppon affection of pompe, and greatnes, or security of theire persons as being commonly in quarrells, the State cannot well stande without it. For that is the common bande of unity between the riche and the poor, bothe by that meanes participating of the benefittes of lande, the one by commaunde, and the other by dependency of the Commaunders trencher. . . .

For this foreign observer in the late sixteenth century, the key question was typically the social order. In Poland it seemed to him solidly based on the 'common bande of unity between the riche and the poore', the latter having been 'interested in the sovereignety . . . [because] the voice of every poore servingman being a gentleman weighes as much in all Conventes and elections as the greatest princes . . .'. At another point he observed: 'it seems that thys poorer sorte desyres not any better state, for they lyve ryotously and gallantly according to the Polish humoure'.[19]

It is rather strange that the author, who (better than many historians today) understood the importance and scale of the patronage of local magnates, under-estimated the consequences of the magnates' growth and could not foresee the two civil wars to come during the seventeenth century. In his opinion the great lords somehow cooled the 'riotous' nature of the lesser gentry[20] and were able to keep them in reasonable order. However, he was aware that the magnates availed themselves of their clients not only 'uppon affectation of pompe, and greatnes', but also 'in quarrels'. He mentioned a characteristic case: 'This [civil war] might well have happened in the quarrell betweene Zamoysky and the

1 Henri III of France and his *mignons*. The King sits under the canopy on the left at the wedding of his favourite, the duc de Joyeuse. Sixteenth-century French school. (Museé du Louvre, Paris)

2 Alvaro de Luna, favourite of Juan II of Castile. His spectacular rise and fall in the fifteenth century epitomized the role of fortune in the career of favourites. (Painting in the Santiago Chapel, Toledo Cathedral)

3 Philip II of Spain: a prince who recognized the dangers of excessive dependence on favourites. Painting by Antonio Moro. (Museo del Prado, Madrid)

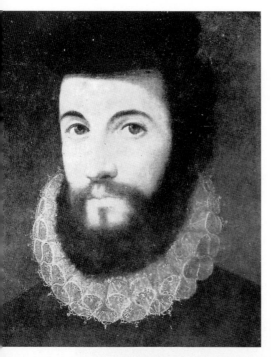

4 Ruy Gómez de Silva, better known as the Prince of Eboli, first and most powerful favourite of Philip II of Spain. (Painting in the collection of the Duke of Infantado, Madrid)

5 Sovereign Mistress of her Grace? Elizabeth I, the 'Armada Portrait'. Painted by George Gower (c. 1588). (Woburn Abbey)

6 Robert Dudley, Earl of Leicester: a favourite too close to the throne? Painting of *c.* 1585–6. (Parham Park)

7 Sir Christopher Hatton, the Lord Chancellor, who danced his way into Elizabeth's favour. Painting of 1591. (National Portrait Gallery, London)

8 William Cecil, Lord Burghley: Elizabeth's Lord Treasurer and devoted servant. (Painting in the Bodleian Library, Oxford)

9 Sir Walter Ralegh: Renaissance courtier whose ambitions for office were thwarted. Painting of 1588. (National Portrait Gallery, London)

10 Robert Devereux, Earl of Essex, the reckless favourite. Painting of 1590 by William Segar (National Gallery of Ireland, Dublin)

11 Charles I of England: the sleeping prince. A broadsheet of 1636. (British Museum, London)

2 Robert Carr, Earl of Somerset: James I of
England's Scottish favourite. Painting of 1611 by
Nicholas Hilliard. (National Portrait Gallery,
London)

3 Jacopo da Ponte, *Beheading of John the Baptist*.
One of the paintings in the Earl of Somerset's private
collection, assembled whilst he was favourite to the
King. (Statens Museum fur Kunst, Copenhagen)

14 Concino Concini: Marie de Médicis'
Italian favourite. (Portrait in the Musée
du Louvre, Paris)

15 Leonora Galigaï: wife of Concino
Concini and confidante of Marie de
Médicis. (Portrait in the Musée du
Louvre, Paris)

16 The marriage of Henri IV and Marie de Médicis at Lyon. The king and queen
are depicted in the heavens as Jove and Juno with the queen's lion-drawn chariot
below. From the Rubens cycle of the life of Marie de Médicis painted for the
Luxembourg palace. (Musée du Louvre, Paris)

17 The duc de Luynes, first favourite of
Louis XIII of France.

SERO, SED SERIO

18 Robert Cecil, Earl of Salisbury:
bureaucrat or favourite? Painting of 1602
attributed to John de Critz. (National
Portrait Gallery, London)

19 James I, King of England. Painting of 1621 by Daniel Mytens.
(National Portrait Gallery, London)

20 The reward of favour: Hatfield House, country home of Robert Cecil, Earl of Salisbury.

Lord Burghley and Robert Cecil, Earl of Salisbury: father and son as royal servants. (Fictional trait, Hatfield House)

22 Matthäus Enzlin, counsellor and favourite of
Duke Friedrich of Württemberg. (Woodcut in the
Württembergische Landesbibliothek, Stuttgart)

I M A G O
Nobilis,& Confultifsimi Viri, Dn.
MATTHÆI ENZLINI, V. I. DOCTORIS, E
illuſtriſſimi Ducis VUrttembergici D. D. FRIDERICI,&c.
Conſiliary intimi, & primary: ac in inclyta Tubingenſi Aca-
demia Profeſſoris excellentiſſimi: Anno Ætatis 41.

'Diſtichon προσονομαστικόν.

Grande DEI DONVM es, Patri.rc̞,Duci.ſ̞,Scholæc̞:
ENS Legum ,& curuiL I N E A recta fori.

E IV

23 Duke Friedrich of Württemberg. (Engraving in
the Württembergische Landesbibliothek, Stuttgart)

Palatyne of Kiovia, (whoe came to the Dyett with 7000 horses) yf it had not ben taken up. For that they twooe as most potent by allies and dependency, would have distracted the state into theire twooe factions.'[21] It is obvious that the anonymous observer was laying stress on the role of the magnates as patrons of the lesser landed nobility (sometimes even defined as 'servingmen'). Their position as great landowners and mighty neighbours was for him more important than the high, even crucial, offices they held.

He also mentions seven members of the Radziwiłł clan entrusted by King Stephan with key offices in the Grand Duchy. He does not suggest that either Jan Zamoyski or the Radziwiłłs were favourites of King Stephan in the *personal* meaning of the word. And indeed a close relationship existed only between the king and Zamoyski, whose career was by any standards spectacular.[22]

Zamoyski's father (1519–72) was a nobleman of modest means, the owner of four villages and part of a fifth in the Palatinate of Ruthenia. He served the king well as a soldier, and probably also won the protection of the first family of Lithuania, the Radziwiłłs, when he was fighting in the grand duchy. As a reward for his contribution to victory over the Muscovites he was granted a large royal estate (the *capitaneatus* of Bełz) and a seat in the Senate as a minor castellan. This placed him on the path to power.

Jan Sarius Zamoyski himself became the sole heir to his father's fortune and position after the death of his elder brother. His early years were complicated by the fact that his father had converted to Calvinism in 1551. Although at the time this was normal, especially among the upwardly mobile nobility, the last quarter of the sixteenth century saw massive reconversions to Rome. Jan was sent away to study in Strasburg and Paris, and finally in Padua, where he studied Roman institutions with Carlo Sigonio, and was elected rector in 1561. In Padua he made valuable intellectual friendships,[23] and, with the help of two of his Italian friends, Sigonio and Paolo Manuzio, of the famous family of printers, he secured the protection of the royal secretary and newly appointed vice-chancellor of Poland, Piotr Myszkowski.

Back in Poland Jan Zamoyski, now a doctor of laws, became a secretary to the king. His duties included the reorganization of the Record Office, and according to his personal secretary and biographer, Reinhold Heidenstein, this 'service to the motherland' brought him both fame and profit. In addition, his close reading of legal texts gave him 'uncommon skill in history and everything concerning the Commonwealth'. He was rewarded by the monarch with grants of land, and, when his father died in 1572, Sigismund Augustus – now terminally ill – transferred his father's leaseholds to him. But, according to his most recent biographer,[24] Zamoyski was not entirely loyal to Sigismund Augustus, and was linked to the Myszkowskis, who were later accused of poisoning the king.

On 7 July 1572, when Sigismund Augustus, the last monarch of the House of Jagiellon, died, the court was virtually dissolved, and court factions lost much of their importance. Although it had long been apparent that no heir would be born, the country was caught unprepared by his death. Zamoyski played a crucial role in one of the earliest county 'confederations' raised by local nobilities for the maintenance of law and order. Some of these were directed specifically against the senators, at a moment when the struggle between the Senate and the Noble Estate as to who represented the Commonwealth was gaining momentum. Zamoyski was on the side of the nobility and openly opposed the senators, but he never became a demagogue; and while it was he who composed the motion that every noble has a right, and duty, to elect the king, he was an advocate of majority voting. The Commonwealth was still far from the *liberum veto*, and the election of a successor to Sigismund Augustus was settled by agreement and compromise, with the election of Henri de Valois, duc d'Anjou, to the throne.

Until the second election and the crowning of Stephan Batory as king in 1576, following the departure of Anjou to assume the crown of France, Zamoyski continued as one of the leaders in the Chamber, and was the principal opponent of the Habsburgs and their Polish faction. Shortly after his coronation, Batory, who had also studied at Padua, appointed him vice-chancellor. Zamoyski's position under Batory is best defined as that of a minister, but he was probably something more. Although he was loyal to the king, there were moments when he had to choose between him and the Chamber of Deputies. His popularity as 'tribune of the nobility' suffered each time he tied himself more closely to the monarch and he appeared to draw the appropriate conclusion after the third royal election, that of Sigismund III.[25]

Continuing as chancellor under the new sovereign, he never won the favour of one whom he defined as a *diabolum mutum*,[26] and consequently was pushed into opposition. Yet the king had no legal means of dismissing him. Few ministers of these times would think ill of the chancellor for having amassed fabulous wealth in landed property, his own estates and low-rent (or free) leaseholds of royal domain. He multiplied his father's four villages into a fortune of many hundreds of manors.[27] This self-made man was among the most accomplished patrons of that age. This was a consequence of his office. When the chancellor's power was petering out, he used his position more and more in defence of his clients for whom he was no longer able to win substantial royal favours.[28] In a sense he was becoming a full-blown magnate. It was his accumulated wealth and prestige, rather than his offices, or his close relationship with the king, which shaped his power. His private empire in the southeast he passed on to the descendants.

Chancellor-Hetman Zamoyski died in 1605, 'possibly too early. We do not know what would have happened,' writes Stanislaw Grzybowski,

> if he had lived until the *rokosz* [the civil war of 1606–7], whether he would have
> become a Polish Cromwell or completed the construction of republican institutions similar to those of Venice. . . . We only know what his faithful pupil and
> best friend, Stanisław Żółkiewski, did. He did not support the king but the law,

defending the full competence of the Sejm to settle political conflicts. He had defeated the rebels but did not pursue them, and put pressure on the king to pardon the defeated.[29]

The conclusion we can draw is that Zamoyski (and, following him, Żółkiewski) regarded himself as a minister of the *Res Publica* rather than a royal servant.[30]

Magnate and Courtier: An Alternative

At the turn of the sixteenth and in the early decades of the seventeenth century, the great houses and ambitious individuals of Poland adopted diverse strategies of advancement. Dr Leszek Kieniewicz, a student of the Senate in the late sixteenth century, has labelled them the magnate–aristocrat alternative.[31] However, these were rather trends than clear-cut strategies.

The magnate strategy was possible only for the nobleman who enjoyed substantial influence in the localities. He dominated the county nobility in a large and/or important region. According to the Nieszawa Statutes of 1454, the king had to win the approval of the dietines in order to impose taxes and to wage war. Their opinions were eventually expressed by the Chamber of Deputies (to which each dietine despatched two deputies). However, the dietines paid close attention to other questions as well. They determined the county by-laws, local taxation and the militia; in questions of law and order they co-operated with the royal *starosta*,[32] who, incidentally, was often a local man of influence.

The magnate extended his strength and increased his political position in several mutually compatible ways. His household was the centre of the social life of the locality; his estates and household troops gave employment to lesser nobles; the latter entrusted their savings to the magnate. A mighty neighbour's support and brokerage was instrumental for lesser noblemen seeking a career in national politics. However, in the seventeenth century, particularly in the western counties, the ordinary nobility was still relatively independent since sharp competition between magnates prevented any one of them from gaining absolute dominance.

Nevertheless, a numerous and loyal clientele in the localities and control over several county Diets was the foundation of magnate strategy. When dignities and honours were being distributed, a mighty patron of county nobility could not be simply disregarded, even if he stood in opposition to the sovereign.[33]

This strategy eventually prevailed in Poland–Lithuania; it represented – or rather it was at the roots of – what may be defined as *dominium politicum*. It was incompatible with *dominium regale*. Polish public opinion tended to regard *dominium politicum et regale* as *absolutum dominium* or simply despotism.[34]

The aristocratic, or rather court-oriented, strategy aimed at impressing and influencing the king directly. In return for valued service, loyalty and devotion, the king would bestow upon the nobleman an office and/or a substantial leasehold on a royal estate (*starostwo*; Lat. *capitaneatus*) on very profitable terms. This was the other face of the Domain State. But it was of crucial importance that the king had no means of withdrawing any material favours he had bestowed. Disloyalty of a grantee was a common, even a typical, phenomenon.

This court-oriented strategy flourished in Poland–Lithuania under the first two Vasas.[35] The first Vasa king, Sigismund III, intensively prepared the election of his son Ladislas (Władysław) to the Polish throne. The household of the prince royal swarmed with young men from great houses competing for lasting friendship with the future sovereign;[36] but, as the future careers of two contemporaries of the prince, Stanislas Kazanowski and George Ossoliński, make clear,[37] initial favour at court did not necessarily determine behaviour in the longer term.

From Favourite to Minister: A Case Study

George Ossoliński (pl. 29) (1595–1650) was a statesman: a successful ambassador to London, Rome and the imperial Reichstag at Regensburg, from 1643 grand chancellor of the crown, the most influential public servant in the Commonwealth, the true kingmaker at the 1648 election and *the* minister of King John Casimir. And yet his early years at the royal court were characteristic of a favourite and gave little indication of his subsequent career as an accomplished statesman.

His father, who was the first member of his family to be a palatine (provincial governor), had been a partisan of the Habsburgs and became an ardent royalist and a supporter of Sigismund III Vasa. A great orator, he persuaded the rebels in 1607 to negotiate with the king. Although his own career was not spectacular, he successfully promoted that of his son, who was handsome and well educated. The young George Ossoliński was also an ardent Catholic, and studied in Jesuit colleges and at Louvain. To secure himself a place at court, he or his father made use of the influence of his uncle, George Firly, the vice-chancellor, of his father's friend, the Bishop of Cracow, and of the premier lay senator, Nicolas Zebrzydowski. The assistance of another relative, *hetman* John Charles Chodkiewicz, was probably decisive,[38] but the entire family supported its promising young member, and in the process made an excellent investment.[39]

In the early stages of Ossoliński's career there were four principal dramatic characters, and the initial scene of the drama was the headquarters of the army moving on Moscow in 1617–18. King Sigismund strongly promoted his eldest son, Ladislas, as a great warlord and a perfect candidate for the Polish throne.[40] The prince (born 1595) was sent to Moscow, or rather against Muscovy, in 1617: during the Time of Troubles a party among the boyars had offered him the Muscovite throne but the opportunity was lost, chiefly because Sigismund himself had his eyes on the throne of the tsars.[41] In 1617 the king and his counsellors decided to try again. However, it was too late. The number of Polish partisans in Moscow had dwindled and the expedition ended with nothing more than a truce signed at Deulino for fourteen and a half years and some territorial gains for Lithuania. Relevant for my theme is what was happening in the prince's entourage. Our principal source of information is heavily biased: Ossoliński's own memoirs.[42] We must not take his complaints and accusations at their face value, and yet his recollections retain a flavour of court life. To cut a long story short let me concentrate upon the different modes of behaviour of particular actors.

The prince's little court on the move towards Moscow was intertwined with the army command. The real commander was the Grand Hetman of Lithuania, John Charles Chodkiewicz, a great warlord, victorious over the Swedes at Kirchholm (1605) and a loyal supporter of the king in the subsequent Civil War. But Prince Ladislas was also accompanied by the whole clan of the Kazanowskis: two brothers Stanislas and Adam, both on close terms with the prince, their father Sigismund, marshal of the prince's court, and their cousin Martin, a military officer.

Young men were inspired by the high stakes of the expedition but seemed indifferent to diplomatic and military progress. Instead, the court-in-the-field swarmed with intrigues. Stanislas Kazanowski and George Ossoliński, who had joined the prince's entourage at the age of twenty-two, were the prince's bed-fellows and spent their days playing cards and banqueting. Ossoliński was bitter when, for reasons which remain unclear, he lost his bedchamber privileges. But soon Stanislas Kazanowski, the closest companion of the prince, lost his favours abruptly. Prince Ladislas tended him during his unpleasant sickness (probably venereal disease) but later unexpectedly transferred his favour to his brother Adam (pl. 30), and Stanislas disappeared from the scene so completely that today he receives no entries in biographical dictionaries. Gossip was intense and the war between the courtiers visibly diminished the preparedness of the army. The prince had no military experience and Hetman Chodkiewicz was not in full control: consequently detachments of troops under diverse commands some-times worked at cross-purposes. The hetman could not stand the prince's 'lovers',[43] who disregarded his orders. Ossoliński openly disapproved of such behaviour and after some unfortunate scenes at the 'court' inclined towards a group of more mature dignitaries who felt a sense of responsibility for the military and diplomatic outcome of the campaign, like the strong disciplinarian Hetman Chodkiewicz, several senators and the young Jacob Sobieski (who would be the father of King John III). The latter group – in this we may believe Ossoliński – strongly disliked what he called the 'silly and almost boorish pride' of Stanislas Kazanowski, whom a castellan compared with a character from Guarini's *Pastor Fido*:

O villano indiscreto e importuno!
Mezzo uomo, mezza capra e tutto bestia.[44]

Ossoliński clung to this group and developed a genuine friendship with some of them. His personal bravery won him respect from the soldiers and officials and we may assume that this was not without impact on his subsequent career as a minister.

The strategy of the Kazanowskis was a clear-cut case of petty court politics: they had no parliamentary or popular support whatsoever (in the sense of *populus nobilium*), and no political programme; they were simply struggling for influence and the prince's favours. Adam Kazanowski 'gratified the prince's whims'. Vindictive and greedy, he was generally disliked at the court; he would make no great political career but concentrated on pressing Ladislas, elected king in 1632, for measurable proofs of his favour. His Warsaw residence was regarded as the most sumptuous palace in the capital.

Ossoliński was poorly equipped for such rivalry: by writing letters home about Kazanowski's doings, he made a monumental mistake, unaware that this was defaming the prince as well. By the time the campaign was reaching its end, Ossoliński had bitterly clear proof of the prince's disfavour – his 'bad heart', as he wrote. So he asked for permission to return to Warsaw for a session of the Diet and disappeared from the court, at that time in Smolensk. Prince Ladislas' letters, which Ossoliński brought to Warsaw, reflected the situation: those addressed to the king alone sang high praise of George (who had distinguished himself as a soldier) whereas one addressed to the king and the queen 'demanded the greatest possible vengeance'. Ossoliński wrote in his memoir: 'the king laughed and wondered about my simplicity in bringing such whips for myself'. Prince Ladislas in his youth visibly encouraged potential favourites, delighted in them and was exposed to their tactics.

Ossoliński did not try again to become a favourite in the strict sense. Fortunately, the prince's criticism did not destroy his position with the king. He was despatched to England to request permission to recruit troops against the Ottomans. Upon his return from Westminster and Denmark – or possibly shortly before – and after his marriage, he apparently made a self-examination and drew conclusions from his experience as a courtier.[45] Probably in 1623 he embarked upon a parliamentary career: he was elected deputy in 1623, 1624, 1625 and finally 1627. In that year he took a radical stand and loudly defended the principles of *incompatibilitas*, or the ban on holding more than one high ministerial post. Ossoliński, although a fervent Catholic, was even prepared to extend this principle to include all archbishops and bishops and did not shirk a stormy conflict with them on the floor of the Diet. Such a political programme was frowned upon by the court but, on the other hand, Ossoliński's popularity with the ordinary nobility could not be ignored, and he constantly underlined his deference to the king – a deference which was not typical of deputies and public opinion in general.

At the king's request he appeased Bishop Andrzej Lipski. The years 1631 and 1632 were critical for his career and demanded all his political skills. In 1631 he was elected speaker (*marszałek*, Lat. *marscalcus*) of the House (testimony to his strong position with the ordinary nobility). This was Sigismund's last Diet and the court was promoting a bill proposing a royal election *vivente rege*. Few if any motions were less popular, even with the magnates: this was a Polish version of the court-versus-country conflict. The motion had no chance in the House; Ossoliński, elected its speaker, complied with the majority but did it so politely that the king did not bear him a grudge and on his deathbed appointed him court treasurer. Prince Ladislas, still only a candidate of the throne, made him his representative during the Election Diet; Ossoliński thanked the electors in the newly elected king's name. The Brandenburg envoy rightly pointed to him as a rising star of the new reign. And indeed in the Coronation Diet Ossoliński took the liberty of contradicting even the grand chancellor, Jacob Zadzik, Bishop of Chełm. Re-elected speaker in 1635, he also successfully undertook several diplomatic missions.[46] In 1636 the king appointed him palatine of Sandomierz. This was his first senatorial office but in two years he would be vice-chancellor and from 1643 grand chancellor. What were his political views? What was his view of *raison d'état*?

Traditionally, historians laid stress on his Jesuit education, his original unpreparedness for court life and his alleged absolutist tendencies. However, both in his early writings and in his diplomatic and parliamentary speeches Ossoliński hailed the principle of *monarchia mixta*, particularly in its Polish – 'republican' – version. Yet there are reasons to suppose that in his opinion the correct balance of state institutions required an increase of royal power and a closer definition of the elite. He was the principal and most steadfast supporter of the project of the Order of the Immaculate Conception (and the lowest-ranking senator on the list of its prospective members). But when the country was flooded with pamphlets hostile to the knights of the Order, and even the king's brother, John Casimir – with an eye on his popularity with the ordinary nobility – declined to accept the distinction, the whole project was doomed.[47]

In the next twelve years, George Ossoliński would be the principal minister of the Commonwealth, the close collaborator of King Ladislas IV, the initiator or executor of his projects, and eventually the author of an abortive political solution to the Cossack crisis of the Commonwealth after the military solution failed. His career differed from Zamoyski's: when Ossoliński entered on the political scene, the lesser nobility's movement for the Execution of the Laws was forgotten, and the Chamber of Deputies was much less independent of the magnates than in the 1570s. For the young Ossoliński's contemporaries the court of the royal prince seemed a promising avenue. On the other hand, the system of *dominium politicum* limited the chances of the prospective favourites. It also shaped the minister's position in a peculiar way. The latter (with the possible exception of the treasurers) was not so much an administrator as a broker between the conflicting interests of the king, the gentry and the magnate factions.[48]

The Rise and Decline of the Magnates:
Poland and the West Compared

The magnates in Poland were gaining momentum as a ruling stratum if not as an oligarchy in the strict sense of the term. It was what Robert Dahl has called 'competitive oligarchy'. This made impossible a minister's career similar to that of, say, Lord Burghley, Cardinal Richelieu, the Count-Duke of Olivares or Axel Oxenstierna. It also diminished the role of the royal court as an instrument for imposing solid discipline on the *vulgus nobilium*. This roughly explains the political assets of the magnate in his relation to the king. The magnate's strength lay in his ability to mobilize and manipulate noble constituencies. The mighty neighbour was able to call together mounted and armed followers – against robbers, for political display and last but not least in defence of 'noble freedom' against the king.[49] In general, whereas landownership was the foundation of magnate power, the patronage of the lesser nobility was crucial for the magnates' identity as a collective group.

Was it wealth in the form of landed property which made a nobleman eligible for a high office and place at the royal court, or rather office and position at court which led to enrichment and influence in the provinces? In most cases landed wealth and traditional domination over a particular area made the great noble an obvious candidate for appointment to high office (ministerial or honorific). Eventually, office was likely to bring him additional power and wealth. A magnate was really strong when he was constantly informed of what was happening at court and when at the same time he was able to control dietines (this could be directly done by his principal clients) and also take part in local country life. He had to run his own court.

While magnate families became solid pillars of the social structure and of the polity of the Commonwealth, there was remarkable mobility among them as a result of their high death-rate, and of patterns of intermarriage. The magnates never became a tightly closed group within the nobility, a *Herrenstand*. They constantly absorbed into their number the ablest members of the lesser nobility, and that link with the rank-and-file nobility contributed to their strength.

In the long run, in Poland the magnate won over the minister and the favourite. Dr Michał Kopczyński has shown how clearly this was reflected in the different behaviour of officeholders in Poland and Sweden.[50] Rule over space – in other words the regional power-base – played a much greater role in Poland than elsewhere in absolutist Europe, when the rise of absolutism was destroying the regional power-bases of the aristocracy.[51]

The magnate could also be a minister. Furthermore, the power and wealth of magnate families demanded that some of their members should hold crucial offices in the Commonwealth. It was good to send their scions to the court. But, from the later seventeenth century, the real struggle for power between 'the mightie famelies' took place in the localities and in the Diet. The role of the favourite had petered out. He lost out to the magnate in Poland, just as he lost out to the minister in the West.

Notes

1. It was called *Rzeczpospolita*, or *Res Publica*, i.e., the Commonwealth.
2. J. P. Cooper writes: 'Though the word noble was usually reserved for the peerage in England . . . in France, Poland and other countries it included those without titles who in England were called the gentry' ('General Introduction', in *The New Cambridge Modern History*, iv (Cambridge, 1971), p. 16). In this paper the term 'nobility' will be used in this comprehensive sense. Its upper stratum will be called 'magnates' (great landowners even if untitled), while the rest of the noble estate will be called 'lesser nobility'. See below, note 20.
3. I am reluctant to restate arguments of relevance which I have discussed elsewhere. The relevant papers written in English were reprinted in A. Mączak, *Money, Prices and Power in Poland, 16th–17th Centuries: A Comparative Approach* (Aldershot, 1994). See also 'The Nobility–State Relationship', in W. Reinhard, ed., *Power Elites and State Building* (Oxford, 1996), pp. 189–206, and 'Lo Stato come protagonista e come impresa: tecniche, strumenti, linguaggio', in M. Aymard, ed., *Storia dell'Europa*, iv: *L'età moderna, Secoli XVI–XVIII* (Turin, 1995), pp. 125–80.
4. Exceptions were the chief military commanders (*hetman*); these, however, usually held some senatorial office in addition to their military command.
5. H. Litwin, 'The Polish Magnates, 1554–1648: The Shaping of an Estate', *Acta Poloniae Historica*, 53 (1986), pp. 5–31.
6. A common method was to buy one or several estates in the county where the magnate aspired to an office or dignity. In Polish, as in English landed society, two or even three generations of residence did not necessarily lead to acceptance by the local nobility of the purchaser as one of their number.
7. I adapt the Eltonian notion of the point of contact to Polish conditions in 'The Space of Power: Poland–Lithuania in the Sixteenth and Seventeenth Centuries', in *Wirtschaft. Gesellschaft. Unternehmen. Festschrift für Hans Pohl zum 60. Geburtstag*, 2. Teilband (Stuttgart, 1995) also *Vierteljahrschrift für Sozial- und Wirtschaftsgeschichte*, Beiheft 120b. pp. 633–40. The Polish language does not distinguish between 'court' and 'household'.
8. E. Opaliński, 'Postawa szlachty polskiej wobec osoby królewskiej jako instytucji w latach, 1587–1648. Próba postawienia problematyki' (Polish nobility's attitudes to the king as an institution), *Kwartalnik Historyczny*, 111 (1984), p. 796.
9. Sigismund III (1598–1632), Ladislas IV (1632–48) and John Casimir (1648–68).
10. I recently treated these questions from various viewpoints in 'Paradoxes of Democracy in Poland–Lithuania', a paper read at the London School of Slavonic and East European Studies in 1994; also 'Stände und Zentralmacht in Polen–Litauen des XVI. Jahrhunderts' (forthcoming).
11. *Elementa ad Fontium Editiones*, xiii: *Res Polonicae ex Archivio Musei Britannici*, pt 1 (hereafter 'Relation'), ed. Carolus H. Talbot (Rome, 1965). The authorship of the manuscript text (British Library, Royal Mss 18 B. 1) has been much discussed. There are two possible authors: Sir George Carew and the Scottish scholar William Bruce. See *ibid.*, pp. xiii–xv; Stanisław Kot, 'Bruce, William', in *Polski słownik biograficzny* (Polish Biographical Dictionary). Notwithstanding the date in the title, the text contains information from subsequent years.
12. Antoni Mączak, 'Tacitus, Aristotle and the Polish Polity in the Later Renaissance', in Bengt Ankarloo *et al.*, eds, *Maktpolitik och Husfrid: Studier i internationell och svensk historia tillägnade Göran Rystad* (Lund, 1991), pp. 27–35 (reprinted in *Money, Prices and Power*).
13. 'Relation', p. 60. The following quotations are from pp. 59 and 60.
14. *Ibid.*, p. 85.
15. *Ibid.*, p. 75; the following quotations are from pp. 80–2.
16. 'Besides those are many officers of Charge and Magistrats for the publike government, not admitted into the Senate . . . other are called Terrestres Officiarii, as belonging to particular provinces wherein they execute theire proper offices, and have some authoritie in the Conventes of them. . . .'

Other officers are secretaries, masters of requests, officers of the household and 'Captaynes', i.e. leaseholders of royal estates (Lat. *Capitanei*, Pol. *Starostowie*, Germ. *Amtsleute*). The British author often uses Latin terms current in Poland.

17. 'Relation,' pp. 83–4. In the following quotation 'Russia' signifies Ruthenia, or the eastern, mainly Orthodox, part of the Commonwealth.
18. 'Tacitus description of the Germane traynes doth most aptly expresse the Polish . . . Hys whole discourse of the German fashions in most thinges fit the Poles.' *Ibid.*, pp. 86, 87. The following quotations are from pp. 86 and 83.
19. On the other hand, the anonymous author frequently stressed the 'tumultous' nature of the Polish lesser nobility.
20. See above, note 2. The anonymous author (1598) did not clearly distinguish between 'nobility' and 'gentry'.
21. 'Relation', p. 95. The palatine of Kiev was Constantine Ostrogski, regarded as the richest magnate in the Commonwealth.
22. Aleksander Tarnawski, *Działalność gospodarcza Jana Zamoyskiego kanclerza i hetmana w. kor.* (The Economic Activity of John Zamoyski, Chancellor and Grand Crown Hetman (Lwów, 1935); Wojciech Tygielski, *Politics of Patronage in Renaissance Poland: Jan Zamoyski, His Supporters and the Political Map of Poland, 1572–1605* (Warsaw, 1990); and 'The Faction Which Could Not Lose', in Antoni Mączak, ed., *Klientelsysteme im Europa der Frühen Neuzeit* (Munich, 1988), pp. 177–201 (Schriften des Historischen Kollegs. Kolloquien 9). The most recent biography of John Zamoyski is Stanisław Grzybowski's *Jan Zamoyski* (Warsaw, 1994).
23. His foreign friends included the anatomist and surgeon Gabriel Fallopius, and at the age of twenty he delivered a funeral oration beside Fallopius' grave.
24. My presentation of the Grand Chancellor's career is based on Grzybowski's very interesting biography.
25. Sigismund Vasa was regarded as an heir of the Polish Jagiellon dynasty because his mother was Catarina Jagiellonica, sister of King Sigismund Augustus (d. 1572).
26. Sigismund III was rather taciturn and reserved; his native language was Swedish.
27. Tarnawski, *Działalność gospodarcza Jana Zamoyskiego.*
28. Wojciech Tygielski, who wrote penetrating studies of Zamoyski's career, distinguished between 'offensive' and 'defensive support'. See his 'A Faction Which Could Not Lose', p. 196.
29. *Jan Zamoyski*, p. 285.
30. This question of the king versus the Commonwealth (*Res Publica*) has recently been analysed in depth by Edward Opaliński. See his summary in 'Die Funktionen regionaler Ämter im Machtsystem der polnischen Adelsrepublik in der zweiten Hälfte des 16. und in der ersten Hälfte des 17. Jahrhunderts . . .', in Joachim Bahicke *et al.*, eds, *Ständefreiheit und Staatsgestaltung in Ostmitteleuropa. Übernationale Gemeinsamkeiten in der politischen Kultur vom 16–18. Jahrhundert* (Leipzig, 1996), pp. 66–7.
31. Leszek Kieniewicz, *Senat Stefana Batorego* (Stephan Batory's Senate) (Institute of History PAN, PhD thesis, 1993, forthcoming).
32. These were *capitanei castrenses*, not simple leaseholders or managers of the royal estates.
33. I analyse this point in *Klientela: Nieformalne systemy władzy w Polsce i Europie XVI–XVIII w.* (The Clientele: Informal Systems of Power in Poland and Europe, 16th–18th Centuries) (Warsaw, 1994), pp. 112–60. For the most interesting case of Chancellor Zamoyski in opposition to Sigismund III, see Tygielski, *Politics of Patronage.*
34. An excellent presentation of the lesser Polish nobility's political opinions is offered by Edward Opaliński, *Kultura polityczna szlachty polskiej, 1587–1652* (Political Culture of the Lesser Polish Nobility) (Warsaw, 1995).
35. The third and last Vasa, John Casimir, abdicated in 1668 after the *rokosz* (civil war) led by George Lubomirski.
36. For the efforts of a great noble to prepare his son for a court career, see *Jasia Ługowskiego podróż do ozkół w cudzych krajach, 1639–1643* (Jaś Ługowski's Travels to Schools Abroad), ed. Krystyna Muszyńska (Warsaw, 1974), p. 33.
37. Ludwik Kubala, *Jerzy Ossoliński* (George Osoliński), 2nd edn (Warsaw, 1924); *Polski słownik biograficzny*, s.v.; Jerzy Ossoliński, *Pamiętnik* (A Memoir), ed. Władysław Czapliński (Wrocław, 1976).
38. Kubala, *Jerzy Ossoliński*, p. 9.
39. The Ossolińskis (a princely family after the Emperor Ferdinand bestowed the title on George) never

belonged to the principal magnate families enjoying political importance. But they remained rich, and pursued intellectual interests in the eighteenth and nineteenth centuries. Joseph Maximilian (1748–1826), prefect of the Imperial Library in Vienna, founded the Ossoliński Library (Ossolineum), one of the two richest Polish collections (now in Wrocław).

40. One has to remember that the Polish monarchy was elective and that since the extinction of the Jagiellons (1572) the king's son had no legal precedence over any other candidate, Polish or foreign. On the other hand, the first two freely elected kings were expected to marry Princess Anna, sister of Sigismund Augustus, and their successor, Sigismund III Vasa, was born in Sweden as the son of Catarina Jagiellonica, another royal sister. The king's children were traditionally regarded as princes and called *królewicz* – literally, son of the king but also prince royal. Notwithstanding the elective monarchy, the myth of dynastic continuity persisted and after the third and last Vasa abdicated (1668) his two native successors were called 'the Piasts', as (symbolic) descendants of the medieval Polish dynasty.

41. He would keep the somewhat incongruous title 'electus Magnus Dux Moscoviae' and during his visit in Italy would be called 'Gran Duca di Moscovia'.

42. Jerzy Ossoliński, *Pamiętnik*. In the following paragraphs I rely on Kubala, *Jerzy Ossoliński*, the respective entries on Ossoliński and the Kazanowskis in *Polski słownik biograficzny* (Stanislas Kazanowski has no entry), as well as Władysław Czapliński, *Władysław IV i jego czasy* (Ladislas IV and his Times) (Wrocław, 1972). I follow Professor Czapliński's revisionist opinion of Ossoliński as a politician and statesman.

43. Hetman Chodkiewicz's expression, although in this case there is no proof of any homosexual relationship. One bed for two men was the norm in European inns. See A. Mączak, *Travel in Early Modern Europe* (Cambridge, 1994), ch. 2.

44. Ossoliński, *Pamiętnik*, p. 62.

45. I am following the argument of Władysław Czapliński in his introduction to Jerzy Ossoliński, *Pamiętnik*, pp. 9–17.

46. In 1633, an embassy to Rome; in 1635 the military governorship of Ducal Prussia; in 1636, an embassy to the Reichstag in Regensburg (negotiations for the marriage of Ladislas with princess Cecilia Renata).

47. 'Mane sparsum fuit Casimirum principem resilire ab equitum regiorum numero creandorum. Varia interpretatio animorum successerit, cum captandae benevolentiae popularis abstinentia ab hac novitate forte deterret, vel in casu arbatae patriae calculum electionis refutatione promitteret.' Albrycht Stanisław Radziwiłł, *Memoriale rerum gestarum in Polonia, 1632–1656*, ii: *1634–1639*, ed. Adam Przyboś and Roman Żelewski (Wrocław, 1970), p. 246, entry of 6 October 1637; Kubala, *Jerzy Ossoliński*, ch. 8. The Order of the Immaculate Conception (which was intended to consist of seventy-two Polish and twenty-four foreign members) was widely regarded as an instrument of *absolutum dominium*. According to the principal senator of Lithuania, Christopher Radziwiłł (a Calvinist), the 'Knights associated with the king may in course of time grow presumptuous and either strive to attain equality with their monarch, or to dominate their fellows'. Kubala, *Jerzy Ossoliński*, ch. 8. The quotation is taken from pp. 107–8.

48. See the comparative essay of Michał Kopczyński, 'Service or Benefice? Office Holders in Poland and Sweden in the Seventeenth Century', *European Journal of History*, 1 (1994), pp. 19–28.

49. This happened in two civil wars (*rokosze*) of the seventeenth century, against Sigismund III (1606–9) and his son John Casimir (1666).

50. Kopczyński, 'Service or Benefice?'.

51. See the discussion of an important case by W. A. Weary, 'Royal Policy and Patronage in Renaissance France: The Monarchy and the House of La Trémoille' (PhD thesis, Yale University, 1972); see also a concise version of his thesis, 'La Maison de La Trémoille pendant la Renaissance: une seigneurie agrandie', in B. Chevalier, ed., *La France de la fin du XVe siècle* (Paris, 1985), pp. 187–212. On the magnate-style use of the clienteles in a major conflict see S. Kettering, 'Patronage and Politics during the Fronde', *French Historical Studies*, 14/3 (1986), p. 421. On the regional power-bases of the aristocracy in Spain see M. J. Rodriguez-Salgado, 'The Court of Philip II of Spain', in R. G. Asch and A. Birke, eds, *Princes, Patronage, and the Nobility: The Court at the Beginning of the Modern Age, c.1450–1650* (Oxford, 1991), p. 207.

Part Three
Representations of the Favourite

11
Favourites on the English Stage

BLAIR WORDEN

If there is a single register of the extent and persistence of the early-modern preoccupation with the power of royal favourites, it is the theatre.[1] Favourites are everywhere on the early modern English stage (though their ubiquitousness has generally escaped the attention of literary historians and critics). Their deleterious influence on monarchs is a large theme of dramatic representation from the later sixteenth century to the early eighteenth. It announces itself as a theatrical subject in the early 1590s, amidst the rise of the public theatre, in Marlowe's *Edward II* and the anonymous play *Woodstock*. A decade and a half later the theme has matured, through plays by Ben Jonson, John Marston, Samuel Daniel, George Chapman and John Day. In the 1620s and 1630s it is a preoccupation of Philip Massinger, of John Fletcher, of John Ford, of James Shirley, of Sir William Davenant. It persists in the (largely royalist) drama put into print during the Puritan suppression of the playhouses, and returns to the theatres after the Restoration, where it figures in plays by Dryden and Congreve and a succession of lesser writers. It persists again after the Revolution of 1688 and into the ascendancy of Walpole. The Licensing Act of 1737, itself a reaction to the theatrical representation of favouritism, then curbs the theme on the stage. In the publication of play-texts, however, it survives well into the reign of George III.

Among the titles of the plays published over that long period we find *The Favourite, The Deserving Favourite, The Fair Favourite, The False Favourite, The Great Favourite, The Loyal Favourite, The Ungrateful Favourite, The Unhappy Favourite* and *The Fool Would Be a Favourite*. There is a much larger number of plays which have a character (or more than one character) listed as a 'favourite' among the *dramatis personae*, and another much larger number where favouritism, though not declared as a theme in the title or the preliminary matter, figures prominently in the text. The favourite is a theatrical type, with a recognizable set of characteristics. While not all theatrical favourites have all those characteristics, most of them have at least many of them.

The characteristics are defined by a vocabulary which establishes, and answers to, a series of generic expectations, and which it is the purpose of this essay, through quotation and example, to recover. Our survey will be broad and will necessarily pass many complexities by. It will be primarily concerned to identify the general tendency of theatrical treatments of favouritism, not the plentiful variations or contrasts to be found among them.

To perceive the vigour of that tendency is to witness the drama's alertness to, and its ability to articulate and intensify, the political concerns of its time. It may indeed be that the drama not only reflects the public preoccupation with favouritism but bears some responsibility for it. Patrick Collinson, in examining, on another early-modern front, the gap between reality and the theatrical representation of it, has suggested that the theatre invented Puritanism: that it shaped the caricature of the Puritan that was so influential at the time and has been so influential since.[2] Did the theatre, in the same sense, invent favouritism? Did it encourage contemporaries to interpret facts of political life in literary or fictional terms? There were many more stage-favourites than stage-Puritans. Like stage-Puritans, stage-favourites were caricatures. The theatre does not dramatize the inherently undramatic. It does not show advisers of monarchs working through their intrays. It does not delineate structures of administration or of patronage. It tells us not about the operation of power but about public perceptions of it. Those perceptions crossed the gulf between literature and life. Time and again the vocabulary which reports them on the stage, and which in doing so heightens or distorts or misrepresents facts of political life, infiltrates the correspondence and memoranda and remonstrances of the political arena.[3]

The perceptions were not always new. Long before the rise of the public theatre, beneficiaries of royal favour had been subjected to some of the terms of disparagement which we shall encounter in this essay. What seems to be novel is the stock image of 'the favourite' – a noun invented in our period – which draws the threads of earlier characterization together and supplies a type, or caricature, to which individuals can readily be judged to conform. Like all types, the type of the favourite reveals at least as much about those who deploy it as about those who reportedly exemplify it.

The drama could invent only so much. It exploited and heightened the topical interest of favouritism, but it did not manufacture it. Yet of the theatrical attractions of the theme, topicality was only one. The others were literary. Being literary, they sharpened the differences between literature and life. First, favourites could meet mechanical needs of plot and dialogue. Plays were conventionally about kings and queens. Favourites were characters in whom monarchs could confide, with whom they could collude, by whom they could be manipulated or betrayed. Second – and in both literary and historical terms more interestingly – there were attractions of characterization. Stage-favourites conformed to dramatic models. In comedy there was the parasite, whose comic scope goes back to Plautus. But in early modern England, favourites are present more often in tragedy than in comedy. In tragedy they tend to conform to one or both of two other types.

First there is the Machiavel. The favourites of early-modern drama are ruthless schemers, quoting or endorsing Machiavellian 'maxims' of statecraft[4] and 'twisting and winding'[5] the more 'credulous'[6] of the rulers who have elevated them. 'Masters' of 'cunning',[7] they pursue 'deep designes' and 'deep ends' with 'deep dissimulation',[8] disclosing their intentions only in soliloquies. They are atheists, scorning the ethical sanctions of religion[9] and making light of 'conscience' (though it sometimes catches up with them).[10] Their goal is 'success', at whatever cost to virtue or justice. The end, they insist, justifies the means.[11] Machiavellian favourites are the equivalents among royal advisers of Shakespeare's Edmund or Iago. Othello's description of Iago as 'honest' is echoed by a number of men duped by favourites on the seventeenth-century stage.[12]

The second theatrical type to which favourites belong provides equivalents to Macbeth or Tamburlaine or Volpone. This is the over-reacher, whose inevitable doom is as spectacular as his ascent. Beginning as the 'creatures' of monarchs,[13] favourites seek first to become their 'partners' or 'equals'[14] and then to 'rule' or 'raign o're' them[15] and 'usurp' their powers; sometimes they aim to 'usurp' their thrones.[16] The motive most persistently ascribed to them is 'ambition', 'fatal' or 'giant-like' ambition[17] (though 'revenge' for some past injury is another frequent incentive[18]). Having 'aspiring' instincts,[19] they 'rise' or 'climb' or 'swell', or are 'raised' or 'lifted' by their rulers, to dizzy 'heights', to 'highest pinnacles'.[20] Ambition or power or favour makes them 'giddy'[21] or 'mad'[22] or 'drunk'[23] or induces a 'thirst' which drinking only intensifies.[24] Favourites aim to master or astonish 'the whole world', only to find that it offers insufficient 'room' for their designs, that 'Empire' is 'too narrow' for their 'souls', that their 'power' runs out of 'opposites' against which to prove or measure itself. So, seeking 'new projects', they 'tread' on 'air' or on 'stars' or reach for the 'skies' or 'the Region of the Sun'.[25]

Even favourites who sense the doom awaiting them are drawn ever onwards and upwards by the logic of ambition and by the logic of tragedy. Once they have begun, once they are 'in', favourites know they must 'goe on', for there can be no 'retiring'.[26] At the peaks of their fortunes they exult in 'the glories of a favourite', in the power, the attention and the servility that their sway commands.[27] Yet the shrewder of them grasp the precariousness of their triumphs. Favourites 'rise first, and commonly fall after', for 'Men born to Greatness, are but born to fall'.[28] Their ambition

> mounts upward,
> Higher and higher still, to perch on clouds,
> But tumbles headlong down with heavier ruin.[29]

In the totality or epic quality of their own destruction they recognize a fitting tribute to their stature:

> Mount, mount, my thoughts! that I may tread on kings,
> Or if I chance to fall, thus soaring high;
> I melt like Icarus, in the sun's eye.[30]

Wanting 'To be sublimely great or to be nothing',[31] they look forward to bringing the whole 'dull' 'world' down with them, rejoicing to think that in their fall their 'large ruins' will crush all beneath them.[32]

The ascent of favourites is social as well as political. Mostly they are of 'base' or 'obscure' or 'mean' origins, 'upstarts', 'raised from the dust',[33] 'mushrooms' that have 'shot up in the night',[34] rising – and falling – 'in a moment', 'on the sudden'.[35] Often (and especially in plays written before the civil wars) they are enemies to the ancient baronage, to 'the noble mind', to 'true born gentry'.[36] Many of them lack not only social roots but that other stabilizing force, age. For although there are some elderly favourites,[37] many more are young, displacing white-haired men of virtue from royal counsels.[38]

Favourites rise not through worth but through the whims of kings who promote them 'accidentally', 'blindly', 'in a good humour', 'without thinking'.[39] They are the playthings of 'fortune', that 'deity' or 'fickle Goddess' which they 'adore'[40] and which raises and then tumbles them. Their careers leave in their wake a trail of Stoic commentary on the frailty and emptiness of fortune, on the superiority of 'virtue' or 'wisdom' or 'fortitude' or 'patience' to it,[41] on the need to be true, amidst the changing winds of prosperity and adversity, to the inner 'self'.[42] Favourites have no constant selves. Constancy is a Stoic virtue. Favourites 'delight in change',[43] its enemy. They are 'Protean', 'putting on' or 'wearing' any 'shape'.[44] Favour proves to be as 'short-lived' as those shapes, to be as mutable as the 'weather'.[45]

The theme of favouritism had a further attraction to dramatists, though one harder to pin down. The noun 'favourite' seems to have carried a *frisson*. Sometimes the word is introduced into a play in a manner which suggests that the audience was expected to perk up at the sound of it. Similes are deployed to insert the noun into surprising contexts.[46] Sometimes, in the lists of *dramatis personae* which were published at the front of play-texts, and which were meant to help the plays sell, characters are described as favourites who barely earn that description in the ensuing action. Or a playwright, in adapting a source or adapting a play by another author, would introduce a favourite or turn an existing character into one.[47] Outside the drama, too, publishers noticed the public appetite for the noun 'favourite'. William Prynne's tract of 1643, *The Popish Royall Favourite*, is not about a favourite, rather about the king's indulgence to papists. In 1689 an account of the career of Judge Jeffreys, whom we do not normally think of as a favourite, was given the title *The Unfortunate Favourite*. The pamphlet drew on the tropes of characterization that theatrical accounts of favourites had established or at least fortified. So did Nathaniel Crouch's historical work *The Unfortunate Court-Favourites of England* in 1695.[48]

In plays, the *frisson* is sometimes sexual. Just as early-modern literature played on the two meanings of 'court' (the one pertaining to politics, the other to love),[49] so it made use of the fact that lovers, no less than kings, distribute 'favours' and have their 'favourites'. Davenant's play of 1638 *The Fair Favourite* is about a favoured lover, not a favoured subject, though political favouritism is a theme of it. In play after play the sexually charged word 'minion' (or 'mignon') is used to describe a political favourite; occasionally the word 'darling' is used as well or instead. Some plays make an explicit connection between political and sexual favour or conduct.[50]

Abusive epithets rain on stage-favourites. Time and again they are 'monsters' or 'villains'. They and their accomplices are 'snakes', 'rats', 'toads', 'spiders', 'earwigs', 'wasps', 'worms'.[51] Yet not all favourites are enemies to virtue. In lists of *dramatis personae* the noun 'favourite' is not expected to carry the imputation of evil – or at least, not a sufficiently vivid one – by itself. An egregious adviser is liable to be described as a 'Villanous Favourite' or 'a Favourite, and Parasite', or a 'politic stout ambitious favourite', or 'a great Favourite: One that by his Sycophantick Counsels misleads his Prince'.[52]

'Favourite' had different resonances for different people or in different contexts. Sometimes the resonances were laudatory. John Day, whose play of 1605 *The Isle of Gulls* attacked political favouritism mercilessly, dedicated another play, without irony, to a group of people whom he hailed as 'honour[']s favourites'.[53] John Dryden, whose plays generally portray favourites unsympathetically, nonetheless commends the Earl of Clarendon for having been a loyal 'favourite' of the doomed Charles I.[54] There are virtuous stage-favourites, who are sometimes undermined by less virtuous ones. That is the fate of the hero of Chapman's *The Tragedy of Chabot*, a 'favourite'.[55] John Fletcher's *The Loyal Subject* has an 'honest . . . favourite', only for the duke to be swayed instead by 'a malicious seducing Councellor', who has standard failings of stage-favourites.[56] There is the heroic central character of Lodowick Carlell's play of 1629, *The Deserving Favourite*, commended to its readers as a 'faire courtly piece' (sig. A2v). It is a general (though not universal) seventeenth-century rule that playwrights with connections at court, or with monarchical or Tory sympathies, were those likeliest to portray favourites sympathetically. There are, it is true, unsympathetically portrayed favourites in two courtly plays of the 1630s, Carlell's *The Fool would be a Favourite* and William Strode's *The Floating Island*. Yet those characters are portrayed not, as most stage-favourites are, as representatives of an unhealthy courtly norm but as aberrations from correct standards, the standards of the court of Charles I. In John Crowne's Tory play of 1679, *The Ambitious Statesman, or The Loyal Favourite*, it is the statesman of the title who is evil, while the favourite represents 'vertue in this dirty world' (p. 35). The leading character of Crowne's masque *Calisto*

(1675) is 'a chaste and favourite Nymph of Diana', though her monopoly of Diana's affections leads an envious rival to ascribe stock shortcomings of 'favourites' to her (pp. 7, 78).[57]

Even dramatists who delighted in portraying bad favourites might acknowledge the desirability of good ones. In Richard Brome's *The Court-Begger* (1640), 'a man rising in the favour royall' is rebuked not for being a favourite but for becoming one 'Before your time, that is, before you had merit'.[58] At the end of Thomas Southerne's Tory play *The Loyal Brother* (1682) the 'Villanous Favourite' is overthrown, and the king restores harmony by appointing a virtuous servant to 'Rise to our favour' in his stead.[59] There are other 'worthily deserv[ing]' favourites too.[60]

Although the relationship between king and favourite usually involves deceit by one or both parties, there are some plays – and some writings outside the drama – where it is honest, at least for a time. Sometimes too there is at least half-sympathy for monarchs and advisers who are caught up in inescapable rules and pressures of power or who need, amidst its loneliness, the consolations of companionship which favourites can provide. As Sir Francis Bacon reminded the future Duke of Buckingham in 1616, 'even the wisest' kings and princes 'have had their friends, their favourites, their privadoes in all ages; for they have their affections as well as other men'.[61] Many stage-favourites are 'friends' of monarchs and – sometimes for better, sometimes for worse – are close to their 'hearts' or 'souls'.[62] The Earl of Orrery's play of 1664 *The History of Henry the Fifth* explores the relationship between favouritism and friendship, and asks how far even a virtuous favourite can be truly a king's friend, since friendship is properly between equals (esp. pp. 2, 17, 32).[63] In a number of plays, bonds of friendship derive or draw strength from bonds of gratitude. Favours are gifts, and gifts are demonstrations of amity, of power, ideally of virtue. Royal 'bounties' bind the favourites who receive them and impose obligations on them. If those favourites betray their masters they are charged, or charge themselves, with 'ingratitude'.[64]

In addressing the theme of favouritism, playwrights were liberal in supplying their characters with generalizations about the qualities and obligations of 'kings', of 'princes', of 'courts'.[65] Truths which had a general application could not but have topical ones. Sometimes playwrights found delicate phrases through which to point their audiences or readers towards the contemporary scene, an art of which Massinger was the subtlest exponent.[66] When suspected of mischievous intent, dramatists offered standard protestations of innocence, claiming that their words had merely followed their sources or had been written before current events had given them an unintended 'application'.[67] There is, however, a change over the course of the seventeenth century. In its first half, audiences were normally left to discern contemporary applications for themselves. In its second, dramatists were readier to draw attention to the present 'parallels' which their plays supplied.[68]

Though contemporary application was only occasionally a playwright's over-riding purpose, it was often one of his purposes. What does stage-favouritism tell us about the political perspectives of the time? First, it reminds us how strong and pervasive was the commitment to the ideal of just kingship, the ideal which evil stage-favourites undermine. Virtuous subjects of misgoverned kings longingly recall the reigns of virtuous ones (often the father of the present ruler) or hope for deliverance by virtuous princes in exile.[69] It is true that many stage-kings are at least as Machiavellian as their favourites. Occasionally they are more so. 'The favourites of Kings', explains a character in Davenant's *The Fair Favourite*, 'are chosen but / To own, and wear their master's worser sins'.[70] Normally, however, favourites 'weaken' or 'eclipse' the merits of kingship, which is rightly 'rich and strong'. 'Royalty' is 'lent out' or 'farmed out' or 'leased', or its 'beams' are 'engrossed'. 'Majesty' is 'trampled on' or made a 'lawn', while the favourite 'grasps the [prince's] sceptre in his stead', leaving him only the 'bare' or 'empty' 'name' of ruler.[71]

The problem of favourites is the problem of 'evil counsel'.[72] Favourites and their followers monopolize and 'abuse' the royal 'ear'.[73] Kings 'hear nothing' but what their favourites want them to hear and will 'hear nothing' against them.[74] Rulers are urged to rely on 'councillors' or 'Counsellors', 'not Favourites', and to choose their advisers not 'for favour, but for parts'.[75] Favourites lead 'factions' which capture the prince for factious purposes.[76] Instead the ruler should 'be / Everybody's king' and 'lend equal ears / To what all say'.[77] One frequent occasion of dramatic conflict is the determination of a favourite's opponent that the ruler be 'told' of the state of his realm and of the abuses to which he has given his authority.[78] Some plays or characters insist that the admonition of monarchs should be 'modest', that rulers must be advised 'with that reverence which to kings is due'.[79] There are warnings against 'boldness' of address. Yet sometimes 'boldness' is a 'duty' towards monarchs,[80] who are almost universally cocooned in flattery and sycophancy. Play after play, especially in the half century before the civil wars, contrasts the artificial, honeyed speech of favourites and parasites around the king with the commitment of their opponents – often representatives of ancient noble houses – to 'honest bluntness', 'honest plainness', 'plain dealing', 'plain truth'.[81]

Plainness of speech against favourites moves rulers to anger.[82] Under regimes controlled by favourites, 'speaking truth' can be 'dangerous'.[83] So 'kings do seldome hear' 'Free speech'.[84] Criticism of favourites, or other 'talk of the state', is held to be 'treasonous'.[85] It is risky to speak 'too loud',[86] for 'spies' and 'informers' are ubiquitous.[87] 'Safety' lies in keeping quiet and in prudent adjustment to the facts of power.[88] In play after play the question is raised whether the opponents of favourites will 'dare' to confront princes with 'the truth'.[89] A common device is to have a spirited critic speak out while a less brave or less prominent figure applauds his courage in an aside.[90]

The sway of favourites is identified sometimes with 'tyranny', sometimes with 'absolute' or 'unlimited' rule.[91] The 'will' or 'prerogative' of rulers, and thus of their favourites, prevails over law or custom or consent.[92] In plays by Jonson and Daniel written in the years around the death of Queen Elizabeth, treatments of impending tyranny corresponded to immediate contemporary anxieties.[93] In those plays too we find a theme which will again be of public concern in the 1620s and 1630s and which will then be developed in the plays of Massinger: the erosion of conciliar or parliamentary or customary liberties and the entrenchment – sometimes the deification[94] – of unlimited monarchical power. As authority contracts towards the centre, so aristocratic rule gives way to absolutism. Councillors and senators become mere 'lookers-on', giving their 'suffrages to that / Which was before determined', shunning topics which are now 'things above us, / And so no way concerne us'. Power has come to reside in 'cabinet counsels', which discredit and destroy conciliar rule.[95]

Though the substance of freedom departs, its forms are preserved. Rulers and favourites pay false-hearted tributes to the liberties they are eroding.[96] Princes, swayed by favourites, claim to welcome candid counsel. In their more prudent moments, indeed, they realize that they need it.[97] Yet in general they soon revert to type. The most subtle observer of that process is again Massinger. In his *The Great Duke of Florence* the duke declares against adulatory forms of address and against the deification of princes, and expresses a wish for 'familiar conference' with those who 'counsel and direct us'. Yet his own 'will' and 'pleasure' prevail, for 'Princes are / As gods on earth'. In Massinger's *The Duke of Milan* the duke urges an adviser to 'use [his] freedome' of address to him. Yet seventy lines later, when a lord of the council has presumed to criticize the ruler's 'especiall favourite', the duke rounds on him for 'speak[ing] thus', calling him 'My vassall'.[98] In the world portrayed by Massinger and other dramatists, 'freedom' or 'liberty' is 'ancient', 'old'. Its antiquity, which is properly its sanction, is too often the mark of its impotence before new systems of power.[99] Few of the enemies of tyranny see legitimate means of resisting its advance. Most of them are instinctively loyal even to the most oppressive of kings. They think it wrong to censure them or pry into their hearts. They are mainly appalled by rebellion.[100]

If the decline of liberty is one feature of modern politics addressed by stage-favouritism, another is the corrupting properties of courts. Though most plays with favourites are set in distant lands in distant times, their authors export to the monarchical entourages of those remote venues the features that were so widely associated with the Renaissance or Baroque courts of their own time: to ancient Greece, ancient Rome, Gothic Lombardy, Moorish Granada, timeless Turkey or Persia, Roman or Saxon Britain, medieval England or France.[101] It is the 'unwholesom', 'infect[ious]', 'poys'nous Air' of courts, their 'foul corruption', that turns apparently honourable men into evil favourites.[102]

Favourites master the 'well known', 'wicked', 'soothing', 'smooth / And subtle' 'arts of court'.[103] They cannot 'leave' courts, for courts and favouritism are inseparable.[104]

It is usually at court that favourites are shown using 'gold'[105] to strengthen their following, or selling posts, or taunting or fleecing armies of suitors and petitioners. The sway of favourites is associated repeatedly with bribery and with the distribution and marketing of offices and places[106] (and often with the allocation of ecclesiastical patronage[107]). In a number of plays the favourite's first appearance shows him selling an office or exacting bribes from petitioners.[108] Through patronage and corruption, favourites build up 'heard[s] of Parasites, Clients, fooles and sutors',[109] of 'creatures'[110] who 'flock, and fawn upon [their] greatness'.[111]

Courts, like the careers of the favourites who thrive in them, provoke a wealth of Stoic disapproval. They are no friends to 'constancy'.[112] Instead, amidst 'the wavering smiles of court', 'cozening fortune holds the scale, which she / Hath ever done in Court'.[113] Faith, morality, opinion, taste, all follow power and its sudden shifts. Men learn to 'laugh' or 'nod', or 'wag [their] tayle[s]', in time with the king or favourite, to 'freeze or sweat, as my Lord is either hot or cold', to 'thinke . . . / As the King thinkes'. They grasp that 'A prince's power makes all his actions virtue', that 'all is good' that the favourite 'make[s] so'. 'It is the bliss of courts to be employed, no matter how', and the way to 'favour' is 'to obey and please', 'Without examining the reasons why'.[114] Criticism of courts is not necessarily criticism of kings. The failings of courts are sometimes presented as facts of political life, with which any monarch, however virtuous, has to live. Even so, the courts of monarchs are vicious places, sinks of venality and luxury and depravity.

They are also enemies to honour and military prowess. Though there are some valiant favourites, who have risen through exploits in war and can be ill-at-ease in courts,[115] the run of favourites and of their adherents are 'cowards' who 'ne're heard / The Canons roring tongue, but at a Triumph'. Wearing silken or effeminate clothes and reeking of perfume,[116] loving 'wantonness and ease', favourites head 'the faction of that home-bred cowardize, / That would run backe from glory'. While brave soldiers go unprovided for, or endure hardships, in distant lands, or 'fill up Hospitalls' at home, favourites monopolize the rewards of office and appropriate the financial gains of war for themselves, a theme of which Massinger is once more the leading exponent.[117] Often it is valiant and loyal generals, all of them experienced and a number of them elderly, who reproach kings for the sway of favourites.[118]

We have been examining preoccupations and language that stretch across a 'long' seventeenth century, from the 1590s to the decades after 1700. Yet there was change as well as continuity.

If, throughout our period, there are plays in which favourites play significant parts, it is mainly in the early part of it that the theme of favouritism produces both theatrical innovation and freshness of political perspective. It is mainly in the early part, too, that playwrights of stature write plays that are *about* favouritism: not exclusively about it, but turning on it in theme and plot.

The pattern is set by two plays of the early 1590s, Marlowe's *Edward II* (*c.* 1592), the title-page of which describes Piers Gaveston as a 'mighty favorite', and the anonymous *Woodstock* (*c.* 1591–4), which is set in the reign of Richard II. Gaveston's lines at the outset of *Edward II*, 'What greater bliss can hap to Gaveston / Than live and be the favourite of a king?' (I. i. 4–5), are not the first recorded use of the noun 'favourite' in the English language. It can be traced back at least as far as 1579, when John Stubbs, warning Queen Elizabeth against marriage to the papist duc d'Anjou, lamented that 'princes . . . commonly' listen not to men who 'dare tell truth' but to 'their chief favourites', who 'study rather for smooth, delicate words than for plain, rough truth'. Three years or so later the fiction of Philip Sidney, who had been Stubbs' literary ally in the campaign against the Anjou match, described the 'favourites' of a tyrant, who were given 'all offices and places'.[119] Between them, Stubbs and Sidney deployed – perhaps created – the tropes of literary favouritism. Marlowe brought them on to the stage. Gaveston's opening soliloquy announces the birth of a theatrical tradition.

In both *Edward II* and *Woodstock*, favourites take control of the monarch, oppress the nobility and commons, provoke rebellion, weaken the country's standing abroad. Both plays set pampered favourites – Gaveston and then the Spencers in *Edward II*; Bushy, Greene, Bagot and Scrope in *Woodstock* – against frugal and warlike barons, who ought to rule in harmony with the crown but whom favouritism has divided from it. In both plays the favourites are of low origin, a characteristic that involved the two playwrights in adjustments to their sources, Marlowe reducing the social standing of Edward's favourites, the author of *Woodstock* omitting the influence on Richard of favourites who were not upstarts.[120] The formulae of characterization and conflict established by the two plays would have an enduring appeal, particularly in the drama performed in the popular playhouses up to 1640.[121]

In the years around 1600, stage-favouritism was given an exciting and risky topicality by the prominence and fall of the Earl of Essex (pl. 10). No other favourite of our period cast so powerful a spell on the theatrical imagination. As a favourite, Essex figures mainly in plays written after his death. Dramatists were interested less in his occupancy of power than in his descent from it. They were fascinated by the combination of qualities that raised him so high and yet cast him so low, a subject to which Chapman boldly points in his plays of 1607–8 about the Biron conspiracy.[122] But while dramatists blamed Essex's failings, they saw him not as an instrument of courtly wickedness but as a victim of it. It was he, after all, who stood for martial prowess and antique honour. He, at least, was no upstart. It was the stay-at-home party, the party of Robert Cecil, that brought Essex down, by methods that repelled not only Essex's followers but neutral observers. Essex, as William Camden said, 'seemed not to be made for the court':[123] his enemies, as dramatists portrayed them, were arch-courtiers. There was thus scope for figuring both Essex and his enemies as stage-favourites.[124]

The fullest exploitation of that dual potential is Daniel's *The Tragedy of Philotas*, published in 1605. Daniel, a former client of Essex, was brought before the council for writing the play, which describes the downfall of Alexander the Great's favourite Philotas, who is executed for treason. During the proceedings against Philotas, he and his opponents are given words borrowed from the confrontation between Essex and his enemies at the earl's trial. The play presents a puzzlingly uneven balance of sympathy, which seems explicable only on the supposition that Daniel altered his text before its publication, perhaps for reasons relating to his brush with authority.[125] Sometimes it seems that the fatal flaw of ambition has lured Philotas into treason: at other moments he seems the victim, perhaps the innocent victim, of courtly 'minions' who have deviously 'intrapt' him (ll. 395, 426). Like Essex, Philotas is unfit for court life and in some respects superior to it (ll. 61–6). He stands for ancient liberties and for what Daniel elsewhere calls 'ancient honour neere worne out of date'.[126]

The ghost of Essex is visible again, if more faintly, in another play published in 1605, Jonson's *Sejanus His Fall*, which apparently got its author, too, into trouble with the council. In *Cynthias Revells*, his satire of the Elizabethan court in 1600, Jonson had already alluded, in what seems to have been an ill-judged bid for royal approval, to Essex's fall from the queen's grace.[127] In *Sejanus His Fall* the imaginative challenge posed by Essex's career is more fully met. Jonson's Sejanus, the 'favourite' and 'minion' of the Emperor Tiberius (III. 243, 640, IV. 364, 454), is an Icarus who, in that respect, resembles Essex. Yet Jonson, like Daniel, distances Essex from the *mores* of the court. The play allocates the earl's values not to Sejanus but to the antique senators who detest the court and lament the seemingly irresistible advance of tyranny.[128]

Sejanus His Fall is a new departure in the theatrical representation of favouritism. Earlier treatments described groups (or a succession) of 'favourites', who had to contend, not always on terms of advantage, with other political parties. Jonson's theme is the dominance and fall of a single favourite. In *Edward II*, it is true, Gaveston has secured a monopoly of royal favour, but that evil soon gives way to others. He does not dominate Marlowe's play as Sejanus does Jonson's. The concentration of Jonson's play on a single favourite enabled him to create, as perhaps no one had done before him, a tragic pattern out of the career of a politician who was not a king.

It also reflected a change of political climate. Until the very end of Elizabeth's reign, no favourite had secured anything like a monopoly of favour. Essex was known as 'a favourite', not 'the favourite'.[129] His fall, and Robert Cecil's swift rise to ascendancy thereafter, aroused the prospect, which would be so prominent a theme of Jacobean and early Caroline politics, of government by a single favourite, at the expense not only of his rivals but of the authority of the crown. A contemporary observer of the twilight of Elizabeth's reign, the time when *Sejanus His Fall* was conceived and its composition begun, noted a change in the character of her rule. Hitherto, by 'feed[ing] the factious affections' of her principal subjects, she had secured their dependence on 'her favour' for 'the raysing of their own greatnes'. She had thus contrived 'to make her own direction the more absolute'. Now, however, 'the queen like Claudius is kept from hearing what is done in the market. All mysteries of state' have escaped her knowledge, and she is left to 'raigne as the moone in borrowed majestie'.[130] That, in Jonson's play, is the fate threatening Tiberius, who has surrendered power and initiative to Sejanus. Later Jonson would allude to the same danger under the early Stuarts: princes who neglect their 'proper office', he wrote, have 'often-times' the misfortune 'to draw a Sejanus to be near about them; who will at last affect to get above them'.[131]

Jonson's play is innovative too in another way: in its depiction of a reign of terror. Earlier dramatists had represented the evils of tyrants: Jonson communicates the evils of tyranny. He is the first dramatist to indicate the resemblances, which impressed and alarmed contemporaries, between the loss of Roman liberties under the early empire and the threat to English and European liberties posed by the monarchies of the late Renaissance.[132] Those themes would make *Sejanus His Fall* a model for a number of seventeenth-century plays in which favourites appear. They would also bring the memory of Sejanus into the arena of political debate, where he would figure most vividly during the supremacy of Buckingham in the 1620s, but long thereafter too, at least until late in the eighteenth century.[133]

One other play from the early years of James I, this one a comedy, shows how powerfully the idea of favouritism held the public mind of that time: John Day's *The Isle of Gulls* (1606), a work which brought severe retribution to the company that performed it. The very title was provocative, recalling as it intentionally did *The Isle of Dogs*, the play of 1597 which had landed its authors, of whom Jonson was one, in prison. Day's play is an adaptation of Philip Sidney's *Arcadia*, a work written around a quarter of a century earlier. Sidney's story has a favourite, Dametas, a buffoon whose whimsical elevation by Duke Basilius illustrates the irresponsibility of absolute power. Yet Dametas and his rise occupy relatively little space in Sidney's romance, where the setting is pastoral, not courtly, the duke having broken up his court. Day transfers the story to a court and makes Dametas, who becomes the monopolist of office and favour, a central character, flourishing while the commonwealth sickens with social and political abuses.[134]

Day spotted his analogical opportunity in two accidents of history: the first, that James I, like Basilius in Sidney's story, was fond of hunting, the activity from which, in the *Arcadia*, Dametas' prosperity takes its rise; the second, that James had written a book with a title, *Basilikon Doron*, that inadvertently aligned him with the name of Sidney's duke. In Day's play as in Sidney's romance, Dametas' elevation is a whimsical exercise of the duke's arbitrary power.[135] Yet where Sidney's main criticism is directed at the duke, Day's is directed at the favourite. We cannot tell whether Day's Dametas is intended to parallel a particular Jacobean politician. If so the target may be Robert Cecil, who was widely attacked in ballads and libels in terms often reminiscent of the depictions of favourites in the drama;[136] or it may be one of the king's Scottish favourites, who were derided in 1605 in *Eastward Ho!*, another play whose authors, Jonson again among them, were put in prison.[137]

One writer is conspicuous by his absence from the list of dramatists eager to dramatize the rule of favourites: Shakespeare. We can grasp the point by setting his *Richard II* beside *Woodstock*, which may have been a source for it, and where the theme of favouritism is so much ampler. In Shakespeare the favourites have minor parts. It is true that the lament of John of Gaunt for 'This royal throne of kings, this sceptred isle' follows the scene which introduces Greene, Bagot and Bushy, and is prompted by the Duke of York's account of the victory won by flattery and 'will' over counsel and of the success of the king's lascivious entourage in 'stopp[ing]' his 'ear'.[138] Yet those revelations are not developed.

With one arguable exception, there are no favourites with major parts in Shakespeare. He might have chosen to make a favourite of Polonius. Yet Claudius, like Shakespeare's other wicked kings – like Richard III, like Macbeth, like Leontes – makes his own way to evil. The arguable exception is to be found in *Henry VIII*, the play Shakespeare wrote late in life with John Fletcher, whose own plays are peopled with favourites. Henry for a time allows too much power to Wolsey, the upstart favourite opposed by the ancient nobility, though the king sees his mistake and recovers from it. When in 1628, a fortnight before the Duke of Buckingham's assassination, the duke attended a revival of *Henry VIII*, observers remarked on his resemblance to Wolsey, that 'lively type of himself, having governed this kingdome eighteen years, as [Buckingham] hath fourteen'.[139] Yet that response tells us about the concerns of the observers, not of Shakespeare.

For there is in Shakespeare none of the appetite for barbed or risky topical allusion, and none of the instinct for political didacticism, that characterize many of his contemporary dramatists.[140] (On the one occasion when he clearly alludes to a contemporary politician – probably Essex – he does not have that politician's standing as a favourite in mind.[141]) The playwrights who wrote about favourites were the ones who got into trouble. Shakespeare did not get into trouble. It is true that the deposition scene in *Richard II*, a play which Essex may have had performed in the hope of winning support for his revolt, had to be omitted from the texts of it published in the lifetime of Elizabeth, who suspected that other accounts of Richard's reign were aimed at her. Sir John Hayward's account of Richard's deposition, published in 1599, led to his fierce interrogation and protracted imprisonment. Yet no one seems to have suspected

Shakespeare of writing *Richard II* with an eye to contemporary politics. His immunity offers a striking contrast not only to Hayward's fate but to the charges levelled at Jonson and Daniel as a result of their plays about favourites.

After the opening years of James' reign, favouritism, though a regular theatrical subject, is never again quite so dominant a one: not even during the supremacy of Buckingham. Certainly the duke was a theatrical target, most vividly and daringly perhaps in *The Maid of Honour*, the play of 1621 or 1622 by Massinger, the client of Buckingham's rival the Earl of Pembroke. Buckingham is unmistakably figured by the 'state Catamite' Fulgentio,[142] the upstart and effeminate monopolist of favour and profit, under whose regime the nation has settled for a slothful peace abroad while the navy has fallen into neglect.[143] At the outset of the play a sharp and extended parallel is drawn between the events that launch Massinger's plot and the refusal of James and Buckingham to give armed assistance to the Elector Palatine. The war party is rousingly led by Bertoldo, who warns the king against 'sycophants, that feed upon your favour' and 'prefer your ease before your honour'. Yet the opening contemporary allusions soon fade.[144] So does the opening impression of didacticism, which yields to the sort of balance of opposing insights that only Shakespeare of the previous generation essayed. Though Fulgentio remains contemptible, Bertoldo's attacks on his regime prove to be the bombast of a morally flawed character.

For in the 1620s and 1630s political drama is changing. The savage satire of courts to be found in the plays of Marston or the early Jonson, or in Donne's early poetry, has largely given way to more subtle, less partisan, less aggressive or acidic writing. The essence of drama is conflict, but there is, in the better drama, a change in the nature of that conflict. Oppositions between good and bad are becoming less straightforward. There are playwrights readier to try to capture the ethical ambivalences of power, and readier to acknowledge the humanity of flawed politicians. The representation of the favourite in Massinger's *The Great Duke of Florence* or Ford's *The Broken Heart* illustrates the trend. There is another change too. Drama which treats of politics becomes less centrally political. It is starting to have proportionately less to do with politics and more to do with romance. Plots and behaviour which begin with the pressures of politics come to centre on those of love.

To us, the great age of favourites may seem to have passed by around 1640. Yet public interest in the subject did not diminish after that date. It was not reduced by the civil wars, or by the Restoration, or by the Revolution of 1688. William III's Dutch favourites were unpopular as James' Scottish ones had been before them. In William's reign, favouritism was as prominent a theme of historical or biographical writing as it had ever been. Nathaniel Crouch's *The Unfortunate Court-Favourites of England* of 1695, which relates the careers of favourites from Gaveston in the fourteenth century to Strafford in the seventeenth, conceives of favouritism as a universal and unvarying phenomenon.[145]

On the stage, too, the preoccupation with favouritism survived the Puritan Revolution and then the deposition of James II.[146] After the Restoration the subject was given fresh topicality by the fall of Edward Hyde, Earl of Clarendon, in 1667 (pl. 70). That event was quickly followed by two plays which touch on it, Orrery's *Tryphon* and Sir Robert Howard's *The Great Favourite, or the Duke of Lerma*. Though the plays were written, as those about Essex had mainly been, after the favourite's fall, Clarendon remained alive and his enemies dreaded his return. Both authors, in their portraits of favourites, use biographical touches to summon Clarendon to their audiences' minds. Howard's play, which reproduces arguments used by himself and by other MPs during the recent attacks on Clarendon, is more closely and conspicuously related to the minister's fall than Orrery's. Yet *Tryphon* carries a clear warning to Charles II which is announced in its opening speech: 'he too much deserves to lose his Throne, / Who makes a Subject's Pow'r exceed his own.'[147] The two plays endorse the view of the courtier who, when Clarendon delivered up the seals of office, told Charles 'that this was the first time he could ever call himself King of England, being freed from this great man'.[148]

The ensuing decades brought many more plays – some Whig, some Tory, some Jacobite, some of no evident political bias – which addressed the theme of favouritism, and in which modern critics, with varying degrees of confidence, have detected topical allusions.[149] In one play of 1691, *King Edward the Third* (perhaps by John Bancroft), the allusions are unmistakable. That work consciously echoes an earlier project. Ben Jonson had begun, but not completed, a play entitled *Mortimer His Fall*, about the favourite of the early years of Edward III. His draft (which was published in his *Works* in 1640) may have been a first attempt by Jonson at the theme of the fallen favourite, for which, in *Sejanus His Fall*, he would choose a Roman setting instead. The draft would have a long afterlife, as would *Sejanus His Fall*. The play of 1691, subtitled *The Fall of Mortimer*, related the sway and fall of that favourite and drew parallels between them and the regime and fall of James II. After a revival in 1719, it was produced in a rewritten form in 1731, now with *The Fall of Mortimer* as its title.[150] Allusions to events of that year were introduced into the text, and the language was brought up to date to enable the medieval barons to speak the language of 'patriot[ism]' and to attack Walpole's use of placemen and mercenary parliaments.[151] The performances of the new version caused a sensation until the government suppressed them. In the same year, perhaps in conjunction with the *The Fall of Mortimer*, there appeared *The Fall of the Earl of Essex*, a revised version of John Banks' *The Unhappy Favourite* (1682). A series of subtle touches conspires to adapt Banks' version to the political vocabulary of the 1730s and to hint at resemblances between Walpole and Essex's rival in the play, Lord Burghley. Other plays, too, joined in the public denigration of Walpole the favourite.[152] Indeed in the years preceding the Licensing Act of 1737 playwrights mocked his ascendancy with vigour and boldness. The theatrical consequences were temporarily exhilarating but soon disastrous. The theme of favouritism, which had been so widespread in political drama since the 1590s, now provoked the suppression of that drama.

Henceforth plays against favourites could (at least normally) appear only in print, not on the stage. Yet print provided a medium of sharp criticism. Jonson's *Sejanus His Fall* was rewritten in 1752, and again in 1770, with contemporary targets in view. The two adaptations protested against what the text of 1770 called 'that dramatic star chamber, the licence office', which prevented their performance.[153] The version of 1770, entitled *The Favourite*, aimed witty shafts at George III's favourite the Earl of Bute, to whom it was mockingly dedicated. So was a play-text of 1763 which *The Favourite* echoed: the republication, at the instigation of John Wilkes, of the text of *Mortimer His Fall* of 1731 and, with it, of Jonson's draft. Bute's alleged intimacy with the young king's mother neatly corresponded to Mortimer's relationship with young Edward's mother, a theme of Jonson's projected play 160 years earlier. Wilkes' saucy dedication (which includes the first usage of the word 'favouritism' recorded by the *Oxford English Dictionary*) invites Bute to produce a still better play on Mortimer. Bute, explains Wilkes, would find that task 'easy', for 'A variety of anecdotes in real life will supersede the least necessity of political fiction.'[154]

Yet if the drama retains, until George III's reign, its power to deride contemporary favourites, the aesthetic decline of such attacks can be dated much earlier. Resilient as the attraction of the theme to playwrights was, topical treatments of favourites produced almost no drama of artistic distinction after the early 1640s. The one clear exception, Sir Robert Howard's fine (if markedly unhistorical) portrait of the ascendancy of the Duke of Lerma, *The Great Favourite*, half proves a rule, for it was based on a play written earlier, certainly before the Restoration, perhaps before the Civil Wars.[155] In the drama before 1640, the contemporary pertinence and the artistic potential of the theme of favouritism fed off each other: thereafter the two went separate ways.

For the historian, however, bad plays can be as informative as good ones. Interest in favouritism, as reflected in the publication of plays and in the writing of fiction and of history, was probably as strong for most of the eighteenth century as it was in the later sixteenth and the seventeenth centuries. It made its slow retreat before a principle which, though it was intermittently advanced in the eighteenth century, was secured only in the nineteenth: a principle which reflected a changed understanding of the proper relationship of minister to monarch. For it was now that the leading ministers of monarchs came under attack not for undermining or usurping the crown's authority, that pre-eminent sin of stage-favourites, but for failing in their duty to restrain it.[156]

Notes

1. In writing this essay I have incurred an exceptionally heavy debt to Dr Paulina Kewes, of the University of Wales, Aberystwyth, for her scholarly guidance and expertise.

2. Patrick Collinson, 'Ben Jonson's *Bartholomew Fair*. The Theatre Constructs Puritanism', in David L. Smith *et al.*, eds, *The Theatrical City. Culture, Theatre and Politics in London, 1576–1649* (Cambridge, 1995), pp. 157–69.

3. Public perceptions of favouritism are helpfully described by Robert P. Shepherd, 'Royal Favourites in the Political Discourse of Tudor and Stuart England', Claremont University PhD thesis (1985), esp. ch. 6.

4. Ben Jonson, *Mortimer His Fall* (in C. H. Herford *et al.*, eds, *Ben Jonson*, 11 vols (Oxford, 1925–52), vii), I. 25ff.; J. D. Jump, ed., *Rollo, Duke of Normandy* (Liverpool, repr. 1969: hereafter *Rollo*), p. xxiv; [Thomas Southland?], *The Ungrateful Favourite* (London, 1664), pp. 24, 71; Joseph Harris, *The Mistakes* (London, 1691), p. 10; cf. Balthazar Gerbier, Baron d'Ouvilley, *The False Favourit Disgrac'd* (London, 1657), p. 19. With the exception of *Sejanus His Fall*, all of Jonson's writings will be cited from the edition by Herford *et al.* D'Ouvilley also explored the theme of favouritism in *Les Effects Pernicieux de Meschants Favoris et Grands Ministres de L'Estat* (The Hague, 1653).

5. Charles Gildon, *The Roman Brides Revenge* (London, 1697), p. 2.

6. Robert Baron, *Mirza* (London, 1655 edn), sigs A6v, A7, and p. 14; cf. John Dryden, *Don Sebastian* (in E. N. Hooker and H. T. Swedenborg, eds, *The Works of John Dryden*, 20 vols (Berkeley and Los Angeles, 1956–), xv), I. i. 57.

7. Ben Jonson, *Sejanus His Fall*, ed. Philip Ayres (Manchester, 1990), II. 155; John Ford, *The Broken Heart*, ed. T. J. B. Spencer (Manchester, 1980), I. i. 42; William Gifford, ed., *The Dramatic Works and Poems of James Shirley*, 6 vols (repr. New York, 1966; hereafter Shirley), v, p. 333; Baron, *Mirza*, pp. 42, 81, 105; John Banks, *The Unfortunate Favourite; or, the Earl of Essex* (London, 1682), p. 5.

8. A. R. Waller, ed., *The Works of Beaumont and Fletcher*, 10 vols (Cambridge, 1905–12; hereafter Beaumont and Fletcher), iii, p. 321; *The Ungrateful Favourite*, p. 57; Bevill Higgons, *The Generous Conqueror* (London, 1702), p. 40; cf. Charles Johnson, *Love and Liberty* (London, 1709), p. 6.

9. Jonson, *Sejanus*, II. 180–1, V. 69–78, 390, 908–12 (cf. Herbert P. Horne *et al.*, eds, *'Nero' & Other Plays* (London, 1888), p. 87: hereafter *Nero*); Baron, *Mirza*, p. 73; Sir Robert Howard, *The Great Favourite or The Duke of Lerma* (in D. D. Arundell, ed., *Dryden and Howard 1664–1668* (Cambridge, 1929)), pp. 226, 229, 270; Elkanah Settle, *Cambyses King of Persia* (London, 1671), pp. 5, 57; John Crowne, *The Ambitious Statesman or Loyal Favourite* (London, 1679), p. 37; cf. d'Ouvilley, *False Favourit*, p. 98.

10. Jonson, *Sejanus*, V. 201; *Rollo*, II. ii. 63–6; Shirley, v, p. 335; Baron, *Mirza*, p. 43; d'Ouvilley, *False Favourit*, p. 71; Thomas Southerne, *The Loyal Brother* (London, 1682), p. 45; Higgons, *Generous Conqueror*, p. 12; cf. Nathaniel Crouch, *The Unfortunate Court-Favourites of England* (London, 1695), p. 45.

11. John Marston, *The Malcontent*, ed. M. L. Wine (London, 1965), V. iv. 73; *Nero*, p. 52; *Rollo*, IV. i. 33–6 (cf. IV. i. 80–1); Beaumont and Fletcher, iii, pp. 309–10; Baron, *Mirza*, p. 43; Roger Boyle, Earl of Orrery, *Tryphon* (London, 1669), p. 1; Settle, *Cambyses*, pp. 5, 67–8; Banks, *Unhappy Favourite*, p. 7[7]; Southerne, *Loyal Brother*, pp. 12–13.

12. *Rollo*, III. i. 254; Lodowick Carlell, *The Deserving Favourite* (London, 1629), sigs B4, G2; *The Ungrateful Favourite*, p. 34 (cf. p. 24); Southerne, *Loyal Brother*, p. 3.

13. Philip Massinger, *The Duke of Milan* (in Philip Edwards and Colin Gibson, eds, *The Plays and Poems of Philip Massinger*, 5 vols (Oxford, 1976, i), I. iii. 282; Shirley, iv, pp. 159, 200 (cf. p. 170); James Maidment and W. H. Logan, eds, *The Dramatic Works of Sir William D'Avenant*, 5 vols (repr. New York, 1964: hereafter Davenant), i, pp. 21, 118, 119, 131; Roger Boyle, Earl of Orrery, *The History of Henry the Fifth* (published London, 1669), 'The Persons'; *The Ungrateful Favourite*, pp. 14, 16; Southerne, *Loyal Brother*, p. 3.

14. Jonson, *Sejanus*, 'Argument' (l. 5), I. 218–19, 529 (cf. Tacitus, *Annals*, IV. ii); Philip Massinger, *The Great Duke of Florence* (in Edwards and Gibson, *Massinger*, iii), I. i. 93; Carlell, *Deserving Favourite*, sig. B4; Baron, *Mirza*, p. 7.

15. Christopher Marlowe, *Edward II*, ed. Roma Gill (Oxford, repr. 1989), V. iv. 48; A. P. Rossiter, ed., *Woodstock* (London, 1946), I. ii. 19; Davenant, i, p. 179; Beaumont and Fletcher, iii, p. 313.

16. J. W. Lever, ed., *The Wasp* (Malone Society, 1974 [1976]), p. 100; Baron, *Mirza*, p. 42; d'Ouvilley, *False Favourit*, p. 97*; Howard, *Great Favourite*, p. 235; Orrery, *Tryphon*, p. 1; Settle, *Cambyses*, p. 70; *The Fall of Mortimer* (London, 1731 edn), p. 12; cf. John Wilson, *Andronicus Comenius* (London, 1664), pp. 64, 73–4.

17. Marston, *Malcontent*, I. iv. 78–9; Jonson, *Sejanus*, 'Argument' (l. 15), I. 241–2 (cf. I. 366, III. 528); Samuel Daniel, *The Tragedy of Philotas*, ed. Laurence Michel (New Haven, repr. 1970), II. 713 (cf. *ibid.*, p. 58); Shakespeare, *Henry VIII*, III. ii. 255–6, 325, 441–2; Beaumont and Fletcher, iii, pp. 359, 367; Shirley, iv, pp. 107, 121, 271; Davenant, i, pp. 106, 121, 179 (cf. i, p. 61), iii, pp. 14, 38,

49; Baron, *Mirza*, sig. A7 and pp. 14, 47–8, 73 (cf. p. 84); *The Ungrateful Favourite*, pp. 21, 24, 52, 57, 61, 64, 7[4], 88; Orrery, *Tryphon*, pp. 1, 2 (cf. Nancy Klein Maguire, *Regicide and Restoration. English Tragicomedy, 1660–1671* (Cambridge, 1992), p. 187); Howard, *Great Favourite*, pp. 221, 236, 255, 278; Settle, *Cambyses*, pp. 5, 83; Crowne, *Ambitious Statesman*, pp. 37, 54 (cf. p. 22); Banks, *Unhappy Favourite*, p. 5; Southerne, *Loyal Brother*, pp. 7, 12; [John Bancroft?], *King Edward the Third* (London, 1691), p. 10; William Congreve, *The Mourning Bride* (in Herbert Davis, ed., *The Complete Plays of William Congreve* (Chicago, 1967), V. ii. 88; Gildon, *Roman Brides Revenge*, p. 12; Higgons, *Generous Conqueror*, pp. 12, 53, 64; *Majesty Misled: or, the Overthrow of Evil Ministers* (London, 1734), p. 18; [Francis Gentleman], *The Favourite* (Dublin, 1770), pp. 21, 26, 45, 49. Cf. *The Unfortunate Favourite* (London, 1689), pp. 3, 4, 6, 9, 10, 11; Crouch, *Unfortunate Court-Favourites*, pp. 7, 45, 99, 156; Edward Hyde, Earl of Clarendon, *History of the Rebellion*, ed. W. D. Macray, 6 vols (Oxford, 1888), i, p. 43; Pauline Croft, 'The Reputation of Sir Robert Cecil', *Transactions of the Royal Historical Society*, 6th series, i (1991), pp. 47, 55.
18. Jonson, *Sejanus*, 'Argument' (l. 8), I. 579, II. 139 (cf. *The Tragedy of Tiberius* (Malone Society, 1914), ll. 1033–4); Massinger, *Duke of Milan*, II. i. 430, V. i. 57–8; Carlell, *Deserving Favourite*, sig. B4; Ford, *Broken Heart*, I. i. 43; Shirley, v, pp. 349, 350; d'Ouvilley, *False Favourit*, p. 88 (cf. p. 91); Howard, *Great Favourite*, p. 270; Settle, *Cambyses*, p. 5; Southerne, *Loyal Brother*, pp. 9, 10, 11; Higgons, *Generous Conqueror*, p. 71; *The General Cashier'd* (London, 1712), pp. 53–4. The third-ranking motive is 'envy'.
19. Jonson, *Sejanus*, I. 556, III. 574; Daniel, *Philotas*, p. 101 (cf. p. 58); *Nero*, pp. 18, 87; *The Wasp*, p. 28; Southerne, *Loyal Brother*, p. 12. Cf. Baron, *Mirza*, p. 47; *The Unfortunate Favourite*, p. 10.
20. Jonson, *Mortimer His Fall*, 'arguments' (l. 2), I. 1; Jonson, *Sejanus*, I. 10–11, II. 403, III. 562, 573, 637–40, 645, 735, 745–8, V. i. 5–9, 572–5, 719, 904–5; Daniel, *Philotas*, l. 445; A. H. Bullen, ed., *The Works of John Day* (repr. London, 1963: hereafter Day), pp. 219, 227; *The Tragedy of Tiberius*, l. 667; Massinger, *Duke of Milan*, I. iii. 272–3, II. i. 18–19, 293–5, IV. i. 22, V. ii. 5–7, 223–4 (cf. Massinger, *The Bondman* (in Edwards and Gibson, *Massinger*, i), I. iii. 187); Ford, *Broken Heart*, IV. iii. 76; Shirley, ii, p. 108; *The Dramatic Works of Richard Brome*, 3 vols (repr. New York, 1966: hereafter Brome), i, p. 186; Davenant, i, p. 128, iii, p. 30; Baron, *Mirza*, sig. A7 and pp. 55, 82, 123; d'Ouvilley, *False Favourit*, p. 89; *The Ungrateful Favourite*, pp. 24, 91; Orrery, *Tryphon*, pp. 1, 4; Howard, *Great Statesman*, p. 236; Crowne, *Ambitious Statesman*, p. 3; Southerne, *Loyal Brother*, p. 7; Banks, *Unhappy Favourite*, p. 17; Harris, *Mistakes*, p. 67; Gildon, *Roman Brides Revenge*, p. 32; *Majesty Misled*, p. 79; *The Favourite*, p. 8.
21. Davenant, i, p. 121; Baron, *Mirza*, p. 123.
22. Daniel, *Philotas*, l. 511; Brome, i, p. 246; Lodowick Carlell, *The Fool would be a Favourite* (in Carlell's *Two New Playes* (London, 1657)), pp. 45, 46; Baron, *Mirza*, p. 123; Settle, *Cambyses*, p. 84; Crowne, *Ambitious Statesman*, p. 54.
23. Marston, *Malcontent*, I. vi. 3; Baron, *Mirza*, p. 73; *The Ungrateful Favourite*, p. 61; cf. Crouch, *Unfortunate Court-Favourites*, p. 49.
24. *Nero*, p. 18; Higgons, *Generous Conqueror*, p. 53 (cf. p. 65).
25. Jonson, *Sejanus*, II. 98–9, 151–3, V. 1–24; *The Wasp*, p. 28; Baron, *Mirza*, p. 42; Howard, *Great Favourite*, p. 221; Settle, *Cambyses*, p. 84; Harris, *Mistakes*, p. 13; cf. Howard, *Great Favourite*, p. 278.
26. Massinger, *Duke of Milan*, II. i. 427–8; Beaumont and Fletcher, iii, p. 359; d'Ouvilley, *False Favourit*, p. 40; John Bancroft, *Henry the Second* (London, 1693), p. 4; Dryden, *Don Sebastian*, IV. i. 74–6; *The Fall of Mortimer* (1731), p. 58; cf. Southerne, *Loyal Brother*, p. 44.
27. Marston, *Malcontent*, I. v. 20–33; Jonson, *Sejanus*, II. 100, v. 1ff.; Day, p. 262; d'Ouvilley, *False Favourit*, p. 13, 89–90; *The Ungrateful Favourite*, pp. 7[4], 91; Southerne, *Loyal Brother*, p. 7.
28. Carlell, *Fool would be a Favourite*, p. 29; *The Ungrateful Favourite*, p. 88; cf. Clarendon, *History*, i, p. 42.
29. Ford, *Broken Heart*, II. ii. 1–5 (cf. IV. i. 72–3; Harris, *Mistakes*, p. 69).
30. Davenant, i, p. 82. Cf. Shakespeare, *Henry VIII*, III. ii. 224–7, 359–64; d'Ouvilley, *False Favourit*, p. 87; Harris, *Mistakes*, p. 19; *The Unfortunate Favourite*, p. 9; *Majesty Misled*, p. 17.
31. Southerne, *Loyal Brother*, p. 13; cf. d'Ouvilley, *False Favourit*, p. 40.
32. Baron, *Mirza*, p. 43; Settle, *Cambyses*, pp. 71–2; Gildon, *Roman Brides Revenge*, p. 12. Cf. Jonson, *Sejanus*, IV. 61–2; Southerne, *Loyal Brother*, p. 21. 'Dullness' is a quality frequently despised by favourites.
33. Marlowe, *Edward II*, I. i. 100, I. iv. 239, 402, III. iii. 20; *Woodstock*, I. iii. 118; George Chapman, *The Gentleman Usher* (ed. J. H. Smith, London, 1970), I. i. 100, 118; Jonson, *Sejanus*, V. 465, 473–

4, 574; Day, pp. 219, 226; *Nero*, p. 13; *The Wasp*, pp. 1, 28; Massinger, *Duke of Milan*, II. i. 237 (cf. Massinger, *Bondman*, I. iii. 187); Beaumont and Fletcher, iii, p. 313; Baron, *Mirza*, sig. A7 and p. 73; *The Ungrateful Favourite*, pp. 4, 50; Settle, *Cambyses*, p. 44; *King Edward the Third*, p. 2.

34. Marlowe, *Edward II*, I. iv. 284; Day, p. 231; George Chapman, *Bussy d'Ambois*, ed. N. S. Brooke (Manchester, repr. 1979), III i. 98; Massinger, *Duke of Milan*, II. i. 86; Massinger, *The Great Duke of Florence* (in Edwards and Gibson, *Massinger*, iii), II. ii. 42; Ford, *Broken Heart*, IV. i. 98, 102; *Majesty Misled*, p. 17; cf. Jonson, *Every Man out of his Humour* (in Herford, *Jonson*, iii), I. ii. 162–3.

35. Chapman, *Bussy d'Ambois*, II. ii. 4–7; Massinger, *Duke of Milan*, II. i. 19; Ford, *Broken Heart*, IV. i. 98, 102.

36. Jonson, *Sejanus*, V. 465–7; Day, p. 226; Martin Butler, *Theatre and Crisis, 1631–1642* (Cambridge, 1984), pp. 206–7.

37. Day, p. 279; Bancroft, *Henry the Second*, p. 3; Congreve, *Mourning Bride*, I. i. 276; *Fall of Mortimer* (1731), pp. 26–7; cf. Dryden, *Don Sebastian*, I. i. 277–9.

38. *Woodstock*, I. iii. 184–92, II. i. 5, 18–20, II. ii. 120ff., 146–8 (cf. Marlowe, *Edward II*, I. iv. 345, III. ii. 168); Daniel, *Philotas*, l. 510; Massinger, *Bondman*, I. iii. 180–4; Ford, *Broken Heart*, I. i. 39, IV. iii. 78, 93; Carlell, *Fool would be a Favourite*, p. 20; d'Ouvilley, *False Favourit*, p. 110 (cf. p. 107); Nathaniel Lee, *The Rival Queens*, ed. P. F. Vernon (Lincoln, Nebr., 1970), I. i. 10, II. 70, 128; cf. Jonson, *Sejanus*, II. 23–4.

39. *The Ungrateful Favourite*, p. 2; Baron, *Mirza*, p. 253; Gildon, *Roman Brides Revenge*, p. 32.

40. Jonson, *Sejanus*, V. 81–4, 203–8, 366–7 (cf. I. 363–5, V. 21–3); *The Ungrateful Favourite*, pp. 36, 72; Gildon, *Roman Brides Revenge*, p. 32. Cf. Settle, *Cambyses*, p. 83; Clarendon, *Rebellion*, i, p. 42.

41. Jonson, *Sejanus*, III. 321–6, IV. 67–76, 115–27, 294–5, V. 739–45; Daniel, *Philotas*, ll. 416ff., 741ff.; Philip Massinger, *The Roman Actor* (in Edwards and Gibson, *Massinger*, iii), III. i. 111–14, III. ii. 95ff.; Carlell, *Deserving Favourite* (London, 1659 edn), sig. N3; Beaumont and Fletcher, iii. pp. 115, 118, 120; Baron, *Mirza*, p. 62; d'Ouvilley, *False Favourit*, pp. 109–10; Howard, *Great Favourite*, p. 269; Crowne, *Ambitious Statesman*, pp. 25–6; *Timoleon: or, The Revolution* (London, 1697), pp. 75–7; Blair Worden, 'Ben Jonson among the Historians', in Peter Lake and Kevin Sharpe, eds, *Culture and Politics in Early Stuart England* (London, 1994), pp. 88–9; cf. Chapman, *Bussy d'Ambois*, I. i. 1ff.

42. Davenant, iii, p. 27 (cf. i, p. 20); Ford, *Broken Heart*, IV. i. 78–9; Massinger, *Duke of Milan*, IV. iii. 71 (cf. Massinger, *Bondman*, I. iii. 100–1); Baron, *Mirza*, pp. 42, 95; Howard, *Great Favourite*, p. 247; cf. John Dryden, *Aureng-Zebe* (in Hooker and Swedenborg, *Dryden*, xii), I. i. 68, 166.

43. Massinger, *Duke of Milan*, IV. i. 67; cf. Blair Worden, *The Sound of Virtue. Philip Sidney's* Arcadia *and Elizabethan Politics* (New Haven and London, 1996), pp. 138–9, 143–4.

44. Marlowe, *Edward II*, I. iv. 410; *The Tragedy of Tiberius*, l. 669; Massinger, *Duke of Milan*, I. iii. 283–4; Shirley, iv, p. 110; Harris, *Mistakes*, p. 77.

45. William Strode, *The Floating Island* (London, 1655), sig. Cv; Settle, *Cambyses*, p. 5; Crowne, *Ambitious Statesman*, p. 25. Cf. *King Edward the Third*, p. 6; *Timoleon*, p. 30.

46. Shakespeare, *Much Ado about Nothing*, III. i. 9–11; Dryden, *Aureng-Zebe*, IV. i. 89–90.

47. Thomas Goffe, *The Tragedy of Orestes* (London, 1633); Nahum Tate, *The History of King Richard the Second* (London, 1681), sig. A1v and pp. 14, 29; William Hemings, *The Eunuch* (London, 1687), esp. pp. 36–8; Thomas Durfey, *Bussy d'Ambois* (London, 1691), 'Dramatis Personae' (cf. Chapman, *Bussy d'Ambois*, p. 3); Ennis Rees, *The Tragedies of George Chapman* (Cambridge, Mass., 1954), p. 161; Dale Randall, *Winter Fruit. English Drama, 1642–1660* (Lexington, Ky, 1995), p. 210; cf. Charles Hopkins, *Boadicea* (London, 1697), 'Dramatis Personae'.

48. See the references to *The Unfortunate Favourite* and *The Unfortunate Court-Favourites* (which was republished in 1706) elsewhere in these notes. The year 1706 also saw the publication of a tract which borrowed from Clarendon's *History of the Rebellion* and which was emphatically portrayed on its title-page as a study of 'favourite[s]': *The Characters of Robert Earl of Essex, Favourite to Queen Elizabeth, and George D. of Buckingham, Favourite to K. James I and K. Ch. I* (London, 1706). See too *The French Favourites* (London, 1707).

49. Catherine Bates, *The Rhetoric of Courtship in Elizabethan Language and Literature* (Cambridge, 1992).

50. Marlowe, *Edward II*, I. i. 5–6; Ben Jonson, *Cynthias Revells* (in Herford, *Ben Jonson*, iv), II. i. 125; Philip Massinger, *The Maid of Honour* (in Edwards and Gibson, *Massinger*, i), I. i. 272 (cf. Massinger, *Duke of Milan*, IV. iii. 275–6; Massinger, *Roman Actor*, I. ii. 20, 36); Davenant, i, pp. 21, 23, 37; Nahum Tate, *The Loyal General* (London, 1680), p. 12; Lee, *Rival Queens*, II. 96ff.;

Dryden, *Don Sebastian*, I. i. 69 and n. (p. 424) (cf. V. i. 274–9); *King Edward the Third*, pp. 3, 10; Hemings, *Eunuch*, pp. 37–8. Cf. Marston, *Malcontent*, II. v. 55ff.; Anne Somerset, *Unnatural Murder. Poison at the Court of James I* (London, 1997), pp. 43, 45, 50.

51. Jonson, *Sejanus*, I. 427 (cf. V. 47); Day, p. 226; George Chapman, *The Tragedy of Caesar and Pompey* (in T. M. Parrott, ed., *The Plays and Poems of George Chapman* (London, 1910)), I. i. 18–25; *The Wasp; Rollo*, p. 75; Beaumont and Fletcher, iii, p. 114 (cf. p. 118); Nathaniel Richards, *The Tragedy of Messallina* (London, 1640), sig. D3v; Baron, *Mirza*, p. 24; Banks, *Unhappy Favourite*, p. 71; Harris, *Mistakes*, p. 15; *The General Cashier'd*, pp. 27, 29; *Majesty Misled*, prologue; cf. Croft, 'Reputation of Sir Robert Cecil', p. 46 (on the Earl of Northampton as 'His Majesty's earwig').

52. Davenant, iii, p. 14; Goffe, *Orestes*; Southerne, *Loyal Brother*; Harris, *Mistakes*; Gildon, *Roman Brides Revenge*; *The General Cashier'd*. In 1709 we have 'a Minister of State: a Villain' (Johnson, *Love and Liberty*, 'Dramatis Personae'), for from the later seventeenth century playwrights more commonly use the noun 'minister' instead of, or alongside, the noun 'favourite': Dryden, *Don Sebastian*, 'Persons Represented' and I. i. 66–8, 278–9, and p. 390; Gildon, *Roman Brides Revenge*, p. 31; *The Fall of Mortimer* (1731), p. 63; *Majesty Misled*, pp. 17, 35, 55; *The Favourite*, pp. 45, 51; cf. Crouch, *Unfortunate Court-Favourites*, p. 40.

53. Day, p. 318; cf. Jonson's *The Underwood*, no. 61, l. 20.

54. Dryden, 'To My Lord Chancellor', ll. 91–4, in Hooker and Swedenborg, *Dryden*, i, p. 40.

55. George Chapman, *The Tragedy of Chabot* (in Parrott, *Plays and Poems of George Chapman. The Tragedies*), I. i. 2, I. ii. 17.

56. Beaumont and Fletcher, iii, p. 76 (cf. p. 138).

57. Mostly the female favourites of women in seventeenth-century drama are virtuous or at least innocuous.

58. Brome, i, pp. 186, 246: quoted by Butler, *Theatre and Crisis*, pp. 220–1.

59. Southerne, *Loyal Brother*, p. 57.

60. Brome, iii, p. 503; d'Ouvilley, *False Favourit*, p. 107; Banks, *Unhappy Favourite*, p. 42. Cf. Shakespeare, *Henry VIII*, V. ii. 29; *The Historical Works of Bevill Higgons*, 2 vols (London, 1736), i, p. 93.

61. James Spedding *et al.*, eds, *The Letters and Life of Francis Bacon*, 14 vols (London, 1857–74), xiii, p. 27 (cf. xiii, p. 14).

62. For this and the previous sentences see Massinger, *Great Duke of Florence*, I. ii. 162; Davenant, i, p. 128; Carlell, *Deserving Favourite*, sig. Fi; *The Ungrateful Favourite*, p. 72; Lee, *Rival Queens*, I. i. 67–8, II. 106, 120, IV. ii. 62; Congreve, *Mourning Bride*, I. i. 271–7, IV. i. 226; John Dryden, *The Conquest of Granada* (in Hooker and Swedenborg, *Dryden*, xi), II. i. 334–5; Dryden, *Don Sebastian*, II. i. 306, V. i. 129ff., 274–7. Cf. John Webster, *The Duchess of Malfi*, I. i. 431–8; Shirley, iv, p. 170; Sir Henry Wotton, *A Short View of the Life and Death of George Villiers, Duke of Buckingham* (London, 1642); Crouch, *Unfortunate Court-Favourites*, pp. 148, 153, 155.

63. Cf. Orrery, *Tryphon*, pp. 2, 16, 25, 26, 32; Shirley, iv, p. 129.

64. Day, p. 286; Chapman, *Tragedy of Chabot*, II. iii. 20–35; Shakespeare, *Henry VIII*, III. i. 161–85; Massinger, *Duke of Milan*, I. iii. 271, 298, II. i. 291–3, V. ii. 5–7; Massinger, *Roman Actor*, I. iii. 29–30, IV. ii. 65–8, 176; Massinger, *Great Duke of Florence*, III. i. 13–19; Ford, *Broken Heart*, IV. iii. 76, 89–91; Davenant, i, pp. 44, 122, 189; Shirley, ii, pp. 105, 108, iv, pp. 168, 170, 182, 271; *The Ungrateful Favourite*, esp. pp. 1–2, 3, 24, 44; Orrery, *Tryphon*, p. 1; Settle, *Cambyses*, p. 54; Banks, *Unhappy Favourite*, p. 23; Dryden, *Don Sebastian*, II. i. 302–11; Higgons, *Generous Conqueror*, p. 65; *The General Cashier'd*, p. 12. Cf. Jonson, *Cynthias Revells*, V. vi. 28–32; Jonson, *The Gypsies Metamorphos'd*, l. 12; Lee, *Rival Queens*, II. i. 324–9; Dryden, *Aureng-Zebe*, II. i. 125–7; Gildon, *Roman Brides Revenge*, p. 31; Somerset, *Unnatural Murder*, p. 226.

65. Marlowe, *Edward II*, I. iv. 390; Marston, *Malcontent*, I. iii. 159–60 (cf. Marston, *Antonio and Mellida*, ed. G. K. Hunter (repr. London, 1965), III. i. 96–7); Jonson, *Sejanus*, I. 434, 537–8, II. 178–9, 383ff., III. 535–6, 632–6, 659–60, V. 621–3; Daniel, *Philotas*, ll. 61–2; George Chapman, *The Conspiracy and Tragedy of Byron*, ed. John Margeson (Manchester, 1988), iii. III. 20; Shakespeare, *Henry VIII*, III. ii. 367–8; Massinger, *Great Duke of Florence*, I. i. 71ff.; Davenant, i, pp. 29, 45, 157, 175, iv, pp. 218–19, 221, 226; Baron, *Mirza*, pp. 23, 24, 40–2, 253; d'Ouvilley, *False Favourit*, pp. 26, 39; *The Ungrateful Favourite*, pp. 2, 4, 14; Crowne, *Ambitious Statesman*, p. 48; Dryden, *Aureng-Zebe*, IV. i. 89–90; Dryden, *Don Sebastian*, II. i. 49–54; Orrery, *Tryphon*, pp. 1, 4; William Whitaker, *The Conspiracy* (London, 1680), p. 18; Nathaniel Lee, *Theodosius* (London, 1680), pp. 36–7; Harris, *Mistakes*, p. 54; Gildon, *Roman Brides Revenge*, p. 32; Wilson, *Andronicus Comenius*, p. 64; *Majesty Misled*, title-page and p. 26.

66. Day, p. 220; Massinger, *Maid of Honour*, I. i. 220ff.; Massinger, *Duke of Milan*, IV. i. 47–8, V. ii.

4–7; Massinger, *Roman Actor*, I. iii. 53–4; Massinger, *The Picture* (in Edwards and Gibson, *Massinger*, iii), II. ii. 149; *King Edward the Third*, p. 2 ('there will be *Mortimer* in every State').
67. Day, pp. 211–12; Daniel, *Philotas*, pp. 155-6. Cf. Hooker and Swedenborg, *Dryden*, xiv, pp. 309ff.; *The Fall of Mortimer* (London, 1763 edn), Dedication; Worden, 'Ben Jonson', p. 79.
68. Baron, *Mirza*, sig. A3v; Lodowick Carlell, *Heraclius, Emperor of the East* (London, 1664), sig. A3v; John Dryden and Nathaniel Lee, *The Duke of Guise* (in Hooker and Swedenborg, *Dryden*, xi), prologue (l. 1) (cf. Hooker and Swedenborg, *Dryden*, xi. 314–15); *Timoleon*, sig. A3v; *Majesty Mislaid: or The Overthrow of Evil Ministers* (London, 1734), epilogue; cf. R. C. Richardson, ed., *Images of Oliver Cromwell. Essays for and by Roger Howell, Jr.* (Manchester, 1993), pp. 39–40.
69. *Woodstock*, V. i. 56ff.; Jonson, *Sejanus*, I. 113ff., II. 472–5 (cf. III. 484–5); Massinger, *Roman Actor*, I. i. 83ff.; Beaumont and Fletcher, iii. p. 78; Brome, iii, pp. 460–1, 503; Howard, *Great Favourite*, p. 235; *Piso's Conspiracy* (London, 1676: an adaptation of *Nero*), pp. 4–5. Cf. Webster, *Duchess of Malfi*, I. i. 2ff.; Wilson, *Andronicus Comenius*, p. 5.
70. Davenant, iv., pp. 218–19. Cf. Massinger, *Maid of Honour*, III. iii. 138–42; Shirley, ii, p. 114; *King Edward the Third*, p. 56 ('And Evill Kings I fear have been the cause'), with which cf. *The Fall of Mortimer* (1731), p. 63 ('A wicked, worthless Minister the Cause').
71. Marlowe, *Edward II*, I. iv. 365, V. i. 28; *Woodstock*, IV. i. 42; Jonson, *Sejanus*, II. 157; *The Wasp*, pp. 17, 100; d'Ouvilley, *False Favourit*, p. 26; Howard, *Great Favourite*, pp. 236, 244–5, 246–7; Banks, *Unhappy Favourite*, p. 62; *King Edward the Third*, p. 2; *The General Cashier'd*, p. 30. Cf. *A Vindication of the Fall of Mortimer* (London, 1731), p. 5; *Majesty Misled*, p. 25; Somerset, *Unnatural Murder*, p. 56.
72. Baron, *Mirza*, p. 40; *King Edward the Third*, p. 2.
73. Jonson, *Sejanus*, I. 433–4; *Nero*, pp. 32, 54; Massinger, *Maid of Honour*, I. i. 26; Massinger, *Roman Actor*, II. i. 70–6; *Rollo*, IV. i. 7, 76; Shirley, iv, pp. 107, 110; Davenant, i, p. 28; Baron, *Mirza*, pp. 41, 123; *The Ungrateful Favourite*, pp. 2, 3, 72; Harris, *Mistakes*, p. 43; *The General Cashier'd*, p. 27; *The Fall of Mortimer* (1731), p. 14; *Majesty Misled*, pp. [iv], v; Butler, *Theatre and Crisis*, p. 236.
74. Jonson, *Mortimer His Fall*, 'Arguments' (ll. 8, 13–14); Shirley, iv, p. 107.
75. *Woodstock*, V. i. 187–92; Baron, *Mirza*, pp. 41, 42.
76. Jonson, *Sejanus*, 'Argument' (ll. 18–19), V. 647; Daniel, *Philotas*, l. 454 (cf. ll. 1968–9); Day, p. 226; Shirley, ii, p. 185; Davenant, i, pp. 28, 124, 168; Richards, *Messallina*, 'The Actors Names'; Baron, *Mirza*, pp. 8, 40; d'Ouvilley, *False Favourit*, p. 27.
77. Howard, *Great Favourite*, p. 247.
78. Jonson, *Sejanus*, I. 259, 425; *King Edward the Third*, p. 2; *Fall of Mortimer* (1731), p. 14. Cf. Beaumont and Fletcher, iii, p. 94; Baron, *Mirza*, p. 41.
79. Robert Davenport, *King John and Matilda* (London, 1655), sigs B3v, B4v; *Rollo*, IV. iii. 19–33; Baron, *Mirza*, p. 41; Orrery, *Tryphon*, p. 4; cf. d'Ouvilley, *False Favourit*, pp. 105–6.
80. Massinger, *Roman Actor*, I. iii. 50; d'Ouvilley, *False Favourit*, pp. 69–70; *The Ungrateful Favourite*, p. 3; Howard, *Great Favourite*, pp. 235, 242, 244; cf. Jonson, *Sejanus*, II. 436.
81. Davenport, *King John*, sigs B4v, D4, H2; *The Ungrateful Favourite*, p. 3; *King Edward the Third*, p. 11; Butler, *Theatre and Crisis*, pp. 206–8, 265–6.
82. Massinger, *Duke of Milan*, IV. iii. 80–1; d'Ouvilley, *False Favourit*, pp. 69–70; cf. Howard, *Duke of Lerma*, p. 235.
83. Jonson, *Sejanus*, II. 436–42 (cf. Jonson, *Every Man out of his Humour*, prologue (l. 124)); Daniel, *Philotas*, ll. 1581–2; Howard, *Great Favourite*, p. 245.
84. Marston, *Malcontent*, I. iv. 159–60.
85. Jonson, *Sejanus*, IV. 30, 354–5; *Nero*, p. 38; Massinger, *Roman Actor*, I. iii. 33–4, II. i. 234–5; Davenant, i, p. 141.
86. Jonson, *Sejanus*, IV. 301; Shirley, iv, p. 200. Cf. Massinger, *Roman Actor*, I. iii. 22–3; Lee, *Rival Queens*, IV. ii. 228.
87. Jonson, *Sejanus*, I. 64–6, 259, II. 444–9, III. 701, IV. 221–4; *Nero*, p. 65; Massinger, *Duke of Milan*, II. i. 85; Massinger, *Roman Actor*, II. i. 112–14, IV. i. 84; Massinger, *Great Duke of Florence*, I. ii. 51, IV. ii. 59; Shirley, iv, pp. 108, 200; *The Ungrateful Favourite*, p. 16; Bancroft, *Henry the Second*, p. 4; Dryden, *Don Sebastian*, II. i. 31; *King Edward the Third*, p. 1; Gildon, *Roman Brides Revenge*, p. 2; Higgons, *Generous Conqueror*, p. 11; Worden, 'Ben Jonson', pp. 79–80, 84; cf. Marston, *Malcontent*, I. vii. 13–21.
88. Jonson, *Sejanus*, I. 433, IV. 14–21, 300–4, 325–6, 522; *Nero*, p. 14; Massinger, *Duke of Milan*, II. i. 12; Massinger, *Roman Actor*, I. i. 79–81, 116–17; Shirley, iv, p. 105.

89. Jonson, *Sejanus*, I. 259, IV. 362; Day, p. 287; *Rollo*, IV. i. 63; Beaumont and Fletcher, iii, p. 87; Howard, *Great Favourite*, p. 242; Southerne, *Loyal Brother*, p. 17; Lee, *Rival Queens*, IV. ii. 233 (cf. II. 299). Cf. Daniel, *Philotas*, p. 152; Shakespeare, *Henry VIII*, IV. ii. 37–41; Webster, *Duchess of Malfi*, I. i. 17–18; Massinger, *Roman Actor*, IV. i. 151; *The General Cashier'd*, p. 35.

90. Jonson, *Sejanus*, III. 286–7; Massinger, *Duke of Milan*, IV. iii. 83; Howard, *Great Favourite*, pp. 244–5.

91. Jonson, *Sejanus*, I. 419–20, II. 390–1, IV. 167–70, 281–2; Massinger, *Roman Actor*, II. i. 135–7 (cf. I. ii. 76; Massinger, *Bondman*, I. iii. 128–32); Baron, *Mirza*, p. 24; *The Ungrateful Favourite*, p. 28; Lee, *Rival Queens*, II. 75–6; cf. Dryden, *Don Sebastian*, I. i. 34.

92. Jonson, *Sejanus*, I. 243–6, IV. 306; Daniel, *Philotas*, ll. 1788ff.; *Nero*, p. 30; Massinger, *Roman Actor*, I. ii. 46–8, 77–87, II. i. 263–4, V. ii. 90–2; Massinger, *Great Duke of Florence*, I. i. 7–8; Massinger, *Picture*, I. ii. 124–4; *Rollo*, I. i. 131–3, 180–2; Brome, iii, p. 459; Davenant, i, pp. 191–2; Baron, *Mirza*, p. 24; *The Ungrateful Favourite*, p. 28; *King Edward the Third*, pp. 2, 3; Johnson, *Love and Liberty*, pp. 2–3. Cf. Marlowe, *Edward II*, I. iv. 9; *Woodstock*, I. ii. 38–50.

93. Worden, 'Ben Jonson'.

94. Jonson, *Sejanus*, I. 379–84; Daniel, *Philotas*, p. 101 and ll. 67–72, 1577–8, 1815, 1968–9; Massinger, *Roman Actor*, II. i. 159–61, III. ii. 5 ('sacred majesty': cf. Worden, 'Ben Jonson, p. 74); Lee, *Rival Queens*, IV. i. 10–11, IV. ii. 110.

95. Jonson, *Sejanus*, III. 16–17 (cf. *Rollo*, I. i. 119), V. 257; Daniel, *Philotas*, ll. 407–8, 940–1, 1767ff. (cf. ibid., pp. 1–2); Massinger, *Maid of Honour*, I. i. 4–6; Massinger, *Duke of Milan*, II. i. 6–12, IV. ii. 21–2; Massinger, *Bondman*, I. iii. 129–32; Massinger, *Roman Actor*, IV. i. 143–5 (cf. I. i. 59–65, I. ii. 13); Howard, *Great Favourite*, p. 244; Wilson, *Andronicus Comenius*, p. 3. Cf. Jonson, *Volpone*, I. ii. 11–12; Baron, *Mirza*, sig. A6v; *King Edward the Third*, p. 3.

96. Jonson, *Sejanus*, V. 566–7, 640–1 (with which cf. III. 472); Shirley, ii, pp. 114, 115.

97. Marlowe, *Edward II*, I. iv. 344–7; Davenant, iv, p. 268; Lee, *Rival Queens*, IV. ii. 20, 224ff.; Southerne, *Loyal Brother*, p. 17 (with which cf. Jonson, *Everyman out of his Humour*, epilogue (l. 13)).

98. Massinger, *Great Duke of Florence*, I. i. 5–8, I. ii. 5–11, IV. ii. 280–2, 295–6; Massinger, *Duke of Milan*, IV. iii. 10, 80–81. Cf. Jonson, *Sejanus*, I. 374–97, 453ff., 503–7; Lee, *Rival Queens*, IV. ii. 120–30; *King Edward the Third*, p. 11.

99. *Woodstock*, IV. iii. 19, 34; Jonson, *Sejanus*, I. 404, II. 312, IV. 138–9; *Nero*, pp. 33–4 (with which cf. Jonson, *Sejanus*, I. 86ff.); Massinger, *Duke of Milan*, IV. i. 39–40; *King Edward the Third*, prologue and pp. 2, 5; Butler, *Theatre and Crisis*, p. 208. Cf. Marston, *Malcontent*, 'Induction', l. 64; Johnson, *Love and Liberty*, pp. 2–3.

100. Marlowe, *Edward II*, I. ii. 61; Massinger, *Roman Actor*, V. ii. 77–8; Beaumont and Fletcher, iii, esp. pp. 154, 160–6; Davenant, iv, p. 225; Orrery, *Tryphon*, p. 3; Crowne, *Ambitious Statesman*, esp. ded. and pp. 85–6; Higgons, *Generous Conqueror*, p. 46; *The General Cashier'd*, pp. 10–11, 12; Butler, *Theatre and Crisis*, p. 209; cf. Dryden, *Don Sebastian*, V. i. 467.

101. Cf. Worden, 'Ben Jonson', pp. 75–6, 85.

102. d'Ouvilley, *False Favourit*, p. 110; *The Ungrateful Favourite*, pp. 24, 52. Cf. *Timeoleon*, sig. A2 and pp. 69–70, 78; Clarendon, *Rebellion*, i, p. 43.

103. Jonson, *Sejanus*, I. 2–6 (cf. II. 399, IV. 290–5); Davenant, i, pp. 45, 49, iii, p. 16 and n. (cf. i, p. 106, iv, p. 22); Gildon, *Roman Brides Revenge*, p. 2; Higgons, *Generous Conqueror*, p. 40 (cf. p. 11). Cf. Richards, *Messallina*, sig. B4; Crowne, *Ambitious Statesman*, 'Actors Names'; Dryden, *Don Sebastian*, I. i. 22; Congreve, *Mourning Bride*, I. i. 215, IV. i. 190; Johnson, *Love and Liberty*, p. 6.

104. Bancroft, *Henry the Second*, p. 4. Cf. *Nero*, p. 13 (cf. p. 32); Southerne, *Loyal Brother*, pp. 9, 12, 45; Dryden, *Don Sebastian*, III. i. 456–7; Albert Tricomi, *Anticourt Drama in England 1603–1642* (Charlottesville, VA, 1989), pp. 125, 171; John Hall, *The Grounds and Reasons of Monarchy*, in J. Toland, ed., *Works of James Harrington* (London, 1700), p. 14; Somerset, *Unnatural Murder*, p. 65.

105. Massinger, *Roman Actor*, IV. i. 93–4; *Rollo*, II. ii. 106–9; Shirley, ii, p. 257; d'Ouvilley, *False Favourit*, p. 98; *The Ungrateful Favourite*, p. 45. Cf. Marston, *Antonio and Mellida*, III. i. 96–7; Davenant, i, p. 175.

106. Daniel, *Philotas*, l. 447; Day, pp. 220, 236–7, 286–7 (cf. p. 276; Tricomi, *Anticourt Drama*, p. 39); Massinger, *Duke of Milan*, IV. i. 43–6; Massinger, *Roman Actor*, IV. i. 63–6; *Rollo*, V. ii. 181; Shirley, ii, p. 157; Davenant, i, p. 124, iv, p. 250; Carlell, *Fool would be a Favourite*, pp. 21, 29; Baron, *Mirza*, pp. 48, 55, 85–6; d'Ouvilley, *False Favourit*, pp. 14, 97*; *The Ungrateful Favourite*, pp. 6, 14; Howard, *Great Favourite*, pp. 248–9; Banks, *Unfortunate Favourite*, pp. 21, 22; Crowne, *Ambitious Statesman*, pp. 4, 21; *King Edward the Third*, p. 12; *Timoleon*, pp. 27, 29–30;

The Fall of the Earl of Essex (London, 1731), p. 5; *Majesty Misled*, p. 66; *The Favourite*, pp. 36–7; Butler, *Theatre and Crisis*, p. 208. Cf. *Woodstock*, I. iii. 182–7; Crouch, *Unfortunate Court-Favourites*, p. 4.

107. *The Wasp*, p. 73; Massinger, *Maid of Honour*, I. i. 34–6; Davenant, i, pp. 126–7; Strode, *Floating Island*, sig. D2.

108. Marston, *Malcontent*, I. v. i; Jonson, *Sejanus*, I. 181–9; Day, pp. 221–2; Massinger, *Maid of Honour*, I. i. 7ff. (cf. II. ii. 90–2); Wilson, *Andronicus Comenius*, pp. 6–7; *King Edward the Third*, pp. 4–5; cf. Howard, *Great Favourite*, pp. 215–17.

109. Massinger, *Maid of Honour*, III. ii. 8.

110. Jonson, *Sejanus*, IV. 457; Shirley, ii, p. 157, iv, pp. 107, 268; Baron, *Mirza*, 'The persons of the Play'; d'Ouvilley, *False Favourit*, 'The Persons'; *The Ungrateful Favourite*, p. 61 (cf. p. 57); Congreve, *Mourning Bride*, IV. i. 428; Gildon, *Roman Brides Revenge*, 'Dramatis Personae'; Higgons, *Generous Conqueror*, p. 53; *The General Cashier'd*, p. 53; *The Fall of Mortimer* (1731), p. 25; cf. Clarendon, *Rebellion*, i, p. 27.

111. Shirley, ii, p. 157; cf. Shakespeare, *Henry VIII*, III. ii. 411–12.

112. d'Ouvilley, *False Favourit*, p. 17.

113. *Nero*, p. 13; Davenant, iv, p. 221.

114. Jonson, *Mortimer His Fall*, I. 18; Jonson, *Sejanus*, III. 715–17, 735; Massinger, *Duke of Milan*, IV. i. 25–6; Massinger, *Roman Actor*, I. ii. 70–1; Massinger, *Picture*, I. ii. 129–30; Shirley, iv, p. 194; Goffe, *Orestes*, IV. i, fol. [19v]; *Timoleon*, p. 24; *General Cashier'd*, p. 58. Cf. Webster, *Duchess of Malfi*, I. i. 119–20; *King Edward the Third*, p. 2 ('smile').

115. Daniel, *Philotas*; Davenant, i, pp. 19, 21, 26, 82–3, 85, 91, 99, iii, p. 16; Massinger, *Great Duke of Florence*, I. i. 67–70; Ford, *Broken Heart*, I. ii. 11–12; *The Ungrateful Favourite*, p. 2; Lee, *Rival Qeeens* (Hephestion).

116. Marlowe, *Edward II*, I. iv. 345–6; Massinger, *Maid of Honour*, II. ii. 137–9 (cf. Massinger, *Picture*, I. ii. 81–5); Davenant, i, pp. 19, 28, 104, iii, p. 6; *The Ungrateful Favourite*, p. 4; cf. Hemings, *Eunuch*, p. 36.

117. Marlowe, *Edward II*, I. iv. 404–5; Daniel, *Philotas*, ll. 453–5; Massinger, *Maid of Honour*, I. i. 43ff.; Massinger, *Duke of Milan*, III. i. 13–17, 22–7 (cf. Ben Jonson, *Everyman in his Humor* (1601 quarto: in Herford, *Jonson*, iii), II. i. 74–5); Massinger, *Picture*, I. ii. 14ff., II. ii. 164–6; Davenant, i, p. 28 (cf. i, pp. 154–5); *The Ungrateful Favourite*, pp. 6, 14, 15; Banks, *Unhappy Favourite*, pp. 21, 22, 40; Harris, *Mistakes*, pp. 2, 28; Southerne, *Loyal Brother*, pp. 8–9; Gildon, *Roman Brides Revenge*, pp. 7, 25; Higgons, *Generous Conqueror*, p. 13; *Timoleon*, pp. 62–4; Christine Gerrard, *The Patriot Opposition to Walpole* (Oxford, 1994), p. 158. Cf. Beaumont and Fletcher, iii, pp. 82, 129; Southerne, *Loyal Brother*, p. 7; Dryden, *Don Sebastian*, IV. iii. 437–65; Randall, *Winter Fruit*, pp. 68ff.

118. Jonson, *Sejanus*, III. 253ff.; Beaumont and Fletcher, iii, pp. 76ff.; Baron, *Mirza*, p. 123; Lee, *Rival Queens*, II. 127, IV. ii. 128ff. (cf. II. 95–6). Cf. *The General Cashier'd*, esp. 'Persons Represented' and pp. 10–11, 13, 20; cf. d'Ouvilley, *False Favourite*, pp. 82, 92.

119. John Stubbs, *The Discovery of a Gaping Gulph*, ed. Lloyd E. Berry (Charlottesville, Va, 1968), p. 30; Sir Philip Sidney, *The Countess of Pembroke's Arcadia (The New Arcadia)*, ed. Victor Skretkowicz (Oxford, 1987), p. 182 (cf. p. 176: 'minions'); Worden, *Sound of Virtue*, pp. 146–7. The young Francis Bacon wrote of the 'favourites' of the French king in 1582: Spedding, *Bacon*, viii, p. 26. The first usage of the noun recorded in the *Oxford English Dictionary* belongs to 1583: the first usage of it recorded by the *OED* to describe people in favour with princes is in Shakespeare's *Much Ado About Nothing* (above, n. 46); but cf. *Henry VI Part I*, IV. i. 190.

120. *Edward II*, p. 20; *Woodstock*, p. 212.

121. For the popular tradition see Butler, *Theatre and Crisis*, ch. 8.

122. Chapman, *Conspiracy and Tragedy of Byron*, Appendix III.

123. William Camden, *The History of the . . . Princesse Elizabeth . . . by way of Annals* (London, 1630), pt iv, p. 189; cf. *The Characters of . . . Essex . . . and . . . Buckingham*, p. 4 (with which cf. Clarendon, *History*, i, p. 28).

124. That technique would be repeated in 1682 in Banks, *Unhappy Favourite*; see too Gerrard, *Patriot Opposition*, p. 164.

125. Cf. Daniel, *Philotas*, pp. 36ff. Daniel, who otherwise draws the martial Essex and the martial Philotas together, surprisingly has an enemy of Philotas charge him, implausibly, with being the leader of the peace party (ll. 453–6).

126. Quoted in Michel's (indispensable) introduction to *Philotas*, p. 4.

127. Herford, *Jonson*, i, pp. 394–6.

128. Worden, 'Ben Jonson', p. 78.

129. Spedding, *Bacon*, ix, pp. 43, 45.

130. Bodleian Library, Smith MS. 17, pp. 42–3.

131. Herford, *Jonson*, vii. 601 ('Discoveries', ll. 1224–6); cf. the similar observation by Jonson's friend Sir Robert Cotton in *Cottoni Posthumi* (London, 1651), 'A Short View', p. 8.

132. Worden, 'Ben Jonson', pp. 85–6; Worden, *Sound of Virtue*, pp. 258–9.

133. Worden, 'Ben Jonson', p. 69; John Trenchard and Thomas Gordon, *Cato's Letters*, ed. Ronald Hamowy, 2 vols, Liberty Fund (Indianapolis, 1995), pp. 112, 115–16, 124, 249, 558, 969; John Thelwall, *The Tribune*, 3 vols (London, 1795–6), iii, p. 303 (cf. P. P. Howe, ed., *The Complete Works of William Hazlitt*, 21 vols (London, 1930–4), vi, p. 303); John Brewer, *Party Ideology and Popular Politics at the Accession of King George III* (Cambridge, 1976), p. 258; below, pp. 173–4. For the legacy of Jonson's play in his own lifetime see Martin Butler, 'Romans in Britain: *The Roman Actor* and the Early Stuart Classical Play', in Douglas Howard, ed., *Philip Massinger. A Critical Reassessment* (Cambridge, 1985), pp. 139–70; cf. B. L. De Luna, *Jonson's Romish Plot* (Oxford, 1967), p. 13.

134. Worden, *Sound of Virtue*, pp. 214, 217–19.

135. Day, p. 219; cf. *The Ungrateful Favourite*, p. 2.

136. Croft, 'Reputation of Sir Robert Cecil', p. 43–69.

137. *Ibid.*, p. 56; Tricomi, *Anticourt Drama*, pp. 31–3.

138. *Richard II*, II. i. 15ff.

139. Butler, *Theatre and Crisis*, p. 201; Somerset, *Unnatural Murder*, p. 90; see too *Henry VIII*, III. ii. 102–5.

140. Blair Worden, 'Shakespeare and Politics', *Shakespeare Survey*, 44 (1991), pp. 1–15.

141. *Henry V*, V. ii. 29–34.

142. Massinger, *Maid of Honour*, I. i. 272.

143. *Ibid.*, 229–30. For the baneful effect of favouritism on the navy see also Marlowe, *Edward II*, II. ii. 167–8; cf. *The Wasp*. p. 73. The literary representation of Buckingham is prominently discussed in R. Little, 'Perpetual Metaphors: The Configuration of the Courtier as Favourite in Jacobean and Caroline Literature', Cambridge PhD thesis (1993).

144. Blair Worden, 'Literature and Political Censorship in Early Modern England', in A. C. Duke and C. A. Tamse, eds, *Too Mighty to be Free* (Zutphen, 1987), pp. 55–7.

145. Cf. Roger Coke, *A Detection of the Court and State of England*, 2 vols (London, 1967), i, pp. 333, 335.

146. In the early 1640s Laud and Strafford were attacked as favourites in the drama and in playlets: Butler, *Theatre and Crisis*, pp. 236ff.; Randall, *Winter Fruit*, pp. 55ff; Joad Raymond, *The Invention of the Newspaper. English Newsbooks 1641–1649* (Oxford, 1996), pp. 201–3. Baron's play *Mirza* (?1655) warns Charles II against favouritism; cf. Randall, *Winter Fruit*, pp. 130–4.

147. George McFadden, *Dryden. The Public Writer, 1660–1685* (Princeton, NJ, 1978), p. 13; Maguire, *Regicide and Restoration*, pp. 127–31, 186–8. In the printed text of 1669, it seems, 'too much' was cautiously replaced by 'almost': *Tryphon*, p. 1; *The Dramatic Works of Roger Boyle, Earl of Orrery*, 2 vols (London, 1739), i, pp. 129, 136. Howard's preoccupation with the evils of favouritism recurs in his *Historical Observations upon the Reigns of Edward I. II. III and Richard II. With Remarks upon their Faithful Counsellors and False Favourites* (London, 1689).

148. *Dictionary of National Biography*, Hyde.

149. Robert D. Hume, *The Development of English Drama in the Later Seventeenth Century* (Oxford, 1976), pp. 221, 223, 456; Derek Hughes, *English Drama 1660–1700* (Oxford, 1996), pp. 264–5, 278–9, 363 and n., 430–1; Susan J. Owen, *Restoration Theatre and Crisis* (Oxford, 1996), pp. 66–71, 131, 167, 268.

150. The story is well told by Lance Bertelsen, 'The Significance of the 1731 Revisions to *The Fall of Mortimer*', *Restoration and 18th Century Theatre Research*, II (2) (1987), pp. 8–25. See too Herford, *Jonson*, vii, p. 53; Robert D. Hume, *Henry Fielding and the London Theatre, 1728–1737* (Oxford, 1988), pp. 80–2.

151. *The Fall of Mortimer* (1731), pp. 4, 22ff. Cf. *The Fall of the Earl of Essex*, p. 5; *Majesty Mislaid*, pp. 56, 70; [Francis Gentleman], *Sejanus, A Tragedy* (London, 1752), p. xiv and 'Dramatis Personae'.

152. Gerrard, *Patriot Opposition*, pp. 78–80, 114, 154–6, 158–60, 163–4; Hume, *Henry Fielding, q. v.* 'Walpole', esp. pp. 77–8; John Brewer, *The Pleasures of the Imagination* (London, 1997), p. 372. I know of no discussion of *The Fall of the Earl of Essex*, a play that would repay closer attention.

153. *Sejanus, A Tragedy*, title-page; *The Favourite*, p. x.
154. *The Fall of Mortimer* (1763), p. xiii.
155. H. J. Oliver, *The Problem of John Ford* (Melbourne, 1955), Appendix.
156. For hints of that change see Peter Whiteley, *Lord North. The Prime Minister Who Lost America* (London, 1996), pp. 218, 225.

12

Francis Bacon: Your Flexible Friend

DAVID WOOTTON

The opening words of *The Prince* provide us with a fleeting glimpse of a Renaissance courtier going about his daily business: 'Those who wish to acquire favor with a ruler most often approach him with those among their possessions that are most valuable in their eyes, or that they are confident will give him pleasure. So rulers are often given horses, armor, cloth of gold, precious stones, and similar ornaments that are thought worthy of their social eminence.'[1] The year is 1516 and Machiavelli is writing to Lorenzo de' Medici. He begins with talk of gifts because what he has to offer is a gift far more valuable than precious stones: 'an understanding of the deeds of great men'; though according to an apocryphal story, on the day when Machiavelli attended on Lorenzo to offer him his book, a rival for the prince's favour presented him with a pair of greyhounds. The book remained unread, while the greyhounds gave Lorenzo much pleasure.[2]

Machiavelli's rhetorical strategy would have been familiar to his sixteenth-century readers. Here is Erasmus dedicating the *Parabolae* to Pieter Gillis in 1514: 'Friends of the commonplace and homespun sort, my open-hearted Pieter, have their idea of relationship, like their whole lives, attached to material things; and if ever they have to face a separation, they favour a frequent exchange of rings, knives, caps and other tokens of the kind, for fear that their affection may cool when intercourse is interrupted.' Erasmus, of course, sends his friend not a cap or a knife, but a book, a token of the meeting of minds. In her delightful essay on books as gifts, Natalie Davis has explored these tropes.[3] Here I propose to read Bacon's *Essayes* as gifts exchanged within networks of patronage and friendship (pl. 31); but I am also concerned with two material gifts of the sort that Machiavelli and Erasmus despised: a plain cup of assay and a bunch of keys. They, we shall see, were gifts as eloquent as any essay. My reading of these gifts, both literary and material, is intended to provide an insight into the changing culture of friendship in Elizabethan and Jacobean England; and in this world, I will argue, the favourite needs to be interpreted as a special sort of friend.

Gifts, as my opening quotation shows, were exchanged not only between friends but also between patrons and clients, and we need to keep this double context in mind if we are to understand the position of the royal favourite in early modern Europe; for the favourite (at least in Jacobean England) was both the king's chosen friend and the universal fount of patronage. From all quarters gifts flowed into his hands: from ambassadors, courtiers, suitors, dependants and, above all, from the king himself. And it was the favourite who handed out not only jewels and rings, but also office, place and position. It was he who arranged lucrative marriages and offered his protection to anxious litigants. Vast networks of gift-giving had his person as their common centre; and through him people unknown to each other were linked in ties of dependence and alliance, ties variously represented as ties of kinship, friendship and service. Bacon's essays on friendship provide a privileged point of entry into this lost world, in which it was through gifts, not salaries, that one hoped to make one's fortune; through patronage, not open competition, that one endeavoured to make one's way in life; and through the praise of loyal friends, not impartial critics, that one aspired to establish an enduring reputation.

Before we can understand these essays as gifts we must elucidate the rules of gift-giving, and it is with these that I begin. My argument then turns to analyse the Elizabethan and Jacobean literature on friendship. With these preliminaries completed, I discuss Bacon's three essays on friendship in the context of three friendships in Bacon's life – with Essex, Buckingham (pls 34–40) and Toby Matthew (pl. 32). The first two of course were royal favourites. I say three essays, although even those familiar with Bacon's *Essayes* may remember only one.[4] The first is Bacon's essay 'Of Followers and Frends', first published in 1597, at the height of Essex's influence with Elizabeth, and Bacon's influence with Essex, in a volume dedicated to Bacon's brother Anthony. 'Of Followers and Frends' reflects the culture of the Elizabethan court in its final decade, and needs to be read alongside essays such as 'Of Sutors', 'Of Faction' and 'Of Ceremonies and Respects'. The second is Bacon's essay 'Of Frendship', published in 1612 in a volume which Bacon had intended to dedicate to Prince Henry, but which the prince's death caused to be rededicated to Bacon's brother-in-law, John Constable. At the time Bacon was struggling to make his way in the Stuart court, the culture of which (quite different from the Elizabethan) is reflected in essays such as 'Of Great Place', 'Of Ambition' (both of which, unlike Bacon's first essay 'Of Frendship', discuss favourites: the first private, the second royal), 'Of Vaine-Glory' and 'Of Counsell'.

The third is Bacon's quite different essay of the same title, published in 1625, after Bacon had fallen from power and been disgraced, in a volume dedicated to his erstwhile patron Buckingham. It is this essay, not that of 1612, which discusses royal favourites (in other words Buckingham himself), while it was natural in Bacon's changed circumstances that another essay new to this volume should be entitled 'Of Adversity', and that the whole volume should end with 'Of Vicissitude of Things'. But the essay 'Of Frendship' itself was privately dedicated to Bacon's close friend Toby Matthew, and thus carried as it were a double dedication. At the same time, beyond this immediate context, Bacon's new essay 'Of Frendship' or 'De Amicitia' was associated with his plan to publish his essays in Latin, so that they might endure long after the English language had been forgotten, as long perhaps as Cicero's essay known by the same title. Thus each of the three major editions of the *Essayes* had an essay on friendship associated with it, and taken together they present three different images of friendship. We may label these three, for convenience, the friend as patron, the friend as royal favourite and the friend as faithful companion.

The Giving of Gifts

Friendship has a thin and ambiguous place in our culture. It has no clear conventions, rights or duties. In the early seventeenth century, however, friendship was a subject which was widely discussed and clearly understood. Every gentleman was familiar with Cicero's 'On Friendship' and with two other classic texts that were also prolonged meditations on friendship: Plutarch's 'How to Distinguish a Flatterer from a Friend', and Seneca's 'On Benefits'. To these had been more recently added Montaigne's essay on his love for Etienne de la Boëtie. Alongside them was placed Psalm 116, 'Quid retribuam?'. These texts made clear what we may call the principles of friendship, principles which were given their clearest modern expression in Marcel Mauss' classic study *The Gift* (1925), a work whose subject matter is identical with that of Seneca, though, strangely, Seneca is never mentioned.[5] Seventeenth-century readers were also acutely aware of certain paradigm cases of friendship and favouritism: David and Jonathan; Joseph and Pharaoh; Sejanus and Tiberius; Gaveston and Edward II.[6]

The insignificance of friendship in our own culture helps account for the fact that the literature on early modern friendship is scattered and unsystematic. In addition to Natalie Davis' essay there are two admirable and wide-ranging discussions by Sharon Kettering, one on gift-giving and patronage, the other on friendship and clientage in early modern France. A number of social historians have seen the relevance of Mauss' work on the gift to an understanding of early modern England. There is an excellent account of Montaigne's friendship with La Boëtie, and a number of other valuable discussions of individuals which take friendship as their theme. There are fine discussions of subjects that bracket mine: Catherine Bates on the rhetoric of courtship in Elizabethan England; Simon Adams on Elizabeth's favourites; Linda Levy Peck on 'benefits, brokers and beneficiaries' in the court of James; Alan Bray on male friendship and sodomy in Elizabethan and Jacobean England; and Antonio Feros on Spanish conceptions of the favourite. Lorna Hutson has written on friendship in sixteenth-century English literature. In the nineteenth century the question of whether Bacon had betrayed his friend Essex by participating in his prosecution was much discussed; Bacon's dealings with Buckingham have more recently attracted some attention; but Toby Matthew still awaits the historian he deserves, and I can find no significant literature on Bacon's three essays on friendship.[7]

We should begin with the fundamental principles of gift-giving (for the gift of friendship is a special case of gift-giving) in Elizabethan and Jacobean England. We may identify them by taking an example from Bacon's apophthegms, a collection of witty sayings, for since wit is culturally specific if we can see the wit in this saying we will have the beginnings of a grasp of our subject: 'Sir Thomas More had sent him by a suitor in the chancery two silver flagons. When they were presented by the gentleman's servant, he said to one of his men: "Have him to the cellar, and let him have of my best wine." And turning to the servant said, "Tell thy master, friend, if he like it, let him not spare it." '[8] More had been offered a gift, and the exchange of gifts is the mark of friendship. He had also been offered a bribe, which he must reject. His actions should be interpreted as a deliberate inversion of the principles of gift-giving: first, a friend must never refuse or return a gift. More returns the flagons, but in doing so he pretends that he has misunderstood their character as a gift, for he returns them with wine in them. He behaves as if, far from being offered a gift, he is responding to a neighbourly request for a cup of sugar. Second, a gift must never resemble a commercial exchange, and so there should be a delay of time between gift and counter-gift, or the two should be simultaneous, so that the giver gives before he knows what he has received (as with Christmas presents). More gives back as soon as he receives. Third, givers should not compete to outdo each other. But More carefully gives more than he has received so that there can be no question of his being in the suitor's debt. Fourth, it is not the gift but the thought that counts, for the gift is a token of devotion. More's suitor does not offer money (at least in appearance), but a token of affection. More too repays with something that has no obvious monetary value, but his gift is perishable, while the ideal gift, like friendship, must be enduring (a jewel, a picture, a book). (In an extreme case, Montaigne himself becomes his friend's picture, Montaigne's book about his friend his gift to friendship.) Consequently – here is the fifth principle – one usually keeps, one does not consume, a gift, but More's gift is to be consumed. (Hospitality is a striking exception here, since it is a gift to be consumed, but hospitality imposes only temporary, not lasting, obligations; gifts intended to embody love and friendship thus tend to take the form of enduring objects: even horses and greyhounds live on in their offspring.)

More's action may be witty, but why is 'Tell thy master, friend, if he like it, let him not spare it' an apophthegm, a witty saying? For two reasons. First, because a gift is a token of oneself, a symbol of the fact that friends belong to each other: More, by insisting that his suitor must not 'spare' his gift, asserts his right not to spare his suitor. And second, because of the seemingly carelessly misplaced 'friend': this friendly transaction, which has gone so awry, is after all not one between friends. More is more friendly to the servant, who has offered him nothing, than to his master, who has tried to purchase friendship.

It may seem strange to interpret this exchange in the context of friendship, but we need to remember that friendship, for Cicero and Seneca, More and Bacon, was first and foremost a pact for mutual assistance, a form of mutual clientage. Friendship, like gift-giving, was inherently paradoxical in nature. It mush be freely given, and yet it represented an obligation. So, just as gift exchanges ought never to resemble commercial exchanges, and must consist both of appropriate objects and of appropriate thoughts, so the ideal friendship would be one in which both offered assistance, but neither knew whether he would end up as debtor or creditor. The ideal friendship was one between equals, who then became unequal, so that one could be dependent on the other and so test his friendship, and in which the inequality was then reversed so that the erstwhile beneficiary could demonstrate his undying gratitude. Such a friendship was a mutual insurance policy on which both parties made a claim, but at different times and under very different circumstances, so that each one by demonstrating loyalty was not merely recognizing an obligation but passing a test of character.[9]

It is such an ideal friendship that Bacon had with Toby Matthew. In exile in 1619, Matthew carried a set of keys to Bacon's house.[10] Bacon had plenty of servants to admit guests (a hundred of them, in fact), so the keys can have had no function.[11] Rather they were a token, a lasting symbol guaranteeing Matthew's access to Bacon's own person and symbolizing that what was Bacon's was Matthew's. The keys were an ideal gift in that on the one hand it was only the thought they symbolized that counted, while on the other they represented a firm and enduring promise of future assistance.

Friendship is thus inseparable, in the early modern period, from alliance, clientage and favouritism – concepts which are to us antithetical to friendship, because in our view friendship is a matter for private life, while public life is ostensibly governed by the revolutionary principles of impartiality and the career open to talents. More, it may be thought, was giving impartiality priority over an offer of alliance; but if so he was not typical. Much ink was spilled in the nineteenth century in debating whether or not Bacon was a corrupt judge. We need only to read a passage in 'Of Sutors' which survived unchanged from edition to edition to know that he saw no shame in avowing partiality, even though he acknowledged there could be no excuse for corruption: 'If affection lead a man to favour the wrong side in justice, let him rather use his countenance to compound the matter than to carry it. If affection lead a man to favour the less worthy in desert, let him do it without depraving or disabling the better deserver.'[12]

The Politics of Friendship

Again and again when discussing social relations Elizabethan and Jacobean authors resort to the language of Machiavelli. It is in the course of an essay on reputation, for example, that we are reminded that 'Fear is a more certain ground than love for maintaining authority, because love is in the power of the lover, fear in him that maketh himself feared.'[13] To see friendship as alliance is to see it as politics, and we should not be surprised to discover that Machiavelli makes his way into discussions of friendship. Thus Machiavelli's famous chapter on conspiracies is interpreted as a discussion of how far one dare entrust secrets to one's friends.[14] But to see friendship in terms of politics was to associate it with fear and with danger.

In this section I want to take five discussions of friendship (four of the five being from volumes of essays written in the tradition of Bacon's own *Essayes*: Cornwallis' *Essayes*, 1600; Johnson's *Essaies*, 1601; Tuvil's *Essaies Politicke and Morall*, 1608; and Robinson's *New Essayes*, 1628) and use them to illustrate what were perceived as the dangers of friendship. One reason for doing this is that Bacon has much less to say about the risks of friendship than most of his contemporaries; it is astonishing to what extent they treat friendship as a focus of anxiety, as the most difficult of all social negotiations.[15] What they offer indeed is a series of commonplaces designed to teach their readers the rules of safe friendship.

First, never be in a hurry to make a friend. Cicero had recommended that you share so many meals with your prospective friend before you risked regarding him as a friend that you consume a bushel of salt together. Second, always test a friendship before relying on it. The cooper first puts water in the barrel before he relies on it to hold wine.[16] Third, beware of a friendship that serves the other's purposes not yours, or you are in danger of being like the oak which supports the ivy, and whose reward is to be eventually consumed by it.[17] ('They are sworn brothers, they will live and die together; but they scarce sleep in this mind; the one comes to make use of the other, and that spoils all; he entered this league not to impair, but to profit himself. . . .'[18]) Fourth, always be careful before entrusting secrets to anyone, even a friend, for this is to place yourself in voluntary servitude, to put yourself in another's power.[19] There are few who can be entrusted with a secret: 'There are few that can say and say truly, as that Grecian of former times did, who being told that his breath did smell, answered that it was by reason of the many secrets which had a long time lain rotting and putrefying within him. . . .'[20] These basic rules are simple and straightforward.

There are others that are more surprising. You should make friends only of those who seem to shun friendship. 'If he be very forward, beware; for either he is a common friend, and so no friend, or else he means to betray you. They are surest that are won with labour, and certainest that are purchased with difficulty: for an open prostitute man or woman is loathsome, and flexible.'[21]

Paradoxically, the friends you can rely on are not those you have helped in the past, but those who have reason to hope you will help them in the future. Thus if you want to have your friend do you a favour you should remind him of your gratitude for previous favours he has done you, never, under any circumstance, of the favours you have done him.[22] It is, in any case, almost impossible to reject a friend's request for a favour, even one that you are in no position to perform, without endangering the friendship. If you say 'no' quickly (while making promises for the future), you may be acting in your friend's best interests, since delay exacerbates disappointment, but you are likely to seem unwilling to help. If you pretend for as long as possible that the request will be granted, eventual failure may suggest ill-faith. But to succeed in doing your friend a favour may also endanger the friendship: to put someone in your debt when they have no prospect of early repayment is to risk turning a friend into an enemy.[23] Wherever you turn, in fact, friendship threatens to turn into its opposite.[24] Thus one should withhold secrets, even from friends; but not to entrust your secrets to your friends is to imply distrust, and to risk turning friends into enemies. Worse still, one should never forget that supposed friends are more dangerous than open enemies: 'Sampson lived safely enough amongst his enemies the giantly Philistines, but in his wife's lap where he thought himself safest he was quickly subdued. . . .'[25] Friendship, it turns out, is close to hatred. Much of this anxiety is summed up in one of Bacon's apophthegms, which reappears in the essay 'Of Revenge': 'Cosmus Duke of Florence was wont to say of perfidious friends: "That we read that we ought to forgive our enemies, but we do not read that we ought to forgive our friends."'[26]

These principles, both obvious and subtle, reflect universal principles of human psychology. But late-sixteenth- and early-seventeenth-century writers believed that friendship had become unusually difficult in their own time for three reasons. In the first place, they believed that they and their contemporaries were peculiarly obsessed with questions of status (although they flattered themselves that in this respect they were all too like the citizens of ancient Rome), and that status anxiety could corrode friendship:

The Romans, not to defraud any man of a due and convenient Congie [greeting], retained certain Admonitors (called *Nomenclatores*) who should suggest the name, quality, and account of every one they encountered, that they might be saluted in a conformable style: for to look strange and disdainful, to be backward in returning these respects procureth hatred even in the dearest friends, so much more dangerous, by how much men can less endure to be despised than injured, because other grievances concern only the body, and bring this comfort, that he is somebody in his conceit who so offended him: but the injuries of contempt are a disreputation, and the offended taketh himself to be accounted nobody, and therefore such omissions can hardly by any means be redeemed. . . .[27]

This preoccupation with status made friendships between equals (traditionally the purest form of friendship) peculiarly delicate, for equality provided the perfect environment for competition and rivalry to flourish.

Second, they believed they lived in an age which, in order to show due respect to status, had become preoccupied with courtesy or court-manners. But where codes of behaviour were strictly defined it was all too easy to slide unintentionally from compliment to insult: 'I have known some affecting courtesy overthrow their labours with not having choice of compliments, but confounding a gentleman and a peasant with the likeness of salutation and farewell. They were to blame to set up shop so ill-furnished. As men differ so must their usages and respects. Not to all "I am the servant of your servant's servant."' Even those who had mastered the language of courtesy stood at a disadvantage when it came to expressing true sentiments, for their language had become devoid of all meaning:

> We accomplement, and civilized, or civeted (for our actions smell like a profound courtier), kiss the hand as if we meant to take assay of it, embrace curiously, and spend even at his entrance a whole volume of words. . . . 'O signor, the star that governs my life in contentment, give me leave to inter myself in your arms.' 'Not so, sir, it is too unworthy an enclosure to contain such preciousness. . . .'[28]

Compliments thus became meaningless forms of flattery, and flattery was the third and final obstacle to friendship which was peculiarly prevalent in their own, self-fashioning day. This was a theme to which contemporaries returned again and again. 'There are some that fashion themselves to nothing more than how to become speculative into another, to the end to know how to work him, or wind him, or govern him: but this proceedeth from a heart that is double and cloven; and not entire, and ingenuous.'[29] 'There was once more certainty, but now policy can put on all shapes, so that the wolf and the lamb are hardly to be distinguished, either by their habit, words or actions.'[30] 'In these our present times . . . flattery is become such a common art and so much practised of most men that almost every rustical companion and illiterate peasant can represent like a looking-glass what man's qualities and conditions he will.' '"Their lips", saith Solomon, "drop as an honeycomb, and their mouths are more soft than oil, but the end of them is as bitter as gall, and as sharp as a two-edged sword. . . ."' In greatest danger of being deceived were the rich and the powerful, who found themselves surrounded by flatterers 'as thick as flies about butcher's shambles'.[31]

Consequently, just as men and women whose hearts had been broken swore off love, so those who had been deceived tried (and similarly failed) to give up the quest for friendship. In the following passage Sir William Cornwallis first denies the existence of friendship, then affirms his faith in it, and then finally adopts the cynical attitude to it he finds so contemptible in others. Was he aware of his own inconsistency? I think not.

There is no love upon the earth. . . . If I could be sure of them, I would say I loved too, and make men say they are my friends: but it is an uncertain trade this loving, and stands upon such a company of circumstances as I like it not. I make no difference between common lovers, and common whores, they both flatter and make the name of love their bawds to serve their particular pleasures. For my choice of friends, virtue shall be the groundwork, and so I may build surely. Let his fortunes be what they will, I care not. Yet if I might choose, I would have him poor, for so I might easiest show my affection to him, and profit myself with least cost: for I hold observation much more precious than wealth, and I will rather give him my purse than my time.[32]

One text may serve as an epitome of this extensive literature on the dangers of friendship. *The Triall of True Friendship, or Perfit Mirror Whereby to Discerne a Trustie Friend from a Flattering Parasite* was written by M.B. and published in 1596. Its epigraph is 'Try ere you trust; believe no man rashly'; its final words are 'Praemonitus praemunitus': forewarned, forearmed.

And one cautionary tale may serve to remind us just what was at stake. In 1616 Bacon prosecuted Somerset (pl. 12) for the murder of Sir Thomas Overbury. The trial was the *cause célèbre* of the age. Why had Somerset and his wife poisoned Overbury while he was held prisoner in the Tower? Because Overbury had dangerous information that he was threatening to use against them. Modern historians have entertained themselves finding different ways of telling the story of the crime.[33] For Bacon nothing could have been simpler: it was a story about the dangers of friendship. Overbury was the epitome of an untrustworthy friend. He had opposed Somerset's marriage 'under pretence to do the true part of a friend (for that he counted her an unworthy woman); but the truth was that Overbury, who (to speak plainly) had little that was solid for religion or for moral virtue, but was a man possessed with ambition and vainglory, was loth to have any partners in the favour of my Lord of Somerset. . . . So all was but miserable bargains of ambition.' Thus Somerset's hatred was not misplaced. And so Bacon was able to conclude that just 'as it is a principle in nature, that the best things are in their corruption the worst, and the sweetest wine makes the sharpest vinegar, so fell it out with them [Somerset and Overbury], that this excess (as I may term it) of friendship [evidenced by the exchange of secrets] ended in mortal hatred on my Lord of Somerset's part'.[34]

Three Friends, Three Essays

There are three friendships which illustrate the real-life underpinnings of Bacon's three essays on friendship.

ESSEX

Recent scholarship has rejected the old picture of the reign of Queen Elizabeth (pl. 5) as a constant struggle between factions, but in doing so has cast into bolder relief her last decade when Essex (pl. 10) and his supporters struggled to wrest power from Burghley and laid claim to a monopoly of patronage.[35] Essex divided the world into friends and enemies, and among his friends was Bacon. In 1595 Essex worked long and hard to have Bacon appointed solicitor general, declaring, 'Upon me [not Burghley] the labour must lie of his establishment, and upon me the disgrace will light of his being refused,' and insisting that 'my credit is engaged in his fortune'. With Essex's support, Bacon had felt confident in pressing his own case 'as long as I have a tongue to speak, or a pen to write, or a friend to use.'

Yet, despite all Essex's efforts, Bacon failed; indeed his friend's support seemed to have harmed Bacon's cause, for the queen was suspicious of Essex's factional behaviour. Essex was thus obliged to rescue his honour by making Bacon a present of some land. Bacon replied by sending him a letter with a remarkable ending: 'For your Lordship, I do think myself more beholding to you than to any man. And I say, I reckon myself as a *common* (not popular, but *common*); and as much as is lawful to be enclosed of a common, so much your Lordship shall be sure to have.' The meaning seems clear: Bacon intends to insist that Essex cannot purchase his loyalty, and that his first obligation will always be to public service. Bacon was declaring his unwillingness to be dependent on a single patron, to become a mere member of a faction. And Essex seems to have understood this, for when he later sought to advance Bacon he insisted that he pressed his case not because Bacon was a friend but because he was dedicated to the public interest ('I would not for the second time hurt him with my care and kindness; but I will commend unto your lordship [Buckhurst] his cause, not as his alone, nor as mine his friend's, but as a public cause').[36] It has been suggested that Bacon's letter was written with the intention that it should be shown to the queen.[37] If so it gives us a good idea of the sentiments that were approved of in Elizabeth's court: Elizabeth herself expected public service to take priority over friendship.

A year later, after Essex had sacked Cadiz, Bacon wrote to him explaining how a favourite of the queen should conduct himself, and urging him not to press too hard on his good fortune, but to imitate his predecessors Leicester and Hatton, and abandon his implicit claim to more favourable treatment than they had received. Essex, he urges, must pay court to the queen; must appear to praise her sincerely, and not merely for form's sake. (In a contemporary essay, 'Of Ceremonies and Respects', Bacon lays similar stress on the politic use of praise: 'And certainly there is a kind of conveying of effectual and imprinting passages, amongst compliments, which is of singular use, if a man can hit upon it.')[38] Essex must make clear that he places loyalty to his queen above loyalty to his friends by deliberately recommending people for positions and then abandoning them. He must not seek to monopolize the position of military leader, but must encourage her to appoint other soldiers to her Privy Council. He must allow others as well as himself to play the role of favourite if he wants to be secure in the queen's favours. The advice is epitomized in the recommendation that Essex should seek the position, not of earl marshal, but of privy seal, for 'it fits a favourite to carry her Majesty's image in seal, who beareth it best expressed in heart'.[39]

Bacon's letter is a helpful account of the qualities Elizabeth looked for in a favourite, and represents a deliberate attempt to steer Essex towards the consensual, conciliar activity which had characterized the major part of her reign, and away from his own factional struggle with Burghley. No individual should appear to monopolize the queen's patronage or policy; the surest road to influence lay through courtly eloquence, not martial deeds; and the queen's favourites must demonstrate that their loyalty to her was greater than their loyalty to their friends. Because Essex would not adapt himself to this advice he doomed himself to a tragic end. In his apophthegms Bacon recorded a remark that could have been his own: 'A great officer at court, when my Lord of Essex was first in trouble, and that he and those that dealt for him would talk much of my Lord's friends and of his enemies; answered to one of them: "I will tell you, I know but one friend and one enemy my Lord hath; and that one friend is the Queen, and that one enemy is himself."'[40] Essex had fatally misjudged the Elizabethan politics of friendship.

It is at around the same time that he counselled Essex on how to be a favourite that Bacon must have written his essay 'Of Followers and Frends', with its criticism of factious followers, glorious followers and pompous and popular followers. Much of the essay reads like a meditation on the conflicts between Essex and the queen. It was Essex who needed to be reminded that 'the most honourable kind of following, is to be followed as one that apprehendeth to advance virtue and desert in all sorts of persons', and was therefore prepared to advance those who were not his exclusive friends. It was Elizabeth who believed that 'To be governed (as we call it) by one is not safe: for it shows softness, and gives a freedom to scandal and disreputation.' Placed in this context, the essay ends with a defence of the Elizabethan court as it had been before the conflict between Essex and Burghley threatened to tear it apart. In the contemporary 'Of Faction' Bacon took the same line. 'Mean men, in their rising, must adhere [to factions]; but great men, that have strength in themselves, were better to maintain themselves indifferent and neutral.' 'When factions are carried too high and too violently it is a sign of weakness in princes, and much to the prejudice both of their authority and business.'[41]

But this endorsement of Elizabeth's court as she herself conceived of it was also a direct attack on Cicero's conception of friendship. Cicero insists a friend is ideally *identical* to oneself. If he is one's superior he must act like one's equal. An excess of resources and power was, he maintained, incompatible with friendship. The limit case was that of the tyrant: 'That is how a tyrant lives –

without mutual trust, without affection, without any assurance of enduring goodwill. In such a life suspicion and anxiety reign everywhere, and friendship has no place.'[42] This contraposition between friendship and tyranny lay at the heart of Etienne de la Boëtie's *Voluntary Servitude*, in which all relationships of inequality were rejected and friendship between equals was presented as the ultimate ideal. It was this idealization of friendship which had first drawn Montaigne to La Boëtie, and it is this egalitarian and republican conception of friendship that Montaigne echoes in his own essay on friendship.[43] Part of this conception was the claim that true friendship was an exclusive relationship: one friend was the most one could have.[44]

Nothing could be more calculated than Bacon's conclusion: 'To take advice of some few friends is ever honourable, *for lookers on, many times, see more than gamesters; and the vale best discovereth the hill.* There is little friendship in the world, and least of all between equals, which was wont to be magnified. That that is, is between superior and inferior, whose fortunes may comprehend the one the other.'[45] In taking the model of friendship as the relationship between patron and client, queen and councillor, where there can be no question of rivalry, Bacon is adapting the ideal of friendship to reflect the realities of court life. In doing so he is implicitly rejecting Cicero's and Montaigne's ideal of the friend as the mirror of one's true self, and as someone who, after death, lives on in oneself. Between client and patron there could be no need for that total sincerity which Cicero and Montaigne had praised. Thus Bacon was in danger of identifying friends with followers, favourites and even flatterers. When, around the time he wrote this essay, Bacon told Essex to give greater appearance of sincerity when praising Elizabeth, he insisted there could be no question of *flattery*, but he intended to be understood as meaning that this was exactly what was needed. For Cicero, by contrast, 'there can be no worse blot on a friendship than fawning sycophancy and adulation'. Elsewhere Bacon quotes Solomon: 'He that praiseth his friend aloud, rising early, it shall be to him no better than a curse' ('Of Praise', 1612).[46] But not here.

In Essex's circle Elizabeth herself came to be seen as a tyrant, and his supporters soon praised friendship as an alternative to courtly corruption. The turning point, the scholarly literature suggests, was the publication of Grenewey's translation of the *Annales* of Tacitus in 1598.[47] Nevertheless, it is tempting to read Bacon's first essay on friendship, published in 1597, as a warning directed at this nascent crypto-republicanism. So too in his 1596 letter advising Essex on how to be an Elizabethan favourite he had advised him to be cautious: 'to take all occasions to speak against popularity and popular causes vehemently; and to tax it in all others: but nevertheless to go on in your honourable commonwealth courses as you do'.[48] Essex's cult of friendship and his taste for faction were already part and parcel of his 'commonwealth courses', and in 'Of Followers and Frends', as in 'Of Faction', Bacon was offering him a courtly alternative. In a later essay, 'Of Praise', Bacon rejected the republican view, so eloquently stated by Machiavelli, that the common people were good judges of political leaders: 'fame is like a river, that beareth up things light and swollen, and drowns things weighty and solid'.[49] Had he said as much in 1597, Essex, who hoped to be borne aloft on a torrent of popular support, might well have taken exception. In Stuart England the case for courtly values could be put more bluntly.

BUCKINGHAM

In Elizabeth's court the queen's bedchamber had been a private, female world. Power lay in the public world of the council. In James' court the royal bedchamber was the locus of power (pl. 19).[50] As Bacon wrote to the future Buckingham: 'you are not only a courtier, but a bed-chamber man, and so are in the eye and ear of your master' (and, unlike other bedchamber men, in his bosom too, he went on to add).[51] Those who shared the daily intimacy of bed, board and hunt determined events. Elizabeth's courtiers had paid court to her: the word had newly come to refer to the blandishments of the lover as well as the insinuations of the courtier. In James' court friendship replaced courtship as the official language of self-advancement, and the result was a new symmetry between the relationship of king and courtier on the one hand and that of patron and client on the other: for, if courtiers could aspire to be the king's friend and favourite, favourites could have their own friends, their own favourites. Public and private were no longer as easily separable as they had been when Bacon had insisted that he was a common, that he was dedicated to the public. These changes soon transformed the language of friendship, and were naturally reflected in Bacon's *Essayes*.

In 'Of Ambition' (1612) he sketched two ways of managing a court, the first of which we can recognize as Jacobean, the second as Elizabethan:

> It is counted by some a weakness in princes to have favourites. But it is of all others the best remedy against ambitious great ones. For when the way of pleasuring and displeasuring lieth by the favourite it is impossible any other should be over-great. Another means to curb them is to balance them by others, as proud as they are. But then there must be some middle counsellors, to keep things steady: for without that ballast the ship will roll too much.[52]

Having grasped James' methods, he was quick to attach himself to Villiers even before it could be said of him 'You are as a new-risen star, and the eyes of all men are upon you.' In what is probably his earliest surviving letter to him he writes: 'I am yours surer to you than to my own life. For, as they speak of the Turquoise stone in a ring, I will break into twenty pieces before you have the least fall.' Soon after he wrote Villiers a detailed document outlining how he should fulfil his role as favourite: 'You are now the King's Favourite, so voted, and so esteemed by all. . . . It is no new things for Kings and Princes to have their privadoes, their favourites, their friends. . . . no man thinks his business can prosper at Court, unless he hath you for his good Angel, or at least that you be not a *Malus Genius* against him.[53] This was to acknowledge that Villiers held a position that no favourite of Elizabeth had ever held, that of monopolist of royal patronage. Naunton was to write in 1633, in his famous account of Elizabeth's reign:

> her ministers . . . were only favourites not minions, such as acted more by her own princely rules and judgment than by their own will and appetites; which she observed to the last, for we find no Gaveston, Vere, or Spencer to have swayed alone during forty-four years. . . . she was absolute and sovereign mistress of her grace and . . . those to whom she distributed her favours were never more than tenants at will.[54]

His intention was evidently to draw an implicit contrast between Leicester as favourite and Buckingham as minion. But it was easy to draw this contrast with hindsight; Bacon certainly failed to realize its full implications at the time.

In 1617 Buckingham planned to arrange a marriage alliance between his own family and that of Sir Edward Coke (despite the opposition of Coke's daughter, who was to be wed against her will). Bacon, long Coke's enemy, opposed the match, which, he insisted, was not in the king's interest. With James and Buckingham away in Scotland, he acted to frustrate Buckingham's plans. Immediately he discovered he had overstepped the bounds. King and favourite both sent him vitriolic letters. It was no good for Bacon to protest that he had acted as a friend, to tell Buckingham, 'parent-like', that 'by my great experience in the world [I] must needs see further than your Lordship can', and to protest to James 'if I should be requested in it from my Lord of Buckingham, the answer of a true friend ought to be, that I had rather go against his mind than against his good'.[55] Our first thought is likely to be that Bacon had misjudged his legal authority or his political influence.[56] But to the participants and the onlookers it was clear that Bacon on the one hand and James and Buckingham on the other had different understandings of what friendship entailed. 'Every courtier', Bacon was told, 'is acquainted that the Earl professeth openly against you as forgetful of his kindness, and unfaithful to him in your love and in your actions . . . not forbearing in open speech to tax you, as if it were an inveterate custom with you, to be unfaithful to him as you were to the Earls of Essex and Somerset.' James, consequently, corrected Bacon by outlining to him the duties of a true friend:

> even in good manners you had reason not to have crossed anything wherein you had heard his name used, till you had heard from him; for if you had willingly given your consent and hand to the recovery of the young gentlewoman, and then written both to us and to him what inconvenience appeared to you to be in such a match, that had been the part indeed of a true servant to us and a true friend to

him, but first to make an opposition, and then to give advice by way of friendship, is to make the plough to go before the horse.

In short, the favourite's friend must act as his servant.

Bacon was nothing if not flexible, and made an abject submission to Buckingham. 'I can be but yours, and desire to better myself, that I may be of more worth to such an owner,' was the language he now knew to adopt. His grasp of the true nature of their relationship was epitomized in the New Year's gift he offered him at the end of the year: 'I am bold to send your Lordship for your New-Year's gift a plain cup of assay, in token that if your Lordship in anything shall make me your [as]sayman, I will be hurt before your Lordship shall be hurt. I present to you therewith my best service, which shall be my All-Year's gift.'[57] Over the next few years Bacon was, as the king desired he should be, Buckingham's faithful servant. When he was impeached in 1621 (when, as Buckingham's assayman, he took upon himself the anger directed at the duke), it was to Buckingham that he naturally turned for the restoration of his fortunes. Yet again he demonstrated that he had not grasped the new rules of friendship. For Buckingham wanted first from Bacon an acknowledgement that everything that was his was Buckingham's. He must hand over York House. Bacon refused: 'York House is the house where my father died, and where first I breathed, and there will I yield my last breath, if it so please God, and the King will give me leave. . . . no money or value shall make me part with it.'

Once again Bacon had failed to play a friend's part. But this time he recuperated his position deftly: even the king praised his 'after-game'.[58] Bacon rejected a request from the Duke of Lennox to purchase York House, saying that since he had refused it to Buckingham he could let no one else have it. And then he allowed Buckingham to determine that Cranfield should have it at any price he chose. If the house was not to be Buckingham's it was to be his to give away. Only then could Bacon begin to travel the long road to a restoration of his fortunes.

When we read the essay 'Of Frendship' Bacon published in 1625 in a volume dedicated to Buckingham, we are entitled to look, as Buckingham would have done, for an endorsement of the Jacobean politics of friendship. And this is exactly what we find:

It is a strange thing to observe, how high a rate great kings and monarchs do set upon this fruit of friendship, whereof we speak. So great, as they purchase it, many times, at the hazard of their own safety and greatness. For princes, in regard of the distance of their fortune, from that of their subjects and servants, cannot gather this fruit except (to make themselves capable thereof) they raise some persons to be as it were companions and almost equals to themselves, which many times sorteth to inconvenience. The modern languages give unto such persons the name of *favourites* or *privadoes*, as if it were a matter of grace or conversation. But the Roman name attaineth the true use and cause thereof, naming them *participes curarum*, for it is that which tieth the knot. And we see plainly that this hath been done, not by weak and passionate princes only, but by the wisest and most politic that ever reigned. Who have oftentimes joined to themselves some of their servants, whom both themselves have called friends, and allowed others likewise to call them in the same manner, using the word which is received between private men.

And Bacon ends his essay with what seems at first a conventional account of how friends can help each other. But the ideal friend turns out to be little more than a great man's go-between, a private ambassador. Of such men Bacon himself had need when he had to make his peace with Buckingham or the king:

> How many things are there which a man cannot, with any face or comeliness, say or do himself? A man can scarce allege his own merits with modesty, much less extol them. A man cannot sometimes brook to supplicate or beg, and a number of the like. But all these things are graceful in a friend's mouth which are blushing in a man's own. So again, a man's person hath many proper relations which he cannot put off. A man cannot speak to his son but as a father, to his wife but as a husband, to his enemy but upon terms; whereas a friend may speak as the case requires, and not as it sorteth with the person. But to enumerate these things were endless. I have given the rule: where a man cannot fitly ply his own part, if he have not a friend, he may quit the stage.[59]

'Of Frendship' was surely intended to be read as an endorsement of Jacobean friendship. Yet, as one would expect in someone who believed himself to have been unjustly treated by his erstwhile friends, Bacon has trouble controlling the tone of his remarks. He devotes a page to great Romans and their friends, but the examples are disturbing. Here we meet, to our surprise, Tiberius and Sejanus, whose intimacy caused the Senate to dedicate an altar to friendship. And later he discusses at length how, if friends are to give good advice, they must have 'the liberty of a friend' to speak their mind, and must be the opposite of flatterers. It can scarcely be a coincidence that Bacon repeats here a phrase he had used, not only in 'Of Followers and Frends' thirty years before, but also less than a decade earlier, when he had tried to justify his opposition to the Buckingham–Coke marriage alliance, and had been told in no uncertain terms that he must not question Buckingham's good judgement: 'As for business, a man may think, if he will, that two eyes see no more than one, *or that a gamester seeth always more than a looker on,* or that a man in anger is as wise as he that hath said over the four and twenty letters, or that a musket may be shot off as well upon the arm as upon a rest, and such other fond and high imaginations, to think himself all in all.'[60] 'Of Frendship' is a complicated text partly because Bacon resented the way Buckingham had treated him. But there is another reason, for we must read it as dedicated not only to Buckingham, but also to Toby Matthew.

TOBY MATTHEW

Toby Matthew was born, son of the future Archbishop of York, in 1577, when Bacon was seventeen.[61] In 1595 he played the part of an esquire in a 'device' written by Bacon for Essex to have performed on the queen's day. By 1604 Bacon was Matthew's patron: Matthew served in Bacon's stead as member of parliament for St Albans, Bacon having also been elected for Ipswich. That same year Matthew left England to travel on the continent, where he converted to Catholicism. He returned in 1606, when Bacon protected him, though he could not keep his friend out of prison. In 1608 Matthew went abroad again, was ordained by Bellarmine (1614), and joined (secretly) the Jesuit order. Meanwhile Bacon faithfully corresponded with him, and sent him copies of his works as they were written. In 1617 he returned to England, again benefiting from Bacon's protection. The next year he published an Italian translation of Bacon's *Essayes*. In January 1619 the king sent Matthew into exile (with Bacon's keys in his pocket) for his steadfast refusal to take the oath of allegiance, but he was permitted to return in 1621.

Matthew had excellent connections at court, particularly with Gondomar and Buckingham's mother. In 1623 he was sent to Madrid to advise Charles and Buckingham on the Spanish match. In these years it was now Bacon who was the client, he the patron. When Bacon was impeached he sent a letter of consolation written in his own hand, 'as if', said Bacon, 'it had been in old gold'. Bacon wrote in reply: 'Your company was ever of contentment to me, and your absence of grief: but now it is of grief upon grief.' In 1623 he describes Matthew in a letter to Buckingham in the conventional terms of friendship: 'to me another myself'. In his will he is 'my ancient good friend'.[62] This was a paradigm case of friendship as I earlier defined it, with each helping the other when he could reasonably expect no help in return.

It is not surprising then that Matthew and Bacon thought of each other when they thought of friendship. In 1623 Bacon wrote to him in Spain to discuss the translation of his works into Latin, 'for these modern languages will at one time or other play the bank-rowtes with books: and since I have lost much time with this age, I would be glad as God shall give me leave to recover it with posterity. For the essay of friendship, while I took your speech of it for a cursory request I took my promise for a compliment. But since you call for it I shall perform it.'[63] Later (as I take it) he writes: 'Good Mr Matthew, it is not for nothing that I have deferred my essay *De Amicitia*, whereby it hath expected the proof of your great friendship towards me.'[64] Here, then, are two further contexts for Bacon's final essay on friendship. It is a work written both for a true friend and for posterity.

Before we look at the essay of 1625 under this double aspect, however, we need to glance back at the original essay of the same title, which stood at the front of Bacon's volume intended for Prince Henry. This too is a conventional praise of friendship ('friendship multiplieth joys and divideth griefs'). Friendship here is quite distinct from the patron–client relationship, indeed its very antithesis: 'Want of true friends . . . is . . . an imposition upon great fortunes. . . . And therefore it is good to retain sincerity, and to put it into the reckoning of ambition that the higher one goeth, the fewer true friends he shall have.' But on the other hand it does not require equality, let alone identity. Bacon carefully redefines true friendship so that it remains within the reach of either a young prince and future king, or a busy middle-aged lawyer still advancing his career. What he describes is something below the level of his own friendship with Matthew: 'Perfection of friendship is but a speculation. It is friendship when a man can say to himself "I love this man without respect of utility. I am open-hearted to him. I single him from the generality of those with whom I live. I make him a portion of my own wishes." '[65] In 1625 Bacon will need to go further if he wants to catch posterity's ear.

I will not analyse in detail here what Lisa Jardine has termed Bacon's 'sensitive and optimistic treatment of friendship'.[66] We have seen already that it has a darker side. Its dominant theme is that 'it is a mere and miserable solitude to want true friends, without which the world is but a wilderness'. Let us note merely two remarkable characteristics of Bacon's essay. The central theme of the Elizabethan literature on friendship had been the danger associated with entrusting secrets to a friend. Even in the 1612 essay Bacon writes, 'A man may keep a corner of his mind from his friend, and it be but to witness to himself that it is not upon facility but upon true use of friendship that he imparteth himself.' Now Bacon longs to unburden himself. 'Those that want friends to open themselves unto are cannibals of their own hearts. . . . A man were better relate himself to a statue or picture than to suffer his thoughts to pass in smother.' For the Elizabethans the second great risk of friendship was the corrupting influence of flattery, but for Bacon 'there is no such flatterer as is a man's self; and there is no such remedy against flattery of a man's self as the liberty of a friend'. Friendship thus appears here idealized, perfected. By the time the essay ends its subject is delicately ambiguous: 'I have given the rule. Where a man cannot fitly play his own part, if he have not a friend, he may quit the stage.' On the one hand, we have seen, the stage stands for court life, where, without friends one can make no headway. On the other hand the stage is life itself: 'For a crowd is not company, and faces are but a gallery of pictures, and talk but a tinkling cymbal, where there is no love.'[67]

One last peculiarity of this essay must be noted. Cicero has Scaevola speak of Africanus. Montaigne had written of his own La Boétie. Bacon never mentions Matthew's name. Could this silence be endured? Surely he intended his Latin 'De Amicitia', the text posterity was intended to read, to link his name to Matthew's, as Achilles' to Patroclus'. In Matthew, Bacon had discovered true friendship. But throughout his career he had sought to adapt the language and sentiments of friendship to the demands of court life, where friendship was inseparable from flattery, patronage and favouritism. At court there was no love without utility, and perfection of friendship was 'but a speculation'. There rulers purchased friendship from their favourites, while favourites sold favours to their friends. If Bacon, ever flexible, had begun to turn away from a courtly conception of friendship it was merely because, now penniless himself, he could no longer afford to purchase friends at court at the going rate.

Notes

1. Niccolò Machiavelli, *The Prince*, ed. and trans. D. Wootton (Indianapolis, 1995), p. 5.
2. Roberto Ridolfi, *The Life of Niccolò Machiavelli* (Chicago, 1963), p. 164.
3. Erasmus quoted from *Collected Works of Erasmus* (Toronto, 1974–), iii: *The Correspondence of Erasmus*, trans. R. A. B. Mynors and D. F. S. Thompson, no. 312, in Natalie Zemon Davis, 'Beyond the Market: Books as Gifts in Sixteenth-Century France', *Transactions of the Royal Historical Society*, 33 (1983), pp. 69–87, at p. 77.
4. For the texts and their publication history, see Francis Bacon, *The Essayes or Counsels, Civill and Morall*, ed. M. Kiernan (Oxford, 1985). The recent literature on Bacon has surprisingly little to say on the theme of friendship.
5. Marcel Mauss, *The Gift: Forms and Functions of Exchange in Archaic Societies*, trans. I. Cunnison (London, 1966).
6. For a lengthy poem on the last of these (obviously written with Buckingham in mind) see Anon., *The Deplorable Life and Death of Edward the Second, King of England, Together with the Downfall of the two Unfortunate Favourites, Gavestone and Spencer* (London, 1628).
7. Sharon Kettering, 'Gift-Giving and Patronage in Early Modern France', *French History*, 2 (1988), pp. 131–51; *idem*, 'Friendship and Clientage in Early Modern France', *French History*, 6 (1992), pp. 139–58. See also Guy Fitch Lytle, 'Friendship and Patronage in Renaissance Europe', in F. W. Kent and P. Simons, eds, *Patronage, Art and Society in Renaissance Italy* (Oxford, 1987), pp. 47–61. For the work of two social historians see Mervyn James, 'English Politics and the Concept of Honour, 1485–1642' [1978], in his *Society, Politics, and Culture: Studies in Early Modern England* (Cambridge, 1986), pp. 308–415 (on friendship), and Felicity Heal, *Hospitality in Early Modern England* (Oxford, 1990), pp. 19–22, 397–403 (on gift-giving). Jean Starobinski, *Montaigne in Motion* (Chicago, 1985), pp. 36–66. Any list of other works in which friendship is a central theme must be somewhat arbitrary, but see Edward Berry, 'Hubert Languet and the "Making" of Philip Sidney', *Studies in Philology*, 85 (1988), pp. 305–20; F. W. Conrad, 'The Problem of Counsel Reconsidered: The Case of Sir Thomas Elyot', in P. A. Fideler and T. F. Mayer, eds, *Political Thought and the Tudor Commonwealth* (London, 1992), pp. 75–107; Susan Brigden, '"The Shadow that You Know": Sir Thomas Wyatt and Sir Francis Bryan at Court and in Embassy', *Historical Journal*, 39 (1996), pp. 1–31. The following studies bracket mine: Catherine Bates, *The Rhetoric of Courtship in Elizabethan Language and Literature* (Cambridge, 1992); Simon Adams, 'Favourites and Factions at the Elizabethan Court', in R. G. Asch and A. M. Birke, eds, *Princes, Patronage and the Nobility* (Oxford, 1991), pp. 265–87; Adams, 'The Patronage of the Crown in Elizabethan Politics: The 1590s in Perspective', in J. Guy, ed., *The Reign of Elizabeth: Court and Culture in the Last Decade* (Cambridge, 1995), pp. 20–45; Linda Levy Peck, 'Benefits, Brokers and Beneficiaries: The Culture of Exchange in Seventeeth Century England', in B. Y. Kunze and D. D. Brautigam, eds, *Court, Country and Culture: Essays on Early Modern British History in Honor of Perez Zagorin* (Rochester, NY, 1992), pp. 109–27; Alan Bray, 'Homosexuality and the Signs of Male Friendship in Elizabethan England', *History Workshop*, 29 (1990), pp. 1–19; Antonio Feros, 'Twin Souls: Monarchs and Favourites in Early Seventeenth-Century Spain', in Richard L. Kagan and G. Parker, eds, *Spain, Europe and the Atlantic World: Essays in Honour of John H. Elliott* (Cambridge, 1995), pp. 27–47. Lorna Hutson, *The Usurer's Daughter: Male Friendship and Fictions of Women in Sixteenth-Century England* (London, 1994) does not displace an earlier work, Laurens J. Mills, *One Soul in Bodies Twain: Friendship in Tudor and Stuart Drama* (Bloomington, Ind., 1937). For an example of the nineteenth-century debate on Bacon and Essex, see Thomas Babington Macaulay, *The Life and Writings of Francis Bacon* (Edinburgh: reprinted from *Edinburgh Review*, 1837), pp. 19–34; [James Spedding], *Evenings with a Reviewer*, 2 vols (London, 1848), i, pp. 91–251; *idem*, *The Letters and the Life of Francis Bacon*, 7 vols (London, 1861–74), iii, pp. 161–2. It is worth remarking that fundamental

to Macaulay's famous attack on Bacon is the rejection of a culture of patronage, friendship and gift-giving in the name of the values of a professionalized civil service. For Bacon and Buckingham, see Roger Lockyer, *Buckingham: The Life and Political Career of George Villiers, First Duke of Buckingham, 1592–1628* (London and New York, 1981), pp. 29–32, 44–50, 70–1, 97–100, 117–19. See also my 'Friendship Portrayed: A New Account of *Utopia*', *History Workshop Journal*, 45 (1998), pp. 29–47.

8. Francis Bacon, 'Apophthegems New and Old', in *The Works of Francis Bacon*, ed. J. Spedding, R. L. Ellis and D. D. Heath, 7 vols (London, 1857–74), vii, p. 128, no. 23.

9. See, for example, [Haly Heron], *A Newe Discourse of Morall Philosophie* (London, 1579), p. 27.

10. Michael Kiernan in Bacon, *Essayes*, p. lxxxix; for evidence of the importance Matthew placed on this gift see his letter to Gondomar quoted in Arnold Harris Mathew and Annette Calthrop, *The Life of Sir Tobie Matthew* (London, 1907), p. 161.

11. Spedding, *Letters and Life*, vi, p. 338.

12. Bacon, *Essayes*, p. 150 (spelling and punctuation modernized, as in all quotations from sixteenth- and seventeenth-century sources).

13. Robert Johnson, *Essaies or Rather Imperfect Offers* (London, 1601), 'Of Reputation', [fol. 52v: handwritten pagination in British Library copy, which has been cropped by the binder].

14. [D. Tuvil], *Essaies Politicke and Morall* (London, 1608), 'Of Cautions in Friendship', fol. 86r–v.

15. Interestingly, the two most optimistic discussions of friendship (prior to Bacon's final essay) known to me are relatively early: [William Paulet], *The Lord Marques Idlenes* (London, 1586), 'Of Friendship and Friends', pp. 36–9, where the main risk is that you might have to judge a contention between two of your friends, 'for to judge between two enemies, the one remaineth a friend; but to judge between two friends, the one is made an enemy'; 'Anonymus', *Remedies against Discontentmet* (London, 1596), ch. 7: 'Of the Choice of Frendes', sig. C7r–C8r, where the main danger seems to be posed by friends who are 'always pensive and ready to sigh upon every occasion'.

16. John Robinson, *New Eassayes* (London, 1628), 'Of Societie and Friendship', p. 203; Johnson, *Essaies*, 'Of Wisedome', [fol. 41r–v]; M. B., *The Triall of True Friendship, or Perfit Mirror Whereby to Discerne a Trustie Friende from a Flattering Parasite* (London, 1596), sig. B1v.

17. Johnson, *Essaies*, 'Of Liberalitie', [fol. 55r]; M. B., *Triall*, sig. C1r–v.

18. William Cornwallis, *Essayes* (London, 1600), 'Of Love', sig. D8v.

19. Johnson, *Essaies*, [fol. 41r]; Cornwallis, *Essayes*, 'Of Friendship and Factions', sig. E3v.

20. [Tuvil], *Essaies*, 'Of Cautions in Friendship', fol. 80r.

21. Cornwallis, *Essayes*, 'Of Friendship and Factions', sig. E3r.

22. Johnson, *Essaies*, 'Of Greatness of Mind', [fol. 2r–v]; 'Of Wisedome', [fol. 43r], 'Of Reputation', [fol. 52r–v].

23. Johnson, *Essaies*, 'Of Affabilitie', [fols 30r–31v]; Cornwallis, *Essayes*, 'Of Friendship and Factions', sig. E4r.

24. Robinson, *New Essayes*, 'Of Societie and Friendship', pp. 204–8.

25. M. B., *Triall*, sig. E4r.

26. Bacon, 'Apophthegems', *Works*, vii, p. 154, no. 206.

27. Johnson, *Essaies*, 'Of Affabilitie', [fols 29v–30r]; see also 'Anonymus', *Remedies*, sig. G1v.

28. Cornwallis, *Essayes*, 'Of Entertainment', sig. F7r–v; Cornwallis, *A Second Part of Essayes* (London, 1601), 'Of Complements', sig. P6v.

29. [Tuvil], *Essaies*, 'Of Cautions in Friendship', fol. 88v.

30. Cornwallis, *Essayes*, 'Of Friendship and Factions', sig. E2v.

31. M. B., *Triall*, sig. B1v (see also Psalm 55), E3v, C1v.

32. Cornwallis, *Essayes*, 'Of Love', sig. E1r–v.

33. For example David Lindley, *The Trials of Frances Howard* (London, 1993).

34. Spedding, *Letters and Life*, v, p. 313.

35. John Guy, 'Introduction. The 1590s: The Second Reign of Elizabeth I', in Guy, ed., *Reign of Elizabeth*, pp. 1–19.

36. Spedding, *Letters and Life*, i, pp. 354, 366, 365, 373; ii, p. 35.

37. Fulton H. Anderson, *Francis Bacon: His Career and his Thought* (New York, 1962), p. 58.

38. Bacon, *Essayes*, p. 158.

39. Spedding, *Letters and Life*, ii, p. 43.

40. Bacon, 'Apophthegems', *Works*, vii, pp. 167–8: ex-*Resuscitatio* (1661), no. 21.

41. Bacon, *Essayes*, p. 155.

42. Cicero, 'Laelius: On Friendship', in *On the Good Life*, trans. M. Grant (Harmondsworth, 1971), p. 204.

43. Michel de Montaigne, *Essais*, I.28: for a recent translation see *The Essays of Michel de Montaigne*, trans. M. A. Screech (Harmondsworth, 1991), pp. 205–15; Etienne de la Boëtie, *Slaves by Choice*, trans. M. Smith (Egham, 1988).

44. M. B., *Triall*, sig. B2r.

45. Bacon, *Essayes*, p. 149.

46. Spedding, *Letters and Life*, ii, p. 42; Cicero, 'Laelius: On Friendship', p. 221; Bacon, *Essayes*, p. 160.

47. Richard C. McCoy, 'Francis Davison and the Cult of Elizabeth', in Guy, ed., *Reign of Elizabeth*, pp. 212–28, at pp. 224, 226; Fritz Levy, 'The Theatre and the Court in the 1590s', in *ibid.*, pp. 274–300, at pp. 277–8; J. H. M. Salmon, 'Seneca and Tacitus in Jacobean England', in L. L. Peck, ed., *The Mental World of the Jacobean Court* (Cambridge, 1991), pp. 169–88.

48. Spedding, *Letters and Life*, ii, p. 44.

49. Bacon, *Essayes*, p. 159.

50. Neil Cuddy, 'The Revival of the Entourage: The Bedchamber of James I, 1603–25', in D. Starkey, ed., *The English Court: From the Wars of the Roses to the Civil War* (London, 1987), pp. 173–225.

51. Spedding, *Letters and Life*, vi, p. 27 (cf. p. 13).

52. Bacon, *Essayes*, p. 116.

53. Spedding, *Letters and Life*, vi, p. 28; v, p. 245; vi, p. 14.

54. Sir Robert Naunton, *Fragmenta Regalia*, ed. J. S. Cerovski (Washington, DC, 1985), p. 40.

55. Spedding, *Letters and Life*, vi, pp. 239, 224, 233.

56. Catherine Drinker Bowen, *The Lion and the Throne: The Life and Times of Sir Edward Coke, 1552–1634* (London, 1957), pp. 339–55; Lockyer, *Buckingham*, p. 45.

57. Spedding, *Letters and Life*, vi, pp. 248, 245; vii, p. 37; vi, p. 288.

58. *Ibid.*, vii, pp. 327, 343.

59. Bacon, *Essayes*, pp. 81–2, 86–7.

60. *Ibid.*, pp. 85, 149; Spedding, *Letters and Life*, vi, p. 239.

61. David Mathew, *Sir Tobie Matthew* (London, 1950) does not replace Mathew and Calthrop, *Matthew* for biographical information.

62. Spedding, *Letters and Life*, vii, pp. 287, 423, 542.

63. *Ibid.*, p. 429.

64. *Ibid.*, p. 344; but Spedding's conjecture about the date is surely wrong. The letter clearly relates to the prospect of a pardon, and must be contemporary with the correspondence of July 1624, reproduced on pp. 518–20, in which Matthew is mentioned.

65. Bacon, *Essayes*, p. 80.

66. Lisa Jardine, *Francis Bacon: Discovery and the Art of Discourse* (Cambridge, 1974), p. 234.

67. Bacon, *Essayes*, pp. 81, 80, 83, 85, 87, 81.

13

Images of Evil, Images of Kings: The Contrasting Faces of the Royal Favourite and the Prime Minister in Early Modern European Political Literature, c. 1580–c. 1650[1]

ANTONIO FEROS

Introduction

Some three decades years ago, Leicester Bradner examined two distinct views held by seventeenth-century English and Spanish dramatists when writing about royal favourites. Spanish playwrights, Bradner noted, sought to 'arouse sympathy for the king and the friend he loves', while the English stressed 'the issues of good and bad government' by presenting the royal favourite as an evil counsellor and a usurper, and the monarch who let him prosper as a weak ruler.[2] Why these disparate treatments of the royal favourite? This query is particularly poignant when we consider that the English and Spanish dramatists believed that they were confronting a similar political phenomenon. Both knew that the rise of the favourite depended on the monarch's whim and that the favourite's fate was determined by the inexorable turn of the wheel of fortune. And, in both monarchies, playwrights used similar examples to portray the favourite, examples taken from the Old and New Testaments (Joseph, Haman and John the Evangelist), Roman history (Sejanus) and the past of their own countries (Gaveston in England and Alvaro de Luna in Spain).

To Bradner, the answer to the above question was simple. The English dramatists denounced favourites whom they viewed as clear evidence of declining standards in the government of the Commonwealth, and as a testimony that seventeenth-century rulers were no longer the 'supermonarchs' whom had dominated the European political scene in the 1500s. In contrast, the Spanish dramatists had become prisoners of flattery, the most malicious courtly depravity. Most modern historians share Bradner's views. For them, the favourite was a political anomaly, the result of the existence of weak monarchs (Henri III of France, Philip III of Spain, James I and Charles I of England). Like the English dramatists, modern historians also believe that the presence of favourites brought political crises, chaos, factional confrontations and ultimately open rebellion.

Early modern Europeans would not have understood modern historians' attempts to demonstrate that only weak monarchs had favourites, nor would they have understood attempts to create the intricate divisions and subdivisions into which modern historians classify favourites – favourite, *privado*, *valido*, private favourite, political favourite and prime minister (*premier ministre*, *ministro principal*). In early modern Europe, these concepts referred to the same court character – a person who enjoyed the monarch's favour and confidence and who as a result played a key role in court policy, the distribution of royal patronage, the appointment of royal officials and other activities associated with the monarch's craft. Early modern Europeans also knew that a royal favourite could rise from disparate political and social milieux, from the ranks of nobility or from the ranks of royal officials.

But, more importantly, early modern Europeans believed that royal favourites were a permanent fixture in personal monarchies. 'There is not a king [who does not have] close to him a *privado* who rules over him,' wrote the Spanish Antonio de Guevara in his *Aviso de Privados*, published in 1539. As long as there are kings there will be favourites, was his prophetic prediction. Fadrique Furió Ceriol, another sixteenth-century Spanish writer, agreed. In his *El Concejo y Consejeros del Príncipe*, written in 1559, Ceriol asserted that to understand a monarchy one has to analyse not only the prince, but also his officials, 'tutors, servants, friends and *privados*'. Guevara and Ceriol were just two of many early modern European writers who claimed that favourites were an integral part of the monarchical form of government. The French Claude de Seyssel, for example, also defended the view that a monarch should have a special confidant, as did Jesus Christ with John the Evangelist, 'to whom He revealed more great secrets than He did to the others'.[3]

In early modern Europe to win the monarch's favour was not considered illegitimate or corrupt, but a legitimate goal of all courtiers. 'The goal of the perfect courtier', Castiglione wrote in *Il Cortegiano*, was to attract the attention of the prince and gain 'the love of his master in such a complete way as to become his favourite'. To receive the king's favour was viewed as a proof of one's virtues and demonstrated that those chosen by the monarch to become their close servants possessed some unique quality. The presence at the royal court of a perfect courtier, or as seventeenth-century writers would say a perfect royal favourite, meant that a 'prince who is worthy of his service, even though his dominion is small, can count himself a truly great ruler'.[4]

It was indeed this view of the royal favourite as a permanent component of personal monarchies – as permanent as princes, royal officials and courtiers – which made the royal favourite an important subject of early modern political writers. These authors were conscious of the diverse relationships between specific monarchs and their favourites as well as of the favourites' diverse social backgrounds, and how the public role of the favourite adapted to each monarch's personality and kingcraft. But, in writing about royal favourites, early modern political writers tried mainly to discover and explain general rules governing the rise and public roles of royal favourites in a political world experiencing profound changes.

The analysis of early modern Spanish, French and English discourses on royal favourites is the subject of this chapter. But before turning to this discussion I want to make explicit some of my methodological premises. I believe that the negative views on royal favourites were similar in the three monarchies and thus I will survey them as a shared discourse. Regarding positive views on royal favourites, however, I consider them to be distinct and thus to merit a separate discussion in each monarchy. My aim is not to persuade the reader that the accepted view of the royal favourite as a force of evil should be replaced by a view of the favourite as a force of goodness. Rather it is to recover the complexity of the discourse on royal favourites in pre-modern Europe.[5]

Evil Counsellors

Negative views of the royal favourite have dominated modern historians' interpretation of the favourite's place in early modern European monarchies. Reflecting the views of authors who opposed favourites and defended assorted opinions on how a monarchy should be ruled, most modern historians have maintained that in early modern Europe the royal favourite was regarded with suspicion and that his presence was considered a danger to the well-being of the commonwealth. That such opposition existed is, of course, well known and, as noted above, reflected similar concerns in the three monarchies. From the fifteenth-century civil wars in England, France and the Iberian kingdoms early modern political writers drew what turned out to be an enduring conclusion: that the civil conflicts resulted from the existence of evil counsellors – favourites, *mignons* or palace servants – who enticed their monarchs to oppress their subjects and prevent participation by other members of the body politic in the ruling of the kingdoms. The immediate result was a very distinctive image of the royal favourite as a person who attained power not because of his virtues and qualities but because of his cunning and ability to flatter the king. Once the favourite saw himself as the holder of the ruler's grace, he revealed his true nature: an avaricious, power-hungry individual whose sole purpose was to expropriate the king's authority. When monarchs let themselves be dominated by such disgraceful characters, the results were disastrous: the monarchs themselves were despised, their subjects rebelled, harmony and peace were destroyed and the entire kingdom was in pandemonium.

To early modern European writers the royal favourite epitomized the capital sin *par excellence*, ambition, what Augustine called 'a perverse desire of height'.[6] The royal favourite appeared as an evil counsellor whose ultimate and secret obsession was to become equal to his master, if not the master himself. The anonymous author of *Leicester's Commonwealth*, for example, warned Queen Elizabeth that the Earl of Leicester's intimated plan was 'to possess himself (as now he has done) of Court, Council, and Country without controlment, so that nothing wanted to him but only his pleasure, and the day already conceived in his mind to dispose as he list both of prince, crown, realm, and religion'.[7] Even if the royal favourite did not attempt to usurp the king's crown, he surely transformed his monarch into a tyrant through his undeserved influence and evil advice. The Spanish Jesuit Juan de Mariana, for example, believed that the worst thing that could happen to a kingdom is that the king let himself be dominated by flattering courtiers and be transformed into a tyrant. Favourites, who dominated the court and gained more authority, favour and wealth than the king's other subjects, believed that 'royal power is greater than the laws and the community, that the king is the owner of his subjects' property, and that everything – including the law – depends on the king's will'.[8]

It was due to their devouring ambition and their intrinsically evil nature that favourites caused continuous confrontations between monarchs and subjects. Sir John Eliot, for example, believed – as did many of his contemporaries – that the relationship between Charles I and his subjects, represented by parliament, was harmonious until the Duke of Buckingham became involved in public affairs. It was Buckingham who 'had cast an alteration in the air', creating a mood of mistrust between Charles I and his vassals, Eliot wrote in *Negotium Posterorum*, composed after the parliament of 1625. Years later, the French duc de Rohan made similar comments when he declared that 'The absolute rule of favourites is the ruin of a state. For either they alter it for their own profit or they give cause to the ambitious to do so, and at the very least they are the pretext for all the quarrels that occur in it.'[9]

According to those early modern Europeans who believed that the ideal form of government was a monarchy in which the monarch was helped and bridled by his counsellors the role of the royal favourite should be clearly limited. 'I do not say', wrote Claude de Seyssel, 'that [the king] cannot have someone familiar with him and above all others in his confidence with whom as with himself he privately shares his lesser domestic affairs and secrets which do not touch the state. . . .' But a monarch should always remember, he continued, that 'it would be a dangerous thing . . . for him to decide matters of great importance, especially matters of state, according to the opinion of one man'.[10] Instead of relying on his favourite, the monarch should rule with the assistance of his counsellors. These counsellors should be 'many, set over thousands, hundreds, fifties, and tens, (one man not engrossing all)'. The worst possible scenario, Sir William Walter continued, is when 'the king's Council rides upon one horse'.[11]

Early modern European writers who believed in the unlimited power of the king expressed similar fears. 'It is an infallible rule', wrote Machiavelli in *The Prince*, 'that a prince who is not himself wise cannot be soundly advised, unless he happens to put himself in the hands of a man who is very able and controls everything. Then he could certainly be well advised, but he would not last long, because such a governor would soon deprive him of his state.' Thus the exist-

24 The favourite naked of interest and clothed with valour: the Count Duke of Olivares. Title-page of *El Fernando* by Juan Antonio y Vera of Figueroa, Count of La Roca. (British Library, London)

25 Philip IV of Spain, painted by Velázquez in 1644, at a moment between favourites following the fall of Olivares. (Frick Collection, New York)

The man of state as the man of God: the triple portrait of Cardinal Richelieu (1642) by Philippe de Champaigne. (National Portrait Gallery, London)

27 Richelieu's successor: Jules Mazarin. Painted by Pierre Mignard. (Musée Condé, Chantilly)

28 Richelieu's château – which he never inhabited – at the new town of Richelieu. Engraving by Jean Marot.

George Ossoliński, Grand
Chancellor of the Crown of Poland.
Painting of 1635 by Bartolomaus
Strobel. (National Museum in Warsaw)

Adam Kazanowski, favourite of
Prince Ladislas of Poland. Painting by
Jan Rij. (Wawel Royal Castle, Cracow)

31 Francis Bacon, Lord Chancellor of England: analyst of favour and friendship.
Painting attributed to Abraham Blyenberch. (Royal Society, London)

32 Toby Matthew: Bacon's ideal friend. Painting of 1616. (National Portrait Gallery, London).

33 The Duke of Lerma, the quintessential favourite, painted by Rubens.
(Museo del Prado, Madrid)

William Larkin, *George Villiers, 1st Duke of Buckingham* (1616). (National Portrait Gallery, London)

Peter Paul Rubens, oil sketch for *Equestrian Portrait of the Duke of Buckingham* (1625). (Kimbell Art Museum, Fort Worth)

36 Peter Paul Rubens, *Equestrian Portrait of the Duke of Buckingham* (1629). (Formerly at Osterley Park, now destroyed)

37 After Rubens, *Glorification of the Duke of Buckingham*. (Whereabouts unknown)

Peter Paul Rubens, *Glorification of the Duke of Buckingham* (before 1625). (National Gallery, London)

39 Peter Paul Rubens,
*Glorification of the Duke
of Buckingham* (1629)
(Formerly at Osterley
Park, destroyed 1949)

40 Gerrit van
Honthorst, *Apollo and
Diana* (1628).
(Hampton Court)

41 Attributed to Velázquez, *Count Duke of Olivares*
(1624). (Museu de Arte de São Paulo)

42 Diego Velázquez, *Count Duke of Olivares* (*c.* 1625). (Hispanic Society of America, New York)

43 Paul Pontius after Rubens, *Count Duke of Olivares*. Engraving of 1626.

44 Diego Velázquez, *Equestrian Portrait of the Count Duke of Olivares*. (Museo del Prado, Madrid)

45 Diego Velázquez, *Riding Lesson of Prince Balthasar Carlos* (1636). (Collection of the Duke of Westminster, London)

46 Juan Bautista Maino, *Recapture of Bahía* (1635). (Museo del Prado, Madrid)

ence of a single counsellor, who could by means of his closeness to the king usurp the ruler's power, was the main threat to creating and conserving strong and stable monarchies. Machiavelli's alternative to this dreadful situation required a king who asked for advice from his counsellors, but who nevertheless ruled alone.[12]

Machiavelli was only one of many political writers who viewed the existence of a powerful royal counsellor as the main challenge to personal monarchies. Three of the most influential early modern political writers, Jean Bodin, Giovanni Botero and Justus Lipsius, shared a similar understanding of an ideal monarch: a monarch who surrounded himself with good counsellors, who listened with respect and attention, who gave his counsellors the freedom to speak the truth, but who ultimately decided alone what was best for the well-being of the commonwealth. As Lipsius wrote, this ideal monarch should consult his or her advisers but not abdicate 'the force of Principality' by referring all things to his councils or by sharing his authority with a single favourite.[13] The king's subjects could not accept a monarch dependent on one single counsellor, claimed Giovanni Botero, because this suggested that the king was weak and unable to assume his responsibilities, and that the favourite thus threatened the monarch's sovereignty. Botero also reminded monarchs that their subjects would sooner or later rebel against the favourites and in doing so they would 'offend the king himself', as was demonstrated by the cases of Edward II of England and Queen Joanna of Naples among others.[14]

Unlike the writers who opposed the presence of a royal favourite because they feared he would promote royal absolutism, the defenders of an all-powerful monarch feared the existence of a favourite or a prime minister for exactly the opposite reason: an influential favourite would reduce the possibility of enhancing the king's power. These theorists believed that the preservation of order and political stability required that the monarch be presented as the unique holder of sovereignty, as a vivid image of God. As a master should never let a servant become too familiar with him, neither could a true monarch let a subject share his authority. Moreover, it was unthinkable that God could create another god. As Bodin wrote:

> royal rights cannot be delegated, and are inalienable . . . and if for whatever reason a Prince communicates his rights to one of his subjects, this subject would became the king's companion and the king would no longer be a sovereign. . . . For as the supreme God cannot make another God equal to himself . . . so we may also say that the Prince, who is for us God's image, cannot make a subject equal to himself.[15]

The same views were echoed by the Spaniard Juan de Vitrián. In the universe there was only one God, in each household one master, in each body one soul, he wrote; the monarch 'as a human god, the master and the soul of the body politic' could only be one.[16]

The conflicts, crises and rebellions in the English, French and Spanish monarchies during the 1620s and 1630s were to many sufficient proof that the presence of powerful royal favourites were leading the monarchies to the edge of destruction. Favourites were indeed the obstacles to a well-ordered and well-ruled monarchy, and the best a monarch could do was to keep them as private companions, far away from state affairs.[17]

The King's Friend and Ministro Principal

The same court character, the royal favourite, was thus viewed as a monster with two faces. In one, the royal favourite appeared as a promoter of absolutism and tyranny; in the other, he appeared as an obstacle to enhancing royal power. But, as Tomás y Valiente's superb study of royal favourites in seventeenth-century Spain demonstrates, to these two images we should add a third. This third image was created not only by flatterers but also by writers who tried to understand the workings of personal monarchies. Many of the authors considered here believed that the presence of a powerful royal favourite and/or a prime minister was not the result of a crisis in the system, or of a weakening in the character of seventeenth-century monarchs, but was a response to new political realities. The new circumstances confronting a monarch after 1570 were well understood at the time. The acquisition of new territories and the increasing confrontations with other European powers meant that a monarch had many more matters to resolve, that an increasing number of officials became involved in public affairs and that new institutions had to be created. A monarch alone could not possibly attend to all matters, remember all problems or control all men under his orders. What the king needed, claimed many political writers, was a man of confidence, a favourite, who acting as a kind of prime minister or chief counsellor could help his master to manage public affairs, protect the monarch against the inevitable complaints against his government and allow him to devote his time to solving the most important public matters.

Yet the favourite's participation in the government of the monarchy had to be accomplished without diminishing the monarch's power and prerogatives. As several modern historians have contended, not all early modern writers viewed the defence of royal favourites as incompatible with theories defending the absolute powers of the king. E. H. Kossman, for example, notes that sixteenth-century monarchs ruled in close collaboration with their councils and parliaments, but when 'these bodies tended to become self-willed institutions, ambitious of independent responsibilities, the absolute king preferred to ignore them and consult only his inner council of ministers'. Kossman, in characterizing royal absolutism as a force endlessly aiming to increase the king's power, reminds us that one of the most common practices during the seventeenth century was to leave old institutions untouched but at the same time 'to superimpose new ideas, institutions and rules upon them and so to create a whole new layer of government, a higher platform of sovereignty'. Late-sixteenth- and early-seventeenth-century monarchs increasingly began to turn for advice to particular ministers who were chosen and dismissed by the monarch and who dedicated themselves to protecting the king's interests.[18] We can characterize the behaviour of sixteenth-century monarchs with Francis Bacon's words about Queen Elizabeth, who 'after the manner of the choicest princes before her, did not always tie her trust to place, but did sometime divide private favour from office'.[19] In contrast, seventeenth-century monarchs tended to prefer the advice of those who enjoyed their private favour and who as a result were placed at the apex of the court hierarchy.

The positive discourse on the royal favourite began to emerge in the 1580s. Until then, there had been, of course, manifestations of support of particular favourites, but these did not amount to a well-formulated positive discourse on royal favourites. What was new after the 1580 was the emergence of powerful favourites who caught the imagination of their contemporaries, and who left their imprint on the politics of their times. In each monarchy, although at different times, one favourite alone came to monopolize the monarch's favour, and unlike sixteenth-century monarchs seventeenth-century rulers publicly recognized that their favourite played a key role in the ruling of the monarchy. The favourites themselves also promoted their position as the monarch's sole favourite or prime minister and their active participation in public affairs. Both developments led to the creation of an extensive positive discourse on royal favourites.

Without doubt, the positive discourse on royal favourites was more complex and prevalent in Spain than elsewhere. It is difficult to pinpoint the exact reason why this was the case, but I believe that one of the main factors that contributed to the emergence of a positive discourse on royal favourites in Spain was Philip II's decision to place a small group of favourites in the apex of the governmental machinery. Between the 1560s and his death in 1598, Philip II (pl. 3) relied on his closest servants and officials (for example, the Prince of Eboli, the Count of Chinchón and especially Cristóbal de Moura in the 1590s) to rule the increasingly complex Spanish Monarchy.

The emergence of this group of powerful favourites did not reinforce the anti-favourite discourse. Few writers, if any, viewed Philip II as a weak king controlled by evil favourites. His reign was a period of political stability and his favourites did not become subjects of court scandals. They did not parade at the court with their scandalous behaviour, as supposedly did Henri III's favourites; nor did they plot against their master, as did the Earl of Essex against Queen Elizabeth. It was under these circumstances that a new generation of Spanish theorists began to make claims that had been unthinkable in the past. They believed, for example, that a royal favourite with an active but clearly limited public role could positively influence the well-being of both the king and the kingdom. The enthronement of a new monarch, Philip III (1598–1621), and the rise of a new favourite, the Duke of Lerma (pl. 33), bolstered the positive discourse on royal favourites. During the first years of Philip III's reign, and as a political comment to Lerma's *privanza*, political authors portrayed the royal favourite as the king's chief counsellor in charge of the everyday government of the Monarchy.[20]

Positive theories on royal favourites evolved even more radically after 1609, when Fray Pedro de Maldonado, Lerma's confessor, completed his *Discurso del Perfecto Privado* ('Discourse on the Perfect Favourite'), which, although an unpublished pamphlet, revolutionized the way in which royal favourites were depicted in seventeenth-century Spain.[21] In writing his pamphlet, Maldonado's first goal was to discredit prior claims against royal favourites. He recognized that those who opposed the presence of a royal favourite did so because they believed that a monarch who depended on one of his subjects could not remain free and eminent. 'I am of different opinion, and believe', Maldonado wrote, 'that if the favourite is how a favourite should be, the royal favourite is the most noble and finest part of the monarchy.' Maldonado did not accept the view that the presence of a royal favourite was simply a lesser evil reflecting the human fallibility of the king, but he firmly believed that a royal favourite was the ultimate good for the well-being of the monarch and the commonwealth: 'the commonwealth is safer with a bad monarch who has a good *privado*, than with a good monarch who has a bad *privado*'. Had tyrants had good favourites at their side the course of history would have been different, he claimed. In Maldonado's views, by having favourites monarchs were behaving according to the laws of nature and God's will. The sun shines on the entire earth, but some parts receive more light than others; the soul gives life to the body, but favours especially the head and the heart; God, who gives life to all humans and creates them in His image, favours some over others. Even Jesus Christ gave singular favour to two apostles: John and Peter.

Although Maldonado's views were extremely important and had a great impact on his contemporaries, his influence extended beyond his times. Until Maldonado, the common definition of a favourite was simple, a courtier who – for whatever reason – enjoyed the king's favour. But, in his pamphlet, Maldonado presented a more complex view of the favourite which greatly helped to justify his role in the day-to-day administration of the monarchy. 'We call *privado*', Maldonado wrote, 'a man whom [the king] has chosen among the rest for a particular kind of equality based on love and perfect friendship.' I have analysed elsewhere the implications of portraying the favourite as the king's friend.[22] For our purposes here, it is sufficient to note that by defining the favourite as the king's friend Maldonado wanted to protect the favourite against being accused of trying to usurp the king's power. As the king's friend, the favourite could be introduced as the king's other self and thus as his echo, his shadow, his public image, and as the intermediary between the king and his subjects.[23]

Contrary to the opinions of many modern historians, I believe that the discourse on royal favourites did not change substantially during Lerma's

(1598–1618) and Olivares' (1621–43) *privanzas*. Olivares (pls 24 and 41–6) was, indeed, both a royal favourite and a prime minister, as Lerma had been before him. Here it is important to differentiate Olivares' public statements claiming that he was not the king's favourite but his minister from theories put forth by his supporters. What Olivares and his supporters attempted, which was not the case under Lerma's *privanza*, was to discredit former favourites, particularly Lerma, but not to question the institution itself. This strategy was clearly articulated by Virgilio Malvezzi, Olivares' propagandist: 'the *privanza* is like the monarchy; if it is in good hands it is very good; if it is in bad hands it is terrible'.[24]

In fact, from the very inception of Philip IV's reign, it was evident that continuity was going to dominate the political discourse on favourites. On 4 May 1621, a few days after Philip III's death, in the presence of Philip IV and Olivares, Fray Gerónimo de Florencia delivered a funeral sermon on the late king, and advised that to protect the well-being of the community the monarch needed at his side a high-ranking servant, whom Florencia called 'the father of the king . . . a *privado* and a confidant who should be in charge of all public affairs'.[25] It was in fact during Olivares' *privanza* that the genre of mirror-for-favourites literature reached its apex. Dozens of books dedicated to Olivares and/or Philip IV continued to proclaim the king's duty to have a favourite–prime minister. Mártir Rizo, an expert on royal favourites, defined the favourite as the king's 'good friend and minister' and contended that an ideal form of government was a personal monarchy as long as the monarch had at his side a just favourite who acted as the king's *alter ego*.[26] Virgilio Malvezzi went even further by presenting royal favourites as perfect and unselfish creatures in the service of crown and country. 'Angels', Malvezzi wrote, 'are the figures of God with us; Favourites, the figures of Angels with Princes; Princes, of God with men.'[27] The positive discourse in seventeenth-century Spain was so strongly rooted in the political culture that, even after Olivares' fall in 1643, many Spanish writers continued to defend royal favourites and their role in the ruling of the Monarchy. This was the case, for example, with Fray José Laínez, who in his *El Josué esclarecido*, a book dedicated to Philip IV, still defined the favourite as 'the king's prime minister . . . a character defined in the Holy Scripture as the King's friend . . . and who is the King's right hand, or better a king without crown'.[28]

Le Premier Ministre

The French case presents both differences and similarities with the Spanish case. We know that in France there were favourites–prime ministers who acquired as much power as and played roles in the ruling of the monarchy similar to their Spanish counterparts. More importantly, some of the concepts and images used to describe and support royal favourites–prime ministers were rather similar, as were the conclusions reached by authors in both monarchies concerning the role of the king's favourite or prime minister. There were, however, some notable differences. A positive discourse on royal favourites developed later in France than in Spain, and some concepts used by Spanish writers – particularly the views of the favourite as the king's friend – were not employed by the French, who preferred, as we shall see, to present the servant chosen by the king to help him rule the monarchy as the king's prime counsellor or *premier ministre*.

Why a positive discourse on royal favourites did not develop until the 1620s in France was at least in part due to the country's special political situation between the 1570s and the 1620s. During Henri III's reign, from 1574 to 1588, royal favourites became the centre of a battle with political and religious implications. The pamphlets, poems, political treatises and satires of this period represent one of the most ferocious campaigns of denigration ever mounted. Indeed, Henri's favourites were depicted as evil counsellors, tyrants, poisoners and Machiavellians, while their master Henri III was portrayed as a weak monarch, a tyrant and a devil.[29] Given such a political atmosphere, it seems obvious that the possibilities for a positive discourse on royal favourites were, to say the least, minimal.

That a king should not rely on favourites became one of the principles on which Henri IV grounded his style of government, which he and his propagandists presented as directly opposed to Henri III's style. The assassination of Henri IV in 1610 led to a new period of political instability, and a new round of anti-favourite sentiments now voiced against Marie de Médicis' favourite, Concino Concini. De Luynes' (pl. 17) short minionship, from 1617 to 1621, also did not lead to more positive views on royal favourites, despite the fact that during those years political stability was the norm, and de Luynes' control over Louis XIII's entourage and council seemed total. After all, as John Holles informed Sir Richard Altham, de Luynes was the greatest 'favourite . . . that ever was in France, since the *maires of the palace*'.[30]

The death of de Luynes in December 1621 precipitated the rise of Richelieu (pls 26 and 47–57) who, as Louis XIII's *premier ministre*, remained in power until his death in 1642. His presence changed the French political discourse on royal favourites. Although most modern historians refuse to consider Richelieu as a favourite, early modern Europeans did not have such misgivings. For them Richelieu was indeed a royal favourite, an individual who enjoyed the personal and political confidence of Louis XIII, and as a result played an important role in the ruling of the monarchy. The Englishman James Howell, whose reports on Spain and France in the first decades of the seventeenth century were particularly perceptive, declared in 1626 that Richelieu 'is grown to be the sole Favourite of the King of France, being brought in by the Queen-Mother'. Peter Paul Rubens also had no problems in comparing Richelieu to other favourites (Lerma and Sejanus, for example), while asserting that Richelieu was a usurper who had taken complete control of the state, transforming

Louis XIII into a simple 'figure-head'. Even some of Richelieu's apologists did not hesitate to present Richelieu as Louis' 'favori', as Mousnier has noted in commenting on François de Colomby's *L'Autorité des roys* (1631).[31]

The most important difference between Richelieu and other favourites is that although Richelieu knew how to play the role of a courtier, as is demonstrated by his relationship with Marie de Médicis, he rose to power not as a member of the king's household, but from his position as a member of the king's council. 'From this vantage point', Bergin has noted, 'he differs from his [French] rivals [and his Spanish counterparts] essentially by the manner in which he succeeded in gradually transforming his initial toehold through the successive, piecemeal conquest of power which eventually made him such a dominant figure in government during the last decade of his career.'[32] Accordingly, the language Richelieu and his followers used to justify his position and influence drew heavily on the theories of the role of the king's counsellors. No reference is made to the king's friendship and love towards his favourite, as in Spain with Lerma and Olivares. It is important to note, however, that many of the historical examples Richelieu and his followers employed to defend his *ministériat* were identical to those used in Spain to defend Lerma and Olivares.

That the discourse to defend Richelieu's position was based on the theories about the king's councils and counsellors is evident in Richelieu's political testament, especially the chapters on 'Le conseil du Prince'. Like many other early modern political writers, Cardinal Richelieu claimed that a good monarch was one who relied on the advice and help of honest counsellors and who refrained from action without their advice. Richelieu's discourse included particular views on the qualities of a good counsellor. He should be wise, incorruptible, knowledgeable about history, honest in his advice and always ready to correct the prince's errors and vices. The king's counsellor should also be loyal to God, the king, the state, and be 'keen on defending the public good'.[33] The theories of Richelieu's supporters were similar. 'If it were permitted to make faire dreams and magnificent wishes' – Jean de Silhon, Richelieu's creature, wrote in his *Ministre d'Estat*, published in 1631 – 'it were to be desired that a Prince alone should make up his council, that he were the sole director of his business, that he were the sole intelligence to give it motion.' But because monarchs were humans and as such imperfect they needed the counsel of others.[34]

Yet Richelieu and his supporters extracted different conclusions from the theories on the ruler's need to receive counsel than did those who opposed favourites and prime ministers, arguing that to impose his authority a monarch needed to have *one counsellor* with superior authority over the rest. As Scipion Dupleix wrote in his *Histoire de Louis le Juste* (1635): 'One does not discuss matters of state with [many ministers] to hear their reasons and sentiments; the decision should be made only between the prince and the general director so that the secret may not be divulged. . . . After all, since political government is organized after the model of the celestial hierarchy, no criticism of it can be made.' Richelieu himself, in his political testament, corroborated this view: to have a well-ordered monarchy the ruler should promote one of his counsellors over the rest, and one whose authority should be 'inferior only to that of his master'.[35]

Richelieu's allies also presented the *premier ministre*'s authority as a reflection of the monarch's will, as the sun reflects God's light and Moses echoes God's words.[36] The *premier ministre* was compared, like the royal favourite in Spain, to Hercules, and many of Richelieu's creatures did not hesitate to depict Richelieu as the prime cause of France's successes, and as a king without a crown: 'Through you,' wrote Jacques Ribier in 1641, 'we are in a happier century, since you have the government of the realm in your hands and you direct affairs as the soul, the genius and intelligence of this great body.'[37]

The Favourite as a Private Companion

As in Spain, political writers in England began to focus on the royal favourite during the last decades of the sixteenth century. This increasing attention given to favourites can at least in part be attributed to the presence of several favourites, whose 'leading characteristic was [their] physical and personal attraction for the queen. . . . They were individuals who both occupied the central positions at the court, and enjoyed an apparently unequaled degree of intimacy with and indulgence by the queen'.[38] It was this physical and personal attraction for the queen that determined how Elizabeth's contemporaries portrayed these favourites. Thomas Blundeville's translation of the word favourite as 'lover' in his English rendition of Furió Ceriol's book on the king's counsellors, a translation Blundeville dedicated to Leicester, is an example of how the language on favourites adapted to the circumstance of a regnant queen with male favourites.[39]

Queen Elizabeth's contemporaries also believed that the queen had given her favourites more power and influence than had been the case under previous rulers, a belief that ultimately led to an extremely negative discourse on favourites. Between 1580 and 1605, English writers published some of the most excoriating attacks against royal favourites with such dramatic force that they continue to sway today's readers. Writers attacked not only courtiers–favourites–lovers (Leicester and Essex) but also counsellors–favourites (Cardinal Wolsey, William Cecil and Robert Cecil), who were all portrayed as evil counsellors with the desire to dominate both crown and country. These works, I believe, discredited the positive concepts that other early modern European writers used to portray the royal favourite. The anonymous *Burghley's Commonwealth*, Shakespeare's *Henry VIII* and Samuel Rowley's *When you see me, you know me*, for example, demonstrated that by permitting one counsellor to have authority over the rest the ruler created a demi-king whose ambition led him to usurp the monarch's power. To term the monarch's favourite as his lover and/or friend did not help. The language of love and friendship used by favourites in *Leicester's Commonwealth*, Christopher Marlowe's *Edward II*, Michael Drayton's *Piers Gaveston Earle of Cornwall* and Ben Jonson's *Sejanus His Fall*, also concealed the true intention of ambitious courtiers who did not vacillate in using the favour of their masters, lovers and friends to gain control over royal power. This anti-favourite, anti-prime-minister discourse had a lasting impact in England and I believe that it affected the ways in which favourites were perceived throughout the reigns of the Stuarts. This is to say not that there were no writers who viewed the royal favourite in a positive light, but that this positive discourse never gained the same prominence in England as it did in Spain with Lerma and Olivares and in France with Richelieu.

During the reigns of James I (pl. 19) and Charles I there were authors who employed a language of love and friendship to describe and justify the role of the royal favourite in public affairs. Even English monarchs themselves resorted to this language to express their confidence in their favourites. Famous are the words of James I when he declared in the Privy Council, 'I love Buckingham more than anyone else, and more than you who are here assembled. I wish to speak on my own behalf, and not to have it to be a defect, for Jesus Christ did the same, and therefore I cannot be blamed. Christ had his John and I have my George.'[40] But, more generally, during the reigns of James and Charles political writers viewed the concepts of love and friendship used to describe the favourite with straightforward hostility or, at the very least, with apprehension. We can point to numerous examples of this hostility, such as Francis Osborne's comments in his *Traditional Memoirs* and the satirical poems published against Charles and Buckingham, which presented a monarch dominated by an irrational, often corrupt, love towards one of his subjects.[41]

Even those who did not oppose favourites and those who openly supported them had misgivings about portraying the royal favourite as the king's friend. Francis Bacon (pl. 31), who in some works supported royal favourites, on occasion used a language rather similar to that used by Spanish authors. In a letter of advice addressed to Buckingham, for example, Bacon asserted that all monarchs had favourites, whom he called 'privadoes and friends'. Monarchs, he continued, had opted to have favourites 'sometimes out of their affection to the person of the man (for Kings have their affections as well as private men), sometimes in contemplation of their great abilities (and that's a happy choice), and sometimes for their own ends'.[42]

Bacon returned to this topic in the 1625 version of his essay 'Of Frendship'. Here, as in his letter to Buckingham, Bacon insisted that all monarchs, weak and wise, had favourites. But, in contrast to his letter to Buckingham, Bacon now called the attention of his readers to the danger that a favourite could pose to the king and the inappropriateness of calling the royal favourite the king's friend. 'It is strange to observe', Bacon wrote, 'how high a rate great kings and monarchs do set upon this fruit of friendship whereof we speak – so great, as they purchase it many times *at the hazard of their own safety and greatness.*' The reason for Bacon's misgivings can be found in contemporary theories on friendship – especially in the idea that friendship created equality. Based on these theories, for a monarch to have a friend implied, as Bacon noted himself, that the king elevates a subject to a position almost equal to the king, 'which many times sorts to inconvenience'. John Speed had already expressed this concern in his *The History of England* published in 1611. By claiming that the root of all problems for Edward II was his friendship with his favourite Gaveston, Speed declared that in keeping such a relationship Edward II forgot that 'those affections, which oftentimes deserve praise in a private person, are subject to much construction in a public'. By making Gaveston 'his half-self', Edward II opened the doors to an extreme civil confrontation which ultimately led to the killing of Gaveston and the dethronement of the king himself.[43]

Despite the fact that Buckingham monopolized royal grace and confidence from 1616 to 1628, the discourse on what role the royal favourite should occupy in governing the monarchy remained radically different in England from its counterparts in Spain and France. The concept of the favourite as the king's friend never became dominant in the English political discourse, and neither did the concept of the favourite as the king's chief counsellor or prime minister, even though there were attempts to portray the favourite as such.[44] Almost all English authors claimed that a king had to have several favourites and not just one, and believed that the favourites should be entirely subject to their monarch's will. Robert Naunton, for example, claimed that Elizabeth's favourites 'were many, and those memorable. But they were only favourites not minions, such as acted more by her own princely rules and judgment than by their own will and appetites'.[45] Behind these views was the belief that while a monarch had the right to have a close companion, a favourite, he should limit the favourite's public role. This was an idea already expressed early in the reign of James I by Edward Forset who, after declaring that 'the counselors of state', and not the royal favourites, should help the king to rule the monarchy, declared that 'The favourites of a Prince may be resembled to the fantasies of the Soule, with whom he sports and delights himself; which to do (so the integrity of judgment, and Majesty of State be retained) is in neither of both reprovable.'[46]

The content of the English discourse on royal favourites and how it differed from that of the French and Spanish discourses is well illustrated by Thomas Fuller's *The Holy State* published in 1642. As its title indicates, in his book Fuller analysed the various components of a personal monarchy, among which he included the royal favourite. In his analysis of the royal favourite, Fuller expressed the prevailing views on this topic – that the favourites should be many, that they should be dependent on the monarch's will and that their public role should be strictly limited. Illustrative of Fuller's views on favourites and their public role were the historical cases he chose to distinguish an evil from an ideal favourite. As examples of evil favourites Fuller chose Cardinal Wolsey and Haman, both accused of trying to usurp the king's authority after becoming the king's chief counsellor. The example he chose for the ideal favourite was Charles Brandon, Duke of Suffolk, one of the favourites of Henry VIII. What made Brandon an ideal favourite according to Fuller was that Brandon always remained the king's boon companion. Brandon, unlike Wolsey and Haman, never attempted to become the king's chief counsellor, and thus was never viewed by the king as a threat to his sovereignty.[47]

Epilogue

In one of the most influential modern studies on English politics during the 1620s, Conrad Russell made an interesting and controversial reference to the topic of favourites. 'The appearance of a "valido", or first minister', Russell wrote, 'was a general phenomenon in many European courts,' and he wonders 'whether the Stuarts' error may not have been the creation of this institution, but the failure to continue it after the death of Buckingham in 1628.'[48] As seen in this chapter, since the late decades of the sixteenth century some political writers had proposed that the king should place more responsibility in the hands of his officials for his own protection. In this context, the royal favourite came to play an increasingly important role by becoming – at least in theory – the monarch's protective shield and chief counsellor.

We also know that favourites were not as successful as their defenders predicted and desired. The reasons, I believe, were not lack of effort by the favourites themselves, or the absence of theories to defend their active role in the government of the monarchy, but the fact that the dominant paradigm on royal power did not change throughout this period. By the late sixteenth century, it was generally accepted that a monarch had to rule alone and this view continued to prevail throughout the second half of the seventeenth century. It appeared impossible for many early modern Europeans to defend simultaneously contemporary theories of royal power and an active role for the royal favourite. This was especially true in moments of crisis, when attacks on royal favourites were perceived as direct attacks on their masters. Philip Sidney cleverly foresaw this possibility, when in his defence of the Earl of Leicester he wrote that those who wanted to subvert the queen's power, 'before the occassion be ripe for them, to show their hate against the prince, do first vomit it out against' her most devoted counsellor.[49]

A favourite and prime minister, Louis XIV claimed in his memoirs, could fulfil a positive function; after all, he wrote, 'if he despoils you of part of your glory, he unburdens you at the same time of your thorniest cares'. But, at the same time, the existence of a favourite–prime minister questioned the royal persona, his power and sovereignty, by transforming the king into a simple figurehead in the eyes of his subjects. The only way to resolve this contradiction

220 Representations of the Favourite

was for the favourite to remain in the shadow of the king. To conserve his power and ultimately to conserve the monarchy, a king had to rule following the example set by Henri IV of France and not by Philip III of Spain, claimed Beaumont de Péréfixe, a tutor of Louis XIV. A monarch must disregard his personal attachments towards his servants and never delegate any of his prerogatives to those he loves. The king 'cannot deceive himself in this, because there is no person more proper than himself, however ignorant he be, to rule his kingdom, God having destined this function to him, and not to others, and the people being always disposed to receive commands when they come out of his sacred mouth'.[50]

Notes

1. I should like to thank the editors John H. Elliott and Laurence Brockliss and those who attended the symposium on the World of the Favourite celebrated in Magdalen College, Oxford, for their comments and suggestions. Special thanks to Irma T. Elo for her insights and help. I wish to dedicate this essay to the late Francisco Tomás y Valiente, murdered by terrorists on 14 February 1996. Professor Tomás y Valiente was an inspiration to many of us through his work, teaching and activities as a defender of democracy in Spain. His book *Los validos en la monarquía española del siglo XVII*, revised edn (Madrid, 1982) first aroused my interest in royal favourites and has been a constant influence in my work.
2. Leicester Bradner, 'The Theme of *Privanza* in Spanish and English Drama, 1590–1625', in A. David Kossoff and José Amor y Vázquez, eds, *Homenaje a William L. Fichter* (Madrid, 1971), pp. 98, 106.
3. Antonio de Guevara, *Aviso de Privados* (Valladolid, 1539), fol. 9v; Fadrique Furió Ceriol, *El Concejo y Consejeros del Príncipe*, ed. D. Sevilla Andrés (Valencia, 1952), p. 100; and Claude de Seyssel, *The Monarchy of France* (1515), trans. J. H. Hexter, ed. Donald Kelley (New Haven and London, 1981), p. 73.
4. Baldassare Castiglione, *El Cortesano*, Spanish trans. Juan Boscán (1534), 2 vols (Madrid, 1985), ii, p. 115, and i, p. 22.
5. I realize that to discuss the discourse on favourites in three monarchies so briefly it is necessary to simplify a very complex theme. This particularly pertains to my treatment of the French and the English discourses on favourites. My purpose here is to give a framework for comparison rather than to provide a thorough treatment of early modern European political discourses.
6. Cf. Arthur Kirsch, 'Shakespeare's Tragedies', in John F. Andrews, ed., *William Shakespeare: His World, his Work, his Influence*, 3 vols (New York, 1985), ii, p. 518.
7. *Leicester's Commonwealth* (1584), ed. D. C. Peck (Athens, Ga, 1985), pp. 187 and 73.
8. Juan de Mariana, *De Rege et Regis Institutione* (1599), ed. L. Sánchez Agesta (Madrid, 1981), pp. 37, 105, 97, 110, 165–6. See also Sir Thomas Smith, *De Republica Anglorum* (1583), ed. Mary Dewar (Cambridge, 1982), bk 1, ch. 7, p. 54.
9. Sir John Eliot, *Negotium Posterorum*, in *Proceedings in Parliament, 1625*, ed. Maija Jansson and William B. Bidwell (New Haven and London, 1987), p. 523; cf. J. H. M. Salmon, 'Rohan and the Reason of State', in his *Renaissance and Revolt* (Cambridge, 1987), p. 106.
10. Seyssel, *Monarchy of France*, p. 79.
11. J. Rushworth, *Historical Collections of Private Passages of State*, 7 vols (London, 1721), i, p. 219.
12. Niccolò Machiavelli, *The Prince*, ed. Quentin Skinner (Cambridge, 1980), pp. 81–2.
13. Justus Lipsius, *Six Books of Politickes or Civil Doctrine* (London, 1594), bk iv, ch. 9, p. 81.
14. Giovanni Botero, *Diez libros de la razón de estado* (1593), trans. Antonio de Herrera y Tordesillas (Madrid, 1613), bk ii, ch. 11, fol. 52, and bk i, ch. 14, fols 17–19.
15. Jean Bodin, *Les Six Livres de la République*, ed. Christiane Frémont, Marie-Dominique Couzinet and Henri Rochais, 6 vols (Paris, 1986), bk 1, ch. 10, p. 299.
16. Juan de Vitrián, *Las Memorias de Felipe de Comines*, 2 vols (Antwerp, 1643), i, p. 31, and ii, p. 114.
17. See Diego Saavedra Fajardo, *Idea de un príncipe político-cristiano representada en cien empresas* (1640) (fac. edn, Murcia, 1985), *empresa* 50, pp. 362–3.

18. E. H. Kossman, 'The Singularity of Absolutism', in his *Louis XIV and Absolutism* (Columbus, Ohio, 1976), pp. 11–12; see also J. Vicens Vives, 'Estructura administrativa estatal en los siglos XVI y XVII', in his *Coyuntura económica y reformismo burgués* (Barcelona, 1969), p. 124.

19. *Sir Francis Bacon his Apologie in certaine imputations concerning the late Earle of Essex* (1604), in Francis Bacon, *The Works*, 17 vols, ed. James Spedding, x (London, 1868), p. 142.

20. On the theories developed during the reign of Philip II, see Antonio Feros, 'Twin Souls: Monarchs and Favourites in Early Seventeenth-Century Spain', in Richard L. Kagan and Geoffrey Parker, eds, *Spain, Europe and the Atlantic World: Essays in honour of John H. Elliott* (Cambridge, 1995), esp. pp. 31–2. On portraits of the royal favourite as the king's prime minister, see Antonio Pérez (Baltasar Alamos de Barrientos), *Norte de Príncipes*, ed. Martín de Riquer (Madrid, 1969), pp. 15–79.

21. Biblioteca Nacional de Madrid, mss 18721/48, no pages.

22. Feros, 'Twin Souls', *passim*; and Antonio Feros, *The King's Favourite: The Duke of Lerma. Power, Wealth and Court Culture in the Reign of Philip III of Spain, 1598–1621* (forthcoming Cambridge University Press), ch. 6.

23. On the influence of Maldonado's definition of a favourite and the implications of defining the favourite as the king's friend, see Feros, 'Twin Souls', pp. 39–42.

24. Virgilio Malvezzi, *Historia del Marqués Virgilio Malvezzi* (1640), in Juan Yáñez, *Memorias para la Historia de Don Felipe III, Rey de España* (Madrid, 1773), p. 23.

25. Gerónimo de Florencia, *Sermón que predicó a la majestad Católica del rey Don Felipe Quarto* (Madrid, 1621), fols 26v–27v.

26. Juan Pablo Mártir Rizo, *Norte de Príncipes* (1626), ed. J. A. Maravall, 2nd edn (Madrid, 1988), p. 64; idem, *Historia de la vida de Lucio Anneo Séneca* (1625), ed. B. de la Vega (Madrid, 1944), pp. 72–3; and idem, *Historia de la vida de Mecenas* (Madrid, 1626), fol. 60.

27. Virgilio Malvezzi, *Il ritratto del privato cristiano* (1635), ed. Maria Luisa Doglio (Palermo, 1993), p. 35; Malvezzi's book was translated into Spanish in 1635 and into English in 1647.

28. José Laínez, *El Josué esclarecido* (Madrid, 1653), p. 506.

29. See, for all the depictions, Pierre Champion, 'La Légende des mignons', *Humanisme et Renaissance*, 6 (1939), pp. 493–528; Jacqueline Boucher, *La Cour de Henri III* (1986), pp. 23–6; and David Potter, 'Kingship in the Wars of Religion: The Reputation of Henri III of France', *European History Quarterly*, 25 (1995), pp. 485–528.

30. Joseph Bergin, *The Rise of Richelieu* (New Haven and London, 1991), p. 163; John Howell to Sir Richard Altham, 1 May 1620, in James Howell, *Epistolae Ho-Elianae: The Familiar Letters of James Howell*, ed. Joseph Jacobs (London, 1892), p. 138.

31. Howell, *Epistolae Ho-Elianae*, p. 222; *The Letters of Peter Paul Rubens*, trans. and ed. Ruth Saunders Magurn (Cambridge, Mass., 1955), pp. 147–9; Roland Mousnier, *L'Homme rouge ou la vie du cardinal de Richelieu* (Paris, 1992), p. 459.

32. Bergin, *The Rise of Richelieu*, p. 261; see also Mousnier, *L'Homme rouge*, pp. 221–33, 262–82.

33. *Testament politique*, ed. Louis André (Paris, 1957), pp. 287–305.

34. Jean de Silhon, *The Minister of State, wherein is shown the true use of Modern Policy* (London, 1658), p. 52.

35. Cf. William F. Church, *Richelieu and Reason of State* (Princeton, 1972), p. 467; Richelieu, *Testament politique*, pp. 305–7.

36. See, for example, Etienne Thuau, *Raison d'état et pensée politique à l'époque de Richelieu* (Paris, 1966), pp. 239–40, and Church, *Richelieu and Reason of State*, p. 220.

37. Malcolm Bull, 'Poussin's Bacchanals for Cardinal Richelieu', *Burlington Magazine*, 137 (1995), pp. 5–6; cf. Church, *Richelieu and Reason of State*, p. 414.

38. Simon Adams, 'Favourites and Factions at the Elizabethan Court', in R. G. Asch and A. M. Birke, eds, *Princes, Patronage and the Nobility: The Court at the Beginning of the Modern Age, c. 1450–1650* (Oxford, 1991), pp. 265–6.

39. Fadrique Furió Ceriol, *Of Councils and Counselors*, trans. Thomas Blundeville (London, 1570), p. 18. On the prevalence of the language of love to refer to the queen's favourites, see Catherine Bates, *The Rhetoric of Courtship in Elizabethan Language and Literature* (Cambridge, 1992).

40. Cf. Stephen Gardiner, *History of England from the Accession of James I to the Outbreak of the Civil War, 1603–1642* (London, 1883), iii, p. 98. Gardiner took this quotation not from an official document produced by the Privy Council, but from a letter of the Spanish ambassador in England, Count of Gondomar, to the Archduke of Austria (12 December 1617); see *Correspondencia oficial de don Diego Sarmiento de Acuña, conde de Gondomar*, 4 vols (Madrid, 1936), i, p. 93. Gondomar was Lerma's ally and he knew first-hand the language used in Spain to justify the favourite's public role, a language based, as we discussed above, on the concepts and language of friendship.

41. See *James I by his Contemporaries*, ed. R. Ashton (London, 1969), pp. 113–14; and *Poems and Songs relating to George Villiers, duke of Buckingham*, ed. F. W. Fairholt, in *Percy Society*, 29 (London, 1851), p. 5.

42. Bacon, *Works*, xiii, p. 14; in his edition of Francis Bacon's works, Spedding published two versions of Bacon's letter to Buckingham, pp. 13–56. I have consulted and used both. Bacon's letters to Buckingham are very similar to Antonio Pérez's letter to Lerma entitled 'A un gran privado' (1594), in Antonio Pérez, *Relaciones y cartas*, ed. Alfredo Alvar Ezquerra, 2 vols (Madrid, 1986), ii, pp. 77–80.

43. 'Of Friendship', in Francis Bacon, *The Essays*, ed. John Pitcher (Harmondsworth, 1987), p. 139, emphasis added; John Speed, *The History of England* (1611) (London, 1623), pp. 668, 670. Speed dedicated this edition to James I.

44. See, for example, Godfrey Goodman, *The Court of King James the First*, ed. John S. Brewer, 2 vols (London, 1839), i, pp. 256–7; and Bacon's letter to Buckingham, xiii, pp. 14–15, 27–8. Bacon's counsels to Buckingham in how to help the monarch to rule the monarchy are very similar to Alamos de Barrientos' counsels to Lerma on how to act as Philip III's prime minister; see Alamos de Barrientos, *Norte de Príncipes*, pp. 15–79.

45. Robert Naunton, *Fragmenta Regalia or Observations on Queen Elizabeth, her Times and Favorites* (1633), ed. John Cerovski (Washington, DC, 1985), pp. 40–1; see also Fulke Greville's 'A dedication to Sir Philip Sidney', in *The Prose Works of Fulke Greville*, ed. John Gouws (Oxford, 1986), pp. 108–9; Henry Wotton, 'A parallel of Robert Devereux, Earl of Essex, and George Villiers, Duke of Buckingham', in his *Reliquiae Wottonianae* (London, 1672), p. 163; and Edward Hyde, Earl of Clarendon, *The History of the Rebellion and Civil Wars in England*, 8 vols (Oxford, 1888), i, pp. 38–9.

46. Edward Forset, *A Comparative Discourse of the Bodies Natural and Politique* (London, 1606), pp. 15–16.

47. Thomas Fuller, *The Holy State and the Profane State* (1642), ed. Maximilian Graff Walten, 2 vols (New York, 1938), ii, pp. 237–57.

48. Conrad Russell, *Parliaments and English Politics, 1621–1629* (Oxford, 1979), p. 10 and n. 3.

49. Philip Sidney, 'A Discourse in defence of the earl of Leicester', in *The Miscellaneous Works of Sir Philip Sidney*, ed. William Gray (New York, 1966), p. 308.

50. Louis XIV, *Mémoires for the Instruction of the Dauphin*, ed. Paul Sonnino (New York, 1970), pp. 130 and 31; Henri de Beaumont de Péréfixe, *The History of Henry IV, Surnamed the Great* (1661), English trans. J. Dauncey, 1663 (New York and Paris, n.d.), pp. 212–13.

14
'Peut-on Assez Louer Cet Excellent Ministre?' Imagery of the Favourite in England, France and Spain

JONATHAN BROWN

If favourites held centre-stage in the European court of the seventeenth century, they have been minor players in recent studies of courtly imagery. Despite the fact that individual compositions have been carefully analysed, there has never been an attempt to define the image of the favourite as a category of court art. The terrain, admittedly, is vast, too vast to be surveyed in a short essay. However, perhaps a start can be made by focusing on three favourites, the Duke of Buckingham, the Count-Duke of Olivares and Cardinal Richelieu. By adopting a comparative approach to a study of their images, it may become easier to perceive the outlines of an iconography of the favourite.

The choice of these protagonists is based on their preponderant roles at three of the major monarchical courts of western Europe; in other words, they were chosen for their political significance. Furthermore, the imagery of these favourites stands out for its quality and quantity alike. These statesmen recognized the importance of visual images as a way to define, enhance and defend their unique position in the public realm. They also recognized that the best artists would produce the most convincing statements of their positions. Thus, in due course, we shall discuss works by Velázquez and Maino, Philippe de Champaigne and Poussin, and, of course, Rubens. These favourites had access to the machinery of production of court imagery and continually sought ways to turn it to their advantage.

Another point concerns the social origins of our favourites. As has often been said, they belonged either to the gentry or to the second rank of nobility. They were *arrivistes* to the inner circle of court and to the upper echelons of societies where appearances, or public conduct, were heavily freighted with significance. The pictures commissioned by our favourites are projections of their altered states of reality. Self-definition is the name of the game, the end of which is to offer burnished, idealized images of these complex, often unloved personalities.

Yet all was not mere role-playing. The three favourites continually struggled against foes and factions who despised them and sought to remove them from power. It follows that some of their images reflect the incessant combat of those who commissioned them. Nevertheless, I do not wish to suggest that a single template will fit all. Distinctive visual codes were elaborated in London, Paris and Madrid before Buckingham, Richelieu and Olivares arrived on the scene, and partly determined how their approaches to representation were fashioned.

Let us begin our tour along *la route du favori* at the court of St James'. In a very useful chapter in his book, *The Great Duke of Buckingham* (1939), Charles Richard Cammell lists some eighty portraits of the mercurial favourite of the early Stuarts.[1] These images can readily be divided into two categories. The largest by far shows George Villiers in full-length or half-length placed against a neutral background. Certainly one of the most spectacular is the version (pl. 34) in the National Portrait Gallery, London, by William Larkin, a fascinating portraitist who worked in the second decade of the seventeenth century.[2] Although stilted in manner, this portrait admirably captures the beauty of face and physique which launched this ambitious son of a Leicestershire knight on a meteoric career. The occasion of the commission was Villiers' installation as Knight of the Garter in 1616, when he was twenty-four years old, and the artist has done his best to create a resplendent image.

Larkin's portrait, which just precedes Villiers' ascent to the status of favourite, hews to the well-entrenched conventions of Jacobean aristocratic portraiture, as exemplified by Robert Peake the Elder (*Henry, Prince of Wales*, London, National Portrait Gallery). This is exactly the point. By appropriating the hieroglyphic pose and painstaking execution of the elaborate finery, which typify what Roy Strong has called the 'English icon', Larkin effortlessly elevates this upstart squire to the highest rank of nobility. Here, as in his later career, Villiers would show himself to be a canny exploiter of visual codes of aggrandizement.

During the early 1620s, the portraits of Buckingham follow the new fashion for Dutch-style imagery introduced into the court by Cornelius Janssen and others. While these portraits are marked by greater naturalism (as well as by the moustache and beard raised by Buckingham after 1620), they are singularly unrevealing of the duke's magnified political power. The only picture to break the mould is the extraordinary work painted by van Dyck in late 1620–early 1621, to commemorate the marriage of Villiers with Lady Katherine Manners.[3] This flashy picture may be considered as either audacious or tasteless, but in any case it certainly is not concerned with Buckingham's political prowess.

It was not until 1625 that Buckingham encountered the painter he required. This was Peter Paul Rubens, arguably the most eloquent court painter of his time. Buckingham and Rubens met in Paris in the spring of 1625. The duke had come to escort Henrietta Maria to London, and Rubens to install the famous series of pictures dedicated to the life of Marie de Médicis (see pl. 16), pictures which Buckingham clearly saw and admired. What Rubens had to offer was rhetoric, a far more effective way to define and, if need be, to defend a position.

And by 1625 Buckingham needed the most persuasive visual rhetorician that money could buy.

Painter and patron agreed upon two works, the *Glorification of the Duke of Buckingham* and an equestrian portrait. Both of these works were destroyed by fire in 1949, but are known from photographs. In addition, Rubens' preparatory oil-sketches survive, and it is through the progression from the preliminary to the definitive composition that we can see an embattled favourite mounting a defence against a determined and growing opposition in parliament and at court.

The *Equestrian Portrait*, for which Rubens was paid the handsome sum of £500, was initially a rather conventional work, as we know from the oil-sketch (pl. 35) now in the Kimbell Art Museum.[4] The pose replicated the one used in an engraving of 1625 by Willem de Passe, to which Rubens has added Neptune accompanied by a naiad, symbols of Buckingham's office of admiral of the fleet. Also included is a multi-purpose personification of a wind god, who holds the trumpet of fame and a laurel wreath of victory. Fair winds promise fame and glory to the triumphant admiral.

The final version (pl. 36), delivered to the duke in the autumn of 1627 (and first recorded in York House in 1635), is now loaded with symbolism directed toward the growing legion of detractors, including the members of the Commons who impeached him in the heated debates of 1626.[5] On the left is Victoria with a laurel wreath and cornucopia, while on the right is Caritas, holding in one hand a flaming heart and dragging with the other the snake-haired and clearly vanquished demon of Discord. The wind gods, now reduced to putti heads, huff and puff to create the favourable zephyrs which will sweep the English fleet to victory and silence the nay-sayers and detractors.

Buckingham's enemies, of course, were not to be rebutted by a mere equestrian portrait. The team of Buckingham and Rubens, therefore, was moved to try again, and the result is one of the most grandiloquent representations of a favourite executed in the seventeenth century, the *Glorification of the Duke of Buckingham*. It now seems that the picture was developed in three stages, becoming ever more grandiose as it progressed.[6] Stage one, known only in a copy after a presumed lost sketch, is again not especially inspired or pointed (pl. 37). Buckingham, holding a standard, is led towards the temple of virtue, assisted by Minerva and heralded by Fame, blowing a trumpet. Beneath are a lion, representing Anger, and Discord, who grasp at Buckingham's leg, trying to pull him down. At the left, the triumphal scene is witnessed by the Three Graces, offering a crown to the ascendant duke.

In phase two (pl. 38), the allegorical apparatus has been conspicuously enriched. Fame is transformed into Mercury, who assists Minerva in leading the duke towards a structure with twisted columns, where Virtue (cornucopia) and Honour (lance) await him. Below, Anger and Discord, repulsed by a female figure, try to impede the duke's ascent. The Three Graces are again present and six putti, holding such attributes as a palm of victory and the trumpets of fame, add grace notes to the paean of praise. One putto holds his trumpet aloft; by abstaining from blowing it, he refers to the withholding of 'ill fame', or the spreading of falsehood. Most audacious of all is the pose of the duke, which has been identified as an adaptation of the Risen Christ in Correggio's *Resurrection of Christ* in the cupola of S. Giovanni Evangelista, Parma.

The final version (pl. 39), octagonal in shape, was intended to decorate a ceiling in 'my lord's closet' (privy chamber?) and involves a further clarification of the allegory. The Graces are somewhat diminished while the temple of Virtue and its guardians are magnified and the numbers of the opposition are increased by the addition of a dragon and harpy. The shriller tone of apology may be seen as a response to Buckingham's enemies in the Commons, who were resorting to extremes of rhetoric. On 10 May 1626, in the course of the debate on impeachment, Sir John Eliot, Buckingham's most outspoken foe, had likened him to 'the beast called by the ancients *Stellionatus*; a beast so blurred, so spotted, so full of foul lines, that they knew not what to make of it'.[7] In the face of such excesses, Rubens' allegory may seem less vainglorious. In any case, actions, as usual, spoke louder than images. The defeat of the English at the Isle of Ré in the winter of 1627 exactly coincided with the completion of the picture and makes Rubens' overblown rhetoric seem an empty, desperate gambit.

This, of course, is the view of hindsight. In 1628, however, Buckingham had come to believe that images could help to shape perceptions of reality. On 16 May 1627, just prior to the duke's departure for the campaign at the Isle of Ré, a masque was presented to their Majesties at York House wherein (as described by the Reverend Joseph Mead) 'first [came] forth the duke, after him Envy, with diverse open-mouthed dogs' heads, representing the people's barking; next came Fame, then Truth, etc'.[8] As this event makes clear, favour depended not on parliament but on the king, who was unshaken in his conviction that Buckingham was indispensable.

The visual testimony of the king's allegiance to his favourite is a picture which stemmed from a royal commission, although it is hard not to see the hand of Buckingham in it too. This is the work by the Dutch painter Gerrit van Honthorst, who arrived in London in April 1628 and immediately set to work on a painting for the Banqueting House (pl. 40).[9] In this masque-like composition, we see Charles and Henrietta Maria dressed as Apollo and Diana, receiving the Seven Liberal Arts, who are introduced by Buckingham, disguised as Mercury. In the lower-left corner, the figures of Envy and Hate are destroyed by Virtue and Love. As Buckingham sponsored the victories of the reign, he now sponsors the arts, which will adorn the peace, glorify the monarchy and stifle the opposition. The familiar trope of the monarch as promoter of the arts of war and peace is appropriated by Buckingham in Rubens' *Equestrian Portrait* and Honthorst's allegory, which accurately reflect his role in the government of Charles I. The *Glorification of the Duke of Buckingham* tacitly acknowledges that the king's subjects viewed these developments with dismay and anger. The abdication of governance to a favourite was viewed by many as a usurpation and contravention of the natural order, and these paintings clearly expose the fault line in rule by favourite.

In some respects, the representations of the Count-Duke of Olivares fall within the parameters established by the imagery of Buckingham. For example, the earliest portrait of the Spanish favourite is the strange, ungainly work painted by Velázquez, or perhaps an assistant, now in the Museu de Arte of São Paulo (pl. 41). Velázquez, whose entry into the court of Philip IV was sponsored by Olivares, received partial payment for this version on 4 December 1624, two years after the count-duke had consolidated his position as favourite, or minister, as he preferred to be known. Olivares' hulking figure fills most of the composition, and the attributes of his position – the key of the privy chamber and the spurs of the master of the horse – are almost blatantly displayed. However, the format is entirely traditional for portraits of Spanish rulers and nobility. Just as Larkin cast Buckingham as an English icon, so Velázquez presents Olivares as a Spanish grandee.

A year or so later, Velázquez revised his image of Olivares as seen in the portrait now in the collection of the Hispanic Society of America (pl. 42). While cosmetically more appealing, this version is given a decided political twist by the inclusion of the long reed whip, held erect in the favourite's right hand. As Antonio Martínez Ripoll has pointed out, this object is not the symbol of the office of *caballerizo mayor*, as traditionally stated.[10] Rather, it is a riding crop, an object with a well-established metaphorical value by which the ruler governs the masses, who are likened to a horse in need of discipline and authority in order to perform its tasks. If this interpretation is correct, then Velázquez has adopted a rather direct means to display the favourite's power.

But then Olivares was not one for subtlety where his image was concerned, and it is here that he parts ways with Buckingham's resort to allegory to promote and defend his policies and reputation. By an extraordinary coincidence, Rubens created a portrait of Olivares at exactly the time he was working on his commissions for Buckingham. However, Olivares seems to have drawn different conclusions about Rubens' value as an advocate for his position.

The work in question is a handsome portrait engraving, designed by Rubens and executed by his assistant, Paul Pontius (pl. 43). Although small in scale, the composition is densely packed with meaning.[11] Without attempting a full exposition of the emblematics, it can be said that the design represents Olivares as endowed with strength and wisdom (the two genii seated on the socle), which enable him, through wise and forceful government (the rudder and baton entwined by a serpent), to bring glory to Spain, as represented by the six-pointed star, Hesperus, which shines over the terrestrial globe, touching Iberia with one of its points. Trumpets and burning torches, symbols of fame, surround the portrait, while swags of wheat, fruit and vegetables indicate the prosperity of a country living in peace.

Upon receiving the engraving, Olivares wrote a warm letter of thanks to Rubens, dated 8 August 1626, expressing appreciation of the work. 'God give me light and strength for this [task of governing], and then it may be thought that I esteem the portrait as it deserves to be, and that its message will not be entirely misplaced.'[12]

Olivares' false modesty appears to have masked true indifference towards Rubens' imagery. Two years later, the Flemish master spent eight months in Madrid, yet received no further commissions from Olivares, who by then could have used the help, now that he was beginning to hear the rumbles of discontent with his ministry. These would grow ever louder in the 1630s.

Olivares' response to his detractors can hardly be called subtle. Around the middle of the decade, as the war with France was getting under way, he commissioned three works, comparable to the ones produced for Buckingham during his period of crisis, which attempt to bolster the power of the favourite and disarm the enemy. One of these is the monumental equestrian portrait by Velázquez in the Prado (pl. 44). Nothing is known of the genesis of this composition, and its date and purpose remain matters of conjecture. Although many writers, myself included, have associated the commission with the Spanish victory at Fuenterrabía in 1638, this is purely a circumstantial argument in that the battle scene in the background is of a generic kind. It could be that the picture owes its origins to the start of war with France, an idea which is supported by the recent technical studies of Carmen Garrido, who dates it to around that time.[13] However, we should not spend time in worrying about the precise date or pretext at the expense of understanding the portrait for what it so patently represents – the count-duke as a confident, powerful warrior. Velázquez, unlike Rubens, chooses to make the point without recourse to symbolism, although both he and Olivares were on familiar terms with Rubens' allegorized *Equestrian Portrait of Philip IV* (copy, Uffizi), which was executed in 1628-9 and hung in the Alcázar of Madrid. Directness, not allusion, is the idiom chosen by Velázquez to glorify the image of military might; even the unlettered could understand.

Much the same approach is applied to a more explicit representation of Olivares as the guiding hand of the destiny of the monarchy – the *Riding Lesson of Balthasar Carlos*, also datable to the 1635-6 period (pl. 45). The scene is set in the courtyard of the Buen Retiro (although it has recently been argued that the tilting-yard of the Alcázar is represented), and the action is a riding lesson of the young prince and heir to the Spanish crown.[14] Equestrian exercises were commonly used as metaphors for governance, so it makes sense that the teacher should be Olivares and not Philip IV, who watches the lesson from a distant balcony, accompanied by the queen. However, it needs to be emphasized that this painting (presumably commissioned by Olivares, although first recorded in the possession of his nephew Luis de Haro in 1647) is a unique record of what might be called favouritism in action. By this I mean that it graphically represents the favourite as protagonist in the conduct of the monarchy, while the king, reduced in size and relegated to the background, passively observes the action. Despite the protests of the opposition, the *Riding Lesson* leaves no doubt that Olivares is still firmly in control of the situation. (However, a copy in the Wallace Collection, London, made after Olivares' dismissal, deletes the count-duke and, for that matter, the sovereigns as well.) It seems evident that Olivares wished to emphasize his *valimiento* and was convinced that forthright representation was again the best way to proceed.

The final work in this triad of visual arguments on behalf of the Olivares ministry is the best documented. In 1635, Juan Bautista Maino received final payment for his remarkable picture, the *Recapture of Bahía* (pl. 46), which was part of a series of twelve battle scenes executed for the Hall of Realms of the Buen Retiro. These paintings depicted the major victories of the reign of Philip IV and, by extension, constituted a defence of Olivares' policies.[15] The Hall of Realms was not only the most important room in the palace; it was also the site of diverse spectacles and festivities. Therefore, Maino's picture was displayed in full view of the court and its message was perceptible by all.

The purpose of the *Recapture of Bahía* as it relates to Olivares is again unmistakably clear, although this time the artist has had recourse to symbolic language. Fadrique de Toledo, the victorious commander of the combined Spanish and Portuguese force which dislodged the Dutch from the Bay of All Saints in Brazil in 1625, addresses the kneeling Dutch soldiers. He points to a tapestry which depicts the king trampling personifications of Heresy and Treachery, while Olivares places his right foot on the chest of that *bête noire* of favourites, Discord. Minerva stands at the left and hands the king the palm of victory. She places a wreath of laurel, the symbol of virtue, on the monarch's brow, ably assisted by the bulbous figure of the favourite.

It is difficult to overestimate the sheer audacity of this composition. In his state papers, Olivares insistently downplayed the importance of his position with respect to Philip IV, often referring to himself as the 'king's faithful minister'. These three pictures seem to make his words so much empty rhetoric. Given the option to use allegory, no less valid a means of communication but certainly less direct, Olivares opted for naked narrative. Perhaps he was reacting to the fury and calumnies of his opponents, although the pictures were calculated to raise their tempers. In any case, these are the final volleys in the visual war of self-defence. Our last glimpse of the count-duke, the portrait by Velázquez of 1638, now in St Petersburg, unblinkingly shows the reality of seventeen years of exhausting labour in a losing cause.

Our final case, Cardinal Richelieu, is the most complex of all. Richelieu was the only one of our three ministers who successfully completed his ministry, defying both assassination and dismissal. Moreover, the imagery of Richelieu is far more extensive, varied and complex than that of Buckingham or Olivares. Perhaps another way to characterize the differences between Richelieu and his counterparts is to note that, whereas the history scenes and allegories made for the English and Spanish ministers have an *ad hoc* quality, those made for the French minster are more deliberate and systematic.

Even before discussing some of these works, it is worth considering why the Richelieu imagery is so markedly different in character.[16] I would like to propose a number of explanations. Richelieu, to begin with, had received training in theology at the Sorbonne and was therefore schooled in rigorous systems of thought. He himself was the author of four religious treatises. I would also like to suggest that Richelieu's religious education imparted a heightened appreciation of imagery as a means of communication and persuasion. Beginning in the late sixteenth century, the Counter-Reformation church had reformed and revitalized the use of images as a means of instructing and inspiring the faithful, and it may be that Richelieu had absorbed those lessons.

More to the point, Richelieu was a patron of learning. In 1624, he became Protector of the Sorbonne, and during the 1630s he extended his patronage to the Académie Française, accepting its letters patent in 1635. It may be that these contacts with the world of learning and language led Richelieu to form a sort of 'Petite Académie', which confected the recipes for his team of image-makers.

A final observation concerns a purely artistic matter. In Paris, unlike London or Madrid, there was a long tradition of printmaking, which was thriving as never before in the years of Richelieu's mandate. This gave him access to a potent means of disseminating his ideas and presenting himself to a public outside the realm of the court. Indeed, the number of engravings bearing the cardinal's message is as formidable as the prints are unstudied, compelling me to present a highly abridged and tentative account of this aspect of the Richelieu imagery.

The visual campaign on Richelieu's behalf did not really hit its stride until after 1630, when he consolidated his power. There is a group of representations clustered around the victories at the Isle of Ré and La Rochelle, which lack the subtlety of thought and refinement of execution of the later works. In one, for instance, a triumphant Louis XIII rides the ship of state across the waters to the Isle of Ré (pl. 47). Fortune is the sail and Richelieu is the pilot of the undersized craft. As for the battle itself, the most ambitious renderings are the monumental engravings by Jacques Callot, comprising six plates (plus borders) and published in 1631. No work better illustrates Richelieu's struggle for control in the late 1620s than one of these, the *Siege of the Citadel of the St Martin on the Isle of Ré*. Two preparatory drawings depict the king and the minister observing the course of the battle.[17] In a third, they are joined by Gaston, while in the print itself Richelieu was erased; the shadowy traces of his figure are visible on the original copperplates, which are preserved in the Chalcographie of the Louvre.

Other prints of the 1620s are more successful, if not exactly subtle. The cardinal's appointment as *Surintendant de la Navigation et du Commerce* in 1627 occasioned an image of Richelieu placidly enthroned on a ponderous triumphal chariot, too heavy to skim over the water but making determined progress nonetheless. An allegory usually dated *c.* 1628 by Jean Ganière (pl. 48) shows

Richelieu protecting the fleur-de-lis while an eagle and lion, the Austrian and Spanish Habsburgs, are subdued and chained to a column. The laudatory inscription below begins with a blatant leading question – 'Peut-on assez louer cet excellent ministre?'

During the 1630s, Richelieu began to put his house of images in order. He found his portraitist in Philippe de Champaigne, whose versions of the cardinal are now familiar. As Bernard Dorival has noticed, Champaigne's portraits, with one exception (Chantilly, Musée Condé), depart from the traditional convention used to depict prelates, namely seated in a chair which is canted diagonally towards the picture plane.[18] Instead they show the cardinal standing, swaddled in the opulent red *capa magna* of his dignity, with his right arm elegantly extended, holding his *biretta* in his hand (pl. 49). In Dorival's reading of the pose, the artist seeks to express Richelieu's dual condition as prelate and peer of the realm.

This typology was invented for one of the cardinal's most ambitious projects, the Galeries des Hommes Illustres in the Palais Cardinal.[19] In the gallery were displayed twenty-four portraits of famous men and one famous woman, eight painted by Simon Vouet, seventeen by Champaigne. Admission to this select circle was predicated on illustrious service to the monarchy, either as minister or as warrior. Three of the ministers, like Richelieu, were ecclesiastics – Abbé Suger; Georges, Cardinal d'Amboise; and Charles, Cardinal de Lorraine. However, it was only in the person of Richelieu that the ideals were conjoined – sage minister, pious cardinal, victorious warrior.

It was also during the 1630s that Richelieu employed the engraver Michel Lasne, who produced both portraits and allegorical compositions. The numerous allegorical glorifications by Lasne and others are an untapped goldmine, and here I can only scratch the surface with a small sample of this sophisticated imagery. While Lasne was often the engraver, the designs were produced by the leading artists of Paris – Champaigne, Claude Vignon, Simon Vouet, François Perrier and others – and were possibly devised by the learned men who enjoyed Richelieu's patronage.

A characteristic example is the engraving by Lasne (pl. 50), designed by Champaigne, which commemorates the concession of the dukedom on 13 August 1631.[20] The cardinal, seated on a dais, receives a genuflecting woman, wearing an ermine-trimmed cloak, who probably represents France. She proffers armour, the ducal crown and a swag of fruit, betokening prosperity. Behind stands a woman with a sail, referring to the superintendency of navigation. To the cardinal's right is Minerva, while at one extreme is a woman holding a sword and the family coat-of-arms. As yet I have not discovered the significance of the figure at the right, holding jewels and accompanied by a lion. Flying in from the left is Fame, offering the ducal crown and a crown of laurel, while a companion, partly hidden in the clouds, blows the trumpet of fame, adorned with the coat-of-arms and the cardinal's hat. At last, Richelieu had found an artist who could do him justice!

An engraving executed by Lasne and designed by Claude Vignon introduces us to an important category of Richelieu imagery, the illustrated frontispieces of doctoral theses presented at the Sorbonne. Here the marriage of image and erudition is consummated and emphasizes the distinctive characteristic of Richelieu's imagery. This engraving of 1635 (pl. 51), which adorned the thesis of Louis de Machault, prior of Saint-Pierre d'Abbeville, is particularly deft.[21] It is hard to improve upon the economical description of the great eighteenth-century print connoisseur P. J. Mariette – 'Geniuses assembling the traits of the greatest ministers who have governed France in order to compose the portrait of Cardinal Richelieu'. The small portraits held by the genius at the right are those of Abbé Suger and Cardinal d'Amboise, two of the heroes in the Galerie des Hommes Illustres.

Without going into detail, but simply to provide a flavour of these remarkable inventions, we turn to Lasne's engraving of 1632 after a design of Abraham van Diepenbeck (pl. 52), in which Louis XIII defends himself with a shield decorated with the image of his minister, and another designed and executed by Grégoire Huret in 1639 (pl. 53), which depicts Robert de Sorbon paying homage to Richelieu as protector of the college he had founded. From the sky above, St Louis, first benefactor of the Sorbonne, bestows his blessing on the assembled company.[22] And, in the background, one of the dark moments of academic life, the dissertation defence, is brought out into *plein air*. The candidate, Jean Chaillou, faces his examiners in front of the building sponsored by Richelieu, which however was still under construction at the time.

The spirit of the allegorical prints can equally be detected in paintings commissioned by Richelieu (as well as in medals). One of the most ingenious is Jacques Stella's *Liberality of Titus* (pl. 54), intended as a chimneypiece for the *cabinet du roi* at the Château de Richelieu, another site which displayed extensive visual panegyrics. In this composition, as John Elliott has explained, Louis XIII, dressed *à l'antique*, is Titus, distributing wooden balls to his subjects, which they can exchange for gifts of food and clothing.[23] Richelieu, swaddled in a toga, stands behind, directing the action.

More extraordinary still is a painting of 1634 by Claude Vignon (pl. 55), which is related to a series of twelve tapestries, executed for the Palais Cardinal. A complete analysis of the symbolism would require several paragraphs; not only the composition, which features Richelieu as Hercules, but also the margins are crammed with allusions to the titles, powers and virtues of the invincible cardinal.[24]

Richelieu, the faithful, wise minister of state and conqueror of his enemies – the imagery tries to persuade us that the cardinal, unlike Buckingham and Olivares, had defeated his enemies abroad and silenced his detractors at home. However, the final major commission of Richelieu's life demonstrates that, for all his skill and success, the voices of dissent were not drowned out in the din of glory. They could be heard and had to be answered.

In 1640, as part of a programme to initiate a new school of court artists, Richelieu summoned Nicolas Poussin, the most renowned French painter of the day, to Paris, and in the next year commissioned him to paint two pictures for the Grand Cabinet of the Palais Cardinal. The first is a chimneypiece, *Moses and the Burning Bush* (pl. 56), which combines two passages from Exodus.[25] In Exodus 3: 1–10, the Lord appears to Moses in a burning bush and commands him to lead his people out of Egypt. In the second passage, Exodus 4: 1–3, Moses is bidden by God to cast a rod on the ground, which is turned into a serpent, a sign that he should persist in his mission despite the incredulity of the Israelites. In the context of the Palais Cardinal, the picture signifies that Richelieu is a French Moses, who will lead his reluctant people out of their misery and into the promised land.

The second picture (pl. 57), which was placed on the ceiling, indicates that the French people might have been less than willing to follow their great leader to salvation.[26] This is a composition with uncanny parallels to Rubens' *Glorification of the Duke of Buckingham* and Maino's *Recapture of Bahía*. Seated on a parapet are Discord, at the left, and Envy, at the right, the implacable enemies, it seems, of rule by favourite. Not surprisingly, all ends well, as Time carries the naked Truth aloft, proving that Richelieu's policies will be vindicated when seen from the lofty vantage point of history.

The apologetic images created by our three favourites – Richelieu's date from but a year before his death – are the other side of the coin of rule by favourite. The recto proclaims his glory, wisdom and power; the verso demonstrates that his hold on power was tenuous. I would argue that the imagery discussed here occupies a unique place in the history of seventeenth-century art precisely because of its apologetic, defensive character. Favourites wielded enormous power, but it was conditional on the monarch, invested by the ruler, not by God. Therefore, the favourites were open to criticism and vulnerable to attack if their policies failed or if they threatened the vested interests. This precarious state of affairs is expressed in the imagery and epitomized by that pregnant rhetorical question inscribed on the print by Jean Ganière dedicated to Richelieu – '*Peut-on assez louer cet excellent ministre?*' This can be interpreted in two ways. Can the great minister be sufficiently praised? and Is sufficient praise ever enough? The insecurity of their position engendered an insatiable need for reassurance in the breasts of the ministers. They hung by a golden thread and this insecurity is woven into their imagery, which ultimately lacks the confidence of works commissioned by natural rulers, even when comparable rhetorical devices and symbolism are deployed.

Rule by favourite, the images tell us, was unnatural and therefore needed to be defended, not merely exercised. Richelieu was confident that he would be vindicated by the judgement of history, and to us his assumption appears to have been correct. However, from the vantage point of 1684, about halfway through the reign of Louis XIV, rule by favourite in France was being perceived in a negative light by the most powerful monarch of the time, as we see in a conspicuous but overlooked verdict on the matter – the central compartment of Le Brun's ceiling decoration in the Galerie des Glaces of Versailles (pl. 58). The composition celebrates the decision of the young Louis XIV to rule without a favourite after the death of Mazarin in 1661.[27] This heroic act, which triumphantly reunites monarchy and governance, is applauded by the gods of Olympus while an inscription, clearly legible from the floor below, explains why they rejoice. It is an epitaph for the age of the favourite: 'Le roy gouverne par lui même.'

Notes

1. Charles Richard Cammell, *The Great Duke of Buckingham* (London, 1939), pp. 372–85. His list is expanded and refined by David Piper, *Catalogue of Seventeenth-Century Portraits in the National Portrait Gallery, 1625–1714* (Cambridge, 1963), pp. 39–42.

2. Roy Strong, *William Larkin, vanità giacobite* (Milan, 1994), p. 112.

3. Reproduced and discussed by Arthur Wheelock *et al.*, *Anthony van Dyck* (Washington, DC, 1990–1), pp. 124–6.

4. Gregory Martin, 'Rubens and Buckingham's "fayrie ile"', *Burlington Magazine*, 108 (1966), pp. 613-18, esp. p. 614; Frances Huemer, *Portraits I*, Corpus Rubenianum Ludwig Burchard, pt 19 (London, 1977), pp. 57–61; Julius Held, *The Oil Sketches of Peter Paul Rubens: A Critical Catalogue*, 2 vols (Princeton, 1980), i, pp. 393–4; Hans Vlieghe, *Rubens' Portraits of Identified Sitters Painted in Antwerp*, Corpus Rubenianum Ludwig Burchard, pt 19 (London, 1987), pp. 66–7.

5. Martin, 'Rubens and Buckingham', p. 614; Held, *Oil Sketches*, p. 394; Vlieghe, *Rubens' Portraits*, pp. 64–6.

6. Martin, 'Rubens and Buckingham', pp. 614–17; Held, *Oil Sketches*, i, pp. 390–3.

7. Cited by Roger Lockyer, *Buckingham: The Life and Political Career of George Villiers, First Duke of Buckingham, 1592–1628* (London and New York, 1981), p. 323.

8. Cited by Martin, 'Rubens and Buckingham', p. 617.

9. Oliver Millar, 'Charles I, Honthorst, and Van Dyck', *Burlington Magazine*, 96 (1954), pp. 36–8; J. Richard Judson, *Gerrit van Honthorst: A Discussion of his Position in Dutch Art* (The Hague, 1959), pp. 181–3.

10. Antonio Martínez Ripoll, '"El Conde Duque con una vara en la mano", de Velázquez, o la praxis olivarista de la Razón de Estado torno a 1625', in *La España del Conde Duque de Olivares* (Valladolid, 1990), pp. 45–74.

11. Held, *Oil Sketches*, i, pp. 398–9.

12. Cited in *ibid.*, p. 399.

13. Carmen Garrido Pérez, *Velázquez: Técnica y evolución* (Madrid, 1992), pp. 309–19.

14. Michael Levey, *Painting at Court* (London, 1971), p. 142; Enriqueta Harris, 'Velázquez's Portrait of Prince Balthasar Carlos in the Riding School', *Burlington Magazine*, 118 (1976), pp. 266–75; Jonathan Brown and J. H. Elliott, *A Palace for a King: The Buen Retiro and the Court of Philip IV* (New Haven and London, 1980), p. 255. John F. Moffitt, 'The Prince and the Prime Minister: The Site and Significance of Veláquez's *Equestrian Lesson of Prince Balthasar Carlos*', *Studies in Iconography*, 12 (1988), pp. 90–120, argues inconclusively that the setting is the Picadero of the Madrid Alcázar.

15. Brown and Elliott, *A Palace*, pp. 141–92, for the Hall of Realms; pp. 84–90, for the *Recapture of Bahía*.

16. For an introduction to the grossly understudied Richelieu imagery, see Jacqueline Melet-Sanson, 'L'Image de Richelieu', in *Richelieu et le monde de l'esprit* (Paris, 1985), pp. 135–47, and the catalogue entries on pp. 307–18.

17. Roseline Bacou, 'Callot, Louis XIII et Richelieu au siège de Ré', *Revue du Louvre et des Musées de France*, 30 (1980), pp. 254–6.

18. Bernard Dorival, *Philippe de Champaigne, 1602–1674: la vie, l'oeuvre et le catalogue raisonné de l'oeuvre*, 2 vols (Paris, 1976), ii, p. 113.

19. Bernard Dorival, 'Art et politique en France au XVIIe siècle: la Galerie des Homme Illustres du Palais Cardinal', *Bulletin de la Société de l'Histoire de l'Art Français, Année 1973* (1974), pp. 43–60.

20. Tony Souval, 'Deux oeuvres peu connues de Philippe de Champaigne', *Gazette des Beaux-Arts*, 57 (1961), pp. 181–2.

21. Paola Pacht Bassani, *Claude Vignon, 1593–1670* (Paris, 1992), pp. 281–3.

22. For the prints of the prolific Huret, see Emmanuelle Brugerolles and David Juillet, 'Grégoire Huret, dessinateur et graveur', *Revue de l'Art*, 117, no. 3 (1997), pp. 9–35.

23. J. H. Elliott, *Richelieu and Olivares* (Cambridge, 1984), p. 169.

24. Pacht Bassani, *Claude Vignon*, pp. 276–8.

25. Humphrey Wine and Olaf Koetser, *Fransk Guldalden: Poussin og Claude og maleriet i det 17. arhunredes Frankrig* (Copenhagen, 1992), pp. 180–7.

26. Pierre Rosenberg, *Nicolas Poussin, 1594–1665* (Paris, 1994), pp. 296–8.

27. For an explanation of the iconography, although without reference to its significance for the imagery of the favourite, see Robert W. Berger, *Versailles: The Chateau of Louis XIV* (University Park and London, 1985), p. 54.

Part Four
The Twilight of the Favourite

15
Nicolas Fouquet, the Favourite Manqué

M. FUMAROLI

At Nantes on 5 September 1661, as the *surintendant* Nicolas Fouquet (pl. 59) emerged from an audience with the king, his chair was stopped by d'Artagnan accompanied by fifteen musketeers.[1] D'Artagnan handed the minister a *lettre de cachet* signed by the king. Fouquet read the missive, and merely remarked 'that he thought that he held a higher place in the king's esteem than anyone else in the kingdom'.[2]

In La Fontaine's poem, *Elégie aux Nymphes de Vaux*, circulated early the following year by the friends of the imprisoned *surintendant*, the poet, imploring the king's mercy, calls on him to witness the 'know thyself' of the favourite disillusioned with favours:

> Voilà le précipice où l'ont enfin jeté
> Les attraits enchanteurs de la prospérité.
> Dans les palais des rois, cette plainte est commune
> On n'y connaît que trop les jeux de la Fortune
> Ses trompeuses faveurs, ses appas inconstants:
> Mais on ne les connaît que quand il n'est plus temps
> . . .
> Jamais un favori ne borne sa carrière;
> Il ne regarde point ce qu'il laisse en arrière;
> Et tout ce vain amour des grandeurs et du bruit
> Ne le saurait quitter qu'après l'avoir détruit.[3]

The 'disgraced favourite' is, as other essays in this volume make clear, one of the commonplace figures in the imagination of the seventeenth century.[4] Deceptive enchantment, the height of vanity, a slippery cake of soap, the inconstancy of the sea winds, all these metaphors of tragic irony make of the disgraced favourite a literary character *par excellence* in the seventeenth century. Nicolas Fouquet, in his own right an accomplished man of letters, adulated by the great writers and poets of his day when he was at the pinnacle of his fame, would possibly receive even greater acclaim after his fall. His charm and misfortune would cast a permanent shadow over the early reign of Louis XIV (pl. 60), and even today they overshadow the radiance of the Great King, just as the prophetic fury of Saint-Simon's *Mémoires* overshadows the closing years of his reign.

The 'favourite', an emblem of transience and illusion, is the antithesis of an institution.[5] In France, apart from the pathetic connotation it might assume in lyrical and tragic poetry, the word 'favourite' designated a political monster: a recipient of the king's personal favours who takes advantage of his master in order to exercise a power in the state which is by definition tyrannical. Nicolas Fouquet would never become a favourite in this quasi-legal sense, though his own destiny would be as tragic. It is this singularity that I wish to examine here.

First of all it is necessary at least to sketch out the typology of the minister and the favourite in France to determine what makes Nicolas Fouquet such a singular case. Louis XIII would have 'favourites' after 1626 in the private sense as the jesuit Bouhours understood it, when he wrote that favourites had no direct relationship to the public sphere. Chalais, Saint-Simon and Cinq Mars were all 'favourites', but they never became ministers. Nevertheless, Richelieu (pls 26 and 47–57), Louis XIII's chief minister after 1624, was dubbed a 'favourite' by the opposition in the sense that, as an agent of royal power, he had wielded it like a Machiavellian prince with Louis XIII's consent. On the other hand, under Henri IV, Villeroy and Sully in particular were never described as 'favourites' but as ministers. They were the servants of a king who governed by himself; they had not taken advantage of the ambiguous favour which originates in the private sphere and spreads out unhindered into the public domain.

As early as 1515, in *De Asse*, Guillaume Budé, the father of French legal humanism, had launched a violent attack on the mismanagement of Louis XII's favourite, Cardinal d'Amboise, who had shown a preference for employing Italians and who had embroiled the king in a disastrous venture in Italy. Budé complained that the kings of France had adopted the disastrous habit of surrendering their power to ambitious and greedy men rather than exercising power by themselves with the love of their people. For Budé, a minister is a man who serves the king while the king exercises full power himself. But a favourite is someone who takes advantage of the king's weakness to misuse royal power and upsets the entire legitimate edifice of the monarchy.[6]

A century and a half later, when another giant of French legal humanism, Pierre Dupuy, wanted to make the name of Richelieu hateful in retrospect, he attributed to him the following maxim: 'No favourite or minister ever perished because he did too little harm, but because he did not do enough.'[7]

In the *Histoire des favoris anciens et modernes*, a posthumous work by Pierre Dupuy published in Leyden in 1660, the only Frenchman mentioned, in an appendix, is Concino Concini, the maréchal d'Ancre, the Italian favourite of

47 Jean Picart after Abraham Bosse, *Le Gallion de Roy flotant sur l'océan.* (Engraving in the Bibliothèque Nationale, Paris)

48 Jean Ganière, *Richelieu as Defender of France against the Habsburgs* (c. 1628). (Engraving in the Bibliothèque Nationale, Paris)

49 Philippe de Champaigne, *Cardinal Richelieu.* (Musée du Louvre, Paris)

50 Michel Lasne after Philippe de Champaigne, *Cardinal Richelieu Receives the Ducal Crown.* (Engraving in the Bibliothèque Nationale, Paris)

EMINENTISSIMO PRINCIPI
CARDINALI DVCI DE RICHELIEV

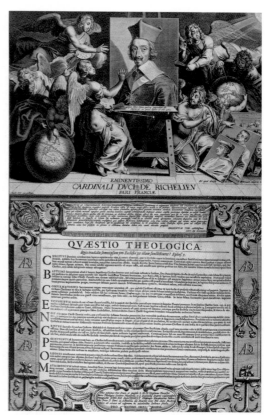

51 Michel Lasne after Claude Vignon, thesis of Louis de Machault, prior of Saint-Pierre d'Abbeville (1635), frontispiece. (Bibliothèque Nationale, Paris)

52 Michel Lasne after Abraham van Diepenbeck, thesis of Laurent de Brisacier (1632), frontispiece. (Bibliothèque Nationale, Paris)

53 Grégoire Huret, thesis of Jean Chaillou (1639), frontispiece. (Bibliothèque Nationale, Paris)

Jacques Stella, *Liberality of Titus* (c. 1637–8).
ogg Art Museum, Harvard)

Claude Vignon, *Triumph of Hercules* (1634).
aisse de Monuments Historiques et des Sites,
ris)

56 Nicolas Poussin, *Moses and the Burning Bush* (1641). (Statens Museum fur Kunst, Copenhagen)

57 Nicolas Poussin, *Time Rescuing Truth from Envy and Discord* (1640). (Musée du Louvre, Paris)

58 Charles Le Brun, *The King Governs by Himself* (1661). (Galerie des Glaces, Château de Versailles)

59 Nicolas Fouquet: the favourite manqué. A engraving of 1660 by Claude Mellan. (Bibliothèque Nationale, Paris)

60 Louis XIV of France painted by Henri Testelon in 1648. (Musée du Château de Versailles)

Jean Baptiste Colbert: Louis XIV's *contrôleur général des Finances*
a member of his ministerial team. Painted by Claude Lefebvre
666. (Musée du Château de Versailles)

Fouquet's château, Vaux-le-Vicomte, a residence fit for a king. Engraving by Israel Silvestre.
bliothèque Nationale, Paris)

63 Prince Ferdinand Portia, tutor and favourite of the Emperor Leopold I. (Engraving in the Österreichische Nationalbibliothek, Vienna)

GIO: FERDINANDO DEL S.R.I. PRINCIPE DI PORTIA
MITTERBVRG, CONTE DI BRVGNARA, ET ORTENBV
SIGNOR IN SENOSETCH, E PREMB, CAV.ᵈᵉˡ TOSON D
MAGGIORDOMO MAGGIORE, E PRIMO MINISTRO DI
LEOPOLDO CESARE,

A.Bloem.del.　　　Co̅. Meÿsens,Fe,Vien

64 Leopold I, Holy Roman Emperor. Engraving.

LEOPOLDUS D. G. ROMAN: IMPERÀTOR
SEMPER AUGUSTUS, GERMANIÆ, HUNGARIÆ,
BOHEMIÆ, ETC. REX. ARCHIDUX AUSTRIÆ, DUX
BURGUNDIÆ.

Peter Schumacher, Count of Griffenfeld, apostle of
solutism. Painting of the early 1670s by Abraham
uchters. (Rosenborg Castle, Denmark)

Corfitz Ulfeldt, son-in-law and right-hand man to the
ng Christian IV of Denmark. Painting of 1638 by
gel Rooswijk. (Det Nationalhistoriske Museum på
ederiksborg, Hillerød)

67 Johann Frederick Struensee, physician to Christian VII and the last Danish royal favourite. Painting by C.A. Lorentzen. (Det Nationalhistoriske Museum på Frederiksborg, Hillerød)

68 Axel Oxenstierna, chancellor to Gustavus Adolphus and Queen Christina of Sweden. Portrait of 163 by D. Dumonstier. (Statens Konstmuseer, Stockholm)

The scapegoats of Charles I's personal rule. A woodcut of 1641 showing Laud imprisoned in the
Tower of London, looking out at the ghost of Strafford.

70 Thomas Wentworth, Earl of Strafford, Lord Deputy of Ireland. Painting of 1636 by Anthony Van Dyck. (National Portrait Gallery, London).

71 Edward Hyde, Earl of Clarendon, Charles II of England's Lord Chancellor. Painting of *c.* 1654 by Adriaen Hanneman. (Private collection)

72 Maximilien de Béthune, duc de Sully, Henri IV's *surintendent des finances*. Engraving, probably from the painting by Ambroise Dubois, in the *Collection d'Estampes*. (Bibliothèque Nationale, Paris)

73 Prince Potemkin, favourite of Catherine II of Russia. Engraving.

74 The Austrian Chancellor Prince Metternich: the last favourite?

Marie de Médicis whom Louis XIII had had assassinated in 1617. The work purports to show, against the memory of Richelieu, that 'favourites' whose absolute power makes a mockery of the laws of the kingdom and who take advantage of the prince's favour are in fact despots opposed to the spirit of French institutions. Apart from the maréchal d'Ancre, the only other contemporary example cited was Rodrigo Calderón, a favourite of Philip III of Spain. To disqualify Mazarin during the Fronde, the *Mazarinades* had described him as a 'favourite'.[8]

Nicolas Fouquet, *procureur général* in the Parlement of Paris since 1650, and *surintendant de finances* in conjunction with Abel Servien since 1651, had made no secret of his ambition to succeed Cardinal Mazarin (pl. 27) as chief minister of the kingdom.[9] During his period as a candidate he was never described as a favourite; and indeed he was neither the favourite of Mazarin, who made a point of pitting him against rivals, first Servien then Colbert (pl. 61), nor did he become a favourite after the cardinal's death during the few months when Louis XIV, although maintaining him in his post of *surintendant*, was secretly plotting his downfall in close collaboration with Colbert. What won him the overall sympathy of the general public and men of letters, who saw him as an innocent victim of Colbert, the real 'favourite', first of Mazarin and then of Louis XIV, was the fact that he neither aspired to be nor became a favourite as Pierre Dupuy understood the term.

Fouquet owed his position as *surintendant* and minister of state not to the favour of Mazarin, who stood in awe of him, but to the immense services he had rendered the queen mother and her chief minister and favourite in the thick of the Fronde of the princes. While Mazarin, unanimously hated, had been forced to flee abroad or stay away from court between August 1652 and February 1653, Nicolas Fouquet, the leader of the loyalist Parlement which had taken refuge at Pontoise – at Fouquet's suggestion – had shown all the intelligence, authority and diplomacy of a statesman, often dictating the conduct of the absent Mazarin and standing in for his disconcerted ministers. His own financial standing and that of his family had already by then enabled him to finance the royal army at home and on the frontiers. It was common knowledge that the crown and Cardinal Mazarin were indebted to Fouquet, who had prepared the triumphant return of the minister to Paris in February 1653 with the help of his brother. On his return Mazarin had no alternative but to nominate Nicolas Fouquet *surintendant des finances* of the kingdom, though he was cautious enough to associate him with Abel Servien in this position.[10]

The real 'favourite' of the cardinal was Colbert, administrator of the cardinal's personal fortune since 1651. He existed through and expected all from him. Fouquet existed by himself and made himself known by himself, through the great political role he had played in the Parlement of Paris at the end of the crisis of the Fronde and by his high standing which made him irreplaceable in the financing of the state. Colbert was the intimate accomplice of his master. This intimacy gave him the means to work against the *surintendant* and nourish the jealousy and irritation Mazarin felt against a man who had become too indispensable. Goaded on by Colbert, the cardinal expected his new *surintendant* to make regular contributions to the financial needs of the state and on occasion also to the rebuilding of his personal fortune at the expense of the state. Fouquet was forced to walk a tightrope. In 1659 Colbert addressed an exceptionally violent memorandum to the cardinal to overwhelm him with the 'irregularities' committed by Fouquet. Mazarin did not want to follow Colbert's lead, and had even entreated the two men to settle their differences.[11]

On the death of Mazarin in March 1661, therefore, matters hung in abeyance. What was needed now was a decision from the young king. Until then Fouquet had not perhaps been sufficiently concerned. Colbert, on the other hand, following Mazarin's advice, had long since gained the personal confidence of Louis XIV, a docile disciple of the Italian cardinal since early childhood. The young king must have been even more aware than his master of the different positions of Colbert and Fouquet: one was an authority unto himself, who enjoyed a power and a popularity he owed entirely to his own personal abilities and services rendered to the state; the other was an obscure *intendant* who could achieve success, as he understood very well, only by keeping out of the limelight and advancing through the king's favour. Mazarin had already made known his preference for Colbert, to which Louis XIV could only acquiesce. Herein lay the weak spot in Fouquet's ambitious plans.

Moral and political issues of the utmost importance were at stake in the impending decision of the young king. He left matters in abeyance between the death of the cardinal on 9 March 1661 and the date of Fouquet's arrest on 5 September the same year.

The first issue at stake for the king was to free his reign of the odour of racketeering which had made Mazarin's ministry so abhorrent. The gigantic fortune accumulated by the cardinal since 1653 implied a management of public money damaging for the state and shocking to the taxpayers.

As Mazarin's *intendant*, Colbert was in a better position than anyone else to know by what means and how much the cardinal had pillaged the state coffers. Ironically, however, it was his position inside the mismanagement of state funds that made his strength and covered him: for reasons of state the accounts of the cardinal, a 'favourite' of the queen mother and the official designer of the victory of the king over the two Fronde uprisings, could not be publicly attacked. On the other hand, Colbert could intimate to the king that his great rival Fouquet, so much more visible in the public eye than he was himself, was the ideal scapegoat for the cardinal's maladministration of finances. By sacrificing Mazarin's over-conspicuous *surintendant des finances*, he could spare the cardinal's memory, and at the same time satisfy public opinion, by showing that the king was determined to break with the criminal financial practices which had so appalled public opinion under Mazarin. The consequence of Fouquet's sacrifice was the political triumph of Colbert.

Nicolas Fouquet was almost defenceless against this plot: as he had in actual
act been responsible for public finances since 1653, he could be accused of
ll the misdealings in the place of his deceased master. He was a wealthy man
n his own right and through his second marriage into the family of président
eannin de Castille, *surintendant des finances* under Marie de Médicis. But
is opulent lifestyle and his generous patronage of poets and artists might
uggest that he was the prime beneficiary of a financial system which the
ardinal had sponsored (pl. 62), which Mazarin had more than anyone else
sed to his own advantage, but from which, for reasons of state, the dead
ardinal must be absolved.[12]

This moral and financial stake linked to the memory of Cardinal Mazarin was
oupled with a political stake in 1661, this time connected with the legacy of
Cardinal Richelieu: the absolutism which the latter had made predominant
n the conduct of affairs of state during his ministry. On the threshold of his
ersonal reign, Colbert and Fouquet represented two opposing options for
Louis XIV, and Mazarin had left it up to his disciple the king to decide between
hem.

Colbert could promise the king that he would accomplish the work of the two
ardinal ministers, crush the seeds of the Fronde once and for all and resume
he construction of the absolute state which had slowed down almost to a
tandstill under Anne of Austria.

Fouquet, on the other hand, let the French public foresee a regime of
econciliation, synthesis and compromise between the restored authority of the
tate and the political forces which had strenuously opposed the excesses of
bsolutism since 1624.

How could Fouquet, so clearly a member of the party that had been victo-
ious in the Fronde, appear in 1657–61 as the candidate for chief minister,
upported not only by former *frondeurs* such as the duc de La Rochefoucauld
ut also by moderate loyalists? The party of reconciliation which he led
esponded to a personal inclination already perceptible in his earlier career, and
o a tradition derived from his personal background. His father, François
Fouquet, first magistrate and then *conseiller d'état*, had served Richelieu well,
lthough with moderation and personal reservations. Nicolas himself, a
onseiller in the Parlement at Metz at the age of eighteen in 1633, was no doubt
ppreciated by Richelieu and his successor. An *intendant* of Dauphiné in 1645,
e had fought off a fiscal revolt with a courage and a humanity that contrasted
harply with the customary repressive habits of royal agents. An *intendant de la
énéralité* in Paris in 1648, then *procureur général* in the Parlement of Pontoise in
650, his loyalty towards the royal cause had always expressed itself with a
reedom of speech and an original stance that heralded a totally different con-
ept of the state from the one held by Mazarin and his ministers.[13] His remar-
iage, to Marie-Madeleine Jeannin de Castille in 1651, did not only make him
member of a very wealthy family: his wife was a cousin of Chalais' widow,
favourite of Louis XIII and an early victim of Richelieu's arbitrary rule.

François Fouquet, the father of Nicolas, had sat in the *chambre de justice* which had condemned Chalais to death. Fouquet had inside knowledge of the arbitrary nature and the violence inherent in absolute power. In 1657 he married his eldest daughter to Armand de Béthune, marquis de Charost, a great-nephew of Sully, whose legend, with its links to the good 'King Henri', was more popular than ever. These indications are consistent with what Fouquet stated in a letter to Mazarin as early as 1652, in which he outlined in no uncertain terms a political programme that was the exact opposite of absolutism.[14]

At the height of the Fronde uprising, he was working towards the victory of the king devoid of vengefulness and without a return to the excesses of authoritarianism that had so disgusted the French. He had opted for Cicero against Caesar, for Sully against Richelieu. The most discerning members of the vanquished *frondeurs* gave their support to him. His candidacy to succeed Mazarin was a response to the overall desire to put an end to extreme government. And he took pains to organize this consensus around his candidacy.

Between 1653 and 1659, when the death of Abel Servien left him as the sole *surintendant des finances*, Fouquet was building up a network of family connections, clients and friendships on all sides of the political divide. It was a real political party as well as a reservoir of funds. Were he to have become chief minister, this party would have enabled him to govern using the same blend of authority, diplomacy and humanity of which he had shown himself capable in 1651–3.[15]

The ramifications of his party were so far-reaching that, in the event of his disgrace, Fouquet could even envisage taking to the maquis and negotiating a 'settlement' with the court from a position of strength. What we have here is indeed a traditional view of monarchy, one with which Richelieu, *nolens volens*, had been obliged to come to terms in his conflicts with the princes or Protestants entrenched in their fortified strongholds. The notorious 'projet de défense' drafted by Fouquet in 1657–8, discovered behind a mirror in the château de Saint-Mandé in 1661, is indeed part of the traditional political game of the monarchy. Mazarin, 'disgraced' by the king against the king's own wishes, had, during the Fronde of the princes, set an example for Fouquet by negotiating his return from a position of strength, first from the fortified city of Sedan, and then from the German town of Brühl.[16]

The death of the Italian cardinal on 9 March 1661 left the succession open. Now for the first time the young king Louis XIV entered the scene at the age of twenty-two. Louis was known above all for his docile behaviour towards his master Mazarin, his talents as a dancer and his appetite for amorous affairs. On 10 March 1661, the young king gathered around him at the Louvre the chancellor Séguier, the *surintendant* Fouquet, the secretaries of state Le Tellier, Lionne, Loménie de Brienne and his son, Duplessis-Guénégaud and Phélypeaux de la Vrillière. According to the *Mémoires* of the young Brienne, to the general surprise of the assembly the king expressed in no uncertain terms his intention to govern by himself.[17]

This proud declaration seemed to correspond to the age-old desire to see the king of France exercise his *potestas* himself, without the services of a self-seeking 'favourite'. This desire had always emanated from the most liberal minds, who expected the king to exercise a moderate and generous power, the antithesis of the Machiavellian excesses committed by ephemeral 'favourites'. The king, it would seem therefore, for the first time since the reign of Henri IV, wanted to do without the services of a favourite and 'govern by himself'. In actual fact the end of his declaration gave Colbert his first opportunity and he became Fouquet's *contrôleur*. It intimated that beneath the ostentatious statement of principle lay the makings of a 'favourite'. No one could have imagined then that the king's avowed desire to 'govern alone' concealed a plan with the aid of the utterly devoted Colbert for restoring the absolute state that had made Richelieu hated and which the Fronde had stopped Mazarin from implementing. Fouquet and his friends were justified in thinking that this statement of aims marked the young king's desire to break with absolutism and therefore with the reign of favourites'.

No one had interpreted the victory of the regent and Mazarin over the two Frondes as a prelude to the restoration of the dictatorship which Richelieu had enforced between 1624 and 1641. The advent of civil peace was the result of a general weariness and Mazarin's able politics, supported by Fouquet. The signing of the Treaty of the Pyrénées in 1659, accompanied by the marriage of Louis XIV to the Infanta Maria-Theresa of Spain, had moreover brought an end to the Thirty Years War in which Richelieu had involved France in 1635, and which had provided an alibi for the cardinal's iron rule. Peace in Europe brought a general amnesty in France, starting with the pardon granted to Condé, the leader of the princely Fronde. Now that peace was restored, it was to be hoped that both inside and outside France a reconciliation between the court, the Parlement and the princes would also be on the agenda.

Nicolas Fouquet's candidacy for the post left vacant by Mazarin embodied this assumption, which benefited from the general approval of men of letters and the members of high society in Paris who had opted for the party of reconciliation. Former repentant *frondeurs* and 'honnestes gens' from all sides of the political spectrum could identify themselves with Fouquet, an accomplished 'honnête homme' himself, a diplomat, a *gentilhomme*, educated, witty, connoisseur of the fine arts and a great patron of the arts of peace. After serving admirably and even saving the court in the dark years, he epitomized the triumph of royal authority and civil order over the aberrations of the two Frondes. His personality at once forceful and yet flexible, his talents as a charmer and his considerate generosity gave assurance that if he were to become chief minister the triumph of the court would in no way aspire to revenge or restoration. In his harmonious hands never again would the exercise of royal authority assume the abrupt arbitrariness and cold cynicism that had so aroused the French against Richelieu and Mazarin.

Thanks to his mother, Marie de Maupeou, co-foundress of the Dames de la Charité with St Vincent de Paul, and thanks to his three clerical brothers and his six sisters who were nuns (three of them had entered the Visitandines), Fouquet had powerful sympathizers in the church. This did not prevent him from gaining the confidence of Protestants.[18] One of his admirers was the Huguenot Turenne, and Pellisson, another Huguenot, became his right-hand man in 1657. His talent for synthesis made Fouquet the heir of the spirit of the Edict of Nantes. He was in all respects the candidate for civil peace and moderation.

All that remained for Fouquet, who had the favour of 'gens de bien', was to obtain the most important favour of all, that of the young king. Nothing at first sight seemed more natural. Until the death of Cardinal Mazarin, the young king had symbolized the return to normality of the institutions of the realm and the expectation of a long-lasting, peaceful and prosperous reign.

If Fouquet were to become chief minister, the king would become, to use the language of the age, the Augustus of a new Maecenas, the Henri IV of a new Sully. Fouquet and his party indeed saw matters in this light. But they had misunderstood the self-pride of a king who possessed neither the moderation of Augustus nor that attributed to King Henri. Fouquet's personal talents, his popularity, his party and even the debts incurred by the crown in his favour were reasons enough to incur the loathing of Louis XIV, a man possessed by 'l'amour de soi-même et de toutes choses pour soi', 'à couvert des yeux les plus pénétrants'. A close friend of Fouquet, the duc de La Rochefoucauld, would devote an entire volume to maxims that analyse the hidden power of self-love, a power which pushed the king towards a concept of 'divine kingship' and placed him above the law.

However, by June 1661, Fouquet had lost his best advocate with the king, the queen mother, whom the duchesse de Chevreuse had succeeded in turning against him. To thwart this intrigue Fouquet had not hesitated to beg pardon from Louis XIV for his 'earlier faults', a polite way of reminding him of Mazarin's involvement in the mismanagement of the state finances: at the end of his audience with the king, Fouquet still had every reason to believe that the second Henri IV would ask him to become his Sully.[19]

But on 14 August 1661 Fouquet, confident of the overtly warm signs of 'friendship' which the king lavished on him, made one fatal mistake: he relinquished the office of *procureur général* in Parlement in favour of the *président*, Achille de Harlay. This office had ensured that, in the event of arrest, he could be judged only by his peers according to the procedures of the Parlement of Paris, immune to pressure from the court. By giving up this judicial office, which was associated moreover with the distasteful memories of the Fronde, he thought he had removed the last obstacle in the way of his political appointment by the king as head of the council. He even went so far as to believe – and the king did nothing to discourage him – that Louis would be gratified to receive, as a political 'wedding gift', the considerable sum arising from the sale of the office of *procureur général*.[20]

No doubt as early as June 1661 he had been forewarned of his impending downfall by his spies. But by then it was too late to do anything. He still wanted to believe in the king's good faith. He could never have guessed how much Louis XIV was irritated by the sympathy of Paris towards him, in particular the Paris of former *frondeurs*: the king never pardoned the rebels who had dared to frighten him when he was an adolescent, and who had defied his nascent authority.

Fouquet was the least satisfactory candidate for a king whose self-love was synonymous with the absolute state. He aspired to be emperor in his own kingdom, not an *optimus princeps* along the lines of the Ciceronian concept. Colbert, the zealous *intendant* of Mazarin's personal fortune, the man behind the scenes, unknown to the public but well known to the king, had the makings of a great minister, which for Louis XIV meant an upper-class domestic servant. Unlike his father Louis XIII, the young king felt no moral or emotional distress at embodying the absolute state. And, unlike Richelieu, Colbert would never presume to dictate reason of state to the king, though he knew how to apply it without hesitation. However absolute and contrary to national customs Richelieu's rule had been, Colbert, this *vir marmoreus*, this 'Nord' as Madame de Sévigné called him, was ready to take upon himself what in Louis XIV's government was abhorrent to all French 'honnestes gens', whether they had been *frondeurs* or loyalists during the regency.

In the months following Fouquet's arrest, the devious trap laid with profound duplicity by the king and Colbert operated like clockwork. As was to be expected, the exasperation of the taxpayers which had been building up during the years of war focused on the sacrificial victim. Mazarin's reputation had remained intact as, on 23 September 1661 in violation of all the legal rules and even without a warrant from the king, Colbert had had taken from the château de Saint-Mandé the letters and papers that could have provided evidence of the rather shameful role Mazarin had played in his administration of public finances. Condemned to solitary confinement, overwhelmed by public loathing, prosecuted not only for embezzlement but also for the crime of *lèse-majesté*, Fouquet seemed destined for imminent death and ignominy.[21]

But a nucleus of Fouquet's most fervent friends, convinced of his innocence and well acquainted with the truth of the matter, were not to be intimidated. As the arbitrary nature of the new regime began to emerge gradually from the *chambre de justice* in charge of the trial, public opinion slowly started to move in the opposite direction. The Parisian world of letters which had acclaimed Fouquet as a new and unparalleled Maecenas, placed all its talent and influence at the service of the *surintendant*'s family and his followers.[22]

The members of the republic of letters in Paris had detested the idea of 'another Tiberius' embodied in Richelieu. They had on the whole 'fronded' Mazarin, who had imported Italian artists to Paris and who had disdained or ignored French writers. They were disgusted to see under the new 'favourite' the reappearance of the Richelieu-style, servile publicists. Much to the disapproval of the king and Colbert, they played a vital role in instigating a real 'Fouquet Affair'. Gilles Ménage, Gui Patin, Pierre Corneille were all the more sympathetic towards the campaign which the family and friends of Fouquet conducted on his behalf because for them the trial of the *surintendant* threatened a principle which they held dear and which had made the Fronde appealing to them: freedom of thought and expression.[23]

The 'pope' of the Parisian republic of letters, Pierre Dupuy, had bequeathed in advance a testament which had laid down the rules for the struggle on behalf of Fouquet. Pierre Dupuy had died in 1651 in the midst of the parliamentarian Fronde, universally venerated by educated magistrates, renowned university professors and scholarly men of letters. He embodied the grand tradition of the French 'politiques', the tradition of Michel de l'Hospital and Jacques-Auguste de Thou. Until 1657, the Academy of which he was the 'prince' would continue to meet in the king's library under the leadership of his inseparable brother, Jacques Dupuy. Pierre Dupuy was, as everyone knew, an historian and a jurist renowned in Europe. He had devoted the last years of his life to a vain attempt to obtain the posthumous rehabilitation of his cousin, François-Auguste de Thou, executed in 1641 at Lyon following a sham trial for complicity in treason with his friend Cinq Mars. The documents for the rehabilitation file had been widely circulated with the aid of the so-called Dupuy Academy, highly influential in parliamentarian circles.[24]

In this series of learned and eloquent *Mémoires*, Pierre Dupuy had examined all the facets of the mock trial which had led to the condemnation and execution of the young magistrate, the pressure exerted on the *commissaires* nominated to condemn him and the stratagems employed by Richelieu's tool, Laubardement, to topple Cinq Mars and his friend, using one against the other. His analysis was not simply an implacable indictment of the tyranny that Richelieu had imposed on France, but was also a plea to restore the rule of law in the kingdom. The De Thou Affair, removed from parliamentarian checks, riddled with irregularities which had enabled Louis XIII's favourite to indulge his thirst for blood and revenge, was a faithful portrayal of the state of violence into which France had been plunged during the cardinal's ministry.

Citing a long list of historical precedents, notably relating to violations perpetrated by Louis XI, Pierre Dupuy, by profession a lawyer, had established that exceptional courts or *commissions de justice* appointed by kings or their ministers and beyond the control of Parlement, usually under the authority of the *chancelier de France*, had on many occasions condemned innocent people, who would be rehabilitated with *éclat* under subsequent regimes. It was just such a rehabilitation that Pierre Dupuy requested in his *Mémoires pour justifier M. de Thou*, sentenced to death for complicity in a plot against the state, having refused to speak rather than make a cowardly denunciation of his best friend.

In his accounts of the execution of de Thou and Cinq Mars that Dupuy appended to his *Mémoires*, both young men are portrayed as Christian martyrs and as the heroic victims of a pagan dictatorship, which one had dared defy and the other had simply detested in silence. Pierre Dupuy drew a striking contrast between this elevation of the soul and the baseness of the publicists who surrounded Richelieu.[25]

Even though the moral intransigence of the old Cato was no longer in tune with the elegant and refined sensibilities of the new generation, it had not lost its authority in 1661 for any truly educated mind or truly Christian soul. It expressed the voice of conscience for magistrates who, like Lamoignon, Pontchartrain, d'Ormesson, Roquesante, summoned to sit in the *chambre de justice* appointed by the king, were nonetheless not disposed to appear in the eyes of their peers and posterity as the accomplices of a new Laubardemont reincarnated in Colbert.

The voice of conscience held sway over highly educated men such as Pellisson, Maucroix, La Fontaine, and their adherence to the moral, legal and political values developed in the *Grande Robe* circles since the age of the Valois kings ensured their affection for Fouquet. The disgraced *surintendant* had made his career within the inner circle of Parlement, where he had so recently been one of the highest magistrates: nothing better demonstrated the arbitrary nature of his trial. As soon as he could answer his judges, he pleaded his case like a great professional lawyer, especially on matters of financial procedure. From behind the courtier, the habitué of the salons, the elegant conversationalist, there emerged in full view a French Cicero, the worthy son of the monarchy's 'Sénat'.

His assistant public prosecutor, Jacques Jannart, conducting his defence in conjunction with Pellisson, who was incarcerated in the Bastille, had in 1659 taken up residence in the Quai des Orfèvres inside the parliamentary enclosure, probably to bring his home and office closer together, and perhaps also to guard against a search by Colbert. When La Fontaine lived in Paris from 1661 to 1663, he stayed with Jannart, in the midst of the frenetic activity of Fouquet's defenders. It was here, at his uncle's house, in the shadow and shelter of the parliamentarian citadel, that the poet composed his *Elégie aux Nymphes de Vaux* and *Ode au roi*.[26]

The *surintendant* and his family benefited, too, from the support of Port-Royal, a notorious victim of the tyranny of Richelieu and Mazarin. One of the most illustrious *solitaires*, Antoine Le Maître de Sacy, had been one of Fouquet's colleagues in Parlement. Another *solitaire*, Robert Arnauld d'Andilly, and his son Simon Arnauld de Pomponne, were so closely connected to Fouquet that Pomponne was exiled to Verdun in September 1661. For the *solitaires*, as for the Parisian educated public, it was imperative to link the case of Fouquet, a victim of Colbert's arbitrary rule, with that of the great Arnauld, the theologian of Port-Royal, victim of an iniquitous condemnation by the Sorbonne in 1656 – a condemnation confirmed by Parlement at the request of Fouquet, who had been forced to bow to Mazarin's orders. The campaign conducted by Pascal in his *Petites Lettres*, printed in secret and circulated with resounding success between 1656 and 1658, had then rallied support from the educated public for Antoine Arnauld's cause and had avenged his honour. Like the *Mémoires pour justifier M. de Thou* by Pierre Dupuy, Pascal's *Petites Lettres* presented a model, a precedent and a method for Jacques Jannart, Paul Pellisson and Fouquet's faithful friends.

In the first weeks of 1662 his friends had boldly seized every opportunity that presented itself. The *premier président*, Lamoignon, who led the proceedings in the *chambre de justice* from 3 December 1661 was a scrupulous magistrate. He owed his office to the *surintendant*, despite their differences of opinion. From the depths of his cell in the Bastille, Pellisson managed to get Jannart to publish secretly a *Discours au roi par un de ses fidèles sujets sur le procès de M. Fouquet*, which was soon followed by other documents.[27] With an eloquence both ardent and moderate, which Voltaire would compare with that of Cicero, Pellisson challenged the extraordinary commission instructed to try Fouquet, demanded that the case be brought within the normal procedures of the realm, and recalled that the entire administration of the *surintendant* was the responsibility of the defunct Cardinal Mazarin.[28] The *Discours*, which ran into at least three editions, made a resounding impact. It was supported by the admirable *Elégie* by La Fontaine, also published secretly and anonymously on loose sheets like the *Mazarinades* and the *Provinciales*.

In July Pellisson launched a second plea, *Considérations sommaires sur le procès de M. Fouquet*, while Fouquet's mother, wife and daughter, the marquise de Charost, appeared before the *grand-Chambre* of Parlement to appeal for its support. The *premier président* Lamoignon, accompanied by a delegation from Parlement, went to present the petition to the king, who could not conceal his anger. The following December, Lamoignon was requested to give up his post as head of the *chambre de justice* to Chancellor Séguier, a long-standing accomplice of Richelieu's exactions.

On 30 July 1662, Fouquet's wife wrote a letter to the king as impassioned against his 'favourite' Colbert as had been Pierre Dupuy's retrospective *Mémoires* against Louis XIII's 'favourite'.[29]

The preliminary investigations, which purported to carry out an in-depth examination of the state accounts during Fouquet's entire administration, dragged on. In January 1663, the prisoner managed to write his own *Défenses* and get them to his supporters; they were printed secretly and enjoyed the same success as had Pellisson's pleas. A first-class lawyer and writer, Fouquet skilfully justified the arduous management of state finances and, above all, recalled the irregularity of the preliminary investigation, in particular Colbert's seizure of 1,600 letters written by Mazarin from Saint-Mandé, which would have easily cleared him of the charges against him. He wrote numerous requests for proceedings to be initiated against Colbert and for the dismissal of judges who were related to the minister or too obviously biased.[30]

On 23 August 1663, Jacques Jannart and his nephew, La Fontaine, too openly compromised in the defence of Fouquet, were sent into exile at Limoges.[31] The most visible pressure was exerted on those judges who had displayed signs of impartiality, in particular Olivier Lefèvre d'Ormesson, a relative of Madame de Sévigné.[32]

When the preliminary proceedings were complete, not without much delay and procrastination, the accused was, on 14 November 1664, brought before the Chamber, which was sitting in the Arsenal rather than the Palais de Justice. Apprised of the ups and downs of the sessions at first hand by Olivier d'Ormesson, Madame de Sévigné would relate them in her letters to Simon Arnauld de Pomponne, in exile at Verdun.[33]

Fouquet, with a perfect mastery of oratory, knew how to mitigate the impression made when the chancellor Séguier read the *projet de Saint-Mandé*, the key document put forward to support the charge of a crime against the state; he reminded Pierre Séguier that he himself during the Fronde of the princes had not been satisfied with the promise of his own eventual escape to safety (as Fouquet had been in a moment of panic), but had agreed to become the mentor of a rebel government, and, with the power as chancellor of France to call on foreign troops to support the revolt (of July 1652), he had effectively betrayed his king. At this same crucial moment, Fouquet, in his own capacity as the king's *procureur général*, had joined the sovereign at Pontoise and played a large part in the final victory of the court. Both Séguier and Fouquet's roles were well-known and fresh in the minds of the general public, but Séguier had since been forgiven by the king.

On 20 December, after hearing the two *rapporteurs*, d'Ormesson and Saint-Hélène, the Chamber stated that it was in favour of d'Ormesson's findings by a majority vote. The punishment was to be exile abroad for life.[34] Exercising his right to grant pardon in reverse, the king commuted this relatively mild sentence to life imprisonment at Pinerolo, where Fouquet would die eighteen years later, in 1680. Of the judges who had shown indulgence towards Fouquet, some, such as Roquesante and Bailly, were sent into exile, others like Pontchartrain and d'Ormesson, were forced to retire. The latter, who received a congratulatory visit from the maréchal de Turenne after the sentence, was generally held in esteem for the rest of his life.

Nicolas Fouquet had paid a high price for presuming to become Louis XIV's chief minister, thinking, like Cicero, that the best credentials for high office were to have saved the state, to be trusted by the worthies and to have given proof of his enormous talents and devotion. When his trial was in full swing, a sermon on ambition preached at the Louvre by Bossuet on 19 March 1662 called on the judges to show no mercy. Gallic theology thus sought to legitimize the political thinking of Machiavelli and Hobbes.[35]

A tragicomedy by Madame de Villedieu, performed by Molière and his troupe before the king in 1665, shows how the memory of the downfallen could be played out at court. The action of the play, *Le Favori*, is set in a mythical Spain. Moncade, the favourite of the king of Barcelona, is tormented by bouts of melancholy which even mar the delights of his castle and gardens. In reply to his prince, who reproaches him for coldness, he says:

Je suis jaloux de ma propre fortune,
Ce n'est pas moi qu'on aime, on aime vos faveurs
Et vos bienfaits, Seigneur, m'enlèvent tous les coeurs,
Ce serait pour mon âme un sujet d'allégresse;
Je sens bien qu'il est doux et glorieux pour moi
De devoir mes amis aux bontés de mon roi.
Je voudrais dans l'ardeur du zèle qui m'inspire
Que je vous dusse aussi tout l'air que je respire;
Que je ne puisse agir ni vivre que par vous,
Tant d'un devoir si cher les noeuds me semblent doux.[36]

Despite his refined expressions of servility, it turns out that Moncade has been so bold as to fall in love with the beautiful lady Lindamire of whom the king is enamoured. Moncade is sent into exile, and his cowardly friends all abandon him. Lindamire, however, confesses her love for him and brings him consolation. In a rage on learning of this the king makes up his mind to take revenge on Moncade. But then he comes to his senses, gives up Lindamire, punishes Moncade's unfaithful friends and reunites the two lovers.

All that remains of the Fouquet Affair in this charming divertissement, which delighted the king, is a witty *courrier du coeur* which strives to play down the *coup d'état* which enabled Louis XIV to become an 'absolute' sovereign. The height of injustice meted out to Fouquet, imprisoned in Pinerolo, was that it explained the cause of his downfall as an amorous rivalry with the king.

Notes

1. There is an abundant bibliography on Fouquet. The most recent synthesis by D. Dessert, *Fouquet* (Paris, 1987), sheds fresh light on the topics of wealth and finance. In addition, we have made extensive use of earlier, broader works, in particular A. Chéruel, ed., *Mémoires sur la vie publique et privée de Fouquet, surintendant des finances*, 2 vols (Paris, 1862); J. Lair, *Nicolas Fouquet, procureur général, surintendant des Finances, ministre d'Etat de Louis XIV*, 2 vols (Paris, 1890, repr. 1980); and on Fouquet's role in the art world, U.-V. Chatelain, *Le Surintendant Nicolas Fouquet, protecteur des lettres, des arts et des sciences* (Paris, 1905, repr. Geneva, 1971). O. Lefèvre d'Ormesson's *Journal*, ed. A. Chéruel, 2 vols (Paris, 1860–1) is particularly useful. We must also mention the excellent and lively synthesis, favourable to Fouquet, by G. Mongrédien, *L'Affaire Fouquet* (Paris 1956). Lastly, see Richard Bonney's recent article, 'The Fouquet–Colbert Rivalry and the "Revolution" of 1661', in Keith Cameron and Elizabeth Woodrough, eds, *Ethics and Politics in Seventeenth-Century France* (Exeter, 1996), pp. 107–18.
2. According to the account by the clerk Foucault mentioned in Chéruel, ed., *Mémoires*, ii, p. 243.
3. 'Elégie pour M. F[ouquet] ou Elégie aux Nymphes de Vaux, pour le malheureux Oronte', in Jean de La Fontaine, *Oeuvres: sources et postérité, d'Esope à l'Oulipo*, ed. A. Versaille, preface by M. Fumaroli (Brussels, 1995), p. 158.
4. A quotation by Firenzuola from the *Vocabolario degli Accademici della Crusca . . .* (Venice, 1612) corroborates the definition of the favourite: 'Abbiti cura della invidia, la quale come palla di sapone, si mette sotto i piedi dei favoriti'. And in Furetière's *Dictionnaire*, La Bruyère is quoted in support of the definition of the illusory favour of monarchs and great men: 'On voit des hommes que le vent de la faveur pousse d'abord à pleines voiles, et à qui elle fait perdre la terre de vue en un moment' (*Dictionnaire universel* (1st edn, 1690; numerous later editions)).

5. The word never appeared in official political discourse, at least not in France. A highly significant passage from P. Bouhours is quoted in Furetière's *Dictionnaire*: 'Les favoris n'ont aucune relation directe avec le public. Toutes leurs fonctions ne regardent que la vie privée du Prince.'

6. G. Budé, *De Asse*, edition used: *Opera omnia*, 5 vols (Basel, 1557, repr. London, 1966), ii, pp. 302–3.

7. [P. Dupuy], 'Mémoires et instructions pour servir à justifier l'innocence de Messire François-Auguste de Thou . . . ', in J.-A. de Thou, *Histoire universelle*, x: *Pièces* (The Hague, 1740), p. 661. It is highly likely that the *Mémoires* were known and circulated in manuscript form.

8. [P. Dupuy], *Histoire des plus illustres favoris anciens et modernes* (Leiden, 1660). Few copies of this work remain.

9. On Fouquet's ambition and his clash with Colbert, see Dessert, *Fouquet*, pp. 232–8.

10. On the nomination of both *surintendants*, see Chéruel, ed., *Mémoires*, ii, pp. 226–38.

11. This was a real project for the re-establishment of the finances, but in establishing a *chambre de justice* he programmed Fouquet's downfall. Fouquet was informed of the project thanks to Gourville and kept a copy; exhibited during Fouquet's trial, it saved him from the death sentence: cf. J. Hérauld de Gourville, *Mémoires*, ed. L. Lecestre, Société de l'Histoire de France, 2 vols (Paris, 1894), i, pp. 153–5. Colbert's plan was edited by P. Clément in *Les Lettres, instructions et mémoires de Colbert*, 8 vols (Paris, 1861–82), vii, pp. 164–83.

12. Dessert has made a good analysis of this aspect of Fouquet's 'necessary sacrifice' as the price to be paid for cleansing Mazarin's memory: *Fouquet*, pp. 231–9.

13. Chéruel, who was not in favour of Fouquet, could not help concluding the first chapter of his *Mémoires*, i, p. 47, on Fouquet's early career with the remark: 'Sans nous faire illusion sur les causes qui déterminèrent le procureur général à s'attacher à Mazarin, nous ne pouvons qu'applaudir à la fidélité avec laquelle il le servit dans la mauvaise comme dans la bonne fortune.'

14. 'J'ai grand déplaisir', he wrote, 'de voir les serviteurs de Votre Excellence déchus de l'espérance qu'ils avaient eue de la voir présentement rentrer dans l'autorité avec l'agrément et la satisfaction de tous les peuples, du consentement des princes, et du Parlement, et dans la réjouissance d'une paix si universellement souhaitée': Chéruel, ed., *Mémoires*, ii, p. 183, letter dated October 1652.

15. What Dessert would call 'le lobby Fouquet', the title of one of his chapters: *Fouquet*, pp. 137–96.

16. Dessert has reproduced the 'Projet de Saint-Mandé' in an appendix to his work, *ibid.*, pp. 354–62. On its composition, see Chéruel, ed., *Mémoires*, ii, pp. 360–4.

17. First, he addressed the chancellor: 'Monsieur, je vous ai fait assembler avec mes ministres et mes secrétaires d'Etat pour vous dire que jusqu'à présent, j'ai bien voulu laisser gouverner mes affaires par feu M. le Cardinal; il est temps que je les gouverne moi-même. Vous m'aiderez de vos conseils quand je vous les demanderai.' Then, turning to his secretaries of state, he added: 'Et vous, mes secrétaires d'Etat, je vous défends de rien signer, pas même une sauvegarde ni passeport sans mon ordre, de me rendre compte chaque jour à moi-même et de ne favoriser personne dans vos rôles du mois. Et vous, Monsieur le Surintendant, je vous ai expliqué mes volontés; je vous prie de vous servir de Colbert, que feu M. le Cardinal m'a recommandé.' L.-H. de Loménie, comte de Brienne called le jeune Brienne, *Mémoires*, ed. P. Bonnefon, Société de l'Histoire de France, 3 vols (Paris, 1919), iii, p. 36. An earlier, more restrained account of the meeting is also to be found in the *Mémoires: ibid.*, ii, pp. 56–60.

18. See Dessert, *Fouquet*, pp. 48–9.

19. The Abbé de Choisy has preserved the memory of his request for pardon to which Fouquet alluded on several occasions in his *Deffenses*. On the evening before his arrest, 'il conta à Brienne qu'á Fontainebleau il avait représenté au Roi que le Cardinal faisant tout à sa tête, et sans observer aucune formalité, il lui avait fait faire beaucoup de choses dont il pourrait être recherché que lui en son particulier avait aussi fait des fautes considérables, et des dépenses excessives; et que pour mettre sa conscience et son honneur en sûreté, il suppliait le Roi de lui pardonner tout le passé, et qu'il était persuadé que sa majesté aveu eu la bonté de le faire . . . ': Abbé de Choisy, *Mémoires pour servir à l'histoire de Louis XIV*, ed. G. Mongrédien, coll. 'Le temps retrouvé' (Paris, 1979), p. 98.

20. The sale of the office to François Harlay de Champvallon for the sum of 1,400,000 livres, of which Fouquet immediately offered the king 1,000,000, put him in debt, but he thought it would open the way to the highest honours: cf. Dessert, *Fouquet*, p. 240: 'Il y a là tout Fouquet: le panache, la passion de la gloire, le besoin de se faire valoir l'emporte sur tout autre considération.' His contemporaries were well aware of what was at stake. For instance, on 12 July 1661, before anything had been settled, Guy Patin wrote: 'Je viens d'apprendre que M. Fouquet a vendu sa charge. . . . On prétend par là qu'il est fort en crédit près du roi . . . qu'il sera ministre d'Etat ou Chancelier

de France, si la corde ne rompt; mais d'autres soupçonnent pis.' Letter quoted by Chéruel, ed., *Mémoires*, ii, pp. 177–8.

21. Serious mistakes had been made early on in the proceedings which moved even those in charge: cf. Chéruel, ed., *Mémoires*, ii, pp. 271–88. Mongrédien, ed., *Mémoires*, pp. 81–96, gives a good summary.

22. On this reversal of events, see an analysis of the manuscript sources in Mongrédien, ed., *Mémoires*, pp. 96–116, 'L'opposition naissante à Colbert'.

23. Chéruel, ed., *Mémoires*, ii, pp. 386–410, points out the role played by Hesnault, Loret, Corneille, La Fontaine and Racine in the case of Fouquet and Pellisson. See also Chatelain, *Le Surintendant Nicolas Fouquet*.

24. They consist of Dupuy's 'Mémoires et instructions', referred to and extensively quoted by Giuliano Ferretti in his edition of Philippe Fortin de la Hoguette's *Lettres aux frères Dupuy et à leur entourage (1623–1662)*, Corrispondenze letterarie, scientifiche ed erudite dal Rinascimento all'età moderna, vol. vii (Florence, 1997), pp. 56–8, 441–2, 444–5.

25. *Ibid.*, p. 661: 'L'esprit du Cardinal enflé d'une si souveraine et absolue autorité, recevoit avec joie les flatteries infâles de tant de petits Poëtes affamés, de tant de plumes vénérables, de tant de misérables panégyristes qui l'ont élevé par dessus tous les mortels, l'ont fait égal à Dieu, et à tout ce qu'il y a de plus saint et vénérable parmi les hommes. Cet esprit si corrompu et altéré par ces continuelles flatteries, ignorait qu'il n'y a que les mauvais Princes et les Tyrans qui se plaisent à ces vaines et fausses louanges.'

26. Cf. L. Petit, 'Autour du procès Fouquet, La Fontaine et son oncle Jannart sous la griffe de Colbert', in *Revue d'histoire littéraire de la France* (1947), pp. 193–210.

27. In his *Etude sur la vie et les oeuvres de Pellison* (Paris, 1859), F. L. Marcou analyses the 'Discours au Roy par un de ses fidèles sujets, sur le procès de M. Fouquet, ou première défense de M. Fouquet', the 'Seconde défense de M. Fouquet', the 'Considérations sommaires sur le procès de M. Fouquet' and the 'Suite des Considérations . . . '.

28. Here is an example of his oratory, quoted by Marcou, *ibid.*, p. 221: 'Ils [les intendants] sont innocents; cependant c'est M. Fouquet qui est criminel, parce qu'il a fait pour des millions, tout à la fois, ce que les autres faisaient pour cent mille écus, parce qu'en son temps la nécessité a été plus grande, qu'il a été plus pressé, qu'on l'ai traité avec plus d'empire, qu'il a mieux obéi, mieux servi, qu'il a eu plus de soumission, plus de courage, dites, si vous voulez, plus de témérité, plus d'imprudence; mais je ne le dirai pas, ni son zèle ne le mérite, ni la bonté et la justice du roi ne semblent le permettre.'

29. Quoted in Mongrédien, ed., *Mémoires*, pp. 114–15: 'Pendant que le roi décharge sa conscience sur les juges, les juges déclarent qu'ils obéissent aux ordres du roi. Mais ce qui va étonner Paris, la France, l'Europe, c'est que Colbert ait eu la hardiesse d'assister au conseil, comme juge de mon mari, lui qu'on sait publiquement être sa plus véritable partie, que personne n'ignore avoir depuis six ans été son adversaire déclaré, avoir inspiré tout ce qu'il a pu de chimérique et de faux contre lui: premièrement, à son Eminence . . . puis à Votre Majesté, où son emploi lui donne moyen d'être à toute heure; pouvaient servir à la justification de mon mari . . . lui qui s'est expliqué, non pas une fois mais plus de cent, comme j'offre de le prouver et vérifier à Votre Majesté . . . que mon mari méritait la mort. . . . '

30. All these papers have been gathered together in *Les oeuvres de M. Fouquet, ministre d'Etat, contenant son arrestation, son procès et ses défenses, contre Louis XIV, roi de France*, 16 vols (Paris, 1668, re-edited 1696). On the impression made by the circulation of these documents during the preliminary investigation, see Mongrédien, ed., *Mémoires*, pp. 119 and 125.

31. The journey lasted from August to November 1663 and, as we know, was the source of La Fontaine's *Relation d'un voyage de Paris en Limousin*.

32. On the pressure exerted directly by Colbert on André d'Ormesson and his son Olivier, who lost the *intendance* of Soissonnais, see the son's *Journal*, ii, p. 139, where he writes: 'M'ôter l'intendance de Soissons, c'était me faire honneur et se charger de honte, en faisant croire que l'on désirait des choses injustes et que j'avais assez d'honneur pour y résister. . . . ' The role of this honest magistrate was capital for the outcome of the trial: cf. Mongrédien, ed., *Mémoires*, pp. 184–91; Dessert, *Fouquet*, pp. 257–62.

33. For example, on 3 December, she wrote to her correspondent: 'Notre cher et malheureux ami a parlé deux heures ce matin, mais si admirablement bien que plusieurs n'ont pu s'empêcher de l'admirer. M. Renard entre autres a dit: "Il faut avouer que cet homme est incomparable; il n'a jamais si bien parlé dans le Parlement; il se possède mieux qu'il n'a jamais fait"': Mme de Sévigné, *Correspondance*, ed. R. Duchêne, Bibliothèque de la Pléiade, 3 vols, i (Paris, 1972), p. 68.

34. 'Tout Paris', the magistrate relates in his *Journal*, 'attendait cette nouvelle avec impatience . . . elle fut répandue en même temps partout et reçue avec une joie extrême, même parmi les plus petites gens des boutiques, chacun donnant mille bénédictions à mon nom sans me connaître. Ainsi M. Fouquet, qui avait été en horreur lors de sa prison, et que tout Paris eût vu exécuté avec joie incontinent après son procès commencé, est devenu le sujet de la douleur et de la commisération publiques par la haine que tout le monde a dans le coeur contre le gouvernement présent, et c'est la véritable cause de l'applaudissement général . . . ': Lefèvre d'Ormesson, *Journal*, ii, pp. 283–4.

35. 'Assur s'est élevé . . . comme les cèdres du Liban; le ciel l'a nourri de sa rosée, la terre l'a engraissé de sa substance; les puissances l'ont comblé de leurs bienfaits, et il suçait de son côté le sang du peuple. C'est pourquoi il s'est élevé, superbe en sa hauteur, étendu en ses branches, fertile en ses rejetons . . . un grand nombre de ses créatures, et les grands, et les petits, étaient attachés à sa fortune; ni les cèdres, ni les pins, c'est-à-dire les plus grands de la Cour ne l'égalaient pas . . . ': sermon quoted in Jean Meyer, *Colbert* (Paris, 1981), p. 79.

36. Madame de Villedieu, *Oeuvres*, 3 vols (Paris, 1720), acte I, scène 6, p. 163.

16
The Demise of the Minister–Favourite, or a Political Model at Dusk: The Austrian Case

JEAN BÉRENGER

This chapter considers the reasons why the office of chief minister was quickly suppressed in western Europe after the so-called 'French revolution of 1661', the year that Louis XIV (pl. 58) established his personal monarchy. Under the system of the chief minister, royal favour was appropriated by an individual, his family and his supporters. The system was ineluctably connected with the wider phenomena of clientage and the court favourite, and for this reason was unacceptable to the aristocracy and the higher clergy who were excluded from political and financial power. In their view, the invention of this new institution in no way improved the administration of the state. We will describe first the decline, or better the suppression, of this office, and then we will examine why it occurred by exploring the justificatory ideology of its seventeenth-century political opponents.

The 'revolution of 1661' occurred after the death of Mazarin, and comprised two moments. First, in March, the Council of State was profoundly reformed with the dismissal of the mere ministers of state, such as Turenne, and members of the royal family, like the queen mother: this moment marked the elimination of the chief-ministerial office. Later, in September, the dramatic arrest of Superintendent Fouquet, brilliantly evoked in the previous chapter by Marc Fumaroli, demonstrated that Louis XIV did not want to rule in collaboration with a new chief minister, even if the candidate had the support of public opinion. This second political crisis at the same time confirmed the emergence of the definitive ruling team which took the place of the chief minister. The new supreme council (*Conseil d'En Haut*) was a smaller, limited version of the Council of State and consisted only of three so-called ministers of state, Lionne, Le Tellier and Colbert, in place of Fouquet. This transformation of the French government represented the demise of the minister–favourite as head of the executive. Louis XIV in his *Mémoires pour l'instruction du Dauphin* explained why he had not taken over the reins of government at an earlier date:

I do not know if I should number among my faults the fact that I did not take upon myself the conduct of my state [from the beginning of my reign]. I can honestly say that this was not the result of negligence or laziness. [It was rather that] I was still quite young, albeit older than the majority of kings whose elevation has been advanced by the laws of the state to avoid greater evils, but not as old as ordinary people are when they begin to control their affairs freely.[1]

The young Louis XIV (pl. 60) did not feel himself able to manage the affairs of his kingdom; he lacked experience and he had great confidence in the capacity and fidelity of his chief minister, whom he considered his best educator and mentor. Nevertheless, he progressively found Mazarin's position a burden and awaited the time when he would be able to govern without such a figure. Although Mazarin had once promised the succession to Turenne, he changed his mind on his deathbed. Instead, he warmly recommended Louis not to replace him with another chief minister but to assume the office himself and rule with the support of some chosen councillors.[2]

The 'revolution' in France was followed four years later by a similar development in Austria on the death of Prince Ferdinand Portia (pl. 63), who had been in charge of the Viennese government from the accession of the Emperor Leopold (pl. 64) in March 1657. Portia was an aristocrat who hailed from Friuli and had had various official careers, as imperial chamberlain, as administrator of Inner Austria and even as a diplomat. His opportunity came when he was appointed to look after the education and supervise the personal court of Archduke Leopold, the younger son of the emperor Ferdinand III, who was brought up to be a future bishop. Portia was a highly educated man and he encouraged the interests of his pupil. He established good relations with the archduke, paying him the deference due a scion of the House of Austria, yet becoming a confidant of the young prince. But Portia was not a second Mazarin. He was a lazy and inexperienced statesman, who was very conservative and proved incapable of sustaining the Austrian monarchy in the serious crisis of the Turkish war of 1663–4. He encouraged his master to be a lover of music, theatre and erudition.

A brief reference to the influence and death of Portia is to be found in the life of Leopold written by the German historian Gottlieb Eucharius Rinck, who was commissioned by the imperial Diet to write an official posthumous biography of the emperor.[3] The death of the high steward and royal favourite in February 1665 seems to have led to a short political crisis which allowed the young Leopold to imitate his French cousin and carry through a political revolution. According to the ordinance of 1527, which defined the chief organs of Austrian central government, the high steward (*obrister Hofmeister*) was the premier privy councillor and chairman of the Privy Council (*Geheimer Rat*), when the emperor was not present at the meeting. In a letter to his ambassador in Madrid, Count Poetting, Leopold declared he would be his own chief minister and explained the reasons for not creating a new one. First, he was young enough to work by himself (Leopold was actually twenty-five). Secondly, he would thereby remain the master, and no other man would be able to boast that everything depended on him. Thirdly, he would be more responsible for his own decisions.[4] In another letter to his cousin at Innsbruck, Archduke Sigismund of the Tyrol, Leopold reiterated that he had taken the decision not to have a new chief minister and claimed that he would govern with the help of some members of his Privy Council.[5] A despatch of the French envoy to the Viennese court, Grémonville, also revealed Leopold's intention,[6] and another a week later from the same source confirmed that no new chief minister had been appointed but that the high steward's office had been given, after negotiations with Prince Auersperg, to Prince Lobkowitz.[7]

Had Leopold wanted to appoint another *premier ministre*, then Auersperg was an obvious choice. He was the former chief minister of the emperor Ferdinand III, in succession to Count Trautmannsdorff, and an extraordinarily talented diplomat who had been a successful negotiator at Osnabrück.[8] But in 1665 Auersperg merely retained his place as a privy councillor. This decision reflected in part the young emperor's dislike for a man considered an able minister but restless and domineering: after all, Leopold had already removed Auersperg as *premier ministre* on his accession and replaced him by his own high steward and tutor, Count Portia. But the decision also reflected court rivalry. If appointed, Auersperg would have exerted an influence upon his master which would have excluded other councillors from power and probably reinforced the authority of the so-called Spanish party.[9] The latter gave unconditional support to the declining Spanish monarchy and paid no regard to the interests of the exhausted Hereditary Lands (Bohemia and Austria), which needed peace for reconstruction.

A further factor affecting the emperor's decision, revealed by the French envoy Grémonville, was the influence of the Jesuits, especially the royal confessor Father Müller, who urged Leopold to follow the French king's example.[10] Auersperg and the Jesuits, it seems, were at daggers drawn. The Society had not forgotten the humiliations that it had once experienced at his hands and therefore supported his enemies.[11] Finally, the decision was also backed by Empress Eleonora, Leopold's stepmother, who gave her approval in a talk with the papal nuncio. Thereby, she believed, Leopold could escape the overweaning influence of a single favourite and finally benefit from the suggestions of different ministers.[12]

Like his cousin Louis XIV, Leopold wanted to conduct diplomacy himself. As Grémonville reported to his master, the emperor would in future receive foreign ambassadors personally and this important task would no longer be left to a member of the Privy Council.[13] In so doing, Leopold imitated Louis exactly, but in his case the burden was heavier because the emperor did not have at his disposal a secretary of state for foreign affairs, as had been the case in France since the beginning of the seventeenth century. For ten years, from 1665 to 1675, Leopold did try to establish such a secretary to the Privy Conference (see below) in the person of the Baron Abele von Lilienberg, but this experiment did not succeed and was abandoned. In reality, conduct of foreign policy was primarily controlled by the imperial Chancery (*die Reichskanzlei*), which dealt with both the administration of the Holy Roman Empire and diplomacy, under the aegis of an imperial vice-chancellor. But the Austrian Court Chancery (*die österreichische Hofkanzlei*) and the Council of War (*der Hofkriegsrat*) were also responsible for some areas: the latter, for instance, was in charge of relations with the Ottoman Empire.

The institutional result of the 'revolution of 1665' was the creation of the Privy Conference, which was always a part of the Privy Council and thus more akin to a Spanish *junta* than the French supreme Council of State (*Conseil d'En Haut*). The project mentioned by Grémonville in the same report – to allocate a department to each minister of the conference – was never realized. Leopold would give ministers the task of studying a particular piece of business, consulting with colleagues and writing reports purely on an *ad hoc* basis. A report would usually receive the emperor's approbation with the words 'placet wie gerathen'.[14] Leopold chose the members of the Privy Conference from among the privy councillors, but their number was always few, only five or six according to the first description of the institution given by the Swedish diplomat Esaias Pufendorf in 1674. Initially they were four: Prince Wenzel Lobkowitz, the new high steward; Prince Weikhard Auersperg; Count Johann Lamberg, a personal friend of the emperor who was promoted lord high chamberlain (*Oberstkämmerer*); and Prince Johann Schwarzenberg, who was chairman of the Imperial High Court (*Reichshofsrat*). None was head of a department. They were then joined by the chairman of the War Council and the Austrian court chancellor.

Transforming Austria into a personal monarchy in the French mould was never going to be easy because the political structures of the two monarchies were so different. The Austrian monarchy was never a centralized and absolute state where the dynasty was served by a relatively devoted administration. Austria in the seventeenth century remained a confederation of states where the landed aristocracy ruled their peasantry without interference. Since the Habsburg victory at the Battle of the White Mountain, the emperors had been able to rule over the Hereditary Lands and the Bohemian crown lands with little restriction, but Hungary jealously guarded its self-government.[15] Political power there belonged to the aristocracy, who dominated the local Diets and the Viennese councils and chanceries which dealt with Hungarian affairs largely unchallenged. In consequence, they had plenty of opportunity to influence Habsburg foreign policy, for instance by restricting financial help.[16]

Nevertheless, Leopold stuck to his resolution of February 1665. He always refused to give his new high steward, Prince Lobkowitz, the title of chief minister, and stayed faithful throughout his reign (forty years) to the system of the Privy Conference, although its inefficiency became obvious to foreign observers in the coming years. In 1669, for example, the nuncio Pignatelli claimed that nobody in the government was able to put the decisions of the Privy Conference into effect because the emperor was unable to manage diplomacy and administration.[17] Two years later, the Venetian ambassador wrote to the Senate complaining about the lack of a chief minister: 'The feebleness and the negligence of an Emperor who amuses and diverts himself means there is no one who keeps a cold eye on affairs of state. . . . There is here neither a chief minister nor a responsible councillor. The prince's good will offers no resistance to artifice; his goodness is incapable of knowing the disorders of the state.'[18]

Even on the eve of the second Austro-Turkish War, a period of real tension, Leopold steadfastly refused to give the position of chief minister to his confidant and confessor, Father Sinelli, the newly promoted Bishop of Vienna, although the latter had been privately counselling the emperor on political matters for more than ten years. As a report to Louis XIV from the French resident at the imperial court, the marquis de Sébeville, makes clear, Sinelli had been angling for the office for some time and was expected to succeed in his quest. Leopold's refusal to take the bait speaks volumes for the emperor's hostility to re-establishing a position he could not tolerate:

Monsieur the Bishop of Vienna has been appointed a councillor of state the day before yesterday and all the evidence suggests that we will soon see him in charge of the Council, although the Emperor is hostile. For some time the Bishop has been encouraging different individuals to complain to the Emperor about the drift in the state's affairs, to make clear that things will not improve unless someone is given the power to lean on those who are entrusted with their discharge and to make them accountable, and to point out that the Emperor cannot get involved in this kind of detail unless someone keeps him informed and lets him know who is doing their duty.[19]

By this time the system of the minister–favourite was roundly condemned by European public opinion. Noblemen, clerics and princes considered it a manifestation of tyranny and a usurpation of the power of the absolute monarchy. The only state where the system remained intact, apart from Muscovy, was the Ottoman Empire, which was considered to be the epitome of tyranny and slavery anyway and was seen as a state where a man of obscure (and unfree) origin could substitute his own authority for that of the legitimate and all-powerful sultan.

The decline of the institution in the 1660s is easily explicable in the light of the many contemporary critiques of the office that promoted this negative view. Much more than Olivares, it was Richelieu (pls 26 and 47–57) who came to symbolize the unacceptable face of the minister–favourite. For instance, one of the main and most brilliant protagonists of the Fronde, Paul de Gondi, from 1651 Cardinal de Retz, went so far as to accuse the cardinal of treason in his *Mémoires*. He compared Richelieu to a Turkish grand vizier, to the

Merovingian mayors of the palace and to the counts of Paris at the end of the Carolingian dynasty. In all these cases royal authority was usurped: the grand vizier was actually in charge of imperial affairs; the mayors of the palace took over the throne at the expense of the legitimate rulers; while Hugues Capet, Count of Paris, replaced the Carolingian usurpers with his own dynasty, which was still ruling France in the seventeenth century.

We know today, through the work of modern French historians, that it is an exaggeration to consider Richelieu a usurper or a mayor of the palace handling state affairs in the place of a lazy king. No one now would accept Cardinal de Retz's assertion that Richelieu 'formed in the most legitimate of monarchies the most scandalous and dangerous of tyrannies which has perhaps ever enslaved a state'.[20] This myth of the lazy king ('le roi fainéant') was given substance by the seventeenth-century historian Mézeray, but it seems to have been common currency soon after Louis XIII's death. Louis XIV in his *Mémoires* (written in the 1660s for the benefit of the dauphin) claimed that even as a young boy he had been shocked by the evocation of the image. Retz maintained that Richelieu, far from reforming the French state, put his own favourites and relatives in the best offices of the royal administration. Moreover, with the creation of the provincial *intendants*, he consolidated his reputation as a tyrant because his subordinates in local government (in fact no more than thirty individuals) were his creatures, who controlled without the least spark of compassion the subjects of Louis XIII – noblemen, clerics or members of the Third Estate.[21] They mercilessly executed the instructions drafted by Richelieu and were always ready to behead rebels ('faire tomber des têtes').[22] In training Louis XIV for kingship, Mazarin insisted upon the dangerous effect of alienating royal power. In theory the chief minister was under the king's control, but in reality he was independent of or even usurped royal authority. According to Mazarin, it was not right that a minister should build up his own clientele by distributing offices, pensions or honours to his own favourites. He recommended the young king to govern with the help of the Council of State but to be its master, taking decisions alone after a discussion without being obliged by a vote of the councillors.

Emperor Leopold was educated according to the same principles. Leopold, too, was taught that the main duty of the sovereign was to make the chief decisions himself, but he had wait until the death of Portia in 1665. The reform he carried through in 1665 was inspired by two confidential documents, produced for earlier Habsburg archdukes. The first is the *Princeps in compendio*, which was written for the future Ferdinand III, and the other a memorandum by Prince Gundacker von Liechtenstein, which was intended to instruct the elder brother of Leopold I, the Archduke Ferdinand.[23]

The *Princeps in compendio* belongs to the 'Mirror of Princes' tradition of political theory (in German *Fürstenspiegel*) that dates back to the Middle Ages. It was written at the request of Emperor Ferdinand II, probably by his clerical favourite, Father Lamormaini, a Jesuit. The latter was officially the confessor of the sovereign and was the inspiration behind the Edict of Restitution of 1629, which brought so much trouble and unrest to the Holy Roman Empire. The work was probably composed in 1632. In 1668 Leopold, after the birth of his first son Archduke Ferdinand (who died a few months later), ordered a second edition of about ten copies.

The tenth chapter of the pamphlet, *De intimo principis*, clearly condemned the institution of the chief minister. The king was not to rely on an all-powerful minister, although Father Lamormaini did distinguish between an honest councillor who could be asked to state his opinion on important matters of government and an evil adviser who abused his influence. Father Lamormaini declared himself hostile to royal favourites because the prince became a puppet in the hands of his creature and could not take any decision himself. The sovereign in the Jesuit's eyes had the right to ask advice from his councillors of state but he had first to choose the questions he wanted discussed and was to keep the processes of giving advice and taking decisions separate. To avoid one minister becoming dominant, the sovereign was to consult in turn each councillor or minister of state at the ordinary meetings of the Imperial Privy Council.

Ten years later an aristocrat composed the second memorandum. Gundacker of Liechtenstein was a privy councillor and the younger brother of Prince Karl of Liechtenstein, the governor of Bohemia after the Battle of the White Mountain, and the man responsible for the merciless repression of the defeated Czech nobility. Both were stalwart supporters of the Habsburgs and the Counter-Reformation, but Gundacker's career was less brilliant than his elder brother's. Like many other Austrian aristocrats, Gundacker of Liechtenstein was a man of good education and culture. Born in 1580, he was originally a Protestant, who studied law and philology at the universities of Basel, Padua and Bologna. He became a Roman Catholic in 1602 and remained thereafter firm in his new faith, refusing in 1609 to endorse Rudolf II's *Letter of Majesty*, which granted toleration to the emperor's Bohemian subjects. He believed that the *Letter* placed too great a constraint on royal authority in Bohemia by giving too much political advantage to the Bohemian estates (comprising the nobility, gentry and the free cities). Gundacker was a specialist in financial matters. As early as 1606 he was appointed councillor of the Court Chamber (*kaiserliche Hofkammer*) or Imperial Treasury and he became its chairman in 1620. As a result, he then became responsible for the financial administration of the whole Austrian monarchy and member of the Privy Council. But his efforts to put the emperor's finances in order at the beginning of the Thirty Years War were unsuccessful and he resigned his chairmanship before the bankruptcy of 1624 (the famous so-called *Münzcalada*). He was nevertheless appointed lord high steward in 1629 and chairman of the Imperial Privy Council, thereby becoming the virtual head of the state apparatus. However, he gave up his office after two years and retired to his large estates in Silesia, rarely taking any further part in the discussions of the Privy Council. In 1636 Ferdinand II called him back to Vienna and made him his chief minister, but again Gundacker surrendered his office, this time to Trautmannsdorff, who occupied it until his death in 1649. In retirement Gundacker turned his attention to political theory. In 1642 he wrote his own *Fürstenspiegel*, entitled 'Gutachten über die Edukation eines jungen Fürsten'.

In this memorandum, Gundacker condemned absolutely the recourse to favourites and recommended that the emperor employ a team of ministers who would study separately the problems of state entrusted to them. It was Gundacker's view that, even if a powerful prince has a servant in his court who enjoyed his master's particular confidence, it was still not possible for that prince to place every matter of state in the hands of a single individual. The emperor must divide the burdens and responsibility of government according to the knowledge and abilities of each minister. When the problem was discussed before the Privy Council, the minister in charge of the affair should read his report first and only then should the other members present express their opinions.[24]

In conclusion, of course, the emperor was invited to put these recommendations into effect. What Gundacker of Liechtenstein proposed in his memorandum was the system Emperor Leopold actually used after 1665. The memorandum demanded a modernization of the system of collegiate government which was in harmony with the aspirations of the Austrian aristocracy and the balance of power in the Habsburg monarchy.

In 1682, when Emperor Leopold was subjected to pressure from Father Sinelli to restore the office of chief minister, another Austrian aristocrat, Count Johann Quintin Jörger, wrote a further sharp critique of the abolished institution. Jörger was the author of a critical history of the Austrian monarchy which remained unpublished in the Viennese archives. In this work, he remarked on the numerous failures and mistakes of the Austrian government; instead, he preferred the collegiate form of government. Like Gundacker, Count Jörger was a distinguished member of the Imperial Court Chamber, where he was successively councillor and deputy chairman, although never a minister of the Privy Conference. He was later appointed governor of Lower Austria (*niederösterreichischer Staathalter*) and was a participant in many executive commissions of the Privy Council.[25]

Jörger's manuscript, which was judged controversial, was confiscated and today still lies in the Austrian State Archives at Vienna under the title 'Different Matters' (*Unterschiedliche Motiven*). In the chapter 'Against chief ministers' ('Excerptiones contra primos Aulae ministros'), he quoted four reasons for abolishing the office. First, a chief minister is not capable of handling all government matters from his own knowledge ('Ministrum sua Scientia non posse cuncta complecti'). Second, chief ministers know no restraint and are the victims of their passions. They become veritable tyrants who use informers, kill illegally ('occidunt praeter leges exemplo Cardinalis de Richelieu qui etiam Regi amantissimos interfeci curavit'), threaten privileges, make unheard-of innovations, and even chase away queen mothers ('more eiusdem Cardinalis') or determine their royal master's marriage, as did Prince Auersperg, who wanted to make the emperor his brother-in-law. Third, chief ministers exhaust the royal treasury by bestowing largesse on their own favourites at the expense of the king's subjects. And here Jörger cited examples peculiar to Austria: Liechtenstein, Trautmannsdorff and Auersperg (the three successive chief ministers from 1630 to 1657).

Fourth, chief ministers are a threat to the sovereign's authority. Here Jörger recalled all the legal indictments of fallen chief ministers and mentioned specifically the dismissal of Auersperg, who was exiled by the emperor in 1669. As a minister of the Privy Conference, Auersperg was in charge of secret negotiations with the French ambassador concerning the partition of the Spanish empire on the expected death of Charles II.[26] These negotiations were a success for French diplomacy in that the Austrian heir to the Spanish empire admitted the rights of Maria-Theresa, Queen of France, notwithstanding her formal renunciation of any dynastic claim in 1659. Auersperg hoped that he would be rewarded by France by being made a cardinal at the next promotion and that his new dignity would lead to his gaining the office of chief minister in preference to Prince Lobkowitz. Unfortunately, he was not supported by Louis XIV, who instead asked the pope to elevate the nephew of Turenne, Cardinal de Bouillon. Auersperg's machinations were then revealed and Emperor Leopold ordered him to retire to one of his Carinthian estates. His public career thus came to an end, although he was never impeached, unlike Cardinal Klesl in 1618 at the beginning of the reign of Ferdinand II. Obviously Auersperg was no favourite of Leopold's, as we have seen. But he was not the only minister to be rusticated by Leopold. Prince Lobkowitz in turn was later exiled to his Bohemian estates in 1674, when his pro-French foreign policy was abandoned in favour of participation in the Franco-Dutch War.

Jörger's argument was clever. First of all, he refuted the essential premise on which justifications of the office of chief minister were based: that the chief minister would be a man of extraordinary intellect who would understand all governmental matters and be an inestimable prop to the prince. He then moved on to discuss the two-fold accusation of tyranny and usurpation. For Jörger the model of a tyrant seems to have been Richelieu, as described by Cardinal de Retz: his chief reproach was directed against the cardinal–minister's judicial execution of Cinq Mars and the exile of the queen mother, Marie de Médicis. He thus followed exactly Retz's Black Legend and ignored the fact that Cinq Mars was not just Richelieu's foe but a conspirator who had negotiated with the Spanish government over ending the war. Cinq Mars was nothing but a traitor and Louis XIII did not need the prompting of his cardinal–minister to send his favourite to the block.[27] Again, in the delicate matter of the relations between Louis XIII, his mother and his chief minister, it was Marie de Médicis who refused to be reconciled after the Day of Dupes, left the French court and fled to the Low Countries, where she hoped to gain support from the Infanta Isabella and her father Philip IV of Spain. When Jörger discussed the charge of usurpation he generally chose Austrian examples. In Vienna, as in Paris, chief ministers created a clientele using public funds, which were even more mismanaged than in France. As an administrator at the Treasury, Jörger had access to the files and knew his facts: he had himself led an enquiry to uncover and check the abuse.

If the *haute noblesse* was on the whole opposed to the office of chief minister, the Catholic church, with the exception of the odd diplomat, was hardly more favourably inclined. Some prelates, such as Retz, were downright hostile. Admittedly, some bishops who were engaged in day-to-day political affairs, especially in the Austrian lands, seem to have wanted a ministerial intermediary with whom they could negotiate quickly and efficiently. The papacy, however, never forgot its difficulties with Richelieu, while the Jesuits seem to have rejected the institution early on, particularly if it is accepted that the *Princeps in compendio* was written by Father Lamormaini. By 1660 Jesuit hostility to the office of chief minister was indisputable. Father Müller, Leopold's confessor, was a quiet man and a scholar, who did not interfere in politics unless the interests of Roman Catholicism were at stake. After 1670 he played an important part in the emperor's attempt to impose the Counter-Reformation on Royal Hungary (that part of the kingdom not under Turkish administration). Yet in the mid-1660s there can be no doubt, as we saw, that he played an important role in persuading the emperor not to appoint a successor to Portia.

It would be interesting to know what the official policy of the Society of Jesus was to the office of chief minister, the theoretical framework in which that policy was couched, and, most of all, what suggestions in case of need were made to the provincials of the order and to royal confessors. What were the motives informing the Society's position? Were they tactical or moral? Did the Jesuits fear the hostility of some chief ministers towards the Society or towards the Counter-Reformation that the order was defending? Did the office of chief minister run counter to the Jesuits' conception of the Christian prince? All these questions can be properly answered only after lengthy immersion in the Rome archives in search of a pan-European solution to the problem.

The Jansenists (always, it must be recalled, a tendency within the church and the French nation, not an institutionally grounded party) never stopped condemning the office of chief minister for moral reasons. The eminent historian of Jansenism in Lorraine and France, René Taveneaux, has demonstrated that the disciples of the Bishop of Ypres were not really political animals. They did, though, have their own opinions on contemporary political problems.[28] It is well known that in France the opposition between the Jansenists and the royal government dated from Richelieu's imprisonment in the Bastille of the founding father of the movement, the abbé de Saint-Cyran, where he remained until the cardinal died. In Richelieu's eyes the early Jansenists were a clerical and judicial elite who were hostile to the all-powerful authority of the state and the absolute monarchy. They in turn came to see the holder of the chief ministerial office as a potential tyrant.

This was the point of view still defended by the abbé Duguet at the extreme end of the seventeenth century. The Oratorian Jacques-Joseph Duguet was a friend of Arnauld and Quesnel. He played a leading role in the Jansenist party and on many occasions successfully counselled moderation. He alone, with Pascal and Nicole, wrote directly about politics. At the request of the abbé de Tamié he wrote a book entitled *De l'institution du prince* for the educational benefit of the heir to the duchy of Savoy.[29] Written in 1699 the book was only published much later at Leiden in 1739 and then was quickly banned in France by Cardinal Fleury for its unequivocal, albeit moderate condemnation of the office of chief minister. Nonetheless the work enjoyed a success comparable to that of Fénelon's *Aventures de Télémaque*.

In the chapter 'Un prince habile et prudent n'a point de premier ministre', Duguet dealt frankly with the problem. He criticized implicitly the role played by Richelieu in granting ministries, offices and gifts to his creatures and he took up the theme of 'lazy' kings ('les rois fainéants'). Like Jörger in Austria, he went so far as to accuse Richelieu of conducting an aggressive foreign policy in order to make himself indispensable. His critique of the cardinal–minister's tyranny was admittedly more discreet, but its general thrust was just as cutting. He concluded the chapter with a condemnation of rule by chief minister even where the favourite was upright and capable.

The sole precaution that prudence can deploy is to place all ministers on an equal footing under the prince, ensure that they are subject to him alone, and not confuse two apparently similar things: full confidence and complete authority. A good man may merit perfect trust but a good man can never be worthy of the prince entrusting his authority to him. And if the prince has a weakness in that direction, not only must he not abuse it, but he must employ all his efforts to prevent himself being degraded by such an act of alienation. If a prince does otherwise he fails in one of his most essential duties.[30]

What is remarkable about the works cited above is the similar structure of their arguments, even though most were not published until the eighteenth century or not published at all. It might be possible, of course, to discover a common textual source for the personal and isolated ruminations of a Louis XIV or a Jörger on the office of chief minister by hunting in better-known literary texts, but in our opinion this would be to miss their point. Do they not represent the shared reaction of different members of Europe's political class when faced by a usurper who has got his hands on the helm of state with the support of his creatures and threatens the prince as much as traditional elites? The chief-ministerial system threatened the monarchy as much as the section of the nobility excluded from power and the wealth accruing from office and service.

At the beginning of the seventeenth century this system was perhaps a positive innovation, designed to make life easier for a lazy or immature sovereign. But the system was quickly and rightly condemned for leading to tyranny and usurpation: both nobles and commoners were its victims and the king its fall-guy. In an age when the monarch was the incarnation of the state, political commentators accused the chief minister of being a barrier between the king and his subjects (like the Ottoman grand vizier). After 1650, these criticisms continued to multiply as all sections of the governing elite felt frustrated by the existence of an individual who deprived them of political power. In consequence, an ideology hostile to the chief-ministerial system was developed, which was shared by princes, clergy, nobles and officials. All these different sections of the governing class felt, albeit indistinctly, that the chief minister was one of their own number who had managed to monopolize political power and its financial advantages for his own benefit. Instead of hundreds of families taking their turn in enjoying the fruits of office and power, there was only one: the *familia* of the chief minister, a clan of relatives and clients who could count on picking up benefices and honours. However, in France, after the 'revolution of 1661', there was but one clientele, the king's, and this fact undoubtedly helped to restore the state's authority. That was the main reason why the new model was adopted by other monarchs, particularly the Austrian emperor, and why the phenomenon of the favourite as chief minister and head of the royal council largely disappeared.

Notes

1. *Mémoires pour les années 1661 et 1666*, ed. Jean Longnon (Paris, 1927), p. 53.
2. 'Mémoire dont le Roy mesme dicta la substance au sieur Rose, secrétaire de son cabinet, et relut tous les articles après les avoir fait entendre en sa présence en la forme ci-dessus', in *Lettres, instructions et mémoires de Colbert* (Paris, 1861), i, p. 535.
3. 'Den 7 Febr. Vormittage zwischen 9. Und 10. Uhr starb des Kaysers Mignon und Obrister hofmeiszter Johann Ferdinand Fürst von Portia, welcher bis anhero des Kaysers Herze in Händen gehabt hatte': G. E. Rinck, *Leopolds des Grossen . . . Leben und Thaten* (Leipzig, 1708), ii, p. 117. Details of his career are given on p. 118.
4. Emperor Leopold to Poetting, Vienna, 18 February 1665, in *Fontes Rerum Austriacarum, Diplomataria*, ed. A. F. Pribram, lvii, 'Denn erstens bin ich noch jung und kann arbeiten, zweitens bleibe ich Herr und kann ein anderer nicht vantieren, dass alles von ihm dependiere, und drittens kann ich besser verantworten, dann alles ich mir selbst attribuierne kann.'
5. Renner, *Wien im Jahre 1683* (Vienna, 1883), p. 6: Leopold declared he would 'nun keinen ersten Minister mehr zu bestellen, sondern sein eigener primado zu sein, und nur einige Räthe beizuziehen'.
6. Grémonville to Louis XIV, Vienna, 19 February 1665: 'On dit pourtant que l'empereur veut établir cinq ministres, qui auront chacun leur département, et qu'il n'y aura plus de premier ministre': see Archives des Affaires étrangères, Paris, Correspondance politique, Autriche [hereafter AAE], vol. 20, fol. 233.
7. Grémonville to the king, Vienna, 25 February (1665): 'L'empereur n'a point fait de premier ministre. Il a seulement conféré la charge de majordome au prince de Lobkowitz'. For Auersperg's ambitions, see Rinck, *Leopolds des Grossen*, ii, p. 118. See also Adam Wolf, *Wenzel Fürst Lobkowitz* (Vienna, 1869), AAE, vol. 20, fol. 251, and H. F. Schwarz, *The Imperial Privy Council* (Cambridge, Mass., 1943), pp. 143ff., 201f.

8. Schwarz, *The Imperial Privy Council*, pp. 143ff., 201f.; Grete Mecenseffy, *Im Dienste dreier Habsburger:* 'Fürst Auersperg', *Archiv für Österreichische Geschichte*, 114 (1938), pp. 225–50.

9. Grémonville to Louis XIV, 25 February: 'On lui [Leopold] fit apprendre que la force de son génie lui ferait insensiblement prendre trop d'empire sur son esprit et sur ses affaires, que quand il ne serait point premier ministre les conférences se tenant chez lui comme plus ancien conseiller d'Etat qu'il en serait comme le maître par le rapport qu'il en devrait faire, qu'il était trop partialement attaché aux Espagnols dont il rendrait Sa Majesté Impériale l'esclave.... Ces raisons jointes à l'aversion naturelle qu'Elle a pour lui le firent résoudre de conférer la charge de Majordome au prince de Lobkowitz, laissant par cette disposition le prince d'Hocsberg [*sic*] simple ministre': AAE, vol. 20, fol. 251.

10. 'Il est assez public que le Père confesseur a toujours persuadé l'Empereur de suivre l'exemple de Votre Majesté, et de ne faire aucun premier ministre. C'est bien jusqu'icy son intention d'user de même': *ibid.*

11. 'Les Jésuites ayant dans les ministères passés expérimenté les rigueurs du Prince Auersberg [*sic*] se sont joints aux ennemys de celluy-ci et ont tant fait que l'Empereur luy a donné l'exclusion, l'ayant persuadé de prendre luymesme la direction de ses affaires à l'exemple du Roy': *ibid.*, fol. 263.

12. Declaration of the Empress Eleonora, widow of Ferdinand III, to the nuncio apostolic in October 1665: see A. Levinson, ed., 'Nuntiaturberichte aus Deutschland', *Archiv für Österreichische Geschichte*, 103 (1913), p. 787.

13. Grémonville to the king, Vienna, 25 February: 'L'ambassadeur de Venise qui eut audience avant-hier, me dit qu'il avait demandé à l'empereur auquel ministre il se devait adresser pour ne se point rendre importun à Sa Majesté, il lui répliqua qu'il vînt à sa propre personne': AAE, vol. 20, fol. 250.

14. Report from the nuncio at Vienna, 12 August 1665: see A. Levinson, ed., 'Nuntiaturberichte aus Deutschland, im 17 Jahrhundert', *Archiv für Österreichische Geschichte*, 105 (1918), p. 241.

15. J. Bérenger, 'La Hongrie des Habsbourg au XVIIe siècle: république nobiliaire ou monarchie limitée?', *Revue historique*, 483 (1987) pp. 31–50.

16. J. Bérenger, *Finances et absolutisme autrichien dans la seconde moitié du XVIIe siècle* (Paris, 1975).

17. Nuncio's report 12 August 1665, in Levinson, ed., 'Nuntiaturberichte', p. 241.

18. Despatch of ambassador Cornaro to the Venetian senate, 15 August 1667: Archivio di Stato, Venice, Senato, Segreta, Dispacci da Germania, filza 129.

19. Sébeville to the king, Vienna, 12 April 1682: AAE, vol. 53, fol. 125.

20. Jean-François Paul de Gondi, Cardinale de Retz, *Mémoires*, ed. M. Allen (Paris, 1950), p. 65.

21. Instruction of the cardinal secretary of state to the nuncio, Scotti, 21 May 1639: see R. P. Blet, *Correspondance du nonce en France Ranuccio Scotti (1639–1641)* (Rome, 1965), p. 96.

22. 'Si Richelieu n'était fort que de la clientèle qui le suivait, cette même clientèle lui suscitait des ennemis': V.-L. Tapié, *La France de Louis XIII* (Paris, 1967), p. 286.

23. *Princeps in Compendio, hoc est puncta aliquot compendiosa quae circa Gubernationem Reipublicae observanda videntur*, 1632, published by Oswald Redlich in *Monstsblätter des Vereins für Landeskunde Nieder-Österreichs* (Vienna, 1906), pp. 105ff.; 'Gutachten des Fürsten Gundacker von Liechtenstein über Edukation eines jungen Fürsten und gute Bestellung des Geheimen Rathes', Vienna, National Bibliothek, MS 10286, fols 14–20.

24. 'Gutachten', para. 5.

25. J. Bérenger, 'Le Conseil d'état autrichien et la politique financière de l'empereur au XVIIe siècle', *Journal des Savants* (1971).

26. *Ibid.*

27. Tapié, *La France de Louis XIII*, pp. 393–6.

28. R. Taveneaux, *Jansénisme et politique* (Paris, 1965), p. 100.

29. Jacques-Joseph Duguet, *De l'institution du prince; ou traité des qualités, des vertus et des devoirs d'un souverain*, i (London, 1738).

30. *Ibid.*, pt 1, ch. xi, pp. 203–5.

17
The Last Favourite? The Case of Griffenfeld:
A Danish Perspective

KNUD J. V. JESPERSEN

Peder Griffenfeld

Peder Griffenfeld (pl. 65), the all-powerful first minister of Denmark, 1670–5, was born Peder Schumacher in 1635, the son of a well-to-do wine merchant in Copenhagen. His father was a first-generation immigrant from Germany while his mother belonged to one of the better families of the capital's bourgeoisie. Physically a weak child, he early showed himself to possess extraordinary intellectual gifts. It was only natural, therefore, that he should choose an academic career, and at the age of eighteen he graduated as a theological candidate from the University of Copenhagen.[1]

Soon afterwards he set out for a lengthy additional education abroad. His long journey took him to several German universities and on to Leiden, where he studied for two years. In 1657 he entered The Queen's College in the University of Oxford, where he specialized in constitutional law and witnessed at close quarters the restoration of the Stuart monarchy in 1660. Having spent a further couple of years in Paris, Spain and Italy he returned in 1662 to Copenhagen and soon entered the service of the absolutist king as a royal librarian and archivist. Those posts brought him into close contact with the king, Frederik III, who himself took a keen interest in scholarly matters. On the strength of this relationship he was promoted in 1665 to the post of private secretary to the king. In this capacity he was entrusted with the important task of working on the text of the Royal Law, the fundamental constitution of Danish absolutism – to my knowledge the only written absolutist constitution in Christendom. He handled this delicate task so well that the road to new and still more powerful positions was now wide open for the ambitious and talented young man.

High in royal favour he was soon entrusted with important key posts in the royal administration and the Supreme Court. At the same time he formed a warm personal friendship with Ulrik Frederik Gyldenløve, the king's natural son, who was viceroy in Norway and very influential in leading circles. This friendship protected him from his enemies at court and at the same time gave him free access to the uppermost circles in the aristocracy.

The real days of glory for Peder Schumacher dawned, however, in 1670, when Christian V succeeded his father on the throne. A powerful alliance of Schumacher, Gyldenløve and Frederik Ahlefeldt – the latter was viceroy in the duchies – persuaded the new king to dismiss the members of the court faction opposed to them. As the two viceroys had to take care of their duties in Norway and the duchies respectively, it was thus Schumacher who became the person in charge of the central administration and the key figure in Copenhagen, the real power-centre of the absolutist state – the new king being still young, inexperienced and of only moderate intelligence.

Schumacher exploited his great influence to carry through a comprehensive reorganization of the state administration, with the result that virtually all power was soon concentrated in his hands, and he alone had access to the king as his sole adviser. This unique position was exploited in several ways. In the first place, he carried through a number of much needed economic reforms after the model of the great Colbert. Secondly, he introduced several measures aimed at finally breaking the influence of the old nobility – a project crowned with considerable success. Finally, he secured for himself, his friends and his family many royal favours in the form of official posts, land and wealth. Schumacher himself was rewarded with extensive donations of land in Denmark and Norway, and eventually, in 1673, he was raised to the ranks of the peerage with the title of Count of Griffenfeld. His position seemed virtually inviolable in the 1670s and his power without limits. It was he who was the real ruler in Denmark, while the formally absolutist monarch seemed to wane in his powerful shadow.[2]

That he was nevertheless precipitated in 1676 from the pinnacle of power into the abyss of utmost humiliation can best be explained by the fact that, intoxicated by his many successes, he allowed himself to forget the basic fact that it was after all the king, and not he, who was the real source of power – even though, ironically enough, he himself eleven years earlier had gone out of his way to emphasize this very fact in the Royal Law. In the turmoil of all his busy activity he forgot that his position, in the end, depended exclusively on the king's grace, and that the king who had elevated him also had the power to throw him away when and if he became a liability. He forgot moreover that a necessary precondition of his power was his ability to maintain at all times a high degree of identity between the king's wishes and the interests of the state. He forgot, in short, that the absolutist king and the state – in the famous phrase of Louis XIV – were one and the same. He had created his splendid career by faithfully serving the king's interests, but, eventually taking greater and greater responsibility for the state's affairs, he ended up acting more and more in accordance with *raison d'état* as he perceived it – which was not necessarily identical with the king's interests and wishes.

It was in the area of foreign affairs that Griffenfeld's fate was finally sealed. The king and the activist generals around him nourished a burning desire for a war of revenge against Sweden which, a few decades earlier, had succeeded in mutilating Denmark, and by the mid-1670s they felt the time was ripe. Such plans were, however, contrary to what, according to Griffenfeld, served Denmark's interests best. He believed a decisive showdown with Sweden to be premature, and worked instead for closer relations with France – Sweden's traditional ally – thus trying to isolate Sweden and destroying the alliance which over the years had caused Denmark so much harm. But his ultimate goal, of weakening Sweden and so eventually regaining the lost provinces, was no different from that of the king and the generals. The difference was one of means: he preferred diplomacy to war.[3]

Things went fatally wrong when Griffenfeld, by means of a diplomatic double-game, tried to force through his own plans even after the king had made his decision and the state of war was a fact. His double-game was eventually disclosed, and his many enemies eagerly persuaded the king to regard it as a clear act of treason. They also saw to it that the king was informed of several cases in which Griffenfeld had manipulated him or even acted directly against his orders. Moreover, the numerous cases of corruption and sales of offices and honours during Griffenfeld's years in power were now also brought into the open.

The conclusion was foreordained: the king had to drop his powerful first minister and former favourite, and Griffenfeld's fall was precipitous indeed. After a show trial in the spring of 1676 he was sentenced to death, but at the last moment pardoned, the sentence being graciously changed to life imprisonment and the loss of honour and property. Griffenfeld spent his remaining twenty-three years alone in prison – at first in the Citadel of Copenhagen and later in the isolated Norwegian fortress of Munkholm in Trondheim Fjord. He died at long last in 1699, sixty-four years old, lonely and forgotten.

Danish Absolutism

The fate of Griffenfeld is a drama involving great triumphs as well as obvious tragedy. It is the story of a young upstart, rising like a star from nothing, illuminating the sky over Denmark for a short while and then disappearing over the horizon into oblivion and darkness.

The necessary preconditions for such a fate were, of course, unusual talents and an exceptional personality – and Griffenfeld certainly possessed both. But it required extraordinary societal conditions, too. And these were indeed present in late-seventeenth-century Denmark. This leads us on to a brief description of the power-structure that conditioned the rise and fall of Griffenfeld, the wine merchant's son.

In the autumn of 1660 Denmark experienced a political revolution which turned the power-structure of the country upside down. Before then, it had been an aristocratic kingdom, like Poland, in which the old nobility exercised the real influence, while the king's power was strictly limited by the constitution. It was the aristocratic State Council that wielded effective sovereignty. An ill-fated war in 1657–60 against Sweden proved disastrous for the State Council's reputation, however, and the result was an absolutist revolution in 1660 during which the monarchy, in alliance with the non-noble estates, deposed the old power-elite and – following other European precedents – invested all power in the king.[4]

It was one thing, however, to grant on paper unlimited power to the king, and an entirely different matter to transform this formal absolutism into daily administrative practice. Certainly the fundamental law of Danish absolutism – the Royal Law of 1665 – firmly stated that the king should personally make all decisions and with his own hand sign all administrative decrees, but in the real world it was of course far beyond the capacity of a single human being – even a king – to make personal decisions on the hundreds of large and small matters handled daily by the royal administration, even down to the appointment of parish clergymen. If the system was to be made workable it was necessary, therefore, to delegate much of the decision-making downwards in the hierarchy.

This necessity confronted the theoretically absolutist king with an almost insoluble dilemma: should he take the words of the Royal Law literally and insist that all business must pass across his desk? If so, he could easily be reduced to the First Bureaucrat of the realm, drowning himself in petty business and thus ending up as a hostage to bureaucratic administration with no time left for more far-sighted, strategic decision-making. Or should the king perceive himself rather as standing above the administration and intervene only in matters of a certain importance, leaving routine business to the bureaucrats? If he did this he risked losing influence over day-to-day administration and thus becoming unable to fulfil the requirements in the Royal Law for unconditional absolutism.[5]

This painful dilemma was a most real one in the first decades of absolutist government, the regime having not yet found administrative routines capable of combining absolutist royal sovereignty with a reasonably efficient and quick administration. The later seventeenth century, therefore, witnessed several experiments in this field. One solution was to insert a strong, competent first minister, enjoying the king's full confidence, between king and administration. The idea was, of course, that such a trusted minister could act as a sort of filter between king and administration and, at the same time, handle routine business on the monarch's behalf, thus relieving him of making numerous trivial decisions without his losing control over the daily administration.

Griffenfeld embodies this solution, the precondition of his power being a great capacity for work and an unconditional loyalty towards the king's person and interests. His capacity for hard work remained intact to the end; his fall, however, was caused by his inability to sustain his loyalty.

Griffenfeld's years as minister–favourite, in other words, represented a difficult transitional phase in the development of the politico-administrative system:

the old pre-absolutist patterns had become obsolete, while the new structures had not yet assumed definite forms. But the question remains whether special importance should also be attributed to the fact that Griffenfeld came from the middle class and was not a born member of the old noble elite. The answer to this question is yes.

In a very real sense the old nobility were the principal antagonists of the new absolutism, representing as they did the old pre-absolutist power-elite, and the old system being almost identical with the noble estate and noble values. No wonder, then, that the early absolutist kings preferred to recruit their most trusted servants from the middle class, their faithful ally during the revolution. In their testaments the monarchs warned time and again of the danger of a noble counter-coup, and strongly advised against ever again allowing members of the old nobility any influence. Loyal to this understanding Griffenfeld, during his years in office, worked hard and successfully to undermine the unity and power of the old nobility by creating a formal order of ranks, founding an entirely new order of knighthood and arranging for a new and elevated class of titled aristocracy – all aimed at weakening the old ruling class and introducing a new rank-determined social structure with the absolutist king at the top. Honoured by the knighthood of the Order of the Elephant and adorned with the title of count, Griffenfeld himself became a prominent member of this new rank-determined structure, built not upon noble birth but upon royal favour and faithful service to the absolutist state.[6]

Griffenfeld, in other words, was typical of a power-structure in the process of stabilizing itself, his great strength being his ability to offer solutions where others were irresolute. Being a brilliantly gifted man with a formidable capacity for administrative work, he was able to lift the heavy burden of decision-making from a king who was young, inexperienced and moreover disliked the dull business of governing. His fatal mistake, however, was that he tended more and more to forget that even his elevated position was conditional on total loyalty to the king – even when the young man on the throne was in his eyes intellectually inferior and a weak personality. This blindness was even more remarkable considering that Griffenfeld himself was the main architect of the new system.

The Last Minister–Favourite?

In a longer time-perspective Griffenfeld was neither the first nor the last minister–favourite in Denmark, nor indeed was he even the first of middle-class extraction. Going back to the years around 1520 we find a rather unusual example of a middle-class favourite exercising a very strong influence with king and government without, however, possessing any formal position. The person in question is the Dutch-born Mother Sigbrit, mother to Dyveke, the mistress of Christian II. For several years this strong-willed middle-class woman exercised a strong influence over the king, forcing his policy into a controversial anti-noble course, thus provoking an aristocratic revolt which resulted in the subsequent deposition and expulsion of the king in 1523, after the failure of several attempts to persuade him to drop her.[7]

It was no accident that Mother Sigbrit's years in power coincided with attempts, supported by the middle class, to secure a foothold in Denmark for the Renaissance state. This experiment failed at the time, because the nobility was still too strong – unlike England, for instance, where the first two Tudor kings, efficiently assisted by favourites like Cardinal Wolsey and Thomas Cromwell, both of humble origin, succeeded in establishing the strong Tudor state.

A somewhat later example of a favourite of a quite different type is Corfitz Ulfeldt (pl. 66), King Christian IV's son-in-law. In the 1640s, when the old king was weakened by old age and bad health, Ulfeldt succeeded in acquiring a power-position which in reality put the king out of the game. By birth, however, he belonged to the uppermost stratum of the nobility and would therefore be regarded as predestined to rule. But what was unusual was the range of his power, which for a few years raised him high above his equals and made him a virtual *alter rex*, until his sudden and dramatic fall in 1652.[8]

It may also be illuminating to draw attention in a much later period to the German doctor Johann Friedrich Struensee (pl. 67), who in 1770–2 was the *de facto* absolutist ruler of Denmark for over a year. The background to this strange episode was unusual. The reigning king, the young Christian VII, was mentally ill and completely incapable of ruling. Dr Struensee was his personal physician and, in this capacity, gained strong influence over his royal patient. Moreover he also became the lover of the young and lonely queen. Armed with such assets he succeeded in squeezing himself into a position where he alone controlled access to the king, while at the same time acquiring full authority to issue cabinet orders in the king's name. He devoted his unique power to carrying through a series of progressive reforms, effectively introducing enlightened absolutism into Denmark. His restless reforms, however, antagonized the established elite, who regarded the foreign upstart with suspicion and disgust. One night early in 1772 he was overthrown in a military coup, in the course of which his enemies seized control of the helpless king's person. Struensee was soon afterwards convicted of high treason and executed in public, while the poor unfaithful queen was hurried off into a lifelong exile in Celle in Hanover.[9]

Those examples are adduced in order to demonstrate that Griffenfeld – in a Danish context at least – was only one in long line of favourites spread over a wide span of time. A common denominator of those favourites is that they all gained so much influence that they tended to outshine the king in the public consciousness, and even stepped into his place. Another common denominator is that their tenure of power was relatively short, and that they all faced a violent and tragic end. On their way up they had crossed, consciously or unwittingly, a number of taboo-lines, thereby challenging the old ruling elites and offending public ideas of legitimacy. For this and for other reasons the reaction was so violent when it finally occurred. Indeed, the case of Griffenfeld differs from that of the others only in one point: he was the only one born in Denmark of middle-class parents.

Preconditions of the Minister–Favourite

As demonstrated, it is possible in Danish history to point to examples of favourites over a time-span much longer than the period singled out as distinctive by Professor Bérenger in his stimulating article in *Annales*, namely the early seventeenth century when the modern state established itself.[10] This prompts a few reflections on the preconditions of the phenomenon in a broader sense, the Danish examples tending to indicate that it was, after all, not specifically located in the first half of the seventeenth century.

Taking those examples as a starting point, two basic preconditions should be suggested. The first, obviously, is that an organized and centralized state-power must be in existence: without this, there can be no ministers – and hence also no minister–favourites. The implication, in a European context, is that the phenomenon belongs in general to the era of the modern state materializing from about 1500 – that is the powerful, centralized state which, while certainly assuming different shapes in different parts of Europe, nevertheless possessed the common characteristic of being far more powerful than any other organization or group of organizations in society.

In England this process gained speed under the early Tudors and fostered in its early stages minister–favourites like Cardinal Wolsey and Thomas Cromwell. In Denmark the same process was initiated under the Renaissance king Christian II, who deliberately sought the support of the middle class in his attempt to build a new state-power. This brought to the fore Mother Sigbrit, the real brains and brawn behind the royal reform policy. But she aroused such intense hatred among the nobility that she provoked an aristocratic reaction which brought the modernization process to a stop. Only after a bitter civil war and the Lutheran church reformation in 1536 could the process be resumed. From then on the Danish version of the powerful early modern state gradually emerged, and eventually transmuted into a genuine absolutist regime with further centralization and concentration of power as its advance continued.

On considering the line of Danish minister–favourites it is evident, however, that a further condition had to be fulfilled before the minister–favourite could emerge: the formal ruler, the king, had to be temporarily weakened or, for other reasons, unable to govern.

Thus Corfitz Ulfeldt appeared on the stage precisely when Christian IV was weakened by illness, old age and private sorrows. Nor was it pure accident that Griffenfeld's time of greatness coincided with the early years on the throne of a young and not particularly bright king. Nor was it accidental that Dr

Struensee's short rule coincided with a marked worsening of the mental illness of the young King Christian VII, which prevented him from carrying out his duties. Yet the duties of ruling had to be carried out all the same, and it thus fell to the king's trusted physician and his queen's lover to run the government in his name. If anything, Struensee was the trusted favourite *par excellence*, who – without a platform in the existing hierarchy of power – came to exercise genuine royal power, with excellent results for Denmark, but with terrible personal consequences for himself.

The case of Dr Struensee underlines the fact that the minister–favourite is also found in a fully developed absolutist state with a fixed bureaucracy and fully fledged administrative routines – indicating, therefore, that the phenomenon may not be quite as closely associated with a specific transitional phase in the evolution of state-power as Professor Bérenger seemed to maintain. Instead it might perhaps be rewarding to look for explanations of a more general nature – explanations, for instance, related to the fact that regardless of how regular and bureaucratic an administration is built up there will always remain a grey zone in its uppermost strata where the process of political decision-making escapes all rules or tends to obey the basic rule of the law of the jungle, the right of the strongest. The minister–favourite belongs to and operates precisely in this zone. In my opinion it is consequently this grey zone that deserves attention in any attempt to isolate and appraise this phenomenon.

Absolutism after Griffenfeld

In conclusion it is worth considering what lessons the absolutist king learnt from his years with Griffenfeld, and following this with a few observations on his and his successors' efforts to resolve the inherent contradiction between absolutism in its purest sense of personal rule and the heavy load of daily business. Inevitably this problem resurfaced with renewed strength as the king, from one day to the next, had to do without Griffenfeld's expert handling of administrative affairs.

On the arrest of Griffenfeld the king declared – obviously inspired by the example of Louis XIV – that from now on he intended to be his own first minister. For this task, however, he had neither the physical strength nor the intellectual capacity. For the rest of his reign, which ended in 1699, he therefore depended heavily on political advisers and strong bureaucrats in the administration. But having learnt from his previous experience he took the utmost care to make sure that the group of advisers changed continually, and he never again vested his full confidence in a single person. He mastered, in short, the noble art of divide and rule.

Moreover he reinforced his council, the closest formal group of advisers, which was to assume an important policy-making position in the zone between the king and his administration. In his last years he even created a series of *ad hoc* commissions with specific administrative tasks in order to prevent the hardening of existing bureaucratic patterns. But the system never came to work in a fully satisfactory way, and King Christian V never found an ideal solution to his dilemma. His administration was marked by many, often unsuccessful, experiments in the fields of policy-making and the handling of business. Intrigue and slander flourished in his court – as the English diplomat Robert Molesworth correctly observed in his famous book of 1694, *An Account of Denmark as it was in the Year of 1692*, with its heavy criticism and frontal attack on Danish absolutism.

Instead it was his son and successor, Frederik IV (1699–1730), who resolved the dilemma, and his solution was personal absolutism. Unlike his father, Frederik IV was intellectually gifted and, at the same time, extremely hard-working. He was thus well suited to put into practice his father's notion that the king should be his own first minister. He insisted from the very beginning that all decisions in vital areas, like finance and defence, should pass across his desk, and for thirty extremely busy years on the throne – and, in particular, behind the royal desk – he managed with an iron-hard working discipline to act as the head clerk of the realm without sacrificing his wider political vision. In a very real sense he was the first servant of the state.

This performance was nothing short of heroic and represented, at the same time, personal absolutism carried to the limits. The hard-working and scrupulous Frederik IV was precisely the type of monarch outlined in Griffenfeld's Royal Law of 1665: ready to work around the clock. None of his successors, however, equalled him as far as hard work and political insight are concerned, and his death in 1730 therefore heralded a new stage in Danish absolutism, that of bureaucratic absolutism. From then on the established bureaucracy gradually took over and saw to it that Denmark was properly ruled, even when the king – like Frederik V (1746–66) – was an alcoholic.

One particular situation, however, was always beyond the range of the bureaucracy, because it was not foreseen in the Royal Law: where the all-powerful king should suffer from a mental illness so serious that he was totally unable to carry out even the most simple act of governing. This contingency became a grim reality with the accession of Christian VII in 1767. The scene was thus set for the emergence of Denmark's last real minister–favourite, Dr Struensee, who was to pay the highest price of all, because he was tempted at a critical time to step into the power-vacuum created by the king's mental illness. In so doing he offended against one of the most fundamental principles of absolutism: that the king, God's anointed, was the sole source of all power in the state.

Notes

1. The most recent biography of Griffenfeld in Danish is Knud Fabricius, *Griffenfeld* (Copenhagen, 1910). Though an excellent standard work for its time, a modern successor is obviously much needed. Works in English with Griffenfeld as the main topic are, to my knowledge, non-existent. He is briefly mentioned in passing in Thomas Munck, *Seventeenth Century Europe, 1598–1700* (London,

1990), pp. 341, 345, 388ff.; in David Kirby, *Northern Europe in the Early Modern Period: The Baltic World, 1492–1772* (London, 1990), pp. 213, 270; and in a few other general English textbooks. In the following the references to Danish literary sources are kept to a minimum as readers of this essay are not expected to be familiar with that language.

2. For a rough outline of the reforms that eventually broke the influence of the old nobility see my article, 'The Rise and Fall of the Danish Nobility, 1600–1800', in H. M. Scott, ed., *The European Nobilities in the Seventeenth and Eighteenth Centuries*, 2 vols (London, 1995), ii, pp. 41–70, esp. pp. 56ff. Readers who find it indelicate of me to refer so often to my own articles in the forthcoming pages will allow me to remark that publications in English on early modern Danish history are actually very few.

3. The endless Danish–Swedish controversies are treated in a wider context in my article 'Rivalry without Victory: Denmark, Sweden and the Struggle for the Baltic, 1500–1720', in Göran Rystad, Klaus-R. Böhme and Wilhelm Carlgren, eds, *In Quest of Trade and Security: The Baltic in Power Politics, 1500–1990*, 2 vols (Stockholm, 1994), i, pp. 137–76.

4. The main features of the political revolution of 1660 and its repercussions are discussed in E. Ladewig Petersen's and my own article, 'Two Revolutions in Early Modern Denmark', in E. I. Kouri and Tom Scott, *Politics and Society in Reformation Europe: Essays in Honour of Sir Geoffrey Elton on his Sixty-fifth Birthday* (London, 1987), pp. 473–501.

5. The parallel texts of the Royal Law in Latin and Danish with related documents are published by A. D. Jørgensen, ed., *Kongeloven og dens Forhistorie* (Copenhagen, 1886, repr. 1973), pp. 38–67. For a summary presentation of its wording and consequences, see Ernst Ekman, 'The Danish Royal Law of 1665', *Journal of Modern History*, 29 (1957), pp. 102–7; cf. also my own article, 'Absolute Monarchy in Denmark: Change and Continuity', *Scandinavian Journal of History*, 12 (1988), pp. 307–16.

6. Cf. the reference in note 2 above. The last will of Christian V written in 1683, seven years after Griffenfeld's fall, is a collection of rules and good advice for his successors and can thus be regarded as a supplement to the Royal Law; it is published by J. J. A. Worsaae, ed., *Kong Christian den Vtes Testamenter som Tillæg til Kongelov* (Copenhagen, 1860). Curiously enough it contains not the faintest reference to experiences from Griffenfeld's time in power, thus perhaps indicating that the king may not have felt his position so threatened by his powerful minister as Griffenfeld's enemies had maintained at the time.

7. For a brief presentation of Mother Sigbrit and a discussion of her role, see Alex Wittendorff, *På Guds og Herskabs nåde, 1500–1600* (Copenhagen, 1989), pp. 77–80 with references.

8. This highly intelligent but deeply neurotic character whose many machinations have left deep traces in Danish history has recently received an excellent biographical treatment by Steffen Heiberg, *Enhjørningen. Corfitz Ulfeldt* (Copenhagen, 1993). Unfortunately the book has not yet been translated into one of the major languages.

9. For Dr Struensee and his time, see the congenial interpretation by Svend Cedergreen Bech, *Struensee og hans tid* (Copenhagen, 1989).

10. Jean Bérenger, 'Pour une enquête européenne: le problème du ministériat au XVIIe siècle', *Annales*, 29 (1974), pp. 166–92; now compare also H. M. Scott, 'The Rise of the First Minister in Eighteenth-Century Europe', in T. C. W. Blanning and David Cannadine, eds, *History and Biography: Essays in Honour of Derek Beales* (Cambridge, 1996), pp. 21–52.

Concluding Remarks: The Anatomy of the Minister–Favourite[1]

L. W. B. BROCKLISS

The underlying aim of the essays in this book and the conference from which they derived has been to take up a challenge issued by the French historian Jean Bérenger nearly twenty-five years ago, and examine an historical paradox.[2] The High Renaissance, roughly the century and a quarter 1550–1675, like the periods that preceded and followed it, was an age of personal monarchy, yet it was also an age in which many, if not most, of Europe's rulers seemed to play second fiddle to their principal advisers. Bérenger believed that this historical paradox was not a quirk of particular national histories but a European-wide phenomenon which merited serious comparative examination. His own pioneering article offered a preliminary exploration of the rise of the principal minister, but his primary intention was to put the problem on the historical map and encourage others to follow his lead.

A quarter of a century on, now that much more is known about the nature of princely authority and government in the different states of Europe during the sixteenth and seventeenth centuries, the sort of careful European-wide examination which Bérenger desired has become much more feasible. As Sir John Elliott pointed out in his Introduction, the essays in this volume do not cover every individual principal minister, let alone every manifestation of the historical problem. Indeed, it was felt unnecessary to provide readers with accounts of the political careers of the most famous principal ministers, whose lives have been studied in detail by historians in recent years. Taken alongside these studies, the essays do, however, make it finally possible to move on from Bérenger's preliminary conclusions and construct a more sophisticated account of the historical phenomenon. This concluding essay is a personal attempt to piece together a picture of the position that we have now reached in the ongoing debate. At the same time, it emphasizes that the jigsaw is still incomplete and suggests a number of areas of future research which will need to be pursued before a satisfactory solution can be reached.

Characteristics

Throughout recorded history, rulers, whatever the system of government, have had their favourites, men and women (wives as well as mistresses and confidantes) whose varying degrees of influence over the affairs of state owed everything to their affective relationship with the fountain of authority and usually next to nothing to any official position that they might occupy in the government hierarchy. Just as Roman emperors and medieval kings had their favourites, so too had and have many popes, presidents, prime ministers and party secretaries. Both Sejanus and the colourful and much maligned Empress Theodora have had many successors. In important respects, Marcia Williams and Nancy Reagan are as much the descendants of the one as Martin Bormann and Che Guevara are of the other.[3] What all favourites share is their permanent access to the ruler, for as long as their favour lasts: they are the persistent voice in the ruler's ear that mixes often contentious advice with the honeyed words of affection. And for this they have been universally execrated by their contemporaries: by insiders because they appear to have usurped the authority of properly constituted officials; by outsiders because they appear to be the source of every ill-fated governmental decision.[4]

There is nothing extraordinary therefore in the fact that the princes and popes of Europe in the century 1550–1650 should have surrounded themselves with favourites. Nonetheless, in the long and ongoing history of the favourite as a political phenomenon, this period cannot but attract especial attention, for it witnessed the rise and then rapid decline of a particularly interesting species of the genus. Admittedly, the century continued to see the star of many common or garden favourites wax and wane – a Ralegh in the England of Elizabeth, a Chalais or Cinq Mars in the France of Louis XIII. However, it also saw the temporary blooming of an entirely new type of favourite, a prickly, dangerous and vigorous brier, not unknown to flourish in the same courtly soil as the more effete hardy perennial. Recently dubbed the 'minister–favourite' by A. Lloyd Moote, this was a new and singular variety that took root for a time in virtually all the large courts of Europe and many of the small ones too, as Ronald Asch's account in the present volume of the rise and fall of Matthäus Enzlin in Württemberg reminds us.[5]

The singularity of the minister–favourite – a term which captures more carefully the aulic origins of the species than Bérenger's modern-sounding *premier ministre* – was displayed in three principal ways. In the first place, the new type of favourite was always a male and his hold over the ruler's affections was not usually the result of attractive looks or manners. Some minister–favourites did begin their rise up the slippery pole by attracting the prince's wandering eye – most obviously George Villiers, later Duke of Buckingham – but most did not. Many were relatively colourless professional pen-pushers and lawyers, such as Burghley in England or Griffenfeld in Denmark. Some were downright ugly: Robert Cecil was a hunchback, while the most remarkable feature of Olivares was his bulbous nose. In this regard then the minister–favourite must be distinguished from the countless consorts, lovers and mistresses who have used their physical allure to pull the strings of state across the ages, or, as Knud Jespersen's account of the pro-active early sixteenth-century Danish reformer Mother Sigbrit reminds us, thrust their relatives (in this case even a female relative) into positions of power.

In fact many *premiers ministres* were not the stuff of classical favourites at all in that they were or became clerics and churchmen – Cardinal Klesl (the servant of the Emperor Mathias), Richelieu and Mazarin, Archbishop Laud, Lerma on the eve of his disgrace.[6] As a result, such minister–favourites could also be legitimately placed in an entirely different and long-standing tradition in Christian Europe: they belonged to the capacious category of the political prelate. Nonetheless, if it was a commonplace in the late Middle Ages and the Renaissance for churchmen to occupy prominent positions in a prince's administration, few ever enjoyed the favour and omnicompetence permitted their successors in the century 1550–1650. The first half of the sixteenth century witnessed the political ascendancy of a number of powerful ecclesiastics, usually lord chancellors, such as Cardinal Duprat in the France of Francis I and Cardinal Beaton in the Scotland of James V. But none except Cardinal Wolsey could be classed as their prince's *alter ego*. Indeed, Wolsey's career is particularly interesting in this comparative context because he was so obviously in many ways the prototype of the later ecclesiastical minister–favourite. Another lord chancellor, he governed England on Henry VIII's behalf for nearly twenty years, completely dominated patronage in state and church to the increasing annoyance of rivals, and conducted with his master's support an ambitious, if only partially successful, foreign policy, aimed at making an under-resourced Tudor dynasty the arbiter of Europe.[7]

These ecclesiastical minister–favourites, it must be stressed, likewise seldom owed their elevation to a close, albeit less physical, relationship with their royal master or mistress in their early careers. Unlike Wolsey in this respect, they had not usually gained the prince's confidence through being his chaplain, confessor or almoner. Most minister–favourites, then, lay or cleric, were not the prince's intimates. They were seldom even natural courtiers, although they managed to navigate the shoals of the court with great success. What earned and retained them the prince's peculiar favour was their perceived competence as administrators. In some cases – usually where elevation to this managerial role initially stemmed from their physical attraction – the ruler or the regent took their capacity on trust and was sometimes sadly disappointed: Robert Carr turned out to be no Robert Cecil and lost his secretarial post in the fall-out from the Overbury Plot.[8] Usually, however, minister–favourites came to the ruler's attention because they had already demonstrated their managerial skills in some office of importance. Cecil had already shown his paces under Elizabeth and had effectively secured James the throne; Mazarin had served Richelieu as a diplomat and negotiator in various contexts in the final years of the reign of

Louis XIII. Even when the future minister–favourite owed his fledgling position to the influence of a patron he usually received the backing of the crown only because his administrative capacity had been already displayed. Thus, the role of Marie de Médicis in Richelieu's elevation to the council in 1624 was clearly crucial but the cardinal had proved himself an able Bishop of Luçon, had already shown his potential as a short-lived minister in the Concini era, and had been an effective factotum to the queen mother in her wilderness years.[9] The ruler, then, did not necessarily love the minister–favourite, although respect and affection could grow over the years under the favourite's prompting, as evidently happened in the case of Philip IV's regard for Olivares.[10]

In the second place, the minister–favourite was much more active and visible in day-to-day government than the favourite *tout court*: the new breed were 'doers'. Historically favourites have tended to hide in the shadows, influencing appointments and decision-making but not putting their name to the documents that flowed from their counsel. The minister–favourite in the period 1550–1650, in contrast, was clearly at the centre of the administrative and patronage machine. He may have been just as venal as the traditional favourite – Richelieu died worth 20 million livres, Mazarin possessing 40 million – but he usually worked tremendously hard, enmeshed in paperwork, often to the detriment of his health. Both Richelieu and Olivares suffered from persistent migraines and Richelieu was prone to nervous collapse.[11] The one obvious exception was Lerma, whose notorious bouts of inactivity may have reflected not so much indolence as periods of deep depression. Sometimes, the minister–favourites held an actual administrative position that justified his role – most notably Chancellor Oxenstierna of Sweden (pl. 68).[12] Normally, however, he was a minister without portfolio, presiding over the prince's council and co-ordinating his administration through his clients and allies who occupied the official posts of secretary of state, treasurer, chancellor and so on. Thus, Richelieu's only right to chair the *conseil d'état* of Louis XIII came from the fact that he was a cardinal, and church dignitaries had precedence by custom.[13]

Total or nearly total control over the patronage and administrative system was so clearly the defining characteristic of the minister–favourites or *premier ministre* that a number of powerful or would-be powerful servants of princes who have been traditionally given the sobriquet should perhaps be deprived of their title. The presence of Charles I's ministers Laud (pl. 69) and Strafford (pl. 70) on the list is particularly problematic. Whatever their ambitions to be the only minister–favourite diarchy and whatever the opinion of later parliamentary detractors, they only ever had a tenuous hold on power and on the king's affections. Archbishop Laud permanently had the royal ear and served on the council, but he was never really a hands-on administrative co-ordinator and he had no clients in the central administration, apart from Bishop Juxon, who served for a time as lord high treasurer. In fact Laud expended most of his energies revitalizing (or undermining – it depends on one's point of view) the Church of England, where he was definitely the administrative co-ordinator from 1628, if only Archbishop of Canterbury five years later. Thomas Wentworth, at least before 1639, was equally powerless, languishing for most of the Personal Rule in the north or in Ireland as lord deputy. If he unofficially tried to advise Charles from faraway Dublin Castle, he had little effective input in decision-making. Charles I was very much a king, we now know, who created his own policies. Laud and Wentworth had to compete with other councillors for the royal ear and usually lost: hence the endless whingeing in their correspondence about the power of 'Lady Mora' (Weston, Cottington *et al.*).[14]

In the third place, the minister–favourite differed from the common or garden variety by dint of his independence of mind vis-à-vis his princely patron. Traditional favourites, whatever contemporaries might have initially believed, were invariably toadies. They did not so much supplant royal authority as encourage it into unpopular channels. It is perhaps not surprising then that the three English medieval kings most remembered for their passion for favourites – Edward II, Richard II and Henry VI – eventually all met the same end as their henchmen. Removing the favourite had little permanent effect, as Piers Gaveston, the Earl of Oxford/Duke of Ireland and the Duke of Suffolk were only singing the royal tune.[15] The minister–favourites, on the other hand, were by and large surrogate sovereigns. To all intents and purposes they took the cares of royal administration completely out of the prince's hands: they not only largely determined patronage decisions (always the most time-consuming part of early modern administration), but they also formulated policy – foreign and internal. Although we are well aware today that the princes in the period 1550–1650 continued to maintain a lively interest in the administration of their realm, even when they left day-to-day business to the minister–favourite, this does not detract from the fact that the favourite educated the prince into seeing the virtue of accepting his advice: he was far more than the prince's favoured servant: Olivares and Richelieu especially had their own radical, reform agenda.[16] Very often the prince was thereby left with little to do but pursue his passion for hunting or warfare. Thus Oxenstierna ran the Swedish Empire, while Gustavus Adolphus sought to expand its size. Sometimes the minister–favourite usurped the ruler's military role as well.[17] Both Buckingham and Richelieu were generals for a short time in the 1620s: the siege of La Rochelle was to prove as much the swan-song of the one as the apotheosis of the other. Both Buckingham and Richelieu were frequently far from their masters' side. But so too were all minister–favourites. The close relationship between prince and favourite was no more based on propinquity than on physical affection.[18] Again, unlike the traditional favourite, the new breed could safely sit in the capital and busy themselves with government while the prince travelled the country showing himself to the people or went abroad in search of *gloire*.

Picked for his administrative competence and appetite for work, not for his looks, the minister–favourite inevitably had staying-power: a number, like Wolsey, controlled the state for twenty years – Lerma, Richelieu, Olivares,

Oxtenstierna, Mazarin. Courtier opponents found them annoyingly hard to remove by the usual methods. They were not to be displaced by bringing to court a handsome man or woman as a lure. Those who successfully convinced the prince of the appropriateness of their policies, even when they failed to deliver the goods, were also frustratingly immune from innuendo or criticism through the estates. Buckingham in 1628 was felled not by opposition in parliament but by the assassin's hand.[19] Even age did not wither them in the prince's affections. While traditional favourites, as James M. Boyden's essay on the genus in Spain before Lerma reminds us (see above, Chapter 2), frequently fell from power when they lost their looks (witness the downfall of Ruy Gómez in the early years of the reign of Philip II), the minister–favourite often grew old with his prince and metamorphosed into a curmudgeonly avuncular crutch, like Burghley – Elizabeth's little pig. Often release came only with the prince's death, when his successor tried to curry favour with disgruntled members of the elite by arranging the minister–favourite's judicial murder, as happened to Enzlin in Württemberg. In normal circumstances, the confessor or chaplain rather than the courtier was the more likely to incite a royal change of heart: hence Richelieu's constant anxiety about the potential disloyalty to himself of the Jesuits who controlled Louis XIII's conscience.[20]

Yet the era of the minister–favourite proved strikingly transitory. Apparently a vigorous plant in full bloom everywhere in Europe in the first half of the seventeenth century, this new variety of favourite quickly withered and all but disappeared after 1660. Louis XIV began the trend by deciding, on Mazarin's death in 1661, that he would take over the reins of government himself. His macho initiative was almost immediately imitated by Leopold of Austria on the death of Prince Ferdinand Portia in 1665, and then by Louis' cousin Charles II of England when he dismissed Lord Chancellor Clarendon (pl. 71) in August 1666.[21] Minister–favourites were still to be found in Denmark and Sweden in the 1670s where, in the first case, Griffenfeld and, in the second, La Gardie monopolized royal authority until their respective downfalls.[22] But they were the last examples in the seventeenth century of the cluster of supernovae whose brilliance had spasmodically dominated the political firmament for a century and a quarter and successfully dimmed and sometimes obscured the hereditary effulgence of their princely patrons. The apparent reinvention of the Merovingian office of mayor of the palace was not destined to last. No European minister–favourite was to gain such a grip on power that he could turn his family into the permanent arbiters of princely patronage and institutionalize the role of administrative *metteur-en-scène*. The Togukawa dynasty in Japan might have succeeded in doing just that at the turn of the seventeenth century and reducing the emperor to a state of permanent powerlessness that would last two and a half centuries, but there were to be no European imitators of their bravura, largely because the political culture of the two parts of the world was so different: there was no European tradition of imperial invisibility.[23] Only one long-lasting father-and-son team appeared in the age of the

minister–favourite – Burghley and Salisbury – and, if the Cecils since 1612 have
played a not inconsiderable part in the political history of the British Isles, none
of their descendants could claim to have run the state again until the premiership of the Marquess of Salisbury at the end of the nineteenth century.[24] Indeed,
if there was any correspondence between the political histories of Europe and
the Orient in this period, it lay rather in events in China. There the Ming
dynasty too in its final hundred years seems to have kept its subjects at arm's
length, leaving the running of the empire to a series of eunuchs. When the
Manchu took over in 1644, on the other hand, as the Ming era collapsed in
anarchy, the new emperor anticipated Louis XIV's decision seventeen years
later: the Ching dynasty ruled as well as reigned, none more so than the
peripatetic K'ang Hsi, virtually the exact contemporary of the Sun King.[25]

Rise

Traditional historiography attributed the rise of the minister–favourite to the
contemporary emergence on the European stage of a string of peculiarly lazy
monarchs. Since the publication of Bérenger's pioneering article in 1974, this
explanation has generally been dismissed in favour of a more structural analysis
of the development of the political phenomenon, but perhaps it should not be
discarded entirely. As Pauline Croft's contribution to this volume reminds us
(Chapter 6 above), the Stuart monarchs at least were not always assiduous
rulers. Charles I may have been a 'hands-on' monarch but James, the father
whom he much despised, had come south in search of the quiet life after years
of struggling with a recalcitrant Scottish nobility. On the other hand, the
detached attitude to their responsibilities shown by James and another prover-
bially laid-back Stuart monarch, his grandson Charles II, especially in the early
years of his reign, may have been exceptional in the period, for the putative
laziness of other European monarchs has not easily stood up to close scrutiny:
it is now recognized that both Louis XIII of France and Philip IV of Spain, for
instance, took a definite interest in the affairs of state and could, occasionally, be
extremely conscientious.[26] There thus has to be a deeper cause of the rise of the
minister–favourite.

Bérenger himself argued that the appearance of the phenomenon could be
traced to the growth of the early modern state. As the feudal monarchy was
replaced by the bureaucratic state in an age of 'military revolution' (to borrow
Michael Roberts' phrase), traditionally trained kings and princes (with the
exception of the better-prepared Philip II of Spain) found themselves ill
equipped to administer the expanding apparatus of government: they needed an
aide-de-camp who would look after the state, while they immersed themselves
in the customary round of war, hunting, courtly ritual and showing themselves
to their subjects. Kings (and queens) were part of an extremely 'active' honour
culture, where the daily round even in peacetime was organized in such a way

as to ensure (in theory) that the prince was in peak condition for performing his primary role as the military protector of his own and his subjects' interests. Being a traditional king was a time-consuming business, which required constant travelling and the constitution of an ox: a prince was destined to long hours in the saddle, at table and (when young) on the dance-floor. Traditional kings did not have the time to immerse themselves in the paperwork thrown up by the burgeoning bureaucracy.[27]

This argument is still very attractive, if only because it helps to explain the relative absence of the minister–favourite in those European states where there was little government expansion in the sixteenth and seventeenth centuries. Poland is a case in point, as Antoni Mączak's contribution to this volume emphasizes (Chapter 10 above). A country with an elective monarchy and a highly decentralized system of government based around noble-controlled county Diets, Poland seems to have produced only one minister–favourite over our period, George Ossoliński, who in the mid-seventeenth century was the right-hand man of Ladislas IV. If there were other ministers who dominated central government at an earlier date, notably the chancellor Zamoyski, they were the creatures of the magnate families who traditionally controlled the king, not the king's personal servants. Of course, Bérenger's argument cannot explain the phenomenon entirely, in that a cluster of minister–favourites did appear in one highly unbureaucratized, albeit juridically and ideologically centralized, country – England.[28] But England across our period was arguably peculiar. Not only, as we saw above, were two of the Stuart monarchs comparatively indolent, but the dutiful Elizabeth was a woman. She needed a Burghley to run her administration, just as in the later part of her reign she needed a Leicester, an Essex or a Mountjoy to lead her armies. In Elizabeth's reign at least, moreover, the English minister–favourite lacked the authority of his continental cousins. As Paul Hammer's essay reminds us (Chapter 3 above), Elizabeth did not want to entrust her realm to a surrogate monarch and she struggled hard to ensure that her minister–favourites operated within a restricted sphere. No one individual ever totally dominated the state apparatus, not even the indispensable Burghley. Those who had ambitions to do so, like the high-flying Ralegh and Essex, found they had been borne aloft on wings of wax which would quickly melt when exposed to the heat of the queen's anger. Elizabeth's minister–favourites were limp insular representations of the European species.

There again, a number of essays in this volume suggest that Bérenger's argument, if useful as a point of departure, needs refining in the light of more recent research on the development of the early modern state. Linda Levy Peck, trying to integrate the exceptional case of England into the general pattern (Chapter 4 above), argues that the real cause of the rise of the minister–favourite lies in the mechanics of patronage, an aspect of early modern government which has received particular attention in recent years.[29] According to Peck the rise of the minister–favourite was not so much a response to the growth of early modern government as a reflection of office-hunger. By the turn of the seventeenth century, the prince was besieged by a legion of place-seekers, anxious to enjoy the rewards of government service. The prince therefore needed a patronage manager who would organize the distribution of royal bounty and protect the crown from the inevitable anger of the disappointed. The appearance of the minister–favourite was therefore the result of a collapse in the equilibrium of the patronage market, as the potential candidates for office grew faster than the number of places. Peck does not offer an explanation for this state of affairs, but it is not difficult to suggest a cause. Presumably, it reflected the broader social effects of sixteenth- and early-seventeenth-century economic growth, which led to an expansion both in the number of well-to-do bourgeois aspiring to government office as an investment and in the number of indigent nobles/gentry who needed to supplement their income by state service. Presumably, too, the bottleneck would have been particularly grave in England, where there were relatively few offices – hence the system of holding offices in reversion from the 1590s.[30]

I. A. A. Thompson (Chapter 1 above) accepts the first part of Peck's analysis. In his view, the emergence of the minister–favourite can definitely not be attributed simply to the growth of the state itself, for there was no cultural reason why princes should not be chief administrators. Rather the phenomenon arose out of the sheer complexity of the administrative system that emerged in the course of the sixteenth century. As early as 1540 in the case of Spain, he insists, there was a need for an administrative co-ordinator who could oversee the disparate and often conflicting branches of the burgeoning bureaucracy. As the effective prince could only be a policy-maker, not a pen-pusher (hence the weakness of Philip II's personal rule), a trouble-shooting intermediary had to be found who would make the system work properly, especially in times of war. This had to be somebody the prince could trust totally – hence the minister–favourite. The latter's power stemmed, however, not just from royal favour. Although Europe's nascent bureaucracies were relatively large by the turn of the seventeenth century, their structures were still not fully formalized: there was as yet no conception of internal promotion ladders. The astute minister–favourite could therefore use the crown's patronage power to insert his own clients into positions of importance and thus gain complete control of the machine.

Both essays clearly help to flesh out Bérenger's original argument, though readers may wonder how far problems of office-seeking and/or administrative complexity played a part in the appearance of the minister–favourite all over Europe. In contemporary eyes, the Swedish bureaucracy was a model of rationality: can the rise of Oxenstierna, therefore, be attributed in any way to its Byzantine structure? More importantly, both essays develop Bérenger's argument in an entirely new direction. It was not that the prince in this period was ill equipped by background and training to manage the new early modern state; it was rather that, if he wished to be a *successful* prince, he was politically wise not to try to do so. There was a need for him to distance himself from his apparatus if he was to make objective decisions and retain the loyalty of his subjects. This argument could be taken further, if contemporary views of good kingship are introduced into the analysis. The good prince at the turn of the seventeenth century, as in the late medieval era, was one who preserved the laws, liberties and customs of his subjects and maintained the true religion. In the period 1550–1650, however, it was more difficult than usual for princes to live up to the ideal, thanks above all to the virtually pan-European breakdown in Christian unity.

This was an era of perpetual religious conflict and little respect for the confessional position of opponents. In many states there were now powerful religious minorities who were ready to resort to civil war rather than give up their faith at the prince's command. Where rulers were in control of multiple kingdoms or principalities, like the early Stuarts or the Austrian Habsburgs, it was often the case that the majority religious preference differed from place to place. The prudent ruler either accepted the wisdom of legalizing to a degree religious dissent (as in France, albeit sporadically, from the time of Catherine de Médicis until the death of Louis XIII) or turned a blind eye to the persistence of heresy (as in Ireland). At the same time, as the pursuit of dynastic ambition became more costly, even the wealthiest monarch was strapped for cash and felt the need to ride roughshod over traditional rights in search of money. Dynastic ambition, as the French kings knew, could also conflict with religious duty. From the time of Francis I, Catholic French kings would ally with Protestant princes, not to mention the sultan, to prevent a Catholic Habsburg hegemony in Europe, even if this meant (as it did in the era of the Thirty Years War) ensuring that the Counter-Reformation would never recapture northern Europe.

Time and again, princes in the period 1550–1650 were drawn into actions that many nobles and ecclesiastics thought were amoral but in the circumstances made perfect sense. Princes then had to protect their flanks from the criticism of the religious bigot and the jaundiced traditionalist. The employment of a minister–favourite was the perfect solution. A Richelieu or Olivares took the flak, while the monarchy generally escaped unscathed. Prince and minister–favourite made an effective double act. The prince presented himself to the world as the good king of yore; the minister–favourite openly pursued a policy of *Realpolitik*. The one carried in his robe Cicero's *De officiis*, the most widely read classroom text of the sixteenth and seventeenth centuries, which stressed that there was only one single morality for both the governed and the governor; the other continually conned the *Annals* of Tacitus (a Latin author virtually ignored before the second half of the sixteenth century and his promotion by Justus Lipsius), and became schooled in the novel art of *raison d'état*.[31]

The success of the tactic can be seen in the contemporary portrayal of the minister–favourite. Bérenger in his original article stressed that minister–favourites were universally execrated: contemporaries portrayed them as machiavels, tyrants and, above all, usurpers of royal authority; they had ceased to be the servants of monarchy and had become its masters. A number of essays in this present volume confirm this view. According to Blair Worden's exhaustive study of the portrayal of the minister–favourite on the English stage (Chapter 11 above), theatre audiences in London at least were continually and exclusively presented with a negative characterization of the political phenomenon. Antonio Feros' general study of the image of the minister–favourite (Chapter 13 above) is admittedly more nuanced in its conclusions, but he too discovers widespread acceptance of the political development only in Spain, a reflection, one might suspect, of the fact that the Castilian monarch from the reign of Philip II deliberately cultivated a more distant relationship with his subjects. Moreover, as Feros' account of writers, such as Maldonado, who argued forcibly in favour of the institution makes clear, even positive portrayals of the *valido* would have done nothing to correct the popular perception that the minister–favourite was a surrogate prince. Maldonado and other Spanish propagandists stressed that the minister–favourite was the lynchpin of the state, a royal intimate and friend, whose advice and judgement in consequence alone could be relied on in a world full of ambitious flatterers. David Wootton (Chapter 12 above) makes much the same point in his analysis of Francis Bacon's understanding of the political phenomenon in England in the reign of James I: royal favourites were not the king's servants but his chosen friends, trusted *participes curarum*. In France, too, Richelieu's hacks equally defended the omnicompetence and authority of the minister–favourite, if they understandably made no attempt to claim that the cardinal was the king's boon companion. According to de Silhon's *Ministre d'état* of 1631, Richelieu was a divine instrument, providentially sent by God to rule over France and clear up disorder. Guez de Balzac even openly extolled the role of the minister–favourite as the prince's protector, an instrument of government who would take unpopular but necessary decisions upon himself and thereby draw the ire of an ignorant and fickle people.[32]

Many minister–favourites themselves only encouraged observers to believe they had usurped the authority of their masters. As the essay of Jonathan Brown effectively demonstrates (Chapter 14 above), three of the leading examples of the genre – Buckingham, Olivares and Richelieu – were committed self-publicists, who used the artist as well as the writer to justify and glorify their power. Richelieu thought nothing of presenting himself as a new Moses saving France (see pl. 56). Furthermore, he unashamedly placed himself on the same level as his king, when he decorated the facing end-walls of the gallery of his palace at Richelieu, the *galerie des batailles*, with two equestrian portraits of himself and his master.[33] Brown surmises that such grandiose statements were more than just reminders to the clients and courtiers who saw the paintings of the achievements and status of the minister–favourite: rather, the constant iconographical hints of opposition in the wings suggest that the paintings were intended to bolster an inner insecurity.

This argument makes sense when it is recalled that the use of art as secular propaganda was revived in Europe in the Renaissance by Italian merchant–princes anxious to consolidate their dominant position in urban oligarchies – notably the Medici. Significantly, it was Marie de Médicis who taught Richelieu the value of art and display. Regardless of the truth of Brown's observation, however, the artistic representation of the minister–favourite can only have further encouraged many contemporaries to look on the political phenomenon with a jaundiced eye. It was of a piece with the favourites' frequently ostentatious, self-aggrandizing lifestyle, which in Richelieu's case put Louis XIII himself in the shade.[34] Inevitably, it was not only jealous and embittered courtiers, like the archbishop of Paris, de Retz, who came to loathe the cardinal–ministers. Even Parisians outside the court's ambit were convinced that Richelieu and Mazarin had usurped the king's power, as the vitriolic correspondence of the Parisian physician, Gui Patin, reveals.[35]

Given the dislike with which the minister–favourite was viewed, it is surprising that any of their number survived in office for long. That several did reflected an uncanny ability to maintain the prince's affection. Constantly the subject of court intrigue and the butt of a nascent public opinion, the minister–favourite owed everything to royal favour. As Sir John Elliott reveals in this volume (Chapter 8 above), Olivares' survival seemed so improbable to contemporaries that it was assumed that he had bewitched his master. In fact, he was just remarkably adept at bolstering Philip IV's confidence and presenting himself to the king as a disinterested minister and counsellor: he eschewed the term *valido*. Minister–favourites were clearly Janus-faced: to the outside world they appeared as demi-gods; in the royal closet they were humble and contrite servants. Richelieu was notorious for his ability to produce tears at will, as his stellar performance before Louis XIII and his mother on the Day of Dupes (11 November 1630), famously reveals.[36] Minister–favourites were master role-players and even the most successful were eventually exhausted by the combined pressure of their political and administrative duties. As the prince's fall-guy in an age of *raison d'état*, they continually had to watch their backs, often literally. Opponents did not wait quietly for the king to tire of his favourite: Buckingham was assassinated and Richelieu the intended victim of several plots.

On the other hand, they played their role so effectively that their princely partners in crime largely escaped scot-free. The only monarchs in the period to be felled by the assassin's knife were Henri III and Henri IV of France. The first was too obviously involved in the murder of the Guise, while the second had committed the cardinal sin of changing his faith for political reasons, not once but twice. Even so, arguably, Henri IV could have deflected the criticism levelled at his *politique* regime more effectively had he entrusted power more completely to Sully (pl. 72). In some respects, Henri IV and Sully formed the greatest double act of them all in the period. While the Gallic Hercules and Catholic convert bought the loyalty of the unruly French nobility by out-whoring, out-drinking and out-gambling his erstwhile Ligueur enemies and pandered to the Counter-Reformation church by patronizing the Jesuits, the Protestant Sully methodically filled the state's coffers by fair means or foul.[37] Unfortunately, the double act was too transparent. Theirs was not the relationship of king and minister–favourite, for Henri IV always made it crystal clear that he was in charge, especially of his state's pro-Protestant foreign policy, with the result that it was the minister not the king who survived into ripe old age.[38] Kings more willing to shelter behind their favourites' coat-tails could pursue with impunity policies that the social elite found controversial.

Being a minister–favourite was clearly an exhausting, debilitating and dangerous business. That Richelieu and Mazarin should have accumulated vast amounts of money and land in pursuing their perilous *métier* is quite understandable. They must have felt that they deserved a share of the prince's estate in return for saving the royal face. Indeed, Orest Ranum's analysis of Richelieu's economic vocabulary (Chapter 9 above) suggests that one minister–favourite at least quite explicitly saw the spoils of office as the legitimate return for services rendered. Although Richelieu remained in many ways wedded to the neo-Stoic discourse of his age which unreservedly criticized venality, he also had a more modern mercantilist concept of wealth. In Richelieu's opinion he had personally increased the material prosperity of his king's state (or tried to), so he was entitled to a commensurate material reward. He was not therefore embarrassed by his great wealth, in contrast to Mazarin who used the more traditional language of a man in his position needing to keep up appearances to justify his riches and exorbitant lifestyle. Of course, many minister–favourites or would-be members of the species may have been quite simply greedy and have taken as much as they could. This was the late C. V. Wedgwood's final verdict on the rapacious behaviour of Strafford (although he, unlike Richelieu, never seems to have directly cheated the king).[39] However, even the greedy as they accumulated offices, honours and land usually did so with an ulterior motive. J.-F. Dubost's study of Concini in this volume (Chapter 5 above) reveals that even a relatively lightweight representative of the genre, who began his career as a traditional favourite, had a strategy of accumulation: he tried to protect his back by building up a power-base in Picardy and having his own personal army, a survival tactic later adopted by Strafford in Ireland.

Decline

Just as in explaining the rise of the minister–favourite, so in accounting for the decline of the phenomenon after 1660 the emphasis has been traditionally placed on changes in the calibre of Europe's princes. If no one has ever suggested that the leadership qualities of Europe's princes suddenly improved *en masse*, it has often been claimed that the era of the dolt and the dunderhead had largely passed by the second half of the seventeenth century (except in Spain).

In the light of the rehabilitation of the princes in the first half of the century, of course, such an explanation can retain little credibility. Yet it would be wrong not to give some weight to individual factors in accounting for the disappearance of the minister–favourite.

One monarch in this new era – Louis XIV (pl. 58) – was particularly talented and influential. When the Sun King, much to the surprise of his entourage, took the decision in 1661 to employ no more minister–favourites, he set an example that Europe's lesser princes definitely hastened to follow. Moreover, Marc Fumaroli's detailed and subtle study in this volume (Chapter 15 above) of Louis XIV's decision to rule alone, emphasizes the peculiar context that led to his taking this momentous step. Fumaroli believes that Louis XIV would in normal circumstances have appointed his *surintendant des finances*, Nicolas Fouquet, to Mazarin's position, and that the king had no long-standing commitment to ruling on his own. Fouquet, however, had an Achilles heel: he was too closely associated with the forces in Paris that disliked the heavy-handed rule of the cardinal–ministers and longed to return to a more consultative absolutist system of an earlier era: paradoxically, then, Fouquet, a jumped-up bourgeois, becomes the unlikely precursor of the two aristocratic critics of the regime of Louis XIV, Fénelon and Saint-Simon. Apprised of this constitutionalist tendency by Colbert (himself too small a fry to inherit Mazarin's mantle), Louis was persuaded to take up the reins of office and bring to an end the era of the minister–favourite in France.[40]

Nonetheless, what Fumaroli's elegant story unravels is the specific context determining the timing of the disappearance of the minister–favourite in France: it cannot explain the general demise of the institution. There were deeper forces pushing Europe's princes, even Louis XIV, towards jettisoning the political phenomenon: the political revolution of the second half of the seventeenth century cannot just be accounted for by princely serendipity and the power of imitation. Bérenger's essay in this collection (Chapter 16 above) suggests that one such force lay in the volatile and fraught political climate that the age of the minister–favourite had itself brought into being. Taking up a point raised in his original article, Bérenger argues that the hostility to the minister–favourite, in the territories of the Austrian Habsburgs at least, had become so great by 1660 that the institution had lost its *raison d'être*. Far from strengthening royal authority, the employment of a minister–favourite now threatened to undermine it. The opposition rhetoric had successfully soured the political atmosphere.

Bérenger's argument is an important one, for it emphasizes the dynamic possibilities of political discourse. The attacks levelled against minister–favourites by sidelined courtiers and ecclesiastics (in Austria's case, Jesuits) not only reflected the success of the institution in deflecting flak from the prince. Perversely, they may also have created a new political environment which reduced the value of the minister–favourite. It may be suspected, however, that Bérenger overstates his case. That there was widespread hostility in court circles to the minister–favourite as an institution cannot be doubted, but how far that hostility was given a wider public airing remains to be seen. Obviously in England, where, as Worden's essay reveals, the evils of the minister–favourite were publicly and continually exposed on the London stage, hatred of the institution must have been widespread. In many other countries, however, one suspects that the critical discourse of the court overflowed into the streets only at moments of political breakdown. In France, for instance, there seem to have been sudden upsurges in the literature of popular complaint only during the crisis of the 1590s, the mid-1610s and the years of the Fronde.[41] Denunciations of individual minister–favourites as tyrants and usurpers were largely the stuff of private correspondence and unpublished political treatises. In normal circumstances, the minister–favourites themselves policed the public sphere too closely to permit the formation of a widely diffused opposition consciousness. If a ruler's horizons were totally defined by the court, then Bérenger's argument makes sense; if not (and the young Louis XIV who set the ball rolling by failing to appoint a successor to Mazarin certainly had some understanding of the wider world), then the political consequences of the opposition rhetoric can only have been a part of the story.[42]

In fact, it is not hard to suggest other contributory factors to the demise of the minister–favourite in the second half of the seventeenth century. A leading factor in producing the phenomenon in the first place, it was argued above, was the difficulty most princes had in reconciling their traditional role as peripatetic action men with the demands of a burgeoning administration. By the mid-seventeenth century, however, combining the two roles had become more manageable, for the concept of traditional kingship had been significantly transformed by noble internalization of early-sixteenth-century humanist ideas of Christian civility and gentility. Princes were no longer expected to be Jaques' soldier–braggart 'seeking the bubble reputation / Even in the cannon's mouth' or periodically risking their necks in tournaments, but rather the epitome of courtesy, self-control and restraint. This was a princely-cum-courtly ideal first popularized even before the age of the minister–favourite in Castiglione's *Courtier* of 1529, a work which transferred the Erasmian concept of the universal Christian soldier to the specific context of the prince's household.[43] However, it took many decades for the new ethic to become firmly rooted at court. If there were several notable individual illustrations of the ideal in the second half of the sixteenth century, particularly Sir Philip Sidney, who expressed the ideal both as a courtier–poet and as a courtier–soldier, the ethic was not widely internalized.[44]

The sixteenth- and early-seventeenth-century court was a violent, frequently murderous place, where courtiers kept their tempers (just) in the presence of their prince but committed acts of affray on its fringes with impunity and often with their lord's connivance. The massacre of the Huguenot nobility that occurred in Paris on 22 August 1572 was admittedly unique in its savagery, but it remains testimony to the burning hatred that often divided factions at court and could rise to the surface when the prince (in this case the mollycoddled Charles IX) allowed the mask of courtesy to slip. Sixteenth-century courtiers still lived, by and large, according to late-medieval concepts of honour. The development of the duel in France and other countries (not England) from the 1580s was an attempt to channel and control the endemic violence of the court, not to outlaw it.[45] It took a further fifty years and Richelieu's notorious martyrdom of Montmorency-Bouteville in 1626 for all forms of physical violence to be banished from the French court. It was only towards the mid-seventeenth century, by which time the new ethic had been institutionalized in a new educational institution – the noble academy – that princes and their courtiers finally began to judge each other by the polish of their manners rather than by their pugnacity and brio.[46]

Princes in the age of Louis XIV, then, were no longer expected to expend their energies in a constant round of travelling, fighting, drinking and whoring. They might continue to hunt and produce a bevy of illegitimate children,[47] but they were now much more discreet in their appetites. Some of their number, too – Charles XI and XII of Sweden, William III of Orange – might continue to lead their armies into battle, but this was no longer *de rigueur*. It was enough to be acquainted with the theory of the art of Mars, to be painted in a military posture and to visit the front from time to time. Instead, Europe's leading princes fixed their court in one particular place, avoided the rigours of campaigning and enmeshed their courtier–nobles in a complex web of ritualized service of the kind most famously orchestrated by Louis XIV at the Louvre and eventually Versailles. Princes no longer earned the loyalty of their magnates by demonstrating their superiority in the traditional martial and courtly arts (as Francis I and Henry VIII had done). Rather, they elevated their persons to a state of semi-divinity and, taking a leaf out of the minister–favourites' book, emphasized their grandeur through extravagant and self-referential patronage of the arts: Augustus had replaced Hercules.[48] Princes, moreover, also came to believe that representations of royalty were more effective ways of retaining their subjects' allegiance than the thing itself. It was the prince's image (served up in a plethora of different forms) that was continually thrust before the eyes of adoring subjects in the second half of the seventeenth century, not the prince's occasional person. Admittedly, earlier princes or regents had not been unknown to promote a positive image of themselves, but scarcely to the same extent, apart from a handful of particularly insecure and usually female rulers, such as Elizabeth I and Marie de Médicis.[49]

The Sun King's image was the most developed and the most bogus. It was not that in his later years Louis XIV's full-length portrait displayed him as a man in his prime when he had gone to fat; he was not the first prince to want to be seen to be eternally young. It was rather that his image-makers presented him as the new Charlemagne, defending Catholic Christianity against the heretic and heathen, when nothing could be further from the truth. Louis wanted to be seen as crusader, ardent to regain Jersualem for the faith, but the heir to St

Louis could not even be bothered to send troops to save Vienna from the Turks in 1683.[50]

The prince in the second half of the seventeenth century, therefore, had much more time to turn to administrative matters. Provided he did not become totally immersed in administrative details, as Philip II had been, the prince could once again bestride both the court and the bureaucracy. Louis XIV (inevitably) was the master of the art, carefully dividing his day between the bedchamber and the bureau. And in his case the routine was never altered. Even when the Roi Soleil received the cataclysmic news of the dauphin's death towards the end of his reign, he retained his self-control: quickly recovering his composure and much to the court's astonishment, he pointedly informed an attendant minister that the council would meet the next day as usual.[51] Admittedly, not every European prince in the second half of the seventeenth century wore such a conspicuous mask of gentility, though those who did not were usually the subject of peer-group censure. When Peter the Great visited western Europe incognito in 1697, he and his entourage behaved little differently in their cups from Henri IV and his cronies a century before. While attending an anatomy lesson at Leiden, Peter even ordered squeamish members of his entourage to tear out the corpse's muscles with their teeth. At the turn of the eighteenth century, however, the Russian emperor was labelled a barbarian.[52]

The prince's new-found ability to balance his two roles after 1660 also went hand in hand with an important change in the political atmosphere. To the extent that the appearance of the minister–favourite can be associated with the contemporary suspicion of the new politics of *raison d'état*, it is surely a significant factor in his demise that by the second half of the seventeenth century hostility to the state's pursuit of an independent secular agenda had greatly waned. The Thirty Years War and the contemporaneous Franco-Spanish struggle had been a bloody and protracted affair which cost the Holy Roman Empire perhaps a third of its population (as many as had been killed by the Black Death of 1348). This orgy of blood-letting might not have taught Europe's elites the futility of war, but it did demonstrate to most Protestants and Catholics (even members of the clergy) that the religious divide was here to stay and that a state's foreign policy should henceforth be conducted purely on dynastic grounds. Cross-confessional alliances no longer raised the ire of the pious. The state, too, frequently emerged from the conflict with an enlarged bureaucracy and standing army. Paradoxically, it now became much easier for the ruler to play his appointed role as defender of the faith in his own territories, whatever the religious complexion of his international alliances. The Thirty Years War and the other conflicts that beset Europe in the middle decades of the seventeenth century ironically finally made it possible for rulers to turn the doctrine of the 1555 Peace of Augsburg – 'cuius regio, eius religio' – into reality. Bohemia became a Catholic state; so too did France in 1685; while Ireland could well have become permanently Protestant had Cromwell lived and his son

Henry continued to pursue his hardline policies beyond 1656. The pious then may have lost their dreams of the religious reunion of Christendom by force but they were frequently wooed and appeased by the prospect of internal proselytization. In such an environment, there was no need for the prince to hide behind minister–favourites: he no longer needed a fall-guy.[53]

The state's attack on its subjects' traditions and privileges in search of money was equally less contested. After several decades of continual warfare the population had largely grown used to heavier and unconstitutional taxation: in pre-industrial Europe changes which lasted long enough to become familiar always ended by becoming acceptable. The process of acceptance was only aided by the fact that the privileged orders were generally protected from the new fiscalism and sometimes even able to benefit from it. In Restoration England, for instance, the introduction of permanent peacetime taxation took the form of an excise on alcoholic beverages which inevitably hit the poor rather than the rich.[54]

Even if the population did not get used to the new tax demands, it still largely kowtowed, for the wars had seen the maturation of an ideology of absolutism which stressed that kings were gods and their commands unquestionable. In both Protestant and Catholic countries the second half of the seventeenth century saw the successful promotion of a novel ideology of sovereign authority, first developed by Bodin in the 1570s and secularized and taken to its fullest extent by Hobbes.[55] To all intents and purposes the much older ideology of the right of rebellion, even tyrannicide, which had been articulated by Aquinas and espoused by both Calvinists and Jesuits in the second half of the sixteenth century, was completely excised from European political culture for over a century, except for its temporary and limited re-emergence in England and the Netherlands in the 1690s with John Locke and Jurieu. Pointedly, in the France of Louis XIV, where future members of the elite were inculcated in the absolutist ideology even while learning classical languages, the most fulsome account of royal power was to be penned by a Huguenot, Elie Merlat, on the eve of the Revocation of the Edict of Nantes.[56]

Thus the rhetoric of disappointed courtiers, a new court culture, a more realistic approach to the division of Christendom and the successful inculcation of a cult of obedience all seem to have combined to hasten the disappearance of the minister–favourite after 1660. As a result his star shone in the political heavens for barely a century. The minister–favourite was clearly the political institution of the High Renaissance. The phenomenon helped the prince negotiate that period of political instability and transition that marked the bridge between the late medieval state and its *ancien régime* successor.[57] The minister–favourite oversaw the transference from the relatively simple, personal and (often cruelly) spontaneous state of the fifteenth and early sixteenth centuries to the much more complex, impersonal and bureaucratic state of the period 1660–1789. The first was effectively described by Machiavelli, although the Florentine grossly exaggerated the amoralism of the princes north of the Alps: they were conventional dynasts who believed that God would bless or damn their cause on the field of battle.[58] The second was brilliantly described by Tocqueville, though his fixation with the administrative centralization of mid-nineteenth-century France prevented him from seeing how corporatist the absolute state really was.[59] No contemporary political theorist-cum-sociologist of lasting significance, on the other hand, ever attempted to define the state of the era of the minister–favourite – Balzac and its other supporters were little more than propaganda hacks.

Unanswered Questions

Although it is now possible to construct a more nuanced picture than hitherto of the rise and fall of the minister–favourite, it remains the case that there are still aspects of the phenomenon that require fuller research. Above all, much more needs to be known about the minister–favourite's relationship to the rituals and structure of the early modern court. In recent years, the court has become a focus of serious historical interest for the first time. Historians no longer contend that the sixteenth and seventeenth centuries witnessed a period of bureaucratic state-building that left the court relatively marginalized. Rather, they have come to understand that the burgeoning administrative apparatus remained deeply embedded in the court. The court, then, was still the epicentre of royal government, even if the prince was peripatetic for most of this period and parts of the administrative machine (usually those concerned most closely with justice) had become permanently fixed. This new understanding of the importance of the court clearly must be taken into account in any attempt to comprehend the phenomenon of the minister–favourite.[60] Retaining the prince's favour and dominating the machinery of state principally required control of the court. How did the minister–favourite achieve this? This present set of essays, it must be admitted, offers no obvious answer, for its authors make little attempt to engage directly with this new history of the court. Yet if, as was earlier pointed out, the *premier ministre* was not necessarily a natural courtier and was frequently absent from his master's or mistress's side, the question of how he retained his authority at the centre of power becomes an even more interesting one.

Given the drift of much of the recent research into the power-basis of the minister–favourite – represented in this volume paticularly by the essay of Sir John Elliott on Olivares (Chapter 8 above) – one would expect a solution to this conundrum to be found yet again through a study of patronage. Presumably, the minister–favourite constructed a ministerial clientele within the court, as he did throughout the wider administration. It may be time, however, for historians of the phenomenon to begin to think about the establishment of the *premier ministre*'s authority in a more imaginative way. It may well be the case that early modern European society was largely held together by the glue of material rewards. To an important degree, it was the honours, offices and cash that princes showered upon their minister–favourites which confirmed the latter's overweening authority, just as the minister–favourite's liberal distribution of patronage among his clients helped reduce the possibility of the disappointed challenging his pre-eminence. There again, this was a society in which obedience and deference were largely engendered through the ownership and exercise of certain rituals of power rather than through the crude monopoly of wealth and physical force. Wealth might help to embellish these rituals but was not strictly necessary: effective rituals do not have to be extravagant *pièces de théâtre*. The sixteenth and seventeenth centuries formed one of the great eras of the invention of court ceremonial. The rituals that orchestrated the relations between an Elizabeth I or a Louis XIV and their courtiers were not aesthetic constructs but statements about princely authority which their enactment created and enhanced.[61] It behoves us, then, to explore whether the appearance of the minister–favourite was accompanied by the development of courtly rituals peculiarly aimed at stabilizing his honour and dignity.

In the case of many minister–favourites the need to construct such a symbolic suit of clothes must have been all the greater in that they were metaphorically speaking semi-clad. As they were seldom personal favourites, their position in the king's affections would not have been continually confirmed by passionate embraces and frequent visits to the royal bed. In a period in which male friendship and trust was publicly and graphically displayed, the personal favourite's authority over the court would have been continually consolidated by acts of intimacy. If this could be a double-edged privilege in that it allowed the jealous to spread rumours of homosexual relations between friends of unequal status, it was still the case that this was a symbol of princely favour to which most minister–favourites had no access.[62] To the extent, too, that many minister–favourites did not hold a major court or administrative office, they had no alternative way of commanding the deference of courtiers. It is no wonder that a Richelieu or a Mazarin prized his cardinal's hat!

It is unlikely, of course, that specific ceremonies were created to clothe the minister–favourite's nakedness, which might be part of the explanation why there were no European equivalents of the Togukawa. What we know of an Olivares or Richelieu suggests that they were interested in using ceremonial to exalt the king rather than themselves. Even Richelieu's famous staged entrances were aimed at emphasizing his ecclesiastical dignity, not his ministerial status. Perhaps minister–favourites felt it sufficient to have their power and deeds frozen once and for all iconographically on the walls of their palaces, rather than referred to repeatedly in a series of gestures and words. But, even if a fuller knowledge of the minister–favourite at court leads to the conclusion that the phenomenon was too dynamic and protean to be defined by a set of rituals (there were certainly ones of a common character, given the heterogeneity of the European court before 1650), it seems more than likely that the individual minister–favourite would have left some mark on his contemporary aulic culture. It has often been noted how careful Richelieu was to be deferential before Louis XIII, always insisting on standing, for instance, in the king's presence even when bedridden with illness. What was the purpose of such courtesy? Obviously, it was part of the cardinal's wider campaign to have royal authority treated with respect: courtiers as well as provincial Frenchmen had to learn that the Lord's Anointed and his servants could not be approached like common mortals.[63] On the other hand, in thereby enhancing the crown's dignity, the cardinal safeguarded his own position. Once the king too had learnt that intimacy with the royal person or his representative was conduct unbecoming, indeed the crime of *lèse-majesté*, the traditional advantages of the personal favourite in the power-game at court were reduced.

Did the minister–favourite, too, devise new ways for the king to bestow his esteem, if traditional methods of physical intimacy were sidelined? Was it Richelieu, for instance, who invented the ritual of the royal *regard* in France, brought to perfection by Louis XIV? If so, the narrative of the Day of Dupes takes on a new poignancy. After Richelieu's tempestuous interview with Louis and Marie de Médicis, the cardinal waited patiently at the bottom of the staircase for the king to emerge from the queen mother's chambers. When he did so and descended the stairs, Richelieu bowed low but the king walked past without bestowing a glance in the cardinal's direction. This, it seems, was the sign that the court had waited for: it was not the sound of the queen mother's anger or Richelieu's tears: the cardinal was finished because he had been ignored by the king. But when and how had the royal *regard* acquired such importance, and what subtle changes in the inclination of the head and the royal mien portended favour or dismissal? The early modern royal physiognomy remains a closed book to historians. Indeed, so too does the broader 'science' of reading a man's character and intentions in his face, despite the fact that it was one of the most widely disseminated belief systems of the age, as Martin Porter's recent doctoral thesis reveals.[64]

Naturally, the minister–favourite not only had to fashion a royal protocol that included a series of gestures which would unambiguously reveal to the court how high he was placed in the king's esteem: he also had to ensure that royal favour continued. Once more, it must be admitted, the essays in this volume add little to existing understanding. We remain locked in the assumption that minister–favourites, who hardly ever won the prince's affections through their looks, had a psychological hold based on their ability to articulate the prince's wishes and put them into effect. Even if this argument is inherently plausible, we need to know much more about the minister–favourite's own reading of his position. Presumably, most minister–favourites for most of the time were very unsure of their domination. Given that success was seldom assured and frequently unachieved, what steps did they take, beyond surrounding the king with their own clients, to ensure that they remained first in the royal affections? Arguably, there is still a tendency to see the minister–favourite as a modern man, the nineteenth- and twentieth-century exponent of *Realpolitik*. This is to forget that they were late Renaissance figures, part of a cultural environment dominated by hermetic and occult ideas.[65]

Sir John Elliott's essay informs us that contemporary Spaniards thought that Olivares had bewitched Philip IV. However absurd such an explanation for the *conde-duque*'s political success may seem to us, the statement needs to be taken seriously. Most educated Europeans before 1650 believed in the realities of witchcraft and possession, and most princes and their advisers consulted astrologers and warlocks. It is by no means improbable that minister–favourites contrived to retain their prince's affection by recourse to magic. Richelieu for one was extremely interested in the occult. How should we read the fact that after the Day of Dupes he imprisoned one of the king's physicians, Semelles, in the Bastille for casting a horoscope predicting that Louis XIII would die in September 1631? Did he silence Semelles because he feared such predictions would give hope to his enemies, or did he really suspect that Semelles might have the power not just to know but to create the future?[66] Even trivial anecdotes about Richelieu's life take on an added importance if we remember his interest in the forbidden arts. On one occasion, he danced the saraband before the queen, Anne of Austria, another of his political enemies. Should this be taken as an interesting insight into the cardinal's 'other' more passionate side, the courtier *manqué* pandering to the queen's Spanish roots, or is it stretching credibility too far to suggest it might signify something more sinister? The saraband was a *sorcier*'s dance. Was Richelieu attempting to bewitch Anne of Austria to win her favour by calling up hidden forces of nature, in much the same way as Henri III and his *mignons* at an earlier date possibly staged magical masques at court depicting the triumphs of peace over civil war with the intention of summoning the support of benevolent spiritual powers? We know much about the minister–favourite as a Machiavellian; we know next to nothing about him as a magus.[67]

Nor do we know enough as yet about the way in which the minister–favourite was perceived by his contemporaries. At present, the species has the solidity of an historical construct. Did the host of contemporary commentators on the phenomenon (usually critical) distinguish the minister–favourite from the more common or garden variety? Several essays in this volume suggest that this was not the case: hostile observers seem to have been more than ready to blacken the reputation of a contemporary *premier ministre* by calling to mind the power and influence of earlier, detested conventional favourites, such as Piers Gaveston. There again, other essays raise the possibility that some critics at least understood the difference. Does the presentation of Sejanus as an archetypal point of reference in the critical literature reflect the newfound interest in Tacitus or a deeper realization that plausible historical parallels from the national past could not be easily found? There was no whiff of intimacy about the relationship between Tiberius and his favourite: the emperor purportedly invited young boys to his bed, not his principal administrative agent.

Clearly more work needs to be done on the contemporary discourse of the minister–favourite to see whether or not he was perceived as a distinctive political animal. A more detailed study of the positive accounts of the phenomenon would be particularly useful. How far did the minister–favourite's 'spin-doctors' actively attempt to fashion a portrait of the *premier ministre* as a novel political figure? Equally, though, we need to pursue the negative portrayal of the phenomenon in much greater depth to grasp more securely the popular perception of the species. The study of the critical literature of the court, however sensitive, is insufficient here. Even the analysis of plays performed on the London stage only touches the surface.[68] We need the minister–favourite to be pursued across the continent through his manifestation in the ballad, broadsheet and woodcut. At the moment only the literary ephemera of the Fronde has been studied in detail. In particular, a deeper acquaintance with this contemporary discourse will throw greater light on Bérenger's suggestion that the minister–favourite disappeared after 1660 because the hostility to the phenomenon outweighed its utility. We want to know how great that hostility actually was. We need, too, to know how far the popular success of the critical literature can be attributed to the manipulation of powerful and disconcerting images in the historical memory. In addition, there is a need to explore how far those images were all the more disconcerting in that increasingly over the period Protestants and Counter-Reformers were attempting to redraw the boundaries of public intimacy.[69]

Finally, while attempting to understand more deeply the historical reality of the minister–favourite in the century 1550–1650, it is important that the extent of his singularity is examined in the light of the apparent reappearance of the species in the second half of the eighteenth century. It is indisputable that the long reign of Louis XIV sees the sudden death of the phenomenon. Yet, as Hamish Scott has reminded us in an essay published in 1996, omnicompetent principal ministers were once again a commonplace in the absolute states of continental Europe after 1750. Pombal in Portugal, Potemkin in Russia (pl. 73), Kaunitz in the Austrian Habsburg Empire, Maurepas and Vergennes in the France of Louis XVI, A. P. von Bernstorff in the Denmark of the mad Christian VII – the names of statesmen in the second half of the eighteenth century who monopolized or virtually monopolized political authority litter the stage of Europe. Only Frederick the Great of Prussia maintained the tradition of Louis XIV and was his own very dedicated principal minister.[70] Indeed, the species began to reappear even before 1750 in France and Russia, where Cardinal Fleury in the first part of the reign of Louis XV enjoyed similar power and influence to Richelieu and Mazarin, and a bevy of minister–favourites, such as Bestuzheff under the Empress Elizabeth, relieved the successors of Peter the Great of the mantle of office.[71]

Scott's point is well taken. In fact, one could extend the list into the first part of the nineteenth century, for some of the absolute states of the Restoration also had their principal ministers. The most obvious candidate for the sobriquet is the 'coachman of Europe', the Austrian chancellor Count Metternich (pl. 74), who ruled the roost in Austria, above all in the realm of foreign affairs, from 1810 to the Revolution of 1848.[72] The re-emergence of the phenomenon clearly cries out for comparative study. Yet, to date, historians of the minister–favourite of the late Renaissance have ignored the resurrection of the species entirely.

At first glance, it must be said, the points of contrast between the two periods seem stronger than the points of comparison. The two sets of minister–favourites definitely shared one important characteristic in that the eighteenth-century principal minister was also not a favourite in a conventional sense. Only Potemkin and Struensee, Bernstorff's predecessor and the ill-fated lover of the Danish queen, owed their elevation to the politics of the bedroom.[73] There again, the eighteenth-century *premier ministre* was much more the officially recognized head of the administration with a definite title and personal sphere of competence (usually in foreign affairs). He was also much more a reformer than a patronage-broker (if he survived long enough to effect significant change). Only a detailed comparative analysis of the two sets, however, will confirm this initial impression. In particular, historians will need to focus their attention on a further apparent point of distinction between the two eras. Whereas the phenomenon of the minister–favourite in the period 1550–1650 was almost universally execrated, in the eighteenth century the institution, if not necessarily the individual representatives of the species, received a much better press. By and large, contemporaries accepted the postion and raised little objection to the concept of royal surrogacy *per se*.

Why did the minister–favourite's second coming cause so little furore? According to Scott, we should attribute the reappearance of the phenomenon to an unprecedented expansion in government activity from the middle of the eighteenth century, as princes and their advisers showed a novel interest in managing the economy and effecting social and educational reforms. As the business of the state expanded, the average prince no longer had the stamina to run the machinery of state himself, and so called in a professional co-ordinator. This explanation obviously derives from Bérenger's original account of the rise of the late Renaissance minister–favourite, and for this reason alone should be treated with caution. If true, however, it might help to explain the relative absence of criticism the second time round. Arguably, the growth in government activity made it abundantly evident to contemporary observers that princes could no longer perform their dual function as heads of the court and the administration, especially in an age which had discovered privacy. Monarchs, like Louis XV and Louis XVI, wanted to spend time on their own or in retreat with their mistress or family.[74] Obviously they had to sacrifice one of their roles and, given their totemic function at the pinnacle of the hierarchical society, they could hardly abandon the court. Only the spartan and probably misogynist Frederick the Great turned himself into a full-time administrator and left the court to be run by his siblings. It was Frederick, too, of course, who originally articulated the novel 'Enlightenment' theory of kingship which declared that the monarch belonged to the state, not the state to the monarch. Other princes later copied him in this profession, but none, apart from Joseph II of Austria, mouthed the sentiment that the prince was 'the first servant of the state' so honestly.[75]

At this stage in our knowledge, though, any answer to the question as to why the minister–favourite was better received in his later manifestation must be pure speculation. This is equally true of another aspect of the re-emergence of the minister–favourite that Scott hints at but does not develop – the British connection. How far should the recourse to a principal minister in a second period of administrative growth and reorganization be in any way seen as an attempt to revivify an ancient, discredited institution? Rather, should it be connected, in an era of relative Anglomania, with the establishment from the second decade of the eighteenth century of the purely British institution of prime minister? Britain's 'first' prime minister, Sir Robert Walpole, of course, had many of the characteristics of a traditional minister–favourite, not least his dependence on Queen Caroline for maintaining his credit with George II, and the office might not have developed so quickly after 1714 had it not been for the Hanoverians' foreign roots. But traditional minister–favourites operated within a court not a parliamentary context, and Walpole ultimately retained the favour of the king only as long as he commanded a Commons majority. Moreover, as a gifted financial administrator, who had lined his own pockets but saved the country at the time of the South Sea Bubble crisis, he had nothing in common with the earlier generation of minister–favourites, who usually had little financial acumen.[76]

Arguably, then, it was Walpole and his successors, whose power was public and challengeable, who were the real models for the continental development of the office of principal minister after 1750, not an Olivares or Richelieu. An institution that the British crown had been forced to foster in order to cope with the complexities of managing Britain's peculiar parliamentary monarchy may have seemed the ideal solution to the complex administrative problems of enlightened despots.[77] Yet, if this was indeed the provenance of the eighteenth-century principal minister, perhaps the likes of Fleury and Bestuzheff should not be included in Scott's list at all. Instead, they should be seen as throwbacks to an earlier era, whose control of power in France and Russia in the second quarter of the eighteenth century is to be explained simply in terms of the laziness of Louis XV and the chance occurrence of a clutch of female Romanovs.

This final suggestion, of course, must be treated with the same caution as its predecessors. To argue that the return of the era of the cardinal–ministers to France had no wider European significance is to assume again what may seem inherently plausible but has yet to be substantiated – that the two sets of minister–favourites are only superficially comparable. The ultimate aim of this concluding essay can only be to set an agenda for future research. If it has offered a more detailed analysis of the phenomenon of the minister–favourite than Bérenger's original article, it makes no claim to present more than a preliminary sketch. Indeed, it is the purpose of the volume as a whole to rekindle an old debate rather than provide a definitive overview. This volume will have achieved the aim of its editors if it has encouraged historians of the early modern period to look more closely at the structure of the European state in the century 1550–1650 and to treat the institution of the minister–favourite as a significant historical phenomenon.

Notes

1. I would like to thank the following friends and colleagues for their help in preparing the final draft of this essay: Joseph Bergin, David Parrott, Clive Holmes, Felicity Heal and Martin Porter.
2. J. Bérenger, 'Pour une enquête européenne: le problème du ministériat au XVIIe siècle', *Annales*, 29 (1974), pp. 166–92.
3. The most colourful favourite at present on the Western political scene is Claude Chirac, daughter of the French president. Dubbed 'Rasputin in miniskirts', it is claimed that 'nobody [apart from the then prime minister] gets a tête-à-tête with Chirac without going through Claude': see *The Times*, 15 March 1997, p. 21.
4. Favourites, even in the twentieth century, have seldom left their own account of their time at the top: they are primarily known through their detractors. In this respect the appearance of Marcia Williams' and Nancy Reagan's autobiographies may mark a new trend: see Marcia, Lady Falkender, *Inside Number 10* (London, 1972); and Nancy Reagan, *My Turn: The Memoirs of Nancy Reagan* (Leicester, 1989).
5. A. Lloyd Moote, 'Richelieu as Chief Minister: A Comparative Study of the Favourite in Early Seventeenth-Century Politics', in Joseph Bergin and Laurence Brockliss, eds, *Richelieu and his Age* (Oxford, 1992), esp. p. 16. Enzlin is not mentioned by Moote.
6. Being in orders was an insurance policy. If and when the favourite fell, his demise was unlikely to be terminal; only Laud among clerical favourites in this period was executed (in 1645).
7. Peter Gwyn, *The King's Cardinal: The Rise and Fall of Thomas Wolsey* (London, 1992), esp. ch. 3, on the 1518 Treaty of London; S. J. Gunn and P. G. Lindley, eds, *Cardinal Wolsey: Church, State and Art* (Cambridge, 1991), intro.
8. Anne Somerset, *Unnatural Murder: Poison at the Court of James I* (London, 1997).
9. Richelieu's political apprenticeship is effectively dealt with in Joseph Bergin, *The Rise of Richelieu* (New Haven and London, 1991), chs 3–6.
10. Olivares' power over Philip IV in the 1620s was based on his role as a father figure to an unsure prince: see J. H. Elliott, *The Count-Duke of Olivares: The Statesman in an Age of Decline* (New Haven and London, 1986), esp. pp. 170–1.
11. J. H. Elliott, *Richelieu and Olivares* (Cambridge, 1984), pp. 16–18. On the fortunes of the cardinal-ministers, see Joseph Bergin, *Cardinal Richelieu: Power and the Pursuit of Wealth* (New Haven and London, 1985), esp. ch. 7, and D. Dessert, 'Pouvoir et fortune au XVIIe siècle: la fortune de Mazarin', *Revue d'histoire moderne et contemporaine*, 23 (1976), pp. 161–81.
12. Oxenstierna was chancellor from 1612 till his death in 1654. The office and its streamlined admin-istration were at the apex of internal and foreign affairs: see Michael Roberts, *Gustavus Adolphus: A History of Sweden, 1611–1632*, 2 vols (London, 1953–8), i, pp. 271–6. There is no complete biography of Oxenstierna in any language.
13. Richelieu's clerical but scarcely political rival, Cardinal Rochefoucauld, presided over the council before him: see Joseph Bergin, *Cardinal de la Rochefoucauld: Leadership and Reform in the French Church* (New Haven and London, 1987), pp. 62–5; *idem, Rise of Richelieu*, p. 253. On Richelieu's control of the central administration through his creatures, see Orest Ranum, *Richelieu and the*

Councillors of Louis XIII: A Study of the Secretaries of State and Superintendents of Finance in the Ministry of Richelieu, 1635–42 (Oxford, 1963), esp. ch. 2.

14. The most valuable studies of the reign of Charles I are now L. J. Reeve, *Charles I and the Road to Personal Rule* (Cambridge, 1989), and Kevin Sharpe, *The Personal Rule of Charles I* (New Haven and London, 1992). Charles' crucial role even in Laudian church reform is emphasized in Julian Davies, *The Caroline Captivity of the Church: Charles I and the Remoulding of Anglicanism, 1625–61* (Oxford, 1992). On Wentworth's difficulties in keeping in touch with the court while governing Ireland, see J. F. Merritt, 'Power and Communication: Thomas Wentworth and Government at a Distance during the Personal Rule, 1629–1635', in J. F. Merritt, ed., *The Political World of Thomas Wentworth, Earl of Strafford, 1621–1641* (Cambridge, 1996).

15. Edward II and Richard II were definitely kings who knew their own minds; Henry VI was weak and inconsistent but he favoured appeasement with France in the 1440s, more so than Suffolk, who eventually took the blame for the loss of Maine and Normandy: see J. R. Maddicott, *Thomas of Lancaster, 1307–1322: A Study in the Reign of Edward II* (Oxford, 1970), esp. ch. 4 (on Gaveston's death and its consequences); Anthony Tuck, *Richard II and the English Nobility* (London, 1973), esp. ch. 7 (on Richard's personal tyranny); Bertram Wolfe, *Henry VI* (London, 1981), esp. chs 9–11 (on the war with France); John L. Watts, *Henry VI and the Politics of Kingship* (Cambridge, 1996), *passim* (on the problems of serving an indecisive king).

16. Whereas Louis XIII and Philip IV were traditionally seen as uninterested in affairs of state, this view has now been largely revised: see the works cited below, note 26. Nevertheless, if Richelieu had to work hard to convince the French king of the rectitude of his foreign policy, it was still his, not the king's, formulation. For a recent nuanced and in part sceptical examination of Richelieu's reform agenda, see Hermann Weber, '"Une Bonne Paix": Richelieu's Foreign Policy and the Peace of Christendom'; Robin Briggs, 'Richelieu and Reform: Rhetoric and Political Reality'; and Richard Bonney, 'Louis XIII, Richelieu and the Royal Finances': all in Bergin and Brockliss, eds, *Richelieu and his Age*, pp. 45–69, 71–97, 99–133. Olivares' personal reform agenda included the creation of a Castilianized, homogeneous Spanish kingdom: see Elliott, *Olivares*, esp. ch. 5.

17. This was inevitable where the ruler was a woman. In the reign of Elizabeth, Leicester and Essex were in many respects traditional favourites who came close to threatening the monopoly of the Cecils only because the war with Spain gave courtier–soldiers the chance to vie with the bureaucrats. On the accession of a woman and minor to the Swedish throne in 1632, Oxenstierna too was forced to become a soldier as well as a diplomat and administrator: he sustained the Swedish war effort in Germany until allowed by the regents to return to Sweden in 1636: see Michael Roberts, 'Oxenstierna in Germany, 1633–1636', in his *From Oxenstierna to Charles XII: Four Studies* (Cambridge, 1991), esp. pp. 8–9.

18. Apparently, Charles I listened more intently to Strafford when he was at a distance! See Merritt, 'Power and Communication', pp. 131–2.

19. Roger Lockyer, *Buckingham: The Life and Political Career of George Villiers, First Duke of Buckingham, 1592–1628* (London and New York, 1981), ch. 10. In the first session of Charles' third parliament in 1628, the opposition had not even renewed the impeachment proceedings of 1626, but simply delivered a remonstrance against Buckingham to the king.

20. The Jesuits obviously disliked the French alliance with Protestant powers. One confessor, Père Caussin, tried to remove the cardinal in December 1637: see Michel Carmona, *Richelieu* (Paris, 1983), pp. 612–17.

21. Clarendon was then impeached by parliament for the country's ineffective performance in the second Anglo-Dutch war: unlike Charles I's defence of Buckingham in similar circumstances, Charles II did nothing to save him, but acutally orchestrated the attack: see R. Hutton, *The Restoration: A Political and Religious History of England and Wales, 1658–1667* (Oxford, 1985), pp. 276–84.

22. Both were victims of their foreign policy: La Gardie got Sweden disastrously involved in the Franco-Dutch war and Griffenfeld was found guilty of not taking advantage of the Swedes' discomfiture. There is no biography of La Gardie in English. Like many favourites he was an ostentatious patron of the arts: see Michael Roberts, *The Swedish Imperial Experience 1560–1718* (Cambridge, 1979), pp. 138–9n.

23. The recent Spanish tradition of *retraimiento* was scarcely similar. Imperial power in Japan had been greatly reduced from the late twelfth century and the establishment of the Kamakura *bakufu*; in fact, the tradition of invisibility went back to the Fujiwara period (858–1160) when the country was ruled by a chief councillor: see Jean-Pierre Lehmann, *The Roots of Modern Japan* (London, 1982), pt 1. On

306 Concluding Remarks: The Anatomy of the Minister–Favourite

the Tokugawa shogunate, see Conrad D. Totman, *Politics in the Tokugawa Bakufu, 1600–1843* (Cambridge, Mass., 1967); also David M. Earl, *Emperor and Nation in Japan: Political Thinkers of the Tokugawa Period* (London, 1981).

24. Also one uncle–nephew combination: Olivares and Luis de Haro. Lerma was succeeded by his son, Uceda, but the latter enjoyed power for only a few years.

25. Jonathan D. Spence, *Emperor of China: Self-Portrait of K'ang-hsi* (London, 1992). See also *idem*, *From Ming to Ching: Conquest, Religion and Continuity in Seventeenth-Century China* (New Haven and London, 1985); Frederick Wakeman, *The Great Enterprise: The Manchu Reconstruction of Imperial Order in Sevententh-Century China*, 2 vols (Berkeley, 1985); and Shih-Shan Henry Tsui, *The Eunuchs in the Ming Dynasty* (New York, 1996).

26. A. Lloyd Moote, *Louis XIII, the Just* (Berkeley, 1989), esp. intro. and ch. 8; R. A. Stradling, *Philip IV and the Government of Spain, 1621–1665* (Cambridge, 1988), esp. pp. 32–5, on historians' changing perception of Philip.

27. Bérenger, 'Pour une enquête européenne', esp. pp. 166–7. The emperor Charles V abdicated at the age of fifty-five or fifty-six, worn out by the burdens of incessantly travelling around his European-wide domains, and died soon afterwards. Michael Roberts' seminal *The Military Revolution, 1560–1660* (Belfast, 1956) was originally delivered as his inaugural lecture at the Queen's University.

28. There were only 1,200 state officials in the early seventeenth century, plus 1,000 unpaid JPs: see Penry Williams, *The Tudor Regime* (Oxford, 1979), p. 107. France had 25,000 officeholders in 1610 and 46,000 in 1665: see E. Le Roy Ladurie, *L'Etat Royal: de Louis XI à Henri IV (1460–1610)* (Paris, 1987), p. 443.

29. Esp. in France: see *inter alia* Sharon Kettering, *Patrons, Brokers and Clients in Seventeenth-Century France* (Oxford, 1987), and Roger Mettam, *Power and Faction in Louis XIV's France* (Oxford, 1988).

30. Williams, *Tudor Regime*, pp. 86–8, 92. Peck's patronage argument is anticipated in Ronald G. Asch, 'Introduction: Court and Household from the Fifteenth to the Seventeenth Centuries', in *idem* and Adolf M. Birke, eds, *Princes, Patronage and the Nobility: The Court at the Beginning of the Modern Age, c. 1450–1650* (Oxford, 1991), pp. 20–4.

31. For the new interest in Tacitus, see Richard Tuck, *Philosophy and Government, 1572–1651* (Cambridge, 1993), chs 2–3. For Cicero in the classroom, see L. W. B. Brockliss, *French Higher Education in the Seventeenth and Eighteenth Centuries: A Cultural History* (Oxford, 1987), p. 136.

32. Etienne Thuau, *Raison d'état et pensée politique à l'époque de Richelieu* (Paris, 1966), pp. 252–62; Guez de Balzac, *Le Prince* (Paris, 1631).

33. Most recently discussed in E. Caldicott, 'Richelieu and the Arts', in Bergin and Brockliss, eds, *Richelieu and his Age*, pp. 217–20. Richelieu's use of art and propaganda is fully explored in R. Mousnier, ed., *Richelieu et la culture* (Paris, 1987), pts 2, 3. Richelieu was a new town in Poitou built to serve the cardinal's château (no longer extant).

34. To be fair to Richelieu, the cardinal did his best to promote the image of the monarchy by organizing the extension and decoration of the Louvre. But Louis XIII showed little enthusiasm for self-promotion: see Caldicott, 'Richelieu and the Arts', pp. 224–6. Richelieu called on Louis to invest in grandeur in his *Testament politique*, ed. Louis André (Paris, 1947), pp. 279–86.

35. *Lettres de Gui Patin*, ed. J.-H. Réveillé-Parise, 3 vols (Paris, 1846), *passim*. His view of Richelieu is examined in Thuau, *Raison d'état*, pp. 159–65.

36. Carmona, *Richelieu*, pp. 502–7. On the cardinal's humility before the king, see Moote, *Louis XIII*, p. 164.

37. The most recent study of Sully's activities is B. Barbiche, *Sully* (Paris, 1978), esp. chs 4–8. For his wealth, see Isabelle Aristide, *La Fortune de Sully* (Paris, 1989).

38. Villeroy not Sully conducted the king's foreign policy. Sully was more like Burghley than the classic minister–favourite. Still the strategy was successful for a decade. There were numerous attempts to assassinate Henri IV before 1600, none in the 1600s before Ravaillac's fatal attack: see R. Mousnier, *The Assassination of Henri IV: The Tyrannicide Problem and the Consolidation of the French Absolute Monarchy in the Early Seventeenth Century*, Eng. trans. (London, 1973).

39. C. V. Wedgwood, *Thomas Wentworth, First Earl of Strafford, 1593–1641: A Revaluation* (London, 1961), esp. pp. 98–9, on Strafford's profiteering from the bad harvest of 1630. Her earlier *Strafford* (London, 1938) painted a much more saintly portrait of the minister–favourite. Her opinion seems to have changed after reading J. P. Cooper, 'The Fortune of Thomas Wentworth, Earl of Strafford', *Economic History Review*, 11 (1958), pp. 227–48.

40. In the eyes of Fénelon and Saint-Simon, Louis replaced rule by minister–favourite with rule by bourgeois ministers, a group of parvenus who fed the king misinformation and shamelessly controlled his decisions. Fénelon in particular sought to introduce a representative element into the

system of Louis XIV: see esp. his *Lettre à Louis XIV*, ed. F. X. Cuche (Paris, 1994). Fénelon's political theory is most fully expounded in F. Gallouédec-Genuys, *Le Prince selon Fénelon* (Paris, 1963).

41. Robert Darnton, *The Forbidden Best-Sellers of Pre-Revolutionary France* (London, 1996), ch. 10 (on politically subversive literature across the period 1560–1789); Jeffrey Sawyer, *Printed Poison: Pamphlet Propaganda, Faction Politics and the Public Sphere in Early Seventeenth-Century France* (Berkeley, 1990); Christian Jouhaud, *Mazarinades: la Fronde des mots* (Paris, 1980).

42. Mazarin had ensured that Louis XIV was not totally cocooned in the French court (as he later certainly became) by *inter alia* ensuring he had experience of life on campaign.

43. Sydney Anglo, 'The Courtier, the Renaissance and Changing Ideals', in A. G. Dickens, ed., *The Courts of Europe* (London, 1977). Erasmus' *Enchiridion militis christiani* first appeared in 1504. For the development of the humanist ethic in and outside the court, see Eugenio Garin, *L'Education de l'homme moderne: la pédagogie de la Renaissance, 1400–1600*, French trans. (Paris, 1968), chs 5, 6, 8.

44. Blair Worden, *The Sound of Virtue: Philip Sidney's* Arcadia *and Elizabethan Politics* (New Haven and London, 1996). For the spread of the new courtly ideal, see Peter Burke, *The Fortunes of the Courtier: The European Reception of Castiglione's* Cortegiano (London, 1990), esp. app. A, list of editions; Burke believed that Castiglione's text was read by at least 300,000 people in the hundred years after its first publication (p. 140).

45. François Billacois, *The Duel: Its Rise and Fall in Early Modern France*, Engl. trans. (New Haven and London, 1990); David Loades, *The Tudor Court* (London, 1986), pp. 89–90.

46. See esp. N. Conrads, *Ritterakademien der Frühen Neuzeit. Bildung als Standesprivileg im 16. und 17. Jahrhundert* (Göttingen, 1987); also Mark Motley, *Becoming a French Aristocrat: The Education of the Court Nobility, 1580–1715* (Princeton, 1990), ch. 3.

47. Augustus the Strong of Poland–Saxony supposedly sired 200 bastards, hence his sobriquet.

48. Louis XIV to all intents and purposes monopolized cultural patronage in France. On the enslavement of the French noble elite to court ritual, see Norbert Elias' tendentious but illuminating *The Court Society*, Eng. trans. (London, 1983).

49. E.g. Roy Strong, *The Cult of Elizabeth: Elizabethan Portraiture and Pageantry* (London, 1977), and S. Mamone, *Paris et Florence: deux capitales du spectacle pour une reine, Marie de Médicis* (Paris, 1990).

50. See esp. Peter Burke, *The Fabrication of Louis XIV* (London, 1995). I owe the observation on Louis the Crusader to my research pupil, Nicholas Dew.

51. *Mémoires de Saint-Simon*, ed. G. Trug, 7 vols (Paris, 1953–61), iii, pp. 813–14 (from the year 1711).

52. V. Klychevsky, *Peter the Great*, Eng. trans. (London, 1969), pp. 25–30.

53. In the long term it became more acceptable that the prince should pursue a secular agenda *inside* his territories, but the development of a more tolerant environment in the eighteenth century did not mean that attempts at *de iure* toleration post-1750 in Britain and other states were not heavily contested. Even the *philosophes* for utilitarian reasons disliked the idea of a multi-confessional society: see Geoffrey Adams, *The Huguenots in French Opinion, 1685–1787: The Enlightenment Debate on Toleration* (Waterloo, Ont., 1991).

54. William Beik, *Absolutism and Society in Seventeenth-Century France: State Power and Provincial Aristocracy in Languedoc* (Cambridge, 1985); Hutton, *The Restoration*, pp. 148–9.

55. J. W. Allen, *A History of Political Thought in the Sixteenth Century* (London, 1960 edn), pt 3, chs 7, 8; Nannerl O. Keohane, *Philosophy and the State in France: The Renaissance to the Enlightenment* (Princeton, 1980), chs 2, 8; Tuck, *Philosophy and Government*, esp. ch. 8; Brockliss, *French Higher Education*, pp. 150–1.

56. Quentin Skinner, *The Foundations of Modern Political Thought*, ii: *The Age of the Reformation* (Cambridge, 1978), pts 2, 3; Guy H. Dodge, *The Political Theory of the Huguenots of the Dispersion, with Special Reference to the Thought and Influence of Pierre Jurieu* (New York, 1947). On the limited influence of Locke's *Two Treatises* in eighteenth-century Britain except among radical Whigs, see H. T. Dickinson, *Liberty and Property: Political Ideology in Eighteenth-Century Britain* (London, 1977), ch. 2. Resistance theory only really reared its head again with the outbreak of the American Revolution and the Declaration of Independence.

57. *Ancien régime* seems a better term than absolutist or Baroque to describe the European state after 1660. An added advantage of its use is that it thereby becomes possible to include the British Isles within the European state system. The British state in the eighteenth century was a representative but also a confessional and corporative polity: see J. C. D. Clark, *English Society, 1688–1832: Ideology, Social Structure and Political Practice during the Ancien Régime* (Cambridge, 1988).

58. Machiavelli sees the unprincipled 'dog-eats-dog' diplomacy of the fifteenth-century usurper princes of the Italian peninsula as typical of Europe as a whole. In so doing, he maligns other

European princes like Ferdinand of Aragon and Henry VII of England who saw themselves as godly rulers.

59. The best account of the *ancien régime* French state is P. Goubert, *L'Ancien Régime*, ii: *Les Pouvoirs* (Paris, 1973).

60. The first serious study of the early modern court was Elias, *Court Society*. More recent works include: Dickens, *Courts*; Loades, *Tudor Court*; D. Starkey, ed., *The English Court: From the Wars of the Roses to the Civil War* (London, 1987); J.-F. Solnon, *La Cour de France* (Paris, 1987); Asch and Birke, eds, *Princes, Patronage and Nobility* (Asch's introductory ch. 1, 'Court and Household from the Fifteenth to the Seventeenth Centuries', is particularly informative).

61. Besides the works cited in note 49 above, see in particular R. E. Giesey, *Cérémonial et puissance souveraine, France XVe–XVIIe siècles* (Paris, 1987).

62. Alan Bray, 'Homosexuality and the Signs of Male Friendship in Elizabethan England', *History Workshop*, 29 (1990), pp. 1–19. Bray is also the author of the important *Homosexuality in Renaissance England* (London, 1982). For male friendship and homosexuality on the continent, see K. Gerard and G. Hemka, eds, *The Pursuit of Sodomy: Male Homosexuality in Renaissance and Enlightenment Europe* (New York, 1989).

63. O. Ranum, 'Courtesy, Absolutism and the Rise of the French State, 1630–1660', *Journal of Modern History*, 52 (1980), pp. 426–51.

64. Carmona, *Richelieu*, pp. 506–7; Martin Porter, 'English "Treatises of Physiognomy", *c.* 1500–*c.* 1780' (DPhil thesis, Oxford University, 1998). The history of any kind of gesture is still in its infancy: the classic account is Jean-Claude Schmitt, *La Raison des gestes dans l'occident médiéval* (Paris, 1990). See also Jan Bremmer and Herman Roodenburg, *A Cultural History of Gesture: From Antiquity to the Present Day* (Cambridge, 1991).

65. The best study of hermeticism at court is still Robert J. W. Evans, *Rudolf II and his World: A Study in Intellectual History, 1576–1612* (Oxford, 1973), esp. ch. 6.

66. *Lettres de Gui Patin, 1630–1672*, ed. P. Triaire (Paris, 1907), p. 23: Patin to Belin, 28 October 1631. Semelles or Senelles seems to have been caught carrying letters containing the horoscope, so he may not have been the author of the prediction.

67. Carmona, *Richelieu*, p. 7; F. Yates, *The French Academies of the Sixteenth Century* (London, 1988), esp. ch. 9.

68. This is not to say that even the most establishment-orientated court literature of the period might not be worth revisiting in search of oblique and disguised references to the phenomenon of the minister–favourite hidden in the convoluted and classical metaphors of court verse. As Kevin Sharpe has shown in his *Criticism and Compliment: The Politics of Literature in the England of Charles I* (Cambridge, 1987), court literature is a politically more ambiguous genre than it might seem at first glance.

69. By the eighteenth century in England at least public signs of male intimacy were judged completely unmanly. We await a good study of the history of same-sex kissing and cuddling in early modern Europe. Useful but not totally germane is John Boswell, *The Marriage of Likeness: Same Sex Unions: Pre-Modern Europe* (London, 1996). For an earlier period, see Yannick Carré, *Le Baiser sur la bouche au moyen age: rites, symboles, mentalités, à travers les textes et les images, XIe–XVe siècles* (Paris, 1992), esp. pt 2, 'Le baiser sur le plan affectif'. Carré notes that kissing on the mouth ceased to play a part in both noble and ecclesiastical rituals in the course of the sixteenth century (pp. 332–6). For the changing culture in England, see the note by Alan Bray appended to the recent article by Cynthia Harrup on the Castlehaven case: *History Workshop*, 35 (1996), p. 22.

70. Hamish Scott, 'The Rise of the First Minister in Eighteenth-Century Europe', in T. C. W. Blanning and David Cannadine, eds, *History and Biography: Essays in Honour of Derek Beales* (Cambridge, 1996), ch. 2. Two recent studies of the eighteenth-century principal minister are Kenneth Maxwell, *Pombal: The Paradox of the Enlightenment* (Cambridge, 1995); Munro Price, *Preserving the Monarchy: The Comte de Vergennes* (Cambridge, 1995).

71. Fleury, like his predecessor Cardinal Dubois who dominated the government of the regent duc d'Orléans, owed his elevation to the fact that he had earlier been his master's tutor. For his rise to power, see Peter R. Campbell, *Power and Politics in Old Regime France, 1720–1745* (London, 1996), chs 1–4.

72. Admittedly, Metternich never dominated internal affairs, where his attempts to reform the Austrian administration were continually frustrated by his rivals for the royal ear, especially Kollowrat after 1835: see Egon Radvany, *Metternich's Projects for Reform in Austria* (The Hague, 1978), esp. ch. 19. Metternich, like Richelieu, left the world his memoirs (English version, 5 vols; London, 1880–2).

73. Potemkin was Catherine's lover for only two years, 1774–6. Isabel de Madariaga, *Russia in the Age of Catherine the Great* (New Haven and London, 1981), chs 22–6.
74. On the growing domesticity of aristocratic life in the second half of the eighteenth century, see esp. Lawrence Stone, *Family, Sex and Marriage in England, 1500–1800* (London, 1977), ch. 8.
75. Friedrich Meinecke, 'Ruler before Philosopher', in Peter Paret, ed., *Frederick the Great: A Profile* (London, 1972). Frederick had his own retreat at Sans Souci but his refuge was a place of work not of leisure: see W. Hubatsch, *Frederick the Great of Prussia: Absolutism and Administration* (London, 1975), p. 36.
76. The most recent biography of Walpole remains Betty Kemp, *Sir Robert Walpole* (London, 1976). Interestingly, the political 'outs' in the Walpolian era attempted to discredit the first lord of the Treasury's monopoly of power by using a time-honoured anti-favourite rhetoric. Bolingbroke talked much of ministerial despotism: see Isaac Kramnick, *Bolingbroke and his Circle: The Politics of Nostalgia* (Cambridge, Mass., 1968).
77. Obviously the office of British prime minister and the continental office of principal minister were not strictly comparable. They were certainly not interchangeable, as was demonstrated in Britain in 1761 when George III elevated Bute, his former tutor, to the premiership. Bute was a principal minister/minister–favourite, not a parliamentary prime minister. He had no parliamentary base and had to resign under parliamentary pressure after less than two years in office.

Index

DATE DUE

GAYLORD	PRINTED IN U.S.A.